D1719409

MAKE MONEY ONLINE

ONLINE

(5 Books In 1)

Learn How to Quickly Make Passive Income on Amazon, YouTube, Facebook, Shopify, Day Trading Stocks, Blogging, Cryptocurrency and Forex from Home on Your Computer

JAMES ERICSON

TABLE OF CONTENTS

DROPSHIPPING
How to Make $300/Day Passive Income, Make Money Online from Home with Amazon FBA, Shopify, E-Commerce, Affiliate Marketing, Blogging, Instagram, eBay, Retail Arbitrage, Social Media, and Facebook Advertising

MAKE MONEY ON YOUTUBE
How to Create and Grow Your YouTube Channel, Gain Millions of Subscribers, Earn Passive Income and Make Money Online Fast While Working From Home

MAKE MONEY BLOGGING
How to Start a Blog Fast and Build Your Own Online Business, Earn Passive Income and Make Money Online Working from Home

MAKE MONEY WITH FACEBOOK ADVERTISING
Learn How to Make $300+ Per Day Online With Facebook Marketing and Make Passive Income in Less Than 24 Hours

STOCK MARKET INVESTING FOR BEGINNERS
How to Make Money Investing in Stocks & Day Trading, Fundamentals to Successfully Become a Stock Market Pro and Make Passive Income in Less Than 24 Hours

DROPSHIPPING

How to Make $300/Day Passive Income, Make Money Online from Home with Amazon FBA, Shopify, E-Commerce, Affiliate Marketing, Blogging, Instagram, eBay, Retail Arbitrage, Social Media, and Facebook Advertising

By
James Ericson

INTRODUCTION

I want to thank you for purchasing this book *Dropshipping: How to Make $300/Day Passive Income, Make Money Online from Home with Amazon FBA, Shopify, E-Commerce, Affiliate Marketing, Blogging, Instagram, eBay, Retail Arbitrage, Social Media, and Facebook Advertising.*

In this book, we will show you how to make money online with the help of many tools available in today's day and age. You have to remember that times are changing; more people are resorting to online shopping and buying digital products online. This means that there is more demand for people looking towards spending money when it comes to online products which also means that there are more opportunities for people looking to start an online business. With that being said, if you are looking to start making $300 a day from online businesses, then there is no better time to start it.

As this industry is new and growing, there is a lot of demand, and soon, it should be filled up. What we recommend is getting into these industries as quickly as possible. This way, you will have a better chance of starting a business and to flourish in this fantastic industry. In this book, we will talk about all the top online businesses you can get into to make money. Also, we will talk about the future of online businesses and how you can be one step ahead of your competition. This will allow you to have a long and prosperous business or businesses, so I hope you enjoy and take action on the information coming your way.

CHAPTER 1
The Basics Of Passive Income

Many people are claiming that they earn $1,000 up to $10,000 a month while working from home. Whereas, other people who work a day job, can't fathom the idea of working from home. You might be asking if it is really possible to make money online and for it to be passive. Plain and simple, yes, and there are many already generating millions. Nonetheless, you will have to learn the right knowledge and implement it before you can start making money. Once you have managed to learn the secrets, you can make money and tons of it. Once you are done reading this book, you will have all the tools you need to make $300 day easily. The results might be different from person to person. Some might make $100,000 the first month, and some might even lose money, but if you play your cards right, you should have no problem making heaps of cash. There are many people already making insane amounts of money from the comfort of their home, and the truth is you can, too. Listen, if you want to live your life on your own terms and want to make insane amounts of money, this book is definitely for you. If any of you are wondering if you can still make money online, then the answer is yes. 100%. Many are making money from these techniques already. You can be making millions of dollar sitting on a beach, and this isn't an exaggeration. Believe in yourself and get to work and you will be there in no time.

Why Make Money Online?
Earning money online is one of the best ways to earn passive income. It is also the kind of opportunity that will allow you to make a decent amount of income even if you just stay in the comfort of your home.
We live in the age of digital technology. It is the golden age of computers. People and businesses now begin to shift from physical to online transactions. In fact, every business these days almost always has some form of an online presence. Many people who are engaged in e-commerce are also on the rise. Indeed, many opportunities become available online. In fact, some people live solely from the profits that they make online. And, mind you, we are not just talking about a $1,000 income, but $100,000 and even higher. This is why so many people these days want to learn how to make money online effectively.
When you make money online, you are also able to minimize your cost. You do not need to rent an office space that costs hundreds of dollars a month. Instead, you can just set up your own domain space on the Internet which costs as low as less than $50 a year. Instead of being tied

to a limited geographical location, you can send all your customers and would-be customers to your website regardless of their physical location. The whole world becomes your market.

Making money online is a new trend. Indeed, people are learning how they can take advantage of the online world to earn a decent income. There are those who successfully make a part-time income, and there are also those who work full time online. But don't think it is as easy as it seems. Indeed, there are also those who fail to generate even $20 when they tried to work online. This is why it is essential for you to build a strong foundation and develop your understanding.

Getting Started

Are you ready to make money online? If yes, then it is time for you to get prepared. When you work online, you can enjoy a good level of flexibility. However, this does not mean that you will only be working for a few hours. On the contrary, if you want to be truly successful, then you should give it as much time and effort as you can. However, if the best that you can do is to give it a few hours in a day, then that will also do but do not expect to be able to establish your business quickly if you do not give it enough time.

Making money online is like a business. As such, you can expect to have some starting capital. However, unlike the traditional business, you do not always need to have significant capital, depending on how you intend to make money. For example, when you make money by blogging, you will only need to have a good-quality computer, a blog domain of your own, and Internet access. All these are very common these days. With respect to having your own URL, it only costs less than $30 a year. Of course, you can also decide to invest a considerable capital, for example, if you choose to invest in cryptocurrencies or trade options. Do not worry. We will discuss all this later in the book. For now, you just have to get ready. So, if it is not really money, what do you need to prepare? You will have to prepare for yourself. Making money online can be challenging in the beginning, especially if you are not that literate in using a computer. However, do not worry as you can learn all these things quickly. You just have to be patient and continue to do your best. For now, you need to be in the right mindset.

If you want to make money online, then you should always be willing to learn. The fact that you are reading this book is a good sign that you want to learn and that you are taking the right actions. Indeed, it is essential to put your knowledge into actual practice. After all, real learning is not just about knowing, but it is more about doing. This book will give you the insight, the keys that you need that can unlock the door to financial freedom; however, it is up to you to put your new-found knowledge into actual practice. Making money online also takes skill. You have to

5

practice regularly. Do not worry; just keep on doing your best and remember that success is well within your reach. Let us now discuss the different ways that you can make money online.

Affiliate Marketing
Many people also earn the right amount of profits through affiliate marketing. This is where you promote other people's products, and you earn a profit on the time a sale is made through your affiliate link. Depending on the affiliate program that you have, you can also earn every time a person clicks on your affiliate link or for every page view. This will depend on the terms and conditions of the affiliate program.

You can message a business, and it may give you an affiliate link that you can use. Usually, people just join an affiliate network like Clickbank. This is the easiest way that you can jump into affiliate marketing. When you enter an affiliate network, you can choose among the different products. Your job is to market and sell your selected products. You can do this by writing something about what you are marketing, such as a product review or comparison, among others. Now, it is easy to have an affiliate link; the challenging part is having people to buy from your affiliate link. This will involve a combination of different things such as having a website, writing posts, promoting on social media, and others. You should also establish and tap your quality followers.

Just how much can you earn? This will depend on the price of the item that you are able to sell, as well as the agreed percentage of your share— your commission. Some online marketers excel at selling affordable products. The key is to sell a massive quantity so that you can earn a decent return. There are also those who like to sell only expensive products. All they need to do is to make one or a few sales a week to earn a decent income. Of course, you can promote both types of items if you want. The important thing is to make a sale so that you can earn a commission.

Although affiliate marketing seems simple, it is not that easy to do. For one, you will have to increase your visibility. This means having to work on your SEO. In order to gain the trust of your audience, you also need to come up with a presentable website or blog, among others. As you can see, there are many things that you need to do to establish yourself as a marketer. Indeed, this takes time, but it is also very much worth it. In fact, when it comes to making money online, successful marketers earn a very high income. It just really requires lots of work in the beginning, especially when you are still building your foundation.

Shopify and Other Online Store
If you are interested in selling things, then you might want to try Shopify and other online stores like Amazon. These sites have millions of

customers and visitors who are looking to spend their money on something. You merely have to sign up for a seller account, and you can start selling right away. Of course, you also have to read and observe specific terms and guidelines. The key here is to follow the number one principle of making a profit: buy low, sell high. If you want, you can even be the one to manufacture the products that you are going to sell.

It is noteworthy that there are now many people who do this kind of business, so you can expect to face some competition. Do not worry; competition is normal and even crucial in business. It only proves that there is indeed a market that has a high demand. This means that there is an opportunity for you to make money. If you want to take this route, be sure only to offer high-quality products. Remember that you are not looking for a one-time sale. Instead, you need to establish a continuous flow of income. Be mindful of the reviews that you get. This is why it is essential to only sell products that have good quality. If a buyer is not pleased with your product, there is a chance that he might write a bad review of the product. This is a sure way to discourage potential customers from buying from you.

You should also have a strong marketing arm. Even if you have excellent products to sell, you cannot make a good income if people do not even know that your business exists. This is why it is essential that you also work on your promotional strategies. These days, businesses usually rely on social media to spread the word about their business. We will talk more about how you can use social media effectively in the next chapter. An online store can significantly cut down your expenses. You would not have to worry about paying office rent. In fact, you may not even need to hire any employees. And, since everything happens online, the store is also open 24 hours a day, round the clock. When you sell items online, remember that it is essential that you offer high-quality products and tap the right market.

Blogging
Blogging is probably the most common way to make money online. What is a blog? Well, a blog is like an online journal or diary that you get to share with the whole world. It is something that you write online, on your web blog, and then people get to read your posts. There are many kinds of blog. For example, if you want to talk about the places that you have visited, then you can write a travel blog. If you are into exercise and nutrition, you can create a health blog. If you are into the latest clothing trends, then you can manage a fashion blog. There is a blog for anything and everything. Okay, but how do you make money from your blog? Well, there are many ways to make money with your blog. One of the most usual ways people make money from blogging is by using ads. When you have a blog, you can have advertisements to appear on a portion of your

blog. You can earn money every time a person clicks on the ad and/or per view. Some people earn a six-figure income just by blogging. Indeed, this can be a highly lucrative venture.

So, how do you get into blogging? Well, the first thing that you need to do is to have a place on the Internet where you can blog. Now, if you just want to test the water, you might want to start with a free website. You might want to check blogger (from Google) or Wordpress. They will give you a free sub-domain that you can use for blogging. However, if you have already decided to pursue a career as a blogger, then you should have your own website blog. This means that you should buy a domain name. For this purpose, you might want to try GoDaddy or NameCheap.

So, what should you blog about? People always say that you should blog about what is currently trending or popular. However, the problem here is that trends change. Instead of blogging about things that you do not even understand, this book suggests that you should blog about what you love. This way you can blog for a long time and appreciate your blog. Since you will blog about what you know, then you can come up with quality content. The problem with many bloggers is that they just want to earn money and blog about things they do not understand, and this leads to poor content quality. Do not worry; no matter what your interest may be, there is undoubtedly a market for you. Do not forget that the whole world is your market.

When you engage in blogging, you have to increase your visibility online. The best way to do this is to optimize your blog for the search engines. This is known as search engine optimization, commonly referred to simply as SEO. When it comes to SEO, it is essential that you learn to use keywords. Gone are the days when you can just use any keyword that you want. Today, you need to be more specific. For example, if you are blogging about gardening, do not just use "gardening" as your keyword. There are now countless articles online that use the word "gardening" many times. You need to be more specific. What is it about gardening that you want to talk about? For example, instead of just "gardening," you can use, "plants to grow during summer."

Another essential point to take note of is the use of long-tail keywords. Long-tail keywords are keywords composed of at least three words. When you use keywords in your blog posts and articles, make sure that your keywords are at least three words long. Also, avoid using generic words. It helps to be specific. However, do not get too specific to the point that nobody else would think of searching for those terms. Take note that the keywords that you use should be those that people type in the search bar when they surf the web.

To know the bests keywords to use, as well as the amount of traffic specific keywords received, you should use the Google Keyword Planner. Google Keyword Planner will not just show you the number of times particular keywords have been searched over a specified time, but it will also offer suggestions for the best keywords that you can use. To gain access to the keyword planner, you should sign up for an Adwords account from Google. Take that this is different from an Adsense account. Adsense is for allowing people to post relevant ads on your blog while Adwords will enable you to be the one to post advertisements for a fee.

Another thing to take note of is quality. No matter how much you promote your blog's visibility, it is still essential that you have exciting and high-quality content on your blog. In fact, it is the quality of your blog posts that will really draw people to your blog. Make sure that every post you make has a good quality.

Another effective way to earn from blogging is by selling an ebook on your blog. Some people do not like the idea of posting ads on their site or blog, and this is understandable. Although they do not make money from Adsense, they earn money by selling an ebook/ebooks on the blog. For example, if your blog is about yoga and you share interesting articles about yoga. If people like what you share and see that you are selling an ebook on yoga, then they will most likely buy that ebook. The articles on your blog will gain the trust of the readers which can then lead to a successful sale of your product.

So, is blogging for you? Well, if you are the type who loves to write and connect with people who share a common interest, then you should definitely try blogging. However, if you would rather keep things to yourself, then you might find it hard to adjust to being a blogger. But, do not be discouraged; being a successful blogger is something that you can learn. Put your heart into whatever it is that you are doing and always do your best.

With that note, we come to the end of this chapter. Remember, in the next chapters, we will show you exactly how to make money from the methods listed in this book, and this chapter was to brief you on what is to come.

CHAPTER 2
Drop-Shipping 101

Hopefully, you now have a clear idea of what drop-shipping is all about. In the previous chapter, we gave you a brief description of it. We will now further talk about it. Currently, there are two different types of drop-shipping. The first one is online drop-shipping, where you just send over the product to your customer from your supplier. Or the next one, where you buy the product in bulk, and you send it over to the companies' warehouse allowing you to drop-ship from there. There are many ways to drop-ship, so let's go into the details on how they all work.

Online drop-shipping
Online drop-shipping is one of the most common ways people decide to start up their drop-shipping business these days. This is the method which comes to mind when people talk about drop-shipping.In this method, you will have to find a supplier which can provide you with high-quality products at a cheap price. One thing you have to make sure about is that he or she will have to ship out the product for you directly to the buyer without you doing any of that. Using this method, you will most likely have to make your own website like using Shopify to make your online store, or if you don't want to create your site, you can use eBay. We will discuss more which websites to choose for your drop-shipping business later in this book.

Now, if you decide to use this method for your drop-shipping, you will have to make sure that you have a safe and secure way of collecting payments from your client. Not only will it help you get paid safely, but it will also make your customers feel safe once they decide to make a purchase on your website or product. If you are thinking about making your website for your products to sell, then make sure you add a trust badge on your site. If you use Shopify as your drop-shipping website, it will show trust badge in the footer menu of your site so don't worry about that if you're considering using Shopify to create your drop-shipping site. One more thing to remember, make sure you have a PayPal account. Most people will use PayPal to make purchases on your site, so if you want to get paid, you need to create a PayPal account.

Now, I want to discuss the benefits of using online drop-shipping for your business. Like I mentioned before, you don't have to hold any inventory. Meaning, there is no need to buy any products in bulk or rent out a warehouse where you can store your products. All you are just going to do is to make a website, upload the product on your site, and once someone purchases the product, you will merely give the shipping information to your supplier, and he or she will mail it out to them! Plain and simple. The only thing you might need investment would be buying a domain name for your website, which I highly recommended. The domain would cost you around $10 a year. Also, if don't do coding for a living, you might have to use a website platform to start selling your products and to collect payments which will cost you additionally $30 to $120 a month (depending on which website platform you decide to use, etc.) If you want, you can pay for the whole year with your website provider which will save you money.

Just like any business model, there are some flaws to this method, so let's talk about them. The main one I see is shipping times, and we live in a world where websites ship products in a day. Most of the times, the supplier you will be working with would be from China, so the orders for your clients will be shipped out from China. For you to actually make a profit on your sale, you will have to use the most cost efficient way of shipping, which will result in slower shipping times. Now, this isn't a total deal breaker, but people are impatient; some more than others.

So, if you don't pick the right supplier and shipping methods, you can expect to get refunds. Don't you worry, not all your orders will get refunded and I will also show you the best tricks and techniques to get fast delivery to your client using this drop-shipping method later in the book, but don't expect shipping times of a day like most big competitors offer as it won't be possible with this technique.

Another drawback or flaw with this business model is that you won't be able to tell the quality of the products which you're going to be selling. So, I would recommend you buy the product before you put it up on your online store. It will lower the risk of your products getting refunded for quality issues. One more thing you have to worry about is driving traffic to your product. Since you won't be affiliated with any big companies, you will have to drive traffic to your own website or storefront using paid advertisement.

Warehouse drop-shipping
This method is similar to online drop-shipping in some ways and different in others. This is a bit confusing so let me explain. This method is identical in the sense that you don't hold any inventory and you don't ship out the products. Where it's different compared to the online drop-shipping method is that you will have to buy a certain amount of products upfront. But the benefit of having products with you would be fast shipping, which will allow you to have fewer chances of refunds and have better customer satisfaction.

So, let me explain to you how warehouse drop-shipping works precisely. First thing to remember is that you will be selling your product on a website like Amazon, you can still use the warehouse drop-shipping method with your site but you will have to rent out a warehouse and shipping would be your responsibly. Companies like Amazon will let you store it in their warehouse and ship the products out for you, which is why it is recommended to work with a big company when doing a warehouse drop-shipping model. So how it works is you find a product for cheap or buy it from a warehouse in bulk then you will ship your inventory to the company's warehouse. Once that is done, you will sit back and see the profits in your bank account, and you don't have to worry about anything like customer service, making a website, or capturing a payment, nothing! The company will take care of everything for you.

But, the upfront investment to start this business model is higher than online drop-shipping. Let me break it down for you. Depending on the product and how much of it you buy, you are looking to spend $1,000 to $2,000 on your inventory. Companies also charge you to have a seller's account that will be around $39.99 or more depending on how many products you sell. Plus a fee for every product shipped. So, as you can see, there is quite a bit more upfront investment compared to the online drop-shipping method. Although this method has a significant upfront investment, it also has some positives to consider.

There are a lot of benefits with this drop-shipping method so let us talk about them. The best advantage of using this drop-shipping method is that you can actually quality check the products before you decide to sell your products. As you know by now, it is imperative that you check your products' quality before you ship them off for your refund rates to be low. Another great benefit with warehouse drop-shipping is that, once you have shipped it to the company's warehouse, you don't have to worry about anything else. The company will take care of the shipping, etc. Another huge benefit with this business model is that you will not have to worry about advertising your product as much as the online drop-shipping method since your product will be listed in the company's website which already gets a lot of traffic. You won't have to worry about promoting your product too much which could mean less paid advertisement and more money in your pocket.

All being said, there is one major flaw I see with this method of drop-shipping. The flaw I see is that there is no guarantee all your products will sell if any. Even though you will be listing your product on a website which gets a lot of traffic, it won't always equate to sales. Remember, there will be a lot of products you will be competing with on the website, so making sure your product sells is crucial if you don't want to lose your investment.

So hopefully, you now know what drop-shipping is and the different ways you can go about starting your drop-shipping business. If you're still confused, then don't worry and keep reading. It will begin to get less confusing as we go along in this book, and hopefully, everyone reading this book now has an understanding of what it takes to start a drop-shipping business. Trust me, drop-shipping is one of the most straightforward business models to scale up and make money on so keep on reading as we will now show you how to start your very own store.

Shopify

For people who don't know what Shopify is, Shopify is an e-commerce company founded in Canada. What Shopify provides is an e-commerce platform or an online store for its users. It was initially established by Scott Lake, Daniel Weinard, and the current CEO, Tobias Lutke. Essentially, what Shopify provides you with is a secure online store where you can sell products to customers online. Most people use this website for online drop-shipping rather than warehouse drop-shipping since Shopify does not provide users with a warehouse. That being said, starting your very own drop-shipping business using Shopify as your platform is straightforward and cost-effective compared to other platforms.

To start making money with drop-shipping using Shopify as your platform, you will need is a supplier, which can ship out the products anywhere in the world for cheap. That's it for the requirements. Now, I want to get specific with a start-up cost of getting started with Shopify as it is not free, but it is really cost-efficient compared to other business models out there.

Now, first things first, you will need to buy a domain name. You really need to make sure that you're website looks legit, and for that to happen, you will need a domain name. Buying a domain name is inexpensive. It will only cost you around $11 to $18 USD per year, depending on the domain name. Now, once you get that sorted, you will now have to sign up on Shopify, and sinceShopify offers a free 14-day trial, I would recommend that you make sure that the store name or brand you come up with is not taken before you buy a domain name for your website or store. Once you have decided your store name, etc., it will now be the time to buy a package from Shopify which will allow you to start selling your products. Shopify offers three packages, which include

- Basic Shopify package ($29.99 USD) a month
- Shopify package ($79.99 USD) a month
- Advanced Shopify package ($299.99 USD) a month

Also to note, if you want to save money, you can buy these packages upfront on a yearly basis. But that's totally up to you.

Now, you might be wondering which one to get started with? Well, let me explain each of them to you. If you're just starting your drop-shipping business, I would like to say right off the bat that you don't need the advanced Shopify package. Once you have your business rolling and if you want to expand, you can do your research on it and upgrade. But for starters, just pick between the basic Shopify package and the Shopify package. If your funds are low, and you want to start making money online, then you can start off with the basic package, but if you have some extra cash to spare, then I would recommend upgrading to the Shopify package as it has some useful benefits.

The valuable benefits this Shopify package provides you with compared to the basic Shopify package is the lower amount of online credit card rates compared to the basic Shopify package. Even though it is minuscule, it adds up once you start making over thousands of dollars a month. Another great benefit of using Shopify package compared to basic Shopify package is that you can start making your own gift cards. As you know, in order to make sales on this platform, you will need to get some traffic first before you can actually make some sales online. So, having these small incentives can add up to more sales in the future. Other than that, these packages are identical. If you are using Shopify for online drop-shipping purposes, you can go with either package which fits your budget. Now, it's up to you which one you want to get started with.

One more thing you can invest in to really make your store stand out is logos, and you will need a logo for your Shopify store. You can get it done professionally by hiring someone on fiverr.com. The logo will not cost you more than $25 USD to get started. One thing to note, you do not need to hire someone to make your logo. It can be quickly done for free by using canva.com to create your free logo. But regardless, free or not free, you will need a logo.

To sum up the total costs of getting started with drop-shipping using Shopify.

- Shopify package $29.99 or $79.99 USD
- Domain name $ 11 to $18 USD
- Logo $0.00 to $25.

So, to get started with Shopify, it will cost you $40.99 + $29.99 USD every month after that and if you go for the cheapest option or $122.99 + $79.99 every month after that. Regardless, the startup should be quite affordable for anyone.

Now, let's talk about the work you will have to put in for your Shopify business to flourish. You will have to make sure your website looks presentable. Now, Shopify provides you with some great themes which can be used to build up your site. But it does require some work to be put in. Another thing you will have to take care of is customer inquiries and complaints. Since it is your brand and company, you will have to deal with everything from complaints to fulfilling an order. So, make sure you have an email created for your store inquiries. Also, as I said before, you will have to emphasize more on getting traffic since no will know about your store except your family and friends. Other than that, you should be fine.

How you get paid on Shopify is simple as well. All you have to do is make a PayPal account since some people might choose to complete their transaction using PayPal. Also, Shopify will make you put in your banking information. So, for the others who use a credit card to make a purchase on your store, Shopify will directly deposit into your account.

The final thing I would like to discuss is how much you can really make using Shopify and online drop-shipping method. Since it is your brand and your company, you can make as much as you want. You can become a millionaire or a billionaire with this method, as long as you build a following for your business, which again, will be talked about in the later chapters. Overall, the sky's the limit! Work hard and be patient; you will get what you desire.

Amazon FBA

If you have been living under a rock, Amazon is one of the biggest e-commerce companies in the world with its founder and owner's net worth is a whopping 150 billion dollars, making him the richest man in the world. Jeff Bezos founded his company in the early 90s, and his goal was to sell books online. Now, Amazon sells everything you can think off. Amazon is the biggest e-commerce company in the world, and its website has one of the highest amounts of online traffic in the world. Needless to say, working with Amazon could make you money.

Now, you might be wondering, what does the FBA stand for? It stands for Fulfillment by Amazon. What you have to do in order to a part of this program is simple, first find a product which you can get for cheap. Second, buy them in bulk, and finally, the third is to ship it to Amazon's warehouse where it can be shipped off to the customer. It is that simple. Now, with that being said, the startup cost with this business model is a little bit higher, so let's break it down.

Buying products in bulk for cheap will cost from $1000 to $3000 USD. If you sell more than 40 items a month, you will have to pay $39.99.

So, on the lower end, you can get started for $1000 USD to $3000 USD plus $39.99 a month if you sell more than 40 products. Plus, there is a charge for each product they ship out, but don't worry, it will only be charged once someone orders a product.

Even though there is a more significant upfront investment in this type of drop-shipping, it still has some benefits like, for example, since your products will be listed on Amazon, you will already be getting free traffic, which would equal higher chances of a sale. Unlike Shopify, Amazon takes care of the back ends like customer refunds, questions, etc. All you do is get the product, ship it to Amazon's warehouse, and you will start earning money.

Now, let's talk about the work you will have to do in order to get this business started from the ground up. The first thing is finding a cheap supplier. For you to actually make some profits, you will have to find products at a cost. Second, buy it in bulk, and third, ship it to Amazon's warehouse. When a business takes off, all you will have to worry about is restocking your products by shipping it to Amazon, so you can make more money. That's all the work you will have to do. As I said, all the back-end stuff, Amazon would take care of such as shipping, customer service, etc.

So, let us talk about how you will get paid on Amazon FBA. It is simple and similar to Shopify. You will first have to make a seller's account on Amazon. Once that is done, you will add your banking information to the account. Amazon will pay you the profits you made right into your bank account, and you don't have to worry about anything else, besides filing your taxes.

The final thing I would like to talk about is income, how much you can make on Amazon FBA. Since Amazon FBA is not a personal brand which you can grow, the revenue will be limited. I know the top earners can produce over two million a year using Amazon FBA. Which for some can be amazing to see this kind of cash. But for others who really want to build their brand, Amazon FBA would not be the answer. Now, the benefit with this business model is that if you do everything right, you can make money faster and could scale up higher. But there is a tap on the amount of money you can make here.

This should now help you really decide which business model you want to try out for yourself. Remember, you can easily make $300 a day with both of these models. Just remember, it takes hard work and the right knowledge. After this chapter, you should be on the right track to becoming successful in either of these business models.

CHAPTER 3
How To Be Successful In Drop-Shipping

Hopefully, by now, you have decided on which type of drop-shipping method and which website you will be moving forward with. Regardless of whichever method you choose, you will need to make sure that your products sell for you to actually make money. So, how will you actually sell products? Well, simply by finding a niche which already has customers and not enough products for all. Here's the cold truth, you will not sell anything or make any money if what you're selling does not have a demand for it. This is why choosing the right niche is imperative for your success in drop-shipping business.

Now, most of you might be wondering what a niche is. Well, to explain it in the simplest manner, a niche is something relating to or being a part of a certain product or service, etc. So, for example, selling something like a dog bracelet to dog lovers would be considered a niche. So, as you can see, having a niche to sell in is imperative for your success in this drop-shipping business. So, in this chapter, what I really want to talk about is how you can find a profitable niche where you can make some amazing profits without wasting money on buying your products in bulk and letting it sit in the warehouse or paying monthly fees and spending money on an advertisement without seeing any profits.

So, from my experience with Amazon, Shopify, and eBay, when you first initially start you won't be able to make a lot of money in niches which are saturated or have a lot of products to sell. Our goal is to get started with minimal money and slowly scale up. The ideal situation for you to make money is to be a bigger fish in a small pond rather than a smaller fish in a big pond. Your job is to find a profitable niche which hasn't been tapped into but you know it has the potential to sell and make you money. So, to find out a niche which will actually sell and make you money, I have created two ways, or rather I should say, two techniques to find a niche and make money online. So, let me first show the websites I use to find a niche which will actually help you make money. The first website I use is Amazon. It is one of the biggest e-commerce websites. So anything that sells well on Amazon will sell anywhere. The second one is Facebook groups and Instagram pages. To find out what you could sell online on these pages will help you tremendously. Now, let's go into the depths of each way to find a profitable niche. We will begin with Amazon.

Amazon

As we know by now, Amazon is the biggest online store right now. So whatever sells in Amazon sells anywhere. So, if your goal is to find a niche which will make you money and is profitable, then you need to review Amazon's products.

If you have been to Amazon's website to purchase a product or anything of that matter, you will see the bestsellers rank under the product description. What that bestseller ranks symbolized is how much the product is being bought. This is very important for you to note. If the product is not selling on Amazon, which is the biggest e-commerce store in the world, it will not sell anywhere. Now, here is what you are going to do in order to find a product that sells.

The most essential thing you are going to do is get on your computer and go to Amazon's website. Now, what I want you to do is to go on to the bestsellers page on Amazon. This page will give you a rough idea on what sells and what doesn't. It also will show you niche products which are selling already. Anything in Amazon's bestseller's page will most likely sell, that is if you can offer it at a cheaper price. Regardless of which platform you will be using for your drop-shipping business, if Amazon has the same product for sale as you do, it will have it for the same price or cheaper than you would. This is the case most of the time, but if you can sell it for cheaper than your competitors then you have a winning product! Congrats.

Now, if that's not the case, it is about time to find an untapped niche. So go to the bestsellers' page on Amazon and look at the top 100 on that list carefully. If you see similar products from the same niche, then this niche is profitable. But it could be hard to penetrate into that specific market or niche. This is where we find a micro-niche. So for example, if the niche is iPhone accessories and there are multiple iPhone accessories on the bestseller list, what we will do is search up iPhone accessories on Amazon search bar. Then, we will go through the top six products and check to see their best sellers list. If the bestseller list showcases a number below 50, 000 for all six items, then this niche is profitable.

Hypothetically, you can sell in this niche and make some great profits. But if the competition is high, then there are fewer chances of you actually making profits. So, if you want to make sure the competition is low, look at the search engine number. If the search engine number has a number less than 5,000 items, then the niche is small and if the top six products have a ranking of lower than 50,000 on the best sellers rank, then you have a winning product and a niche to get into. So, if you search up iPhone accessories and it has 20,000 items for sale, it would be harder for you to tap into. On the other hand, if you search up iPhone phone cases and it has lower than 5,000 items for sale and the top six items best seller rank is lower than 50,000, we have a winner at hand. So this is how you use Amazon to find a profitable niche.

Facebook groups and Instagram pages

This is another place where you can find niches to sell. A lot of Facebook pages and Instagram pages are made to share videos and contents online for people to look at simply because they are a big fan of it. They have a special connection to this niche for some reason. It could be personal, business, who knows. But you can use this fan page or groups to offer them something they can't refuse.

Think about it, if you are a big fan of dogs and you loved dogs, wouldn't you want to buy a $25 t-shirt which says I love dogs? Of course, you would because you are a super-fan. Now, the best part about this method is that the people you will advertise your product to will most likely buy it, and there are a lot of pages online where there is a big following but no products to sell. So, in order to find these pages, all you have to do is search and think outside the box, as there are some pages waiting to be sold I love "something" t-shirt. So, look around and search and once you find your niche, you will be making some serious profits.

With that being said, let me share with you some niches which have made me money in the past.

- Dog lovers
- Cat lovers
- Lion lovers
- Car lovers
- Electronic accessories

These niches are still quite profitable, so do your research and if you like, then sell items from these specific niches.

Supplier

Finding the right supplier or the right wholesalers for your drop-shipping business is imperative, meaning that you can't "cheap out" or not care about this aspect. As you can imagine, your business will revolve around your supplier quite heavily. Truth be told, if you don't have any products that you can sell, then it would honestly be impossible for you to make any money which would therefore equal to no profits. Whereas, if you decide to "cheap out" and sell low-quality products, chances are people will return the products. Even though we discussed the importance of finding a proper niche to the importance of advertising the product the right way etc., it can't be overridden by an unreliable or a cheap low-quality product.

Finding the right supplier for your drop-shipping business purposes is imperative, for both quality purposes and shipping purposes. Now, if you are going to be using Amazon FBA or a similar type of drop-shipping method, then shipping times do matter in order for you to stock up your products, but it isn't the biggest of the deal for that drop-shipping model compared to drop-shipping methods using Shopify. Now with all that being said, quality is the biggest factor you have to worry about when selling your products. So, today, we will go through the top websites from where you can find great suppliers for your business. We will also talk about how to build a great relationship with them. And finally, for everyone using the method online-drop shipping, I will reveal a secret to getting the fastest shipping anywhere in the world so your customers stay happy and fewer refunds are being made.

We will break this chapter into two phases. First, we will talk about how to find suppliers for people using online drop-shipping. We will go through everything from finding the product, building a relationship with the seller, getting it shipped fast, and of course, making sure the product is of high quality. Then we will talk about finding a supplier or a wholesaler for warehouse drop-shipping method.

Online Drop-Shipping
So, finding a supplier for people using online drop-shipping as their business model could be challenging. Since most of the time, you will be going by assumptions, what your job with this process is to take out as much of the guesswork as we can and find the winning supplier which we are looking for. Now, there are a lot of websites online where you can find products for cheap. But from my experience, AliExpress has one of the best quality products and shipping times. If you have been doing some research online, you might have heard things like "AliExpress is dead" or things of that nature. But I am here to tell you that Ali Express still works amazingly and will help you make some serious profits online. There are some tips and techniques you need to know before you fully start using AliExpress as your sole supplier.

Now, if you don't know what Ali Express is then let me clarify it for you. Think of Ali Express as the Amazon of China. There are a lot of people selling products online on this website, mostly from China and as we know most of the products are manufactured in China. This means that the mark up on the products would be a lot less. Meaning you can easily sell it online for a higher price in the North American market, and to make things even better, the products on AliExpress are mostly similar types of products which are sold or are popular in the North American market. The point I am trying to make is this, people selling on AliExpress are selling it to people specifically who want to start their drop-shipping business.

There are some guidelines you need to follow before you start to use AliExpress to drop-ship products from, as there are some flaws. The things we need to look into before we start selling products using AliExpress are as follows:

- Suppliers review
- Product photos and description
- Epacket
- How many orders sold

Now, if all these points are checked out, then your supplier is good. So, let's begin with the supplier review. To find out if the supplier is good, the first thing you will need to do is check the reviews. Make sure the review on his or her store is at least 95% positive. If that's not the case, then either the product's quality isn't good or the product is something else when it gets delivered. Another thing to worry about is photos and the description. If the product has great photos and description, then most of the time, it shows that the seller actually cares about what he or she is doing and will do whatever it takes to keep his customers happy.

Another thing to take care of is shipping. If the seller offers a shipping method known as e-packet, then the shipping times would be a lot faster than other suppliers. Normally, epacket delivers the product in 2-3 weeks, which are the fastest shipping times you will get on AliExpress. So, make sure your supplier provides you with e-packet. Also, to make sure this supplier is reliable, check out how many orders he/she has had. If it is higher than 500 orders, then they are in the clear. If all the points I just described to you are checked out, then the supplier is a good supplier and you can truly start to grow your business with him or her. And if the supplier doesn't check out on all these points, then find a new one.

One more tip I would share with you is that Ali Express tends to take some time when processing a payment. It could take up to three days. It is done simply for their security. If you want to expedite the process of processing the payment for your order to be shipped even faster, then I would recommend using Ali pocket. Ali pocket is similar to a gift card. It is like a safe credit card for Ali Express. So, if you buy Ali pocket in bulk and use it to buy the product which you will be shipping it out to your client, then there would be no time to waste for processing payment and the order would be shipped right away.

Now, AliExpress is great for selling new trending stuff. But if your goal is to sell fan t-shirts and things of that nature then, it might not be the right choice for you. AliExpress has a lot of things to sell online, but the products it sells are not specific to niches and people. This is where print-on-demand t-shirts come in.

What is print-on-demand, you might ask? Well, print-on-demand is a service where you come up with a logo. Pick out a plain t-shirt sweater or whatever they have, and then what will happen is that the company will use your logo, put it on a t-shirt, etc., and directly ship it out to the customer or the buyer. That is what print-on-demand is. Now, there are a lot of websites to choose from. But the one I highly recommend is Pillow Profits. It is amazing. Not only do they have your good old t-shirts but they also offer things like pillowcases, shower curtain, or bed sheets which can be sent to a customer with your logo on any of those things.

Now, print-on-demand is ideal for those super-niche fan pages we talked about before. Since those fan pages are unique and hard to find, you need to be really unique with your products just like the page you are promoting it to. So, if your store is based on super-niche products, then it would be hard to find products on AliExpress and this is where Print-on-demand comes in.

Print-on-demand will offer you cheap supplies with whatever you want on it and fast shipping. Most of the print-on-demand websites have a really fast delivery since most of them are based in the United States, so you don't need to worry about shipping or any of that. Just make sure to pick out a print-on-demand website you like and come up with a logo.

Let's talk about building relationships with your suppliers. It is imperative that you build a great relationship with your supplier. Not only will it help you make more profits, but it will also help you get faster shipping times. What I am about to tell you applies more so to Ali Express rather than print-on-demand websites. Regardless of which website it is, you need a great relationship with your supplier. So, in order to build great relationships with your suppliers, here are the ways you can do so.

- Give them business
- Be accepting
- Leave them great reviews

So, giving them business is quite self-explanatory. If you want to build a great relationship, you have to give them business. You can't expect to be their "special customer" if you don't buy anything from them. So, make sure you first buy at least 20-25 items before you can think about asking them for a discount on your products. Another thing to be mindful about is making sure you don't get angry at them for a shipment which is a couple of days late or things of that nature. You have to remember that they are trying their best to keep you happy, just like you are trying to keep your customers happy. So make sure you are accepting and not making a big deal about small things like these. The final thing is to leave a positive review because let's face it, everyone cares about positive reviews. If you follow all these steps, you will start to build a great relationship with your supplier and you can slowly start to ask for things like discounts on your orders which would mean a higher profit margin for you. So make sure you start to build a great relationship with them.

With all that said, that is all for finding a supplier for people using online drop-shipping, let's talk about finding suppliers for people using Amazon FBA or warehouse drop-shipping. It is a little bit different but shares some of the same principles.

Warehouse drop-shipping

To find suppliers or products for this type of drop-shipping is a little bit easier compared to online drop-shipping. Since you can inspect all the product before you start selling makes it one step easier compared to the others. So, in short, there are three ways you can go about finding a supplier. The first one is using sites like Ali Express, the second one is to find a warehouse where they are selling the products for cheap, and finally, buy products on special sales and re-sell them.

Now, you already know how to find the right supplier on AliExpress, but let's talk about how you can use AliExpress for warehouse drop-shipping. So right off the bat, once you find a product that you would like to sell, I would highly recommend you buy one of the products and really check it's quality. Once you have checked it out and made sure that the quality is of a high caliber, then you should contact the supplier and work out a deal. You see, since you will be buying the product in bulk, there would be higher chances of you actually getting it for a further discounted price, so make sure you ask for it so you can make even more profit. Finally, once that is all done, ship it to the warehouse and start selling.

That was using AliExpress. Now, let's talk about using warehouse or special sales to find your supplies. People don't realize that there are a lot of warehouses like Costco where you can buy stuff for cheap and sell it on Amazon. So, the way this process works is simple. Go to a warehouse like Costco, find a product in bulk for really cheap, and then transport it to Amazon's warehouse and start selling. Trust me, I have found so many cheap products on Costco for sale which have made me some great profits! Make sure you find these products and start selling them on Amazon.

Finally, one of the ways I have made tremendous amounts of money on Amazon FBA is by waiting for sales like Black Friday and things of that nature. I would buy products on sale for 50% to 70% off, and after the sale is done, I would sell it on Amazon at its original price. Although this method is not as frequently occurring as the other two, it will yield you a lot of profits so make sure you wait for these sales to make some real cash.

Finally, one secret method I have used before is finding listings on Craigslist and Facebook market places for products and supplies. Most of the times, you will find brand new stuff for sale near you, and the seller would be selling it off for next to nothing. So this would be your time to shine, find something in bulk for really cheap on these websites, work out a deal and sell it off on Amazon for a great profit. Now, if you found something for cheap but the quantity is low, then I would recommend using eBay to sell it on. I remember finding a brand new iPhone for super cheap. So, just like anyone else would do, I bought it and sold it off on eBay for a great profit. So, whatever you can find on these websites for cheap, make sure to act on them as soon as possible before they are gone. With that note, we come to a conclusion of this chapter. I hope it was quite informative as we went thru a ton. We showed you how to find products the right way and where to source it from. This will allow you to become very successful in your business. Remember, if you follow the steps in this book, then you will be in a very good place when it comes to making money with this business.

CHAPTER 4
How To Market Your Drop-Shipping Store

By now, this book has been through everything regarding drop-shipping from the different types of drop-shipping businesses, how to start your own drop-shipping business, and how to pick out the most profitable niche and products. You see, everything is essential for your business to flourish, but if you can't get people to come into your page/website or to drive traffic to it, then nothing in this book will help you get sales. It's simple if no one is there to see your product or what you're selling, then no one is going to buy your products. It's just going to sit there and do nothing. So for you to make sales, you need to drive some traffic to your store or page, and that is what we will be talking about in this chapter; how to drive traffic to your store or page.

Learning how to drive traffic can be a challenging task. There is no right or wrong answer in this method. For some people, using websites like Facebook and Instagram could work amazingly, and that is all they do to drive traffic, whereas, for other's using free traffic techniques could be working beautifully making them some serious sales. So, it is more so of trial and error than getting it right in the first place.

When I started my drop-shipping business, I tried everything from Facebook ads to free traffic techniques like creating blogs and sending out emails. But all my drop-shipping businesses work differently, and sometimes, one business would work great on getting Facebook traffic and only that while others might work great on blogs traffic or emails, so it really just depends. For you to find out what works and what doesn't, you need to try it out and see for yourself. There is no way to tell if a specific add will generate you millions of dollars or not.

We will talk about the three most significant ways to drive traffic to your product page or website, which would be Facebook ads, Instagram shout outs, and finally, free traffic utilizing blogs, emails, etc. Try all of them out before you knock on one or the other. Like I said before, some might work beautifully for you compared to the others to make you try them out completely. With all that being said, let's tackle the hardest one first, Facebook.

Facebook

Facebook has a lot of users, over 2 billion of them to be exact. There are a lot of people on Facebook who would be interested in buying your products. The Facebook advertisement has been used by almost every drop-shipper you can find to drive traffic and this method is probably the cheapest and the most effective way you can use to drive traffic to your product page or store. Now, there are some steps you need to go through before you start advertising your product the right way in utilizing Facebook, which we will be going through this chapter.

First things first, when you create your Facebook ads account, you will need to make sure you add your website pixel on it. This is more important for people using the online drop-shipping method. Here is the thing. If you don't add your store pixel onto your Facebook ads account, it will not be able to collect data for your website and products. The pixel will receive things like what kind of people are checking out your product page and what kind of people are actually purchasing your product which would equal to a better ad campaign in future, as you would be able to target specific people to your product page or website. Now, after you have created your Facebook ads account and added your pixel to your Facebook ads account, we can now start to advertise your products. Here is what we need to take care of before we start advertising on Facebook.

- Finding products like yours
- Finding big companies' Facebook ads
- Targeting to a particular age group and country
- Amazing product photos
- Amazing caption
- Split testing

I know that there are a lot of things to worry about. But believe it or not, these are just the basics we need to take care of as there are a lot of other advertising methods which can be used. But for now, worry about the basics.

So, let's start off with the first step. Finding a similar product to yours on Google is essential to look for, as most of the times, it will show you the top sellers of your niche. When you start your Facebook ads campaign, it will ask you ad pages or companies related to your niche. What our job is quite simple, yet important. The first thing we will do is go online and search up our product. For example, if I am selling a car, I will look up "cars for sale," then I want you to click on all the websites which sell your products. So, in this hypothetical scenario, I would be clicking through Honda, Toyota, etc., so after you do that, I want you to write down all the websites which are related to your niche or product that you are going to be selling.

After you have written all the top websites, I want you to log into Facebook, then after that is done, I want you to search up the sites' Facebook pages. Once you have gotten that done, check to see if their Facebook likes are over 500,000 and if so, you have found a winner. You see, what Facebook does with that information on your campaign is that it will promote your product to the specific people on that page. So, let us get back to my hypothetical scenario. If I am selling a car and I add Honda to my targeted Facebook advertisement, it will then specifically target people who are interested in Honda. So, find a product and Facebook page which has over 500k followers, and then advertise the product to the people involved in that page.

Now that you have the keywords and the specific people you will be advertising your products to, it is now time to create an eye-catching advertisement. Since most of you haven't created a Facebook advertisement I assume, so in order for you to make sure your publication converts into sales, you will need to make sure your ads look good. Now, there are many tips and techniques out there spilled out by "supposedly" drop-shipping gurus, but some of you might have heard the phrase "if it ain't broke don't fix it" meaning that if there are big companies advertising their products successfully then there is no need to come up with your own unique way of doing it, as that trial and error could hurt your wallet.

If you did your research and tried to find big websites or companies specific to your niche, then there is a high chance that you might have seen their Facebook ads pop-up. The next time you see it, I want you to examine their advertising and see what kind of videos or images they are using. This will help you build your own advertisement, so make sure you review the ads and copy what they are doing. Trust me; it will work a lot better than you create your own special one.

Let's talk about finding age groups and country for your advertisements. If you know what your product provides to consumers, you would know what kind of people would be interested in purchasing your products. Before you start your first campaign on Facebook, it will ask you to put an age range on your advertisement. So, if you are going to be selling a car like I am, then I would probably set the age range around 25 to 65 as most of the people. Since most 18-year-olds won't be buying one by themselves and anyone over 65 won't either. So our goal is to target it to people who are most likely to buy your product. So, this takes some research and guesswork involved, but if you really specify the age, you will save the right amount of money and get more sales.

Whereas, for picking out the county or region to advertise it to, I would recommend you advertise it to the U.S.A only if your budget is small. Most of your buyers will be coming from the United States so no need to worry about advertising it to any other people. Now if you have some spare change left over, then you can further your audience to Canada which could get you more views and get you more sales.

After you have done all of this research, it is now time to create your advertising image and caption. People don't realize how important it is for you to have the right image and caption for your post. This will either make your post or break it. So, picking out the right photo and caption is imperative for your advertisement to be a success. Now, how do you pick out the right image for your advertisement? Simple, if you did your research correctly looking up big companies websites, then you would know the specific type of photo or caption to use, so mimic their advertisement.

Now, after you have decided upon the photos and captions you will be going with, it is now time to add a picture to your campaign. Two things to remember are to make sure the photo is high-definition. If it's not high-definition, then it won't stand out from the crowd, and it would also look unprofessional. Also, make sure the picture is compatible with smartphones advertisement. For you to check out what it would look like on a smartphone, just click on the smartphone advertisement option. It will show you what it looks like.

Now, let's talk about the caption. In order for you to get people clicking on the caption, you need to make sure that it is also eye-catching. For you to deliver that, you need to make sure you offer your clients with some incentives, like get this now for 50% off or only 50 in stock. Just like the big companies, you will need to make sure you create urgency by adding an incentive.

Finally, when everything is good to go and ready to be launched, you will utilize a tool called split testing. What you have to do is create two similar advertising campaigns with slight changes. For example, one ad could have an age group of 18-50 and the other 25-65. After the add has been running for some time, it will show you which one works better compared to the other, and this will help you optimize your ad campaigns in the future. This is optional but highly recommended.

That is all for Facebook advertising. Let's now talk about Instagram influencer advertising.

Instagram

Instagram is a great place to market your products and they have an enormous number of users, and most of the time, they are more engaging as compared to Facebook. So, if you are thinking about dismissing the idea of advertising on Instagram, think again as you would be leaving a lot on the table. Note that advertising from Facebook does go on onto Instagram, but it isn't as potent as it should be. So, when advertising on Instagram, we use a method called "Instagram influencer." It is quite simple. First, you will find an Instagram page which is related to your topic. Second, you will ask them to promote your product on their Instagram page and finally see sales come in. I have used a lot of methods, but this one always works! If you want quick sales on your

Instagram account, use this method. Now, let's talk about the things you need to worry about before you start advertising on Instagram.

- Find the right influencer
- Make sure they don't have any BOTs
- Engagement

So, here is the thing for you to make sales and rack up some reasonable amount of cash from your sales. You need to make sure that your influencer would have the right audience. Meaning you cannot expect to make sales off of a dog bracelet if the page is about "I hate dogs." Do you see what I am trying to say? Make sure the product you are trying to sell is related to the people who are on that specific page. So, for example, if I want to sell a fishing rod, I would look up I love fishing pages to promote on that.

Now, before you go out finding your influencer page, you need to make sure that the page has at least 300k followers. If it doesn't, then you are not going to get the engagement which you are looking for.

Next thing to take care of would be making sure the influencer you are thinking about working with has a high engagement rate. If people are not tuning into his/her page, they probably won't see your ads as well. There are some tools you use to find that out, but if someone is not getting at least 5-10% of their followers' likes, meaning if they have 100k followers and they are not getting at least 5-10k likes, then the chances are the followers are not engaging.

This would also show you if the followers are BOTs or not, meaning if they have bought followers or if they are real followers.

Now, let's talk about how to get a shout from these Instagram pages. Message them directly saying that you want a shout out. Then once you guys work out a deal, ask them for a "story shout out" as those work the best and ask for a 12-hour story shout out, all the followers will see your advertisement within the 12 hours so no need to advertise it longer than you should.

With that being said, let's now discuss the third method.

Blogs and Emails

This method works great! If someone has already bought from you once, and they liked the product or your services, odds are they will buy from you again. Using tools like creating your own blogs or anything of that nature can work beautifully for you to get sales and or to get some traffic onto your store. So, there are a lot of ways you can get free traffic. We will only be talking about the two main ones today which would be creating a blog and collecting an email list. Now, there is a downside to this method, and it could take some time to get traffic to your blog and collecting email list so don't consider this method if you want fast results.

Using blogs and email list to promote your products and services have been used for some time now. A lot of successful drop-shipping businesses solely use this method for advertising their products and services. So it works, and it works great! Just remember, it won't work right away as it takes time. Now with that said, here are the three things that you need to worry about before you start advertising with this method.

- Create a blog
- Get traffic on the blog
- Collect email subscribers
- Email them not SPAM!

The first thing you need to do is to create a blog. You will need to create a blog in order for you to actually start collecting emails. So, how you going to actually collect emails is quite simple. Once you have created a blog, I want you to begin publishing about the niche or subject with relates to your store or product. For example, if your online store or your product is about fishing, then write a blog about "how to ice fish" etc. Make sure the blog you write is filled with knowledge. People would not want to subscribe to a blog if it is not exciting or providing them with great tricks and tips about the niche.

Now, once you have created a blog and written your first blog, you will now need to start promoting your blog to the right people. This can be done for free. All you have to do is go on Google and search up similar blogs posted in the 24-hour mark time. Go on their blog's comment section and tell every reader to check out your link! It works excellent and equals free traffic.

After you have started to get some traffic onto your website, it will now be time to collect some emails. In order for you to receive emails, offer them something. So, if your blog and store are related to fitness, offer them a free workout plan if they enter their email! Everyone wants free stuff, so make sure you provide it to them. This should help you collect your email list, and I have personally built up around 10,000 email lists using this technique, so make sure you use it.

Once you have a decent amount of emails, you can now start promoting your products, But there is one thing you should remember, that is not spam! People do not like to see a sales email every day so make sure you space it out. Ideally, here is how you should go about emailing your potential client. For the first four days, send them an educational email like "how to fish" or "how to work out." Again, something related to your website, and then, on the fourth day, you can try and promote your product. This strategy works typically for me, and I am sure that it would work for you.

With all the tools provided to you, you should now be able to start your very own drop-shipping store. Remember, it takes time and effort to get to where you want to. But once you do get to a point where the money is coming in, it will become very passive and will overall help you to live the life you had always wanted to.

CHAPTER 5
Blogging 101

If you are on the fence about starting a blog or you have just started one, let me tell you why you have made the right decision of starting your very own blog or if you are about to. I think advanced readers can agree that blogging is one of the most creative ways to express one's thoughts. I remember starting my blog just to help people and express my views with the help of the internet.

Fortunately for me, blogging helped me with the needs I was looking for. It helped me express my opinions just the way I wanted to, and it honestly made me more creative. My first blog was related to the "how to make money online" niche, and I remember the first month I uploaded it, I got around 180 visitors to my site. I know for some people this isn't a lot of traffic, but for a beginner merely trying to express his thoughts into words, it was an accomplishment, to say the least.

Truthfully, the main reason why I started this blog was to promote my business and get some sales. Also, I just wanted to expand my brand and spread my knowledge in the niche I was in. Well, I didn't know that you can make money out of blogs until a couple of months into it. So, as I started to connect with people online, one of the bloggers told me to add Google Adsense to my blog to earn some cash. So, I took him up on his advice. So, a couple of months in, I was already getting some traffic to my blog and once I started using paid ads on my blog, I began to make money! I remember my first payout was $100 and I was so excited. It was my first time making money online, hence, the excitement.

As the months went by, my blog began to grow and start making more money. Little did I know I would be making money from a platform which I was merely using to promote my business. So, by now, I am making more than $1,000 a month from this blog. Which I know isn't much, but hey, I am making money for free and while promoting my business.

Then, after some time, a company messaged me and asked me to promote their product on a blog post, and they will pay me $400. I thought to myself, if I keep getting these leads at least twice a month, I can easily make $2,000 a month by merely writing 3k words explaining what the product is capable off and giving my opinion on it. I can't lie; this blogging stuff is really starting to grow on me. I am making money online! That's the dream.

After a year of blogging, I discover something called affiliate marketing. For those of you who don't know what affiliate marketing is, it is merely a commission you get if someone buys a product through your link. The exact words to myself were "well I get a lot of traffic to my blog anyway so why not make some extra cash." Well, I made the right decision. Within a couple of months, I went from making $2,000 a month to almost $15,000 a month by simply becoming an affiliate marketer with the help of the traffic to my blog.

What started as a simple way to promote a business turned into something which is now making me enough money to give up my business overall. Not only did blogging provide me with a platform to express myself and also to help promote my business, but most importantly helped me make a living.

Now, for any beginner here wanting to quit blogging or not start blogging, in general, let me ask you a question, do you want to connect with people with your ideas and thoughts while making a great living? If the answer is yes, then start your blog now or after you are done reading this book. And if the answer is no, then pass on this book to someone starting a blog. Listen, I know it's hard to make that decision of getting started but once you do, there is really no looking back here. You will soon be living the life you want to live by taking action now and not one year from now. Look at me after some years of blogging, I now entirely make a living out of my blog, and it is the best decision I have made so far.

Truth be told, you don't have to waste your time working a 9-5 in order to make money and live for the weekend. Look, I can say with no hesitation that blogging is the way to go if you want to make money fast and make a living while working. If you follow the steps in this book, you will get there quicker than I did.

Niche
Picking out a niche is probably one of the most important things you need to consider when you are first starting out your blog. The best way to decide which niche to pick for you and your blog would be to find all your interests, what do you like to do in your spare time? Is it fishing or skateboarding? Whatever you decide to write your blog on needs to be something you're truly passionate about as it will show on your writings. If you're not interested in a topic your blog is on then, you won't get a lot of traffic, as compared to your blog's topic being on something you are genuinely interested.

As by now, you can see the importance of picking out the right niche. Once you have picked out the right niche, which truly resonates with your personality and who you are, then we are ready to go! Now, once you have decided on which niche your blog will be based in, it would be the time to investigate it even further.

As a blog writer, the first thing you need to make sure of would be to find out everything you can about the niche you will be writing on, and it is imperative that you do so as it will only lead to further success with collecting your ideal prospects. Now, if you followed the first step by picking out a niche you are already passionate about, then it would be easier for you to find information about the niches' latest news, etc. But regardless, there are a couple of ways to go about finding absolutely everything about your niche which we will be covering today in this chapter.

More specifically, we will be discussing the three ways on how to find out everything about your niche in order to stay up to date with trends and new topics. The first thing you can do in order to find out more about your niche would be to use social media fan pages, as they do talk about the latest news and updates. The second method would be to read up on the top blogs in your niche, and the third one would be to learn more historical things about your niche as I will show you how it can help you.

Social media

Now, social media is one of the most powerful ways to stay connected with the latest news online. Especially for niche-based topics, I think we can all agree on the fact that the general population now relies on social media for the latest news rather than using traditional methods like newspaper or news channel. Not saying that newspapers or news channels are dead or useless, but most of the time, social media delivers the news to us faster than any news channel or newspaper would.

Well, it is a no-brainer for most of the bloggers to stay up-to-date with the news and latest trends utilizing social media as their tool. Now, there are three leading social media websites which I would recommend you use, and the first one would be Facebook. As we all are aware, Facebook is one of the biggest and most popular social media websites. If there is anything even remotely related to your niche, Facebook will have news and updates for you. The second one would be to use Instagram, and I would highly recommend using Instagram to stay up to date with any news or controversies regarding your niche.

Finally, the third social media platform I would recommend to be used would be Snapchat. Recently, Snapchat has started to use its platform to provide its users with some news and updates on the most niches you can think about. Quite frankly, the stories are subpar at the most, but sometimes, they really help you keep the mind flowing and do more research on a specific topic. With that note, let us get into the specifics on how these three platforms can be used to your advantage.

Let's first discuss Facebook. By now, Facebook has around 2.27 billion active users, so it is safe to say that Facebook has every news and up-to-date trends you can think about. More specifically, if your goal is to learn more about your niche and its latest trends, then consider joining fan pages related to your niche. Facebook has a lot of fan pages in a lot of different niches, so don't worry, and you will find a fan page related to your niche. The reason for having a fan page on Facebook is to provide the fans with its latest news and updates regarding what is happening in that niche, so definitely start using this platform to your advantage.

Instagram is a platform everyone has heard about by now. Slowly but surely, Instagram is starting to take over Facebook and become the next most prominent social media platform. The reason is simple. It is because it is so fun yet easy to use. Similar to Facebook, there are a lot of fan pages with every single niche you can think of. Use this tool to keep yourself updated with all the latest trends and topics related to your niche.

Thirdly, we will be covering the platform known as Snapchat. Some of you might know about this social media platform, but it is mainly used by many to share photos which they might have taken. Snapchat has a feature known as "the story." The main reason for having stories on the Snapchat page is relatively simple. It is to provide users with the latest news and updates, but the only drawback is that the niche section isn't as "filled up" as something like Facebook. But as I previously said, it gets the mind flowing. The niches covered on Snapchat are very broad niches, granted this is a relatively new feature, so we cannot expect it to compete with Facebook and Instagram.

Top blogs

Yes, you read it right. Using other blogs related to your niche for inspiration to get ideas and stay up to date with your blog works excellent. Quite frankly, this method sometimes works even better in comparison to using social media to stay updated with news related to your blog. So, how you utilize this method is very straightforward. The first thing you will do is to make sure the blog you are reading up on is highly respected in your niche. Secondly, you will try and see what the latest trend is in the blogging community.

For instance, if your blog is about health and fitness, then read up on all the top blogs in that niche and see what they are posting. Most of the time, they will post controversial post on the latest topics in that niche, which will not only keep you up to date with the niche but it will also give you some great ideas on how to write your blog post. Just make sure to cross-reference information in the blog post, as sometimes, bloggers can "twist up" the news. Just make sure you have the most accurate information.

Finally, using recent articles or latest updates from big news websites will work, too. Articles are very similar to a blog post, but just a little more authentic. Use the most recent articles which provide you with the latest news or discoveries in your niche to further your knowledge. Most of the time, the information provided will be accurate. That is if the website is of a big news channel. So, definitely consider using this platform.

History

Finding out the history of your niche can help you a long way when it comes to creating new topics. Now, it is essential that you stay up to date with the latest news in your niche by using the methods provided above. But if your goal is to become a true master in your niche, then it is not only important, but it is necessary that you know about every single thing there is about your niche, which of course includes the history.

Being aware of the history in your niche will help you with a lot of things when it comes to creating your content, more specifically, two things. First of all, help you understand newer information better, and secondly, help you create your own original content. So, first of all, knowing the history of your niches will help you identify the latest news better. Since most of the latest news or findings are sort of related to a prior history of the niche, let's take the health and fitness niche as an example. In the health and fitness industry, most news and research are cross-referenced with older information, since you might have heard or read of blog titles such as "Forty-year-old information was correct after all."

If you only decided to read up on the latest news and had not considered reading up on the history of the niche, then chances are you might not know anything about the information in the latest news which might have been historical before. Can you see why knowing everything including history is essential? It is because trends play itself out every time. Trust me, everything thing done in the past will be back in trend sooner than later. For instance, if you look at fashion, you will notice that the latest trend is inspired or is ultimately brought back from past trends.

I will keep saying it again and again; you need to get yourself aware and knowledgeable about the events that took place in the past related to your niche. If you want to make your blog stand out and have some great content flowing, then there is no shying away from learning the history of the blog. I know history could get boring, but if you want to grow your blog and get those potential leads, then your information needs to be of the utmost quality. People who are genuinely interested in the niche your blog is in will know the ins and outs of the niche, and to turn these beautiful people into potential customers, you basically need to become an expert in the niche you are in. If you follow the steps in this book, you will become one of the experts in no time.

My recommendation would be to read up on older blog posts and forums to find out more about the history of your niche. You can even read older books on your topic if you prefer that. Just make sure you have some time throughout the day to look up the history of your niche and absorb as much knowledge as you can.

This chapter should give you a clear idea on how to start your very own blog, more importantly, why. Blogging is one of the best ways to earn a lot of money online and to even get up to $300 a day. I hope this chapter was informative to you and we will see you in the next chapter.

CHAPTER 6
How To Make Money From Blogging

Affiliate Marketing
Believe it or not, affiliate marketing is one of the most common ways to make money from your blog. The truth is that bloggers make most of their money from affiliate marketing. It is very easy to start collecting your commission checks from your very own blog post, as we will show you how to do so. The top main affiliate programs to go with would be Amazon and Clickbank, as they will allow you to have a vast majority of the products to advertise, and also, this will allow making more money. Finding products to sell won't be so hard. It will be marketing which will be the problem. The best way to go about marketing would be to collect emails.

Email Marketing
Hope you're excited; we will be discussing how to create a vast email list from a single post. I just want to remind you of the fact that having an extensive email list doesn't mean that you will get a whole lot of sales, it is much better to have 1,000 emails which are engaging rather than having 10,000 emails which aren't as engaging. Either way, you need to make sure that you have the right amount of participating email addresses in order to start earning some money quickly.

For some people who don't know how this works, collecting emails gives you the ability to contact people. Meaning that you will reach people if you have something to sell, so if you have around 1,000 emails and you email a product to sell to the 1,000 emails, you have an affiliate or a product of your own. Let's just say that your product or affiliate product is worth around $40 in profit to you, and you only have 10% of the people from your email list buy it. You have now made $4,000 in one day. Let's say you have 10,000 engaging emails, and only 10% of your email list buys from you, you have now made $40,000 in one day!

Hopefully, by now, you're getting the idea of how powerful collecting an email list can be concerning making money rather quickly. That said, let's go through some tips and tricks on how to grow your email list rather swiftly and effectively. Before you get into tips, let's first discuss how you will be storing these emails. There are two websites or tools you can use to do so, and the first one would be to use mailchimp.com. It is free up to 1,000 emails, and then you have to pay after. If you're a beginner with no money, then this might work a little better for you, if not, then there are plenty of other apps you can use online to collect email.

Either way, you need to figure out how you will be collecting these emails for your blog. So, without further ado, let us talk about the three things we need to make sure of before we can start to make money with one singular post. Now, there are two most prominent ways to do so. First would be to use a technique where you offer something of value to the readers also known as an ethical bribe. The second method would be to merely have a pop-up show every time they visit your page. These are two simple yet effective techniques.

Ethical Bribe

We have all done it before, and we had all entered our email previously because someone was using this method correctly. Look, you can never go wrong using this method to collect emails. This is by far the easiest most effective way to receive emails without a doubt, and yes, as the title says, we are talking about using the ethical bribe to collect some profitable email. Now, how this works is when someone enters your blog or website, a pop-up will show up. What that pop-up will do is offer a gift to the people reading the blog. So, for instance, if your blog is about health and fitness, you will provide them something like a free eBook on different types of workouts you can do online. So, in order to unlock the gift, they will have to enter their email. Simple enough, you offer them something they want or like for free, and all they have to do is open their email.

I think we can all agree on the fact that we have entered our email to an ethical bribe. Now, there are two ways to go about it. First would be to make sure that whatever you're offering in exchange for the email is relevant to your blog's niche. The second one would be to provide something they can't refuse. Let's talk about the fitness niche again. If your blog post is about fitness and you offer them a basic workout, then chances are a lot of people won't enter their emails since they can find basic exercises everywhere. Instead, provide them with a guide book on how to create their own workouts based on their problems and needs.

Do you see the difference? Instead of giving them a cookie cutter workout which they can find anywhere, you have managed to provide them with something they can honestly take some knowledge out of, essentially offering them something of value.

One other way to offer an ethical bribe would be to give your readers a chance to win a free product if they enter their emails. I know some people who have used this method to collect a lot of money, but mostly, this is how it works. The first thing you will do is offer readers something they can't resist. It could be money or it could be a chance to win a free iPod to one lucky winner.

What this would do is create a great buzz around the blog and more people would enter in their email to simply win money or iPod. Make it a draw, so people get excited and spread the word around. Unfortunately, you might have to invest some money upfront but it works, and it is totally worth it. Again, you don't have to use this method. It just merely works great, that's all. Don't worry; the free eBook method also works great!

Pop-ups
The second thing I would like to talk about would be to use generic pop-ups. It is quite simple and effective. Very similar to the ethical bribe, all you have to do is just ask them to enter their email, and they will be getting updates on whenever you post a new blog. This pop-up can show up anywhere on the blog website, and it doesn't have to be on the home page. It could show up on the homepage, literally anywhere until they add their email to the pop-up. Just make sure you have a great pop-up so they don't miss it and they don't second-guess adding their email.

So, to make sure your pop-up looks great, make sure you pick the right color. Using colors like plain white won't work as they don't pop so much. Use colors like red to really attract people's attention so they genuinely can't miss out. Another thing to consider would be the caption, thus again making sure that you don't input in something bland like "enter your email here." It simply sounds boring; say something like "enter your email to get updates on new amazing blogs uploading every day." This sounds better and would work better, so definitely make sure to add the right colors and the right choice of words.

Mostly, it would help if you got readers emotionally attached to the blog for them to enter their email. In order to do that, first, you need to make sure to offer them something for free which is of value to them. Again, if your blog is about fitness, you can't provide them with a cookie cutter workout plan. It needs to be of high-quality for them to enter their emails. Secondly, you need to make sure your pop-ups look amazing, and you can't expect to get a bunch of people to enter their emails if your page looks bland. So, make sure to have bright colors on your pop-ups and also make sure have the right caption which hits them emotionally. I remember seeing this pop-up where it said something along the lines of "No thanks, I don't like free stuff" if someone decided to opt out of entering their email. That line or quote gets most people emotionally. That being said, make sure that the pop-ups have a line or quote where it gets the readers emotionally. But don't have a line like "enter your email, or you will remain fat" as it will just make you look like an insensitive person.

Hopefully, this helped you figure out how to collect emails regarding the use of these techniques in order to store emails and the ethical bribe and the pop-up techniques. Now, let us briefly touch up on how to actually make money using the email list.

How to make money?

There are two simple steps to remember in order to make money. First of all, the product or affiliate product which you will be selling has to be of the utmost quality. So, if you are selling a treadmill, for example, or if you're affiliated with a company that sells treadmill, you need to make sure that the product isn't "junk" as it will lead you to lose trust in your readers.

Now, for the most crucial step to cover. For you to actually get more people to buy from your email list and help you make heaps of money with just one post and one email, you need to make sure to email them and not spam them. Truth be told, no one likes a blogger or a marketer who makes it difficult for readers to trust them. If you keep sending them emails regarding a product or a sales pitch. Then chances are they will unsubscribe, and you need first to make sure to gain their trust and how you do that is very simple.

I like to use a technique where I email the readers informational stuff, so again if your blog is about fitness, send them one email every two days regarding new information or something helpful. Like "how to get fit in 30 days" or "ketogenic diet recipes" etc., and you need to make sure the information you provide is actually helpful to the readers. Now, here is the trick, after you have sent out at least four informational emails with no sales pitch, you can send your sales pitch on the fifth one.

So, a day before you can email your email list, ask them to check out the new blog you are about to post in 24 hours, and then once you have posted a blog, you can have the product links in that blog. Then, after 24 hours of you posting you're a blog, you can send them another email regarding the products you have to offer. Just make sure you have captured the most amounts of buyers.

This method works great, and it isn't pushy. Just make sure only to send them a sales email every four emails. Meaning the first four have to be informational and the fifth one can be a sales pitch. If you follow these two steps, you will not only grow an engaging email list, but you will also get the most sales. In order to make this even more profitable, slowly "hype up" your email list a couple of days before saying things like "make sure to check out the post in 4 days as it will blow your mind". This will further enhance you're sales and make you a lot of money. Again, get the readers as excited as you can in order to make some serious money on that one post.

With that note, I would like to conclude this fantastic yet informative chapter. Remember, that in order to make money with your email list, you need to make sure you have a place to store your email. You can use mailchimp.com or any other server; it is entirely up to you. Second, you need to make sure that you offer them an ethical bribe, and also to make sure that the bride is of high quality. It cannot be anything of a cookie cutter.

The third thing to make sure is to have a fantastic choice of color on your pop-up. Anything red works. Also, make sure you're caption hits them emotionally. Once you have managed to do that now, it would be the time to email them. Make sure your first four emails are of high-quality emails, so they become more engaged. Finally, it would be best if you made sure that the fourth email is about a product you want to sell or are affiliated with. Also, remember the fact that the product is of high quality. Remember to excite them up for your blog post a little bit in every email as it will lead them to read it more likely, and after another 24 hours, send them another email regarding the product you want to sell.

Trust me, and these techniques work like a charm. If your goal is to get the most out of your email list, you most definitely need to follow these methods listed above. With that being said, see you on the next page

CHAPTER 7
Become A Pro-Blogger

In the previous chapter, we briefly discussed the benefits of having an email list. We went into details on everything from how to build an email list to all the way on how to utilize the email list correctly in order to make the most money out of it. Now, needless to say, in order to collect email and make money, you need traffic. Currently, there is no better way to gain traffic than to make sure you're content is golden. You can't expect to gain notoriety without having great content.

So what does creating great content mean? Well, there are two ways to produce great content. The first and the most obvious way would be to make sure you're content adds value to the readers. You can't expect to make money or get traffic with a blog if you can't make the readers feel like it's worth their time. So, making sure you have value in your content is the key. The second way to attract more traffic to your blog would be to add some controversy.

Now, truth be told, everyone loves to read up on the controversy. Even if it doesn't provide them with any benefits, people will still read up on it. If you have a fashion blog, people would much rather read up on the latest gossip regarding the most trending superstar than to learn about the latest trends going on in fashion. Do you see my point? If you want to create a blog post which helps you get a whole lot of traffic, then it is best to write about the latest controversies in your niche.

There are some flaws to this technique though. Even though creating a controversial blog can help you gain a lot of attention, you need to make sure that it is done tastefully or you're brand name can be jeopardized. We will further discuss the reasons why it needs to be written or portrayed tastefully, but just remember that using this method could affect your brand image so be aware of that.

Controversy

Now, there are two types of controversies. The first one being a the debate controversy and the second one being the shocking or taboo controversy. For example, having a campaign which is belittling racists would be considered a debate controversy. Most people could agree with the fact that racism is not the best thing to partake on. Except for racist people, everyone else would find your post humorous and shareable to their friends. This would be considered a safe controversy.

Another yet so famous controversy was created by United Colors of Benetton, which made them famous. They posted a photo of a nun kissing. The idea behind it was to "unite" and have more multicultural acceptance. This would be considered a shocking or taboo controversy, and if not portrayed correctly, it could bring your brand crashing down. It's recommended to have a positive message if you want to use this type of controversy safely.

With any controversy posts, the point is this. You need to make sure whatever type of post you put up on your blog needs to have a "debatable" level to it in order to get noticed by people. But remember being debatable isn't enough. You need to make sure to correlate it with your brand to grow and get traffic.

If you need some ideas on how to make your blog post or banner more creative, there are plenty of amazing designs you can choose from in order to come up with a plan which will help you have a better understanding of which one to pick for the blog post.

So, now you have an idea on how to get traffic with posting some highly controversial post, remember to do it tastefully. My recommendation would be to, first and foremost, make it controversial, and secondly, make it so that it has a positive message, and it is imperative to do so as it will most likely not come along with negative stigma. One more thing to remember: if you really want to boom, your post should have a super controversial photo like United Colors of Benetton had.

Snowball effect

By now, you should be ready to create your controversial post. But you're not done yet, as you know, by far, the best way to get publicity to your blog would be through the use of the superpower which is social media. Social media has been used by so many people to boost their blog post to a whole nother level, so now; it's time for you to do the same.

Your controversial post will gain popularity with the help of social media and the snowball effect. Now, if you don't know what snowball effect is, then let me explain. The snowball effect is where you're blog post starts to become famous on social media and gets shared and promoted for free by users on social media. For some people, the snowball effect is a breakthrough for their blog post which will get a whole lot of traffic.

Let us not forget, most people online only use the internet for social media. Social media is the new way to get notoriety. So, if you can manage to get the snowball effect rolling and which you will with the help of social media and your controversial post, then your blog will get the traffic you want and need!

Now, there are three ways to create a snowball effect onto you're a blog post, but before we start this process, you need to make sure that you have you're blog posted and ready to go. Once your blog is posted and ready to go, you can now start to create a snowball effect. Our goal with this blog post is to make sure that it is indeed "debatable" and controversial. If it is controversial and debatable, then you don't need a lot of traffic from your end, as it will create some dangerous traffic with the help of social media and other people reposting your link on their page.

So, there are three things you need to do to get the snowball rolling. The first one would be to create backlinks. It is super-easy to do so, and I will show you how. The second thing you need to take care of would be to email all the email contacts you have on your latest upload. Finally, you need to make an effort to post your blog link on to every Facebook page there is related to your niche.

Let's talk about the first method which is to create some backlinks. Now, you should be building backlinks for your blogging regardless, but make sure to create as many backlinks as you can in the first three days of posting your blog. So, how you can create backlinks is relatively simple. What you do is go onto more famous blogs or even you're competitor's blogs and merely post a link to your blog. Now, unfortunately, most of the comments get deleted, so in order to avoid that, you need to make sure to post your link correctly.

In order to post your blog link correctly, you need to make sure you sound like a reader rather than a promoter. Instead of writing a comment saying, "Hey, check out my blog" you need to say "Check out this blog! Where they talk about blah blah what do you guys think?" Do you see the difference? You need to make sure that you sound like a reader instead of a blogger trying to create backlinks. This will work and only work if you make sure to look interested. Also as a reader, another thing to remember is that if your blog is going to have that controversial post, then you will get people promoting your blogs online and the backlinks you would have created would work wonders.

So, make sure to write comments on every blog you can find related to your niche and make sure to write predominantly on post or blogs which are trending and have been uploaded at least a week before the day you decide to comment on them. Since the blog will be new, it will get a lot of traffic and so will you with the backlinks created.

The second method would be to use your email list. Obviously, make sure you keep emailing your list a couple of days before you post your controversial blog online. This will help you get your readers excited and ready to read your blog on the day it is published. So, make sure you keep your email list updated, and once the blog is live, make sure to email them right away and see your blog post blow up.

Now, the third and final method, which is also very important, would be to post your blog links onto Facebook pages related to your niche. This works like a charm concerning getting traffic to your post and creating that snowball effect. So you need to make sure that in order to get some considerable traffic to your blog, you will have to post it on social media pages related to your niche.

Now, similar to creating backlinks on other blogs, posting on Facebook pages is the same. You can't get away with merely posting your blog onto the Facebook page as it requires your post to be approved by the admin of the page. So, in order to get your post approved, you have to do similar things as you did before, which would be to act like a follower/reader rather than just a promoter. Saying things like "check out this blog where they talk about blah blah" would work a lot better.

Make sure to post on social media platforms carefully, and make sure to only post it on to pages which are related to your niche. As posting it on random niche pages will merely make you look like a promoter, even if you post like a reader. Again, make sure you do use this social media platform as it works wonders and will get you're snowballing effect rolling faster.

In conclusion, remember that in order to get a whole lot of traffic and make money out of your post, you need to do a couple of things. First of all, it would be to create a controversial post as it will yield you the most results concerning gaining traffic. Again, make sure that the post is done tastefully as it can bring your brand name crashing if not done so, another thing to pick before you create your blog post would be to consider the two options you have, first one being debate controversy and the second one would be taboo or shocking controversy. Ideally, I would go with debate controversy as it is safer.

Secondly, you need to make sure that the post has been promoted correctly, and for you to do that, you need to take care of three things. The first one is creating backlinks on blogs. This works great if done right and will produce the snowball effect right away. The second one would be to email your list. This also works great, and most definitely needs to be exercised, and finally, let us not forget the power of Facebook pages. Make sure to promote your blog link just like the way this book has taught you to do so. After all that has been said and done, you should start to see the snowball effect in action right in front of your eyes. Just remember that it may or may not work for you the first time but keep trying. Eventually, it will. These methods listed in this chapter are the fastest ways to get traffic, so keep pushing and keep going at it; you will get your fame soon.

The PAS method

Hopefully, by now, you should have gotten something great concerning how to write a blog the right way and how to market it. Now, it is time to touch upon copywriting, and truth be told, copywriting isn't something which can be created by writing some things here and there, hoping to have some power magically. You can't expect to follow a formula and expect to have this beautiful copyright to follow. What these copyright formulas give you is a starting point or a framework which you can make as your own.

So, today, we will be talking about one of the most famous and useful copyright formulae. It has been used for some time now and still works great. Of course, we are talking about P.A.S: Problem-Agitate-Solve. It's an all-time favorite for most people as it works on everything for all kinds of marketing, landing pages, and flyers. Hopefully, by the description, you could have guessed what Problem-Agitate-Solve is all about. So without further ado, let us get into the topic and truly dissect this method.

Problem

Now, when we are talking about problems, you need to make sure that you get into the emotions of the readers and make them feel like they need to make the change to fix the problem. You need to make sure that you remind them of the problem and make them feel the pain as they are reading through the post. For example, if you're post is about a fitness tool like a foam roller, you would write, "Tired of using traditional foam rollers were getting the right spot is not only hard but impossible?"

Now, do you see what I am trying to say? You need to make sure that you bring up the problem which makes them feel like they definitely need a change. You will merely attach the problem and make them feel emotionally connected to what you wrote, plain and simple.

Agitate

Moving on to part two of the method, since you have now managed to get the readers agitated and ready to go in terms of getting them emotionally involved, it would be no time to attack the problem even further and get the readers more emotionally attached to the post. Now, one thing to make sure, you cannot wallow too much as it will fend off a lot of people. Just add some salt to the wound, while still making them feel like they have a way out.

An example would be "While you use the foam roller, it just seems like it is not helping you get to your problem areas, which can get annoying, and quite frankly, make you want to give up on foam rolling overall, but there is a way to fix this." Did you see what I did there? I really "added some salt" to the wound, and made the readers feel like they most definitely need the thing or product I am about to offer them.

Solve

Now finally, we will be discussing the final phase which would be to solve the problem. Since you have managed to get the readers more engaged and aware of their issues, it would be now time to fix the problem. This is very simple, but it has to be done the right way, you cannot sound like a salesman. Look, you need to be subtle with your closing meaning that you can't be too aggressive. If you end up being too aggressive, then the Problem and Agitate will go to waste.

Now, to make sure you don't sound too aggressive or rather like a salesperson, you need to make sure that you're more of a friend by helping them fix their problems rather than closing a sale. Here is an example, "No worries, with the help of this new foam roller, you can hit those hard to get areas! Try it out". As you can see, I was talking to my readers like I would be talking to a friend, simple and not too pushy. That is what you should be aiming for.

Example PAS

We have all been there, trying to wake up early every day so we can get more stuff done and get closer to our goals. But somehow, we end up waking about 4 hours after when we're supposed to.

Truth be told, these regular alarm clocks don't work anymore. Every day, you get one step away from achieving your goal. These snooze buttons are just not the way to go and are indeed holding you back.

But there is a way out, and luckily with the new alarm pillow on the market, it will vibrate your head until you wake up. I know I don't need old technology anymore! I'm going with snooze pillow. Get it today at snoozepillow.com.

Do you see how great this PAS is? It is really attacking people's problems and is genuinely here to fix the issue in no time. The best part is that you don't sound like a salesman. Just a friend who is helping another friend to fix the problems he or she may be facing. Hopefully, you get the idea by now.

People, just remember two things. Readers don't want to be sold to and also don't like it when they are sold to, and the readers love it when you bring out the problem and help them find a solution.

With that note, I would now like to conclude this chapter. Remember, using PAS is one of the best ways to get sales and recognition to your blog post. So, I would highly recommend that you use this method to get the most out of your post. Remember to not sound like a salesperson, instead, make sure you sound more like a person who truly wants to help your readers solve the problem which they might be facing. So make sure you bring up the problem, agitate it further, and offer your readers with a solution and the rest will be history.

CHAPTER 8
Instagram 101

In this chapter, we will be talking about Instagram and YouTube, and how you can make money out of it. The reason why the chapter only has Instagram at the top is that it is the most used platform out there. But if you combine all three platforms together, you can make some serious money. Most of the users make money from affiliate marketing, but in later chapters, we will show you how you can make even more money dabbling with different methods out there to earn more money. But for now, we will show you how to make money from this method and how to combine it with three other methods which will allow you to earn even more. Let's talk about affiliate marketing if you have no idea of how it works.

Affiliate Marketing
The best way to describe affiliate marketing would be to use an analogy. Let us say you are the president of your university and every single student in that university listens to your voice. Since you are the president of this university, a majority of the people in that university follows your advice and recommendations. When suddenly, a professor of the university offers you sell his textbook, and in return, you get a commission or a percentage of the textbook sale by promoting the professor's textbook to your audience or following.

So, in essence, this would be an example of affiliate marketing. Just what you have to do in order to get sales would be to first create a big following and then promote a product to that audience. Simple enough, right? Well, there are some tricks involved in this method in order to become successful in affiliate marketing which we will be discussing in this chapter. Now, there are a lot of ways you can start to market a product to make a commission; we will be considering how to do so by using the best methods for you to start affiliate marketing.

Now, the methods which will help you to start making money with affiliate market will be YouTube, blogging, and Instagram/Facebook page. Now, these three are the best ways to get started with your affiliate marketing business. There are some pros and cons to each of these tools; you might have to try out all three methods before you can see which one works for you and which one doesn't. Now, without further ado, let's begin with YouTube.

YouTube

YouTube was founded on February 14th, 2005, created by three former PayPal employees Chad Hurley, Steve Chen, and Jawed Karim. YouTube, at first, was created by the founders to share videos easily without facing any problems while doing so. Fast forward to November 2006, YouTube was sold to Google for USD 1.65 million. Ever since then, YouTube has not stopped growing. According to some sources, there is at least 1 billion hours' worth of videos that are being watched every day on YouTube. That goes to show how big YouTube is. Now, you might be wondering since this website is so popular, you could easily start promoting affiliate products and earn some great commissions.

Well, there are some tricks involved to do so, although there are a lot of videos watched on YouTube. On any given time of day, there are still some things you need to make sure. One is to check from your end before you can really start to promote your product on this website. Don't worry it isn't hard, just like any business; it will take some time and effort to get started.

The first thing you will need to do is to create a niche. Really think about what you are interested in. For example, if you are interested in fitness, then make a fitness channel. If you are interested in science, create a Science channel. The main thing you need to consider before you start your very own YouTube channel is to make sure that whatever your channel is about, it needs to be something you are genuinely interested in. This is the reason why people can see through everything these days. If you hate fitness and you decide to make a fitness channel, they can tell that you don't like fitness-related stuff, and therefore, don't subscribe to your channel. Making sure you have love and passion for the circuit you will be building on YouTube is imperative.

The second thing we need to worry about is growing your channel or following, and if you don't have an audience on your YouTube channel, then chances are your affiliate marketing endeavors might go to fail. So, you first need to grow your YouTube channel before you can start selling affiliate products. With that being said, let us discuss how you can build your YouTube channel fast and efficiently.

Now, there are a lot of ways to do so, but the best way I would recommend is to come up with unique content. I know it sounds very cliché, but it works! Think about it. Why would someone want to follow you if you don't have something different to offer them? So, there are a lot of ways to be compatible with your content, but the first technique to make different material is to think outside the box and into the future like what would be the "new thing." Once you have figured it out, make sure you are the first one to start the trend.

Another way to start getting some more views and followers would be to have an exciting caption and clickbait. Let me give you an example of a clickbait. Recently, big YouTubers would do things like "My yearly income" and a photo of them with money as the clickbait on the video. Since everyone is curious about how much these big YouTubers make, these YouTubers directly elude people into their video and start to rank up the views, but they never reveal their income. As I said, it is merely clickbait. Now, this technique does work, but you can't use it every time, as it will lead to some drops in your followers, etc. so, use it with caution. Finally, the last technique I would recommend would be to collaborate with YouTubers who already have a big following. Before you work with one of the big YouTube channels, make sure their channel is related to your channel. Collaborating with a more significant channel won't be easy or free. I would say 1 out of 10 will agree upon doing a "collab video" with you and finally work out a deal either by an upfront payment or a shared partnership of the video. There is some money involved, but it is totally worth it as this technique works the best in order to grow your YouTube channel and business.

Now, after you have managed to grow your YouTube channel to a substantial level—ideally, a 100k followers or subscribers—it would take no time to promote products from which you can earn an affiliate commission. Again, remember to promote a product which is related specifically to your YouTube channel. Don't expect to sell a PlayStation 4 on a channel connected to fitness. It is not that people won't buy—they probably won't—but it makes you look like a salesman, which is not the look that you should be going for. So, if you want to earn some affiliate commission, make sure the product is related to your channel and niche. There are many websites you can use to start earning an affiliate commission, but the two leading sites I would recommend is ClickBank and Amazon. Let us cover ClickBank first. ClickBank is an online video course website that sells courses from a health-related niche to a making-money-online niche, so as you can see, it has a broad spectrum of courses available on its site. You can earn up to 75% of the commissions on each sale, and it is straightforward to do so if you have a following. All you have to do is review the video course and give your audience an honest review of the product. Make sure you add your affiliate link in the description below of the YouTube channel in order to earn commissions.

The second one is Amazon. As we know, Amazon is the biggest e-commerce website in the world right now. On top of that, they sell anything you can imagine, so it doesn't matter what niche you are in. You can find a related product to your niche. That said, there are some pros and cons to this website. The disadvantages are that the commission rates are lower compared to ClickBank. There is no exact percentage of commission you will get, but 75% of commission on Amazon is super hard to find as compared to ClickBank. Now, the positive is that once someone even clicks your affiliate link, you will be getting a commission on everything they buy for the next 48 hours. This is where the lower commission rate makes up for Amazon. Again, if you decide to use Amazon as your source of the affiliate partner, make sure you try out the product and give a proper review.

Instagram/Facebook Page

This is also a fantastic technique to start earning those affiliate commissions. So how this works is quite similar to YouTube. You will first need to attract a following to your page, and then you can start to promote your products slowly. Now, to explain this process instead is this: no audience = no sales. Therefore, our primary goal is to start getting our Instagram page bigger, which would equate to more affiliate commission.

The first method would be setting up a Facebook page which would be specific to your niche. Now, after you have created an Instagram account and a Facebook page, start promoting both pages only by purchasing shoutouts from bigger pages related to your niche. After that is done, you will slowly begin to grow your Instagram/Facebook page, but one thing to remember is that you don't want to stop posting content on your Instagram/Facebook page as it will result to a drop of followers and engagement rate.

The second method to grow your Instagram page is to use a technique known as "follow-unfollow." It is pretty self-explanatory. What you have to do is follow users hoping that they would follow you back and then eventually unfollow them. This technique works if your goal is to gain some following quickly. That said, this is not the best way for long-term growth so keep that in mind. Start following people and unfollow them after three days or so.

Finally, let us talk about how to make money with affiliate marketing on Instagram. So, after you have a following off around 100k, you will then start to notice people will pay you money to have their product on your page. You can also do affiliate marketing with ClickBank, but it just works better when you promote on Instagram using the "shoutout" technique.

Using all three at once

Now, ideally, this is how it should be. Using YouTube, Blogging, and Instagram all at once will yield you the best results. So, if you really want to make some serious cash with affiliate marketing, here is how you do it. You will first create a brand. For example, if you're into fitness, you will create a YouTube channel, blog, and Instagram/Facebook account with a brand name that you came up with. Now, you will merely use all the techniques listed in this chapter to make sure all three sales channels—YouTube, blog, and Instagram—grow and flourish.

How much money can you make?

Now, this is a question that can't be answered straight away. You see, if your goal is to put in minimal time and make it as passive as possible, you can realistically make anywhere from $100 to $1,000 a month. But if you really want to make some serious cash and if you utilize all three sales channels while using the techniques above, you can make $100,000 to $1,000,000 a month. I have personally seen some pay stubs of the top affiliate marketers, and they surely make more than a million dollars a year, so if you are willing to put in the hard work, you can seriously make some fantastic cash.

All that said I would now like to conclude this chapter by saying this: With affiliate marketing, the choice is yours. You can choose to make an extra $1,000 a month by doing some work here and there, or you can honestly take your income to the next level! Again, the choice is yours.

CHAPTER 9
How To Make Money From Instagram Page

If you remember previously, we talked about how to make money from Instagram and YouTube. In this chapter, we will show you all the opportunities out there, which will allow you to make tons of money. Affiliate marketing is a great way to make money; however, making your own Instagram page to grow and to make money out of the niche people who follow you can be one of the best ways to make money. One of the ways to do that is to make cool merchandise based on your Instagram or Facebook page, allowing you to make the most money.

Now, you might have heard of this topic before, but if not, let me explain to you how this works. Selling merchandise is merely selling a t-shirt with a distinctive logo to a client. It could be anything like shoes, pillowcases, etc. But most of the time, this is used for selling t-shirts. How this works is simple. Specific websites or apps allow you to add any logo your heart desires and sell it to customers. It is similar to drop-shipping, since you don't have to see the products, and it ships out directly to your customers. This method is probably the most trending right now regarding making money online since it is so new, you can make money with it rather quickly. Now, there are a couple of things we need to take care of before you can go ahead and start your very own business of selling merchandise. Now, there are a lot of platforms you can use to start you're very personal shop such as Amazon Merch, Redbubble, Tasty, and your very own Shopify. It is entirely up to you which website you use to get started with, and luckily, the start-up cost for all is very cheap and reasonably affordable, so you don't need to worry about investing a lot of money into it. All you need to worry about is the monthly payment of websites and the cost to get a logo design done, that's all.

With that said, here are three things you need to take care of before you can start your business of selling merchandise. 1. Find a niche 2. Make an Instagram/Facebook page 3. Advertising. So, all these things are essential if you want to be successful in this business. So, without further ado, let us get into it.

Finding a niche

Finding a niche is very important for you to actually to make this business profitable. Think about it? Why would someone want to buy your t-shirt? It is merely a t-shirt. Whereas, if you make a meme t-shirt, everyone who is a fan of memes would be interested in buying your product. It is essential that you find a niche you would want to sell into.

Now, there are a lot of niches to get into. Your job is to find one where you can sell t-shirts relating to the niche. Now, there are a lot of examples of this. But I will use one for the readers so they can get a better idea. So, if you ever stumble upon fitness gurus or fitness channels on YouTube, these guys solely use these methods to make and distribute it to the buyers, since they have a large following of people who want to buy from them.

The beauty of finding a niche in this business model is that you can make any topic or niche profitable business. So, if you like bowling, you can create cool bowling logos and sell it to people who would be interested in bowling. As long as you have a cool logo, you can sell your t-shirts. Also, you need to get traffic on you're the page, but we will get into that topic later on in this chapter.

Listen, you don't need to find a specific niche. You can enter any niche your heart desires and sell it on there as long as the logo looks cool and you have people in that niche become aware of your t-shirt or any merchandise for that matter.

YouTube

Now, making a YouTube account is very easy. If you have a Gmail account, then chances are you already have a YouTube account for you to upload on. Once you have the YouTube account, pick a niche and start to advertise your page on there. YouTube is one of the hottest social media out there, in regards to building an audience. Essentially, your goal is to build up audiences all around your niche's specific page like YouTube, blog, Instagram page, so you have more places to reach a potential audience.

Growing a YouTube audience is a bit complicated, which is why we recommend you start by building both Instagram and YouTube pages simultaneously. That way, you can get your viewers to grow faster and to get more benefits out of it. Another way you can actually make money from YouTube would be to start monetizing your videos. Once you reach 1,000 subscribers, you will have the ability to monetize your videos. Hence, allowing you to make money from it. Then, once you have achieved 1,000 subscribers, you can then start to sell your merchandise. This way, you will be making money from YouTube, and you will start to get sales for your merchandise. As always, you can even begin to promote products to earn an affiliate commission.

That way, you can make money from three different avenues from one source. Remember, it is always good to have as many streams of income as possible in this day and age. Really try and capitalize on as many income avenues as possible. That way, you can start to earn more money sooner and you will have better chances of scaling up even higher. This goes for any income stream listed in this book. Hopefully, that helps you to make more money.

Make Instagram/Facebook page

Now, once you have found out which niche you will be getting into, it would soon be time to make an Instagram and a Facebook page on that subject. Now, most people don't talk about this, but making a niche specific page and growing it to a big following can get you a bunch of sales. As this would be targeted advertising, you will first gain people's trust by posting amazing photos and logos on your page, so people follow. And once it grows out to be a more prominent page, you can then start selling merchandise to them, and it will sell.

There are a couple of ways to grow your Instagram page. One of them would be to buy followers online. However, that isn't effective if you want to improve your brand and get more sales. Remember, it is much better to have 1,000 followers that are active than 10,000 followers that are inactive. Our goal is to make an Instagram page which will help you make money, not boost your ego. Now, to organically grow your Instagram page, here are the top 5 things to do: 1. Be active on your account 2.Follow and unfollow 3. Post high-quality photos 4. Get paid promotions from bigger pages 5. Join an engagement group.

So, the first thing we will be covering would be being active on Instagram, being active on Instagram means that you are continually liking and commenting on photos and videos on Instagram. What this does is to get your account out there and be visible to the people who might be interested in following you. Once you start liking and commenting on the photos and videos on a more prominent Instagram page, often you will begin to notice your channel is getting free publicity and people will start to follow you. So, make sure you are doing this religiously every day to grow your Instagram page.

The second thing would be to use a method known as "follow-unfollow." Essentially, what your goal with this method is to follow as many active users as possible, and then unfollow after three days or so. There are some online tools which will take care of this process for you, so you can either go that route, or you can go the other direction and do this manually. If you do go manually, make sure to write down their names, so you can unfollow them after three days or so. This technique still works to gain quick followers in a hurry. Make sure that you are utilizing it, especially in the beginning.

The third method would be to make sure you provide users with some high-quality photos, and this is crucial for your Instagram to grow. If your page is about camping and outdoor activities, and you post landscape photos, they can't be of and quality. You need to make sure you have high-quality images, and you can use other Instagram pages photos which are of high quality but always make sure to tag them on your post. One company who has done this successfully is outdoor_hack. They are a Shopify-based account, and even though they don't have any photos taken especially for them, they still have managed to grow and make money. So, if you are looking for some inspiration, I would check that page out on Instagram.

The fourth thing you can do would be to use bigger pages online to promote your page. How this works is that you pay them money for a 24 hour or 12-hour shout out. Most of the time, they post it on their story or feed. This works great if you have some money to invest, merely getting shout-outs from bigger pages can help you grow your page quite rapidly.

Now, finally, we will talk about engagement groups. This is the method most people use to take their page/pages to the next level. This method will make your page skyrocket in followers, and of course, more sales for your merchandise business. An engagement group is a group of pages similar in size. What everyone in this group will do is whenever you post a photo, they will like and comment on it the picture, and you will also have to love others photos and comment on them.

Every engagement group has different rules, but most of them pre-decide when everyone is going to post online. Everyone in the group has to like and comment on that specific post within the allotted time period of typically 30 minutes, and if you don't follow the rules, you will be kicked out of the group, period. So make sure to follow the rules, and finally, make sure to follow all the four steps above so you can actually utilize this tool correctly and get the most out of it.

Now, most of my readers might be wondering, why did I ramble on growing a niche based Instagram account? Here is the reason why most people won't tell you this, but this business model won't work correctly if you don't have a niche based Instagram/Facebook page. So, if you want to make money out of this business model, having a niche page with a big following is a big part of your success. Now, this takes time. If you want to get quick sales fast, you will have to advertise your product.

Advertising

Now, once you have created a Facebook page, you can use that page to utilize Facebook's advertising services to promote your products. It is the exact same process as the one described in chapter 6 so make sure to check that out. However, we again come back to Instagram advertising to make money. It just works so much better than any other method.

Instagram, as I said before, is a great place to advertise your products, especially for the merchandise business since it is such a niche based one. So, if your goal is to get quick sales on your page, you can use this method. When we advise on Instagram most of the time, you will use a technique called "Instagram influencer."

Similar to promoting your page for more followers you will find an Instagram page which is related to your topic which also has a big following, then you will get a paid shoutout from them and see the sales come in. People who are in the business of selling merchandise online can say this is one of the fastest ways of getting sales. There are three things you need to take care of before you start advertising on an Instagram page.

- Finding the right influencer
- Making sure they don't have any BOTs
- How much engagement are they getting

As you know by now, in order to get sales and make money, you need to make sure you are promoting your product to the right audience. So you cannot promote a fitness shirt on a page that is about global warming, Make sure the page you decide to encourage on is about what you are trying to promote.

Just a little side note, make sure whichever page you choose has over 300k followers. Now, this depends from niche to niche, but this a good rule of thumb to follow when picking out your influencer.

Now, finding an account in your niche with over 300k followers is tremendous but what's their engagement like? The truth is some pages have "BOTs," meaning they have bought followers for their page. There are a couple of ways to find out if that's the case or not, but if someone is not getting at least 5-10% of their followers like their post, meaning if they have 100k followers and they are not getting at least 5-10k likes, then the chances are their follows have been bought.

So, in order to get a shout from these Instagram pages, you will have to message them directly saying something along the lines of wanting a shoutout. Once you have decided on a price, you can start to promote your product on their page once they receive the payment. One thing to remember is that there is no need to get a 24-hour shout out for a product ad. All of the followers on the page will see your advertisement within the 12 hours, so no need to advertise it longer than you should.

How much money can you make?

Now, this totally depends on you, but you can make as much as $1,000 to as much as you want. The sky is indeed the limit. This is the same as Shopify. You can make a lot of money with this method, make sure you have a niche brand and also make sure to grow it as big as you can. You can become a millionaire, if not a billionaire, with this method. But if you want to make some extra cash on the side, it would be very easy to do so with this method.

So, remember to follow everything that is said in this chapter if you want to start earning some cash. The biggest secret revealed is to grow your very own Instagram pages. This is something that isn't talked about so much. Creating logos and other aspects of the business is very easy to do but if you want to grow your business and take it to the next level, make sure to create and improve your Instagram account as quickly as possible. Also, make sure to pick a niche in which you have interest and passion for it will more likely grow bigger for you as compared to others.

CHAPTER 10
Future Of Passive Income

If you thought that we were going to tell you something like "new way to make money online," then you are entirely wrong. When people think of passive income, they think about sitting at home collecting money. All the methods we talked about so far in this book where passive, but the two main ways we are going to talk about in this chapter as the most passive methods out there. These methods will ensure passive income. That means you will make money while sitting at home. These two streams of income have been used in the past, and I believe the future of passive income.

Stock Market

A stock market is also a form of trading. It has been used by big investors like Warren Buffet to make some serious cash. The stock market was founded on March 8th, 1817 in New York City U.S.A. The stock market was created for people to start investing in companies for the company to get more funds for growth. Eventually, as the companies would grow, the stock prices would go up for the specific company. So, for the people who had some money invested in the company, they would sell those stocks for a profit which would mean more money in their pockets. So, in a nutshell, that is how stock market trading was invented.

Now, this method has some pros and cons to it so let us go through them. To start with the advantages, the first positive is, of course, you can make money using this process. The second positive would be it is entirely passive compared to other methods in this book. All you have to do is check up the stock market frequently, and you should be good. Just like anything in this world, there are some cons. The first significant con would be that you can lose you invested money. It is imperative that you do your research on the company before you decide to invest in that company.

The second con would be irregular, what I mean by that is this. Let us say you buy a stock at $1.30 a piece and a couple of days go by and the stock is now $2.00. Most of the people would rather wait, but sometimes, the stock would come plummeting down to $0.80 a piece which would make you lose money. Or if you decide to sell it at $2.00 per share, you would still make good money, but if the next day it shot up to $3.00 per share, you would be regretting your decision.

Look, what I am trying to say is this. Utilizing the stock market to make money is like a rollercoaster ride. You will have your ups and downs, and you will face some significant losses sometimes or some significant gains. Although there are ways to avoid the considerable injuries with the methods I will provide, the main thing to remember is not to get greedy as it might make money sometimes, but you can come crashing down.

There are two methods to make money utilizing the stock market which we will be going through today. The first one is "Growth stocks" and the second one would be "Mutual funds."

Growth Stocks

Growth stocks, also known as "buy low sell high" is one of the most common techniques used by many investors. Although this method takes time and effort, it can yield you with some good returns. Now, the principle behind this method is this, find a company with cost per stock that is low, and then once it goes up, sell it and enjoy the profits you made. Simple enough, right? Well, there are some things to be learned before you go about doing so, specifically three things.

- Research about the company
- Patients and discipline
- Continued research

To begin with, let's talk about how to research the company you will be investing in. As we know, there are a lot of companies in this day and age. Picking out the right company to spend it can be somewhat tricky. So, this is where the extensive research comes in before you pay in one. To be clear, there is no right or wrong company to be investing in. There are a lot of companies which will go up, and you have to pick the one you believe in. To find out if the stocks of a particular company will go up or not, it requires a couple of steps. The first thing you need to do is to check out last year's report on the company and their stock prices.

Check to see if the stock prices have steadily been going up or not and are it still continuing on. The second method would be to make sure that the company is up is to do something big which will help the company grow, for example. Canada made marijuana legal which equated to all the marijuana dispensaries stock prices to go up in Canada. So, what I mean by doing research is to see if anything significant is happening to the company or the market the company is in.

Being patient and having a certain amount of discipline is imperative for your growth and success in this market in order for you to make money and not to lose money while investing in stocks. Truth be told, you can make some severe cash overnight with this method or make some fantastic returns a couple of years down the road. Don't get impatient and sell your stocks when you have an idea of the company and if it is going to be making significant moves soon.

61

On the other hand, don't get greedy. If the stocks are coming up fast, then they will come down just as soon in most cases. Don't get greedy wanting for more money. Sell it once you have made some good money out of those stocks. This would be where your discipline comes into factor. Finally, I would like you to remember that investing in stocks requires some "gut feeling." Not everything is going to be calculated in stock market spending. After you have done your research and decided to buy stocks, you might have to go by gut feelings sometimes to sell your shares. Finally, what you will have to take care of is continued research on the company. Now, making sure to stay up to date with the company's news in which you invested in is imperative for your growth and success. This will give you an idea of when to sell and when not to sell your stock. For instance, let us say you find out the company you invested in might notice a drop in its stock price. Merely make sure to sell it before you lose money or vice versa. Continued research and updates will give you an idea of when to sell and when not to sell.

Mutual funds
This method is a little bit easier to get started with as it comes with a lower risk. Mutual funds are when your money is managed by professionals and is invested in different companies by them. Although there is a cut taken by the professionals, in the end, it is still a safer and effective way if you want to make money as compared to "Growth Stock." Since you won't have to worry about doing research online and checking out every little detail about the company, it will be more of a "passive investment" which will make you money later on.
So, if you want to make money without spending too much time doing research and other things which are related to "growth stocks" as it is less of a risk, go ahead, but you won't make as much money as you could be making with "growth stocks."

How much money can you make?
Now, this would depend entirely on the market and how much you put in. The stocks game is "the more you put in, the more money you will make," so if you want to make more, you will have to invest more. There is no estimate on how much you can potentially make, and you can make $1,000 profit up to a $1,000,000 profit. It depends on luck and how much you invest in the company. Like I said previously, if you want to play it safe, I would recommend you invest in some mutual funds, even though the returns won't be as good as "growth stocks," it will still yield you some good money without the risk.
Remember that investing in the stock market is a gamble. You might make some money or lose some money. If you do what is advised in this book, chances are you will make money. Many full-time day traders make

money solely off the stock market. But you need to remember that the market is unpredictable and anything could happen anytime, so if I were you, I would invest some money on the side rather than to make this a full-time job as it is not so secure.

Once you do spend, don't forget to do your research and to make sure that you don't pay more than what you can afford. Again, if "growth stocks" scare you, then invest in some mutual funds. Sometimes, it is good to take some risks as you don't know where it will take you. Remember to be safe and smart with your money and don't get too greedy as it could lead you to lose your hard-earned money which is the last thing we want to do.

Options Trading

Just like the previous method, this method will also be a bit "theoretical," so please read it a couple of times if you don't understand it fully the first time. Now, there are two types of options trading. One is the call options and the other is the put options. So, in this chapter, we will be going through the two options. We will discuss how they work. So, without further ado, let us get into it.

Call options

To explain the call options, we will be using an analogy. Let's say you work in the automotive industry. You know the ins and outs of it. You also know exactly how much a specific car is worth and if it will go up in price or not in the future. Now, you get some insider news that the 1996 corvettes will be going up in prices in 6 months from now. Just like anyone in the interest of making some profits, you start looking for a 1996 corvette, and lo and behold, you find the perfect example of one for sale. Now, it will cost you $20,000 to buy one, and you only have $5,000 to spare. But you do know that you will be getting a bonus in 6 months for $20,000 which will cover the cost of the car, but unfortunately, it will be too late by then as the prices will go up. So, what you do is this: offer the seller $5,000 as a down payment for the car. You will tell the seller that you will have the full amount of $20,000 in 6 months from now for the car. Until then, you will take the car off the market and in 6 months you will buy it for a fixed price of $20,000. If you can't fulfill the cost of the car in the six months' time, the seller keeps the vehicle and the $5,000, and if you do have the funds ready in 6 months, you can buy the car for the fixed price of $20,000.

Let's now talk about how this would work in the stock trading market. For example, if a stock is trading at $10 and you think it will go up to $20, what you can do is buy $15 "call option" for $0.10. If your predictions were right and the stock did go up to $20, then you could buy the stock at $15 even if the stock is at $20 netting you a profit of $4.90. But like in the analogy above, there is a time limit. So let us say the stock didn't go up until $20 by the time you had predicted it to go up, then you are out $0.10 and the seller keeps the $0.10.

Put options
Now, we will be using the same analogy for the put option as we did for the call option. So, let us say you ended up buying the Corvette for $20,000. To keep yourself and the car safe, you decide to buy insurance at $1,000 for a year's coverage. In case of an accident or theft, the insurance company will cover your losses. Let's just say a year goes by and nothing happens to your car. You are happy that nothing happened, and you bought the insurance for your peace of mind and the insurance company is satisfied that nothing happened to your car and they get to keep the $1,000.

In another example, let's say your car has been damaged and it will cost you $4,000 to fix the damages. You decide to use your insurance to cover your losses, and the insurance covers your losses as promised. In the final example, your car gets stolen. Now, you are out $20,000! Don't worry. The coverage is more than happy to cover your loss of $20,000 as it happened within the year. You see, the insurance company doesn't mind paying out $4,000 or $20,000 for your damages when you only paid $1,000 as it is getting the $1,000 premium from multiple people. They would need to pay out $20,000 in that year, but they got $1,000 premium from 100 people, which means they made $80,000 profit in a year.

Now, let's use put option in a trading scenario. So, if a stock is floating around $15 per share and you have a feeling that it will drop down to $10. As a safety net, you could buy a $12.50 put option for $0.10. If the stock drops down to $10, you will still have the possibility of selling it at $12.50 even if the stock is at $10. Netting you a profit of $2.40, on the other hand, this would leave the person at a loss of $2.40 who sold you the "put option." Now, if the stock never drops down to $10 in a certain amount of time and the "put" expires, then the put buyer is out $0.10 and the seller keeps the $0.10 as profit.

It is a gamble.

You are now well-educated on options trading, and you know that it can be a gamble. Therefore, I would not recommend making this your sole income as the cash flow is unpredictable. Exercise this method on the side to make money.

How much money can you make?
Just like stocks, you cannot put a number. People have made millions of dollars from options trading, and some have lost millions of dollars on

options trading. So like I said, there is no fixed rate of pay you will be getting, but also, there is no cap on how much you can make.

Now, before you go and try out your luck in this, please remember to know what kind of risk you are putting yourself into. There is no guarantee that you will make money or lose money, it is a gamble. For you to make it less of a chance, find out everything about the stocks you will be buying, know if it will be going down or up in price and then make your call. Just remember to make this your side income stream rather than your sole income as it could lead you to lose some money if not all. So, remember, practice with smaller amounts of money and have the discipline to stop when you feel like you are going into deep.

CONCLUSION

With that note, we come to the conclusion of this book *Dropshipping: How to Make $300/Day Passive Income, Make Money Online from Home with Amazon FBA, Shopify, E-Commerce, Affiliate Marketing, Blogging, Instagram, eBay, Retail Arbitrage, Social Media, and Facebook Advertising.* Remember, the methods in this book, when followed correctly, can yield you amazing results when it comes to making money. However, you need to act on these methods as soon as possible to ensure that you make a great living from it sooner than later. The last thing you want to do is to procrastinate, that will only hold you back from achieving optimal results. Once you have read and understood the chapter, act on it as soon as possible so you can get going. You will be in a much better position if you act on it as quickly as possible, as compared to waiting for the perfect storm. There will be no ideal time to act on your dreams and goals than now, so make sure you start that business and learn as you go. That is the only way to succeed.

You can read all the books that you want, but if you don't take action, then you will never perfect the skills that allow you to make money. Go ahead and pick a method from this book and start working on it. I am sure that you might fail a couple of times, but eventually, you will succeed. Remember, the difference between a winner and a loser is how many times they have failed. Both have failed, but the one who got back up is the real winner.

DESCRIPTION

In this book entitled *Dropshipping: How to Make $300/Day Passive Income, Make Money Online from Home with Amazon FBA, Shopify, E-Commerce, Affiliate Marketing, Blogging, Instagram, eBay, Retail Arbitrage, Social Media, and Facebook Advertising*, you will find several ways on how to earn money passively while you are at home or doing your daily job. The techniques are explained in detail to ensure readers has understood what they have read about.

Have you always wanted to make money, more specifically, make money while you are in the comfort of your own home, or better yet, traveling? Well, I have a solution for you. In this book, we will show you the top trending ways to make money online and more specifically making money with minimal work. Depending on your goals, you can make $300 a day up to whatever amounts you can think. We say $300 a day because that is the sweet spot for passive income, in this book you will learn.

Introduction: Talk about the book and what the audience should expect to get out of the information provided in this book.

Chapter 1 - The Basics of passive income: Talk about all the new and working methods which will allow you to make money passively

Chapter 2 - Dropshipping-101: Talk about all the ways you can drop-ship such as thru eBay, Shopify, and Amazon.

Chapter 3 - How to be successful when drop-shipping: All the things you need to know in regards to being successful in all the three drop-shipping methods.

Chapter 4 - How to market your drop-shipping store: Talk about Facebook ads, Instagram influences to get sales, and to make money.

Chapter 5 - How to make money from blogging: Talk about a way to make money from blogging, such as utilizing Google ads and affiliate marketing.

Chapter 6 - Blogging 101: The things you need to do to have a successful blog primed to make money.

Chapter 7 - Become a pro-blogger: Which niche to pick, how to write a blog post, and how to market it the right way to make money.

Chapter 8 - Instagram 101: Talk about how to make an Instagram page and grow it to a high following.

Chapter 9 - How to make money from your Instagram page: Talk about affiliate marketing and promotions you can do to make money from this page.

Chapter 10 -Future of passive income: Talk about the future of making money online and passively, allowing you to see what will work in the years to come when it comes to making money.

As you can see, this book is packed with information, allowing you to make money online with minimal effort. More specifically, proving you with the right information, and giving you the tools to make your business profitable from the get-go. Look, we get it. You have been way too tired of spending your time living your life on someone else's term. 9 to 5 jobs aren't for everyone, so if you are tired of living a life in a cage, then you need to get this book now before it isn't accessible to you. If you want to change your life for the good, you need to take action now and make your dreams come true. Now, stop reading the description and start reading this book now! Then go live your life on your terms.

MAKE MONEY ON YOUTUBE

How to Create and Grow Your YouTube Channel, Gain Millions of Subscribers, Earn Passive Income and Make Money Online Fast While Working From Home

**By
James Ericson**

INTRODUCTION

Congratulations on purchasing *Make Money On YouTube* and thank you for doing so.

The following chapters will discuss how you can turn YouTube in a career for yourself. Not just a career, but a fruitful one, one that will keep your head above the water for years to come.

YouTube has gone from a simple video sharing platform to a huge money machine for many different people, and you can totally be one of them. In this book, I'm not just going to outline the trick to making your video platform work, I'm going to make a point of including how exactly you can make money.

There are many different ways to make money on YouTube, to the point where there's no book that covers each and every way. But this book will give you a great look into it, and step by step instructions on how to make the most of each of them. You could even follow every single one on this book, although I'd recommend you never do more than one at a time before you master the next.

Making money with YouTube is the perfect way to take control of your career and livelihood, you're able to talk about the things you love and enjoy. Who could ask for a better job, spending all your day talking about the things you love?

There are plenty of books on this subject on the market, thanks again for choosing this one! Every effort was made to ensure it is full of as much useful information as possible, please enjoy!

CHAPTER 1
What Is Youtube

YouTube is one of the most popular websites in the world. You'd be hard pressed to find somebody who has never watched a YouTube video, mostly because it's everywhere. It's people's go to platform for when they want to post a video, whether it's something silly they want to send their friends or something full of information that they want to send out to the world. It's the number one place to go when you want video content, good or bad. As of 2019, it has nearly two billion monthly users, and that's not even counting all of the people who watch the site without an account. YouTube went from a tiny startup to an everyday part of our lives, similar to many other social media out there such as Facebook or Instagram.

YouTube started in 2005 when creators Chad Hurley, Steve Chen, and Jawed Karim all worked at PayPal, which at the time was another internet startup. Following the eBay buyout of PayPal, the three men used their bonuses that were received by it. There are rumors that the site initially started off as a dating website idea. This idea was scrapped after three separate occasions occurred where a video website would be useful: the first being that Karim was unable to find footage of the infamous Janet Jackson's Super Bowl wardrobe malfunction, the second that Hurley and Chen couldn't send footage of a dinner party, thanks to email's miniscule attachment limits at the time, and the third being a devastating tsunami that occurred on the Indian Ocean.

So, February 14th, Valentine's Day of 2005, they registered the website YouTube.com. The first ever YouTube video was uploaded several months later, April 23rd, 2015. It's a home video of Karim at the San Diego Zoo, titled Me At The Zoo. It's still online to this day. It's legitimately just a 19 second clip of Karim standing in front of the elephant pen and talking about their trunks.

It didn't take long before YouTube caught the eye of the internet, and people began flocking to the site. It gathered so much attention that Google eventually started investigating. They offered Chen, Hurley, and Karim $1.65 billion dollars, which they accepted. By May of 2010, the site was getting more than 2 billion views every single day, and by March of 2013, they were getting 1 billion monthly active users.

These numbers just kept growing. In 2019, the site has nearly 2 billion logged in monthly users and is now considered an essential part of our entertainment. 6 out of 10 people would rather watch online video over TV, and it's the number one entertainment service for millennials and generation Z. It's the world's second largest search engine, only out taken by its adopted father, Google, and is the third most visited website on the internet. Every day, more than 1 billion hours of content is watched.

But, it's not just the numbers that are so incredible about YouTube. YouTube was the start of the influencer culture. For those who don't know, influencers are people online, who post pictures, videos, and more to a large online following. The majority of beginner online influencers, such as PewDiePie, Shane Dawson, Tyler Oakley, Jenna Marbles, and Grace Helbig, starting posting just for fun, or to share silly videos with their friends. Before long, they had amassed online followings, and companies, and YouTube sat up and started to take notice. As time went on, more and more people started following and enjoying these creator's content. Many of the users had migrated over from Myspace, having had a ton of friends on that platform as well.

So, Google, who had begun running ads on the platform soon after it was bought, began offering these content creators a slice of the ad revenue. This was done to encourage YouTubers to not only make good content, but to make a lot of it, and to make it quickly. YouTube saw the value in these people and saw that they would bring a lot of people to the platform, rather than the person building their own website. And so it went, more and more people signed on to become YouTubers.

Many of them are household names now. It's launched the careers of many Hollywood stars, artists, makeup artists, musicians, athletes, and even comedians. Names include Jeffree Star, who now runs a huge makeup brand worth $75 million on top of a YouTube channel, Justin Bieber, who was discovered on the platform by accident, became the youngest person to sell out Madison Square Garden and is now worth an estimated $265 million, and the infamous Logan Paul who posted a dead body from Tokyo's "suicide forest", who apparently made about $12.5 million in 2017.

Yeah, that guy made 12.5 million dollars.

Needless to say, YouTube has officially cemented its way into not just to get a lot of subscribers, but also a way to make serious income. And there's a reason why. Who wouldn't want to make 12.5 million dollars a year? So, people flocked to the site, and to this day, people are still trying to get YouTube famous. There are only a few problems with that.

One, the competition is insane. An average of 400 hours of video is uploaded to YouTube every minute. That means that if your video happens to be 5 minutes long, you're competing against 399 hours and 55 minutes' worth of content. That's over one million seconds worth of content. So, this means that you're competing with all of that content, so yours has to be pretty spectacular to stand out.

Two, it's hard work. Yes, the idea of sitting at home and writing and making videos all day may sound like a good time, especially if you're writing about something you love. But, it can be hard work. You had to write the script, usually 2 or 3 times to make sure that it's the best it can be, you have to do any recordings, and then you have to post it. This may not sound like a lot of work, but it can be tough, especially if you're doing it alone.

Third, it can be lonely. One thing that YouTubers are constantly struggling with are feelings of loneliness and worthlessness. Depression is a common problem among them. As a YouTuber, you're often spending long hours alone in front of a computer, and many find themselves obsessing over their amounts of subscribers and putting out content on time. I'm just going to say it: this is the same with a lot of freelance work; the trick is to make sure that you're not letting your entire worth reflect on views and subscribers. Especially make sure that it doesn't take over your entire life. We'll talk more about that later.

Now, this may sound as if I'm trying to talk you out of becoming a YouTuber. Actually, quite the opposite. I'm trying to be honest with you about what you're getting into, and how this will affect your life. You'll be spending long hours in front of a computer, spending a lot of time alone, and not only that, but it can take some time.

There are YouTubers out there who are starting out right now who will be making their living from YouTube in less than 2 years. You could absolutely be one of them. There are stats that work in your favor, after all: Every year, the number of YouTube channels who are making 6 figures worth of income doubles. YouTube accounts for two-thirds of online videos among millennials. Searches of "How To" videos are especially popular; every year, the number of searches increases by 70%.

Those crazy numbers should be what convinces you to take the next step into YouTubing, whether you choose to do it as a full time career or just a part time thing to do for fun. In this book, we're going to tell you how to build a profitable YouTube channel, no matter what your topic. Just know, it may be a bit of an uphill battle.

Now, let's get started.

Make Money on YouTube

Of course, the first thing you need to know about making money off of YouTube, is, well, how exactly do you make money off of YouTube.

We're going to start off this book by talking about how to build your profile, the things you'll need, what your day to day will look like, things like that. Knowing how to manage all of these things will really help you create an effective, money making YouTube channel. After all, even if you're just getting into YouTube because you want to spend your day talking about what you love, or making content that you'd want to see, making money would still be nice.

So, here we are going to list all the ways you can make money. We'll be getting into several of them in more depth in later chapters, so here is just a very brief overview.

1) Use monetization. Monetization from ads has gotten more difficult in the past few years. YouTube, in an effort to take out bad apples in their community, has removed the ability to monetize for a lot of YouTubers. Advertisers now have the ability to choose what kind of content their ads appear on.
2) Use it to bring traffic to your own website or blog. There are plenty of YouTube channels out there, especially recipe or beauty ones, who also have blogs on top of their channel. YouTube is a great place to show off some of your content while keeping the rest on your blog.
3) Sell products. One way that a lot of businesses out there have done is to create products and sell them online. Many YouTubers has taken this step to make extra income, and some have just started to YouTube just to promote their brand.
4) Do affiliate marketing. If making your own products isn't really your deal, affiliate marketing is the way to go. We'll have an entire chapter dedicated to this later on, but for these who don't know here's a textbook definition: affiliate marketing is the act of you talking about a product from a company on your channel and for every person who goes to buy that product, you get a cut from that company.
5) Crowdfund. This is becoming more and more popular these days, especially with the introduction of websites such as Kickstarter, Patreon, and Indiegogo. It can be a great source of money, but it

only works if you have truly good content and a large enough following. You really need to sell your ideas if you want to do this and be able to sell an idea. But, it is a great way to revenue projects for the future. More and more YouTubers are turning to this idea as using ad monetization to make money gets more and more difficult.

We'll be getting farther into each of these topics later on this book, but let's just get this out of the way: you don't have to just do one of the things on this list. In fact, many YouTubers choose to partake in more than one. Having your own stream of revenue that is completely in your hands depends on you looking into as many different forms as possible. Now, it's time to really get down to the important stuff.

In the following chapter, we're going to be talking all about making your channel, your google page, all of the equipment you'll need, skills you may need, and a comprehensive guide to all of YouTube's amazing features. Let's go.

CHAPTER 2
Making Your Channel

You're not going to get anywhere on YouTube without knowing how to build your profile, knowing the kind of skills and equipment you're going to need, and understanding exactly what a YouTube account can give you. Without these things, you're going to get nowhere. That's just a fact.

So, the first thing before you get started with making a YouTube channel, you're going to have to make a Google account. There are plenty of amazing features that Google has to offer, including Google Drive, Google Plus, and of course YouTube.

Thankfully, signing up for an account is an easy and quick process, and you can't get anywhere without on, at least on YouTube. Follow the easy steps below:

1. Open the google webpage. You can do it from the main Google page (google.com) but you can also do it from other places such as Gmail, Google Plus, Google Drive, YouTube, or whatever other pages you can think of. Just simply click on the sign up button, which will take you to another page, where you'll start to input your information.
2. Come up with your username. This username is different from your YouTube channel name. This is what you will use to make your new Gmail email address. You can't create a YouTube page without a Gmail account. If you've already chosen your channel name, use that. Be prepared to change it in case it's already been taken (Google will provide you with similar options if this happens).
3. Put in your information. Enter your first and last name, your gender, your birthday, your country of residence, your phone number for verification purposes, and another email address for more verification.
4. Agree to the privacy policy. Check the box that you agree.
5. Click next. The next page will be your Google plus creation page. This is where you add a picture to your account and write in some information about yourself.
6. Get started. Quickly click the "get started" and you're golden! Just be sure to verify your account.

Now that you've got a Google account! Take your time to adjust yourself to all of their features, including the drive (this will be a great place to keep scripts and collaborate with other YouTubers!) and Gmail (if you so choose, your followers can contact you here!).

Now, let's get into the real fun: creating your YouTube channel.

Now, to be clear, you technically already have a YouTube channel. You get one automatically the minute that you get a Google account. But, you're going to need a business channel if you're there to make content. The process is incredibly simple, and there's only a few clicks and typing involved.

Simply go to your YouTube page, and click on the user icon at the top right of the screen. You want to go to settings, which is the gear icon. There you'll find "create a new channel". Simply click on it, and then find "use a business or other name". Simply add your channel name.

The most important thing to remember about creating your brand name is that it must be short and sweet, or at least catchy. Something that will be remembered easily. Remember, this is not your username, so you don't have to input numbers unless you feel you absolutely have to. Just be sure that it's unique (checking this only requires a quick google search), and go right ahead.

Next, it's time to start filling out your profile.

The first option you see after your channel's creation will be your channel description aka your "About Me". This is where you'll describe your channel, including what you're going to be posting and what your brand is all about. You should also be posting your social media links, any website you may have, and your email where people can get a hold of you. This will be appearing in more than one place on your channel, so make sure to make sure it's good, and regularly update it as time goes on and things change.

Next, put your channel art up.

Go to any professional YouTube channel in the world, and you're greeted with a large banner at the top of their profile displaying the channel's name, plus a design that represents who the brand is. This is known as your banner art, and you can make it as extravagant or as minimal as you wish. The most important thing you can do here is showcase who you are as a brand.

To be sure that you're getting the right sized image, YouTube's recommendation is 2560 x 1440 pixels, the maximum size file being 4 MB. They also offer a template that you can use as your base on their help page. Simply google "YouTube channel banner template" and you'll get many different results. You don't have to be a Grade A designer to have a good one. There are plenty of amazing photo apps that you can use out there. PicMonkey, which is online and can be used from a computer, is a great one. You could also consider hiring a graphic designer, but I would only consider that if you have the cash to spend.

Now, you have your YouTube channel. But, before we get to posting, let's go over some of the other things you'll probably need. For one, you'll need to know your niche. We're going to get into that next chapter, as we're just focusing on the practical stuff here. So, let's get into what you need to make sure your videos are the best they can be.

What you need to make truly great videos on YouTube is greatly over exaggerated. A lot of YouTubers like to show off their fancy cameras and their amazing studios and some of them even have a camera crew. This is not needed, or used, by the majority of YouTubers. In fact, many of them just choose to use their smartphones. If you have a great personality, and your content is truly one of a kind and well put together, you can get away with that. Lots of amazing equipment doesn't necessarily equal good quality content. In fact, many beginner YouTubers (and filmmakers, for that matter) make this mistake and buy expensive equipment, and their videos/films are still not great because they never learned how to use the basic stuff first.

Not only that, but a lot of YouTubers out there will tell you to just focus on the simple stuff when you're just starting out. Why invest a ton of money into something that might not be making you a ton of money for the foreseeable future?

But, then again, we've already talked about how incredibly competitive YouTube is. It's a platform that is built on competitiveness. Whoever gets the most views gets the most money; that's how it works. What does this mean? That you most likely can't get away with just using your smartphone to make videos. Good quality is good quality, and to make truly good videos, you will need to invest at least a little bit of money.

How much you invest is based on two things: the type of content you plan on bringing into this world, and how much money you're willing to put into it. I don't know your financial situation, but I'm going to say this: pick a budget, stick to it, and be practical. Don't buy anything unless you're absolutely sure you're going to need it. That's all, carry on, and here's the list:

- Camera
- Tripod
- Microphone/sound equipment (optional)
- Lighting
- Video Editing Software (optional)

Again, what you buy off this list is entirely up to your choosing. If you want to buy a $4,000 camera, spend $800 on a tripod, and invest in a complete sound and lighting studio, that's up to you. I'm going to advise against it if you still don't know how much money you're going to be able to make, but again, it's up to you.

Now, let's get a little more into each of these things:

Camera

This is 100% the most important piece of equipment you will buy for your channel. Even if you don't plan on having a channel where you appear on camera, I would strongly advise that you at least have access to something that can record high quality video (at least 1080p).

Now, don't just straight away buy an expensive DSLR or mirrorless. These are great for investments later down the road where you're ready for an upgrade. For now, you should probably stick to a quality camcorder or webcam, depending on what your needs are.

Microphone/Sound Equipment

You need good sound. That's just a fact. While you could get away with bad camerawork, you won't be able to get away with bad sound. If you're audio is terrible, it will ruin the whole thing. That's just a fact. While many cameras come with an internal microphone, and it will probably serve you well, it gets more tricky if your video is heavily relying on your dialogue. Not only that, but mics that are built into cameras or laptops usually are not able to record or eliminate ambient sounds effectively. Make sure to do some research into good mics, and ask the person at your local tech store for more information. For YouTubers, USB microphones are the most popular, easy to use and are generally affordable. Of course, there are other options on the market, such as shotguns, and lavaliers, but you may want to upgrade to these later on as they can be more expensive.

Tripod

Tripods are a game changer if you want to create quality content. Unsteady footage can turn your viewers off of watching your content. Another option is something called a Gimbal Stabilizer, which is a lot easier to carry around than a tripod. This, of course, will depend on what kind of content you'll be making, but tripods are generally more affordable. This would be one area where I really press that you invest your money, considering that you need them to be durable and sturdy. This ensures the safety of whatever equipment you're using. A gimbal, on the other hand, is perfect for vlogging. They're stabilizers built specifically with weights or motors, and carefully balance your camera. This makes your videos look more smooth, and even if you make sudden movements, it will still remain smooth. Gimbals only do what they're supposed to do if you have a lightweight camera, like a GoPros. While you can find more heavy duty ones, they're generally a lot more expensive.

Lighting

I would say lighting is only necessary if you find yourself without a good spot to shoot that has no good daylight shining through, or the only times that are available to you are when it's dark out. Or, if you can afford it. Lighting, like sound, is pretty powerful. It can create moods, and even out your whole videos. There are plenty of different kinds of lighting out there, and I would recommend extensive research before you make a choice. You might not even need it at all. I certainly wouldn't tell a beginner YouTuber that they absolutely must need it.

Video Editing Software

I know what you're thinking: why did you label this as optional? Of course, you need good editing software to make good videos. I'm not saying you don't. What I'm debating is whether or not you need to purchase it.

There is no point in buying a program like Adobe Premiere Pro or Apple's Final Cut Pro unless you actually know how to use it, or need to use it. There are plenty of programs that will do all that editing for you that don't cost ridiculous amounts of money and that can do everything that you need. This is especially important to realize if your videos won't require a lot of really complicated editing, like color correcting and being able to process and edit huge, feature movie length files.

Not only that, but video editing programs definitely have a learning curb to them. I'm not saying that you shouldn't learn how to use them, you probably should, but just get used to posting content on your channel first. Once you have gotten into the groove of editing, then you can try something else. Adobe Premiere Pro is a great place to start, and it costs about $20 (USD) a month.

And that's pretty much it for things you'll need to get started on your YouTube channel. Now, just having these items doesn't automatically mean you know how to use them. That's the next step; the skills you need.

Running a YouTube channel will take a bit of a learning curb. Things like being able to organize your time and understand all of YouTube's features will you be able to run a successful YouTube channel. Of course, you can probably run a YouTube channel without a few of the skills mentioned below, but if you want to make money, you'll make more this way.

1) You need to understand the platform. While we're going to go into every single inch of the platform and how it works in this book, it's important to understand that you need to understand it. While this is hardly a complicated platform, there's still a lot to learn.

2) Keyword research. Any YouTuber that puts out quality content on a weekly basis understands that they need to do research, and do it well. You're going to have to spend a lot of time on conversation sites such as reddit, and pay attention to what's going on online in your niche. Not only that, but understanding keyword research will help your videos get the maximum amount of views thanks to search results.

3) Video editing. This is a no brainer. While some YouTubers choose to hire a production team including a camera crew and editing people, your budget may not allow for that at this moment. For editing programs, don't go any more complicated than you feel you need to go. For beginners, using something like iMovie or VideoPad, both of which are perfect for people who don't have much experience editing videos. Of course, if you do choose to go for the bigger software, there are plenty of tutorials online which will be able to help you out.

4) How to use a camera (properly). If you just plan on using a basic camcorder or a phone this shouldn't be a huge deal but if you're going all out for a DSLR, understanding things like shutter speed, ISO, and white balance will help you out in making sure your videos look amazing.

5) Use of other social media accounts. We're going to talk more about this in this book on how to promote your videos onto other social media accounts, but it is of vital importance. Even if you're just available on one or two other websites, you'll be able to reach a wider audience. What social media presence you choose to use it up to you, but it will depend on your niche. For example, beauty and fashion will find more success on Instagram and Snapchat, while gamers will do better on Twitter and Twitch.

6) Willingness to work hard with endless patience. While there are YouTube channels that grew big within only six months of being on the platform, other big channels took 10 years to get big. It really depends on two things: luck, and your content. There's a lot of amazing content on YouTube. You can't deny that. So, going big often depends on your luck rather than your skills. That doesn't mean that you can't make money off the platform before you gain 1 million followers. It just means that you may have to get creative and be willing to put in some very hard work.

Now, that we've gotten these necessary skills out of the way, let's talk about all of YouTube's great features that they have.

YouTube's Features

Of course, this isn't a complete list of all of the features that YouTube has. I didn't bother with the ones that are obvious, like uploading videos and things. This is more these features that people don't bother taking the time to explore, but are important to you as a content creator, as they'll drastically impact the number of views that you get.

You must keep in mind that for a lot of features that YouTube has, such as monetization, live streaming, and making longer videos, you do have to get verified to do this. The verifying process usually isn't that hard: you can use your cell phone number, or you may have to take YouTube's creator's course to get it. This is so YouTube knows that you're serious about the content you post, and you're not going to fill their airways with spam.

So, now that we've gotten that out of the way, let's get into it:

1) Cards and End Screens. The majority of popular YouTube channels utilize this feature and even the not so popular ones. They work similar to call to action buttons, and they can direct people to subscribe, look at merchandise, or a fundraising campaign. End screens are easily customizable; all you have to do is go to video manager, select "edit", before clicking on "end screen and annotations" from the drop-down menu. Easy. This is where you can play with different backgrounds and templates. To choose where you plan on sending your viewers, you just have to click "add element". This will take you to a list of videos. As for cards, which are found by simply clicking the "I" in the in right hand upper corner of your screen, the card expands and will give you a link to another video or a product. To add a card, simply head to your Video Manager, click edit, and choose cards from the menu. From there, you decided where in the video you want the card to appear, and what you want it to appear.

2) Creator Studio. There aren't too many creators that actually use the creator studio, but it's full of useful things. You'll find advanced video editing techniques that can usually only be found in programs like Final Cut Pro and Adobe Premiere Pro, such as color correction, time lapse, and slow motion. It also has a huge array of sounds available, free to use for any YouTuber. You won't find any big artists, but you'll definitely find music that matches the tone you're looking for.

3) Live streaming. One of these things that more YouTubers need to be aware of, live streaming is a great way to get more subscribers and create a connection with the ones that you already have. With the introduction of other live streaming platforms like Periscope, Facebook Live, and Instagram Live, it's only going to become more popular. Live streaming on YouTube is slightly more difficult than other websites. You have to download software and set it up first. To get the software, log into YouTube, click the "live-streaming" button on the right hand side of the screen. Click "get started". YouTube will make sure your channel is verified, and you'll have two options, "Stream now" and "Live Events". Which one you pick is up to you, but "Stream now" is the more popular option. You may also stream from mobile devices, but you need 10,000 subscribers to do so.

4) YouTube advanced settings. In YouTube advanced, you can do many things to help get more views to your channel. One of these is you can add your channel keywords. Basically, any word that has anything to do with your channel goes there. You can also go to channel recommendations and click on "allow my channel to appear in other channel's recommendations". This means that

YouTube will actually allow your videos to appear in recommendation lists. You can also see your Google Analytic. You have to connect your YouTube ID to your Google Analytics page, but this lets you see all sorts of information, like what time people are most active on your channel and how long they usually spend on it. This can be useful information when you're choosing what content to put up.

5) Custom URL. If you want to have an easy-to-remember internet link to get your channel, having a custom URL is a great way to go. You can use pretty much anything you want for this, but there are some catches. One, you need 100 subscribers, be at least 30 days old, have channel art, and a profile picture. You also need to be sure that that's what you want for your custom URL. You can't change it afterward. Simply go to YouTube settings and click on advanced in your name section. If you're eligible to get a custom URL, it will tell you under channel settings. Simply agree to their terms of service and click "change URL" to make it official.

Basically, these are all the basic technical stuff you need to know...for now. Of course, you're probably not wanting to get into YouTube to be technical. You're getting into YouTube to chat about all the things that you love. Well, that's what the next chapter is going to be all about: how to find your niche, your audience, and all the different kinds of videos you can make.

CHAPTER 3
Finding Your Voice

When you first start out on YouTube, it can be easy to just post whatever you want, but this really doesn't work with audiences. When audiences follow you on YouTube, they want to know exactly what kind of content to expect from you. You may be a person with a lot of different passions and a lot of different things that you want to talk about, but that doesn't work for audiences.

This means that you have to find your niche, and you have to stick to it. I would say before you've even posted your first video, you should have your first 10 planned out and prepared. I'm serious. Having all of your videos planned out, and prepared will give you a lot of breathing room of getting used to YouTube, and not only that but give you some time to prepare for the next ten. Having a plan will really help you adjust more easily and get you into the flow of posting.

But first, let's talk about your niche. Here are just a few tips on how to find a topic that you want to talk about day to day.

5 Tips On Finding Your Niche

1) Make a list of all the topics that you love. This is a topic that you're going to be spending a lot of time discussing, thinking about, and making videos about it. People will be subscribing to your channel based on the topic that you eventually land on to make your channel about.

2) Choose a niche with a lot of subtopics. This is a mistake that a lot of beginner YouTubers make, where their niche is so strict and solid that they cannot get more than maybe 50 videos out of it. Your niche topic should be broad enough that there are plenty of subtopics to address. For example, let's say that your chosen niche is "lifestyle". Well, this can mean things like health, fitness, beauty, remodeling, parenting, finance, and a variety of other topics.

3) Make sure it's either something you're well versed in or you want to become well versed in. Now, to be clear, there are plenty of YouTubers out there who are far from experts on their chosen topic. In fact, a lot of their charm is in the fact that they're learning as they go along. You're a beginner, just like your audience. Now, the downside of choosing a topic that you don't know much about

is the fact that the amount of research goes up considerably, so if you're not willing to spend all that time researching that topic, don't do this. You need to be able to put content out there that is correct, as this will be the key to making sure that your channel gets the attention that it needs to grow.

4) Look into what other people are doing (and do it better). One thing that makes people turn away from starting a channel is the fact that there is already so much content out there. But, this can also be a good thing. If you can find a side that hasn't been addressed yet, jump on that. Not only that, but if you want to make a film review channel, and there are people who love to watch film reviews, they're not likely to just go to one source for them. They want a bunch of different sources. If you can do something differently from anyone else, that content will be valuable.

5) Find an idea that nobody else is doing. If out of one of your ideas there's an idea that nobody else is doing, jump on that. If there is no competition, you have struck gold. This doesn't mean that you have to have a completely new idea. You just have to have an idea that is different from all the rest, one with a twist. You just have to find a gap that hasn't been covered yet.

6) Try to solve problems. The search for "how to" videos goes up higher and higher every year. And besides that, every single popular web page or YouTube video in the history of the internet goes back to some kind of need. Vlogs, it's a feeling of needing to be a part of their life. For review channels, it's the feeling of your choices needing to be valid. YouTube isn't about you. It's about fulfilling the needs of somebody out there. Keep that in mind, and finding your niche and starting your channel will be off to a great start.

What Kind Of Videos Do I Want To Make

Now, I know what you're thinking. Isn't the niche the same thing as the type of videos I want to make?

Well, yes and no. Yes, because a niche can definitely decide what kind of videos you'll be posting, but sometimes, there is a wide variety of things you'll be posting. Let's say you want to talk about movies. Are you going to be analyzing them? Reviewing them? Doing top 10 lists? What?

So, to help you get some ideas, here are the top 20 videos that get the most views on the platform. Don't feel as if you have to make these types of videos to get a lot of views, but it definitely doesn't hurt to have these on hand for yourself.

1) Product reviews. I was shocked that it wasn't cat videos. Straightforward product videos are basically just a person in front of a video talking about what they think of a certain product. The more brutally honest, the better. Anything from technology (which is the most popular) to movies to make up to restaurants can be done. Why are they so popular? Well, more and more people are turning to the internet to know other people's reviews on products. They're much more likely to trust an online influencer with thousands of subscribers who haven't been paid off by the company, rather than an ad that is made to make the product look like the best product ever. This makes a lot of sense.

2) How Tos/Tutorials: the second most popular search engine in the world is YouTube, and one of the most popular searched things on the web is "how tos". If there is something that you can do well, you may have a future in YouTube tutorials.

3) Vlogs: blogs, but in video form. Quick, fun, and casual, they can cover a variety of topics of day to day life. They're usually more on the light side but can delve into more serious topics, and many do.

4) Gaming: this kind of YouTubing is often looked down upon, thanks to the eternal question "why would you want to watch someone playing when you could just do it yourself?" Well, there isn't really an answer to this question, but you can't deny how popular the concept is on the website. YouTube even launched a site just for video game streams, that's how big it is.

5) Comedy/Skit Videos: this is another comedy niche that can be hard to make money off of, but they can be fun to make. You can also raise money for them through Kickstarter. These can really go from anything to improvised silly bits to full on productions.

6) Hauls: these videos have no middle ground, they're either loved or hated by a person. Basically, you go out and buy a bunch of stuff, then show off what they bought in a video. Not only that but once you get enough views, you won't have to buy anymore, as brands send you things for free in hopes you'll talk about them.

7) Memes/Tags/Challenges: these can be varied, and will go from very silly to more serious. Draw-my-life, the boyfriend tag, cinnamon challenge, ice-bucket challenge, and more. You could even start your own and see if it takes off.

8) Favorites/Best Of: in this kind of video, you basically showcase what your favorite things are, based on a certain topic, or what the best of the best is. It can be anything from what your favorite

movies are to what are the best makeup brands there are right now. Anything goes.

9) Education: pretty self-explanatory. These are just videos that are made with the intent of someone learning from them on a particular topic. Bonus points if you can make them easy to digest and designed for students.

10) Unboxing: basically, if you enjoy shopping and love unboxing things, this is for you. Any product can be unboxed on camera, and people will want to watch it. You generally have to have an idea of what kind of products you'll be unboxing (toys, technology, makeup, clothes, etc.). People like to watch these because it shows them exactly what to expect when they order something.

11) Q & A be online long enough, and eventually, your followers are going to want to know more about you. This is a great way to interact with your following. Simply ask your followers for questions, usually through Facebook, Twitter, or Instagram, and pick the best ones to answer in a video.

12) Collections: really not much to say here. Just a person showing off their collection of whatever items they collect, whether it's a single type or a group based on a theme. They then explain where the item comes from.

13) Pranks: Pranks aren't nearly as popular on YouTube as they were back in the day, but they're still there. Anything from super intense, controversial stunts to staged jokes done with other creators to silly, simple practical jokes are on the website.

14) Funny animals: there aren't a lot of people who can see a picture of a cute dog or a cute cat doing something silly and not at least smile. It's just not possible. Cute and funny; nothing bad here.

15) Celebrity Gossip: this can be a big difficult to break into, but if you can, do it. It also takes a lot of research, and you risk the chance of a lawsuit if you get something really wrong. However, just because of these, doesn't mean you shouldn't give it a try if you're willing. People may like to say that they're above celebrity gossip, but the majority of them really aren't.

16) Parodies: these are very popular on YouTube mostly thanks to the fact that people want to laugh. But, it's a lot harder to make money off of them, with many trying to profit but very few of them actually doing so. This is something that you should only do if you're going to actually have fun doing so.

17) Self Improvement: this is pretty much self-explanatory. These videos are meant to help people improve themselves in sometimes simple, sometimes complicated ways. They can

address topics like nutrition, self-love, and how to handle depression.

18) Covers: Nobody who is in the YouTube world can forget the fact that YouTube took a 12 year old kid living in a small Canadian town named Justin Bieber to international stardom. It's because of this that many other musicians have taken to the platform to promote their own music, usually by covering popular songs.

19) Couple Vlogs: think of that one couple that you know that is super cute and everyone tells them so, and pick up the phone and tell them they may have what it takes to become a successful couples vlog channel. They do things like post about their dates, their adventures together, couples tags, and day to day life. The type of videos that make you feel all fuzzy inside.

20) Cooking: cooking channels that show recipes step by step are popular, mostly thanks to the amount of creativity they allow. Creative channels are big on YouTube, especially ones that do things you're not expecting. Tasty, which is owned by Buzzfeed, is especially known for putting out some crazy food ideas. Not only that, but who doesn't want to learn how to cook easy, some healthy, some not-so-healthy, and delicious recipes?

The Importance of Quality of Quantity

Quality over Quantity is a concept that was probably taught to you when you were a child. But, it's hard to adjust to, especially in today's world where putting out as many products as possible is what you're supposed to be doing. It's widely regarded as the quicker you can put out content, the more money you will make.

While this is true, and this is a system that many companies have implemented in an effort to make as much money in the shortest amount of time. This is the best business model: the quicker you can make a product, the more money you will save and the more money you will make. Unfortunately, crafting products that are high quality are expensive and time consuming, and if your goal is to put out content as fast as possible, you may find yourself running yourself dry.

But, when you're putting out content like video content, quality is so important. Bad audio, blurry videos, crappy lighting, bad research, all of these things will degrade the quality of your channel and make people want to go somewhere else for content. This is the last thing that you want. You want a channel that generating revenue, and to do that, you need people to actually watch your channel.

So, try to only upload one video a week, at least at first. That means you can put all of your time, energy, and money into making that video the best of the best. Every video that is sent out you should have the feeling of "I gave it my all". While there are plenty of businesses out there that can get away with not following this philosophy, YouTube is not one of them. Don't ignore it.

CHAPTER 4
Growing

Of course, you won't have any success on YouTube without doing the one most important thing: and that's posting. But don't just go crazy and start posting videos right now.

What a lot of beginner YouTubers don't realize is that there are not only ways to make posting easier for you, but also ways to make sure that it's getting the most views as it can possibly get. There are more effective ways to post, and in this chapter, I'm going to tell you how.

Other things in this chapter are reasons why, that despite numerous people doing it, you probably shouldn't be buying YouTube subscribers, no matter how much of an easy shortcut it is. Not only that, but we're going to talk about how you can grow organically, plus a guide in how to get past that creative block if you ever find yourself struggling. Let's get started, shall we?

Guide to Posting Effectively

Read this simple guide to uploading if you don't care about views or money:

1. Log into your account. If it's from the Google homepage, click on the YouTube icon in the corner.
2. Select the upload button. It's in the top right corner at the beginning, a silhouette of a video camera with a plus sign.
3. You have two options on how to go from here: you can drag and drop the file, or you can select to upload.
4. Enter the description, tags, privacy information, and add a thumbnail if you want to.
5. Share the video.

That's it. Simple, right? YouTube is designed to be simple, after all.

Now, let's go through all these steps one by one, shall we? Especially if you want to make some money.

Now, before we get into the actual posting, let's first start with this easy fact: timing.

When you choose to upload a video, your timing actually matters, believe it or not. This occurs on every social media page: there is always the best time to post so your blog/page/video/post/picture gets the most views, likes, comments, and basically engagement possible.

For YouTube, thankfully there is always a model you can follow, and that's TV. When does TV air the most episodes? Nighttime. When does all their prime content air? Usually weekend times, from Thursday to Sunday. People generally are more likely to check out YouTube during the weekends (or in the evenings) because that is when they're home and scrolling through their feed looking for something to watch.

Thursday and Friday have proven to be the best, with it starting to spike up on Thursday, before peaking on Saturday and dying down on Sunday. This is as people prepare for their week. Of course, this is up to you when you want to post.

The next thing you need to really worry about is step 4. This is where you basically set all the settings of your video. There are privacy settings, the thumbnail, adding your tags, and putting it into a playlist (if you so choose).

YouTube offers four different privacy settings; unlisted, private, public, and schedule. Private is obvious, meaning that only you can see it. Unlisted means that only people with whom you have a link to the video that you can see it.

Public means that anyone can view or search for the video. They can share it as much as they want. Any subscribers you have will see it in their feed. This is the obvious choice for YouTubers. But the schedule is honestly the one that I'm going to discuss here.

Schedule means that you can set a time and date for when you want your video to go public. This means that you could literally have weeks of content in your folder and simply schedule it, meaning that you won't have to worry about anything, just coming up with ideas.

Then, we're going to talk about filling out your description, tags, etc. You can fill out a lot of this information while you're uploading, actually, which will save you a bit of time.

Title: Quick and simple. As you're filling this out, remember this. Keep it simple. The shorter, the better. Just stick to what exactly your video is.

When people search for your video; that is what your title should be. At least less than 10 words.

Description: If there is something that you can't squeeze into the title, this is where you can put it. Really consider keywords here, as descriptions will also register on YouTube's and Google's search bar, and don't forget to make it really long and descriptive. The more words you hit, the more likely you are to show up on Google. You should also include any links to important information, such as your other social media pages or business email, here. To make this process easier for you, you can add defaults for whenever you upload in Settings. Under YouTube's advanced settings, you can set a description template, meaning that you won't have to fill it all out every time, making the process a lot more streamlined.

Tags: similar to posting on Instagram or Twitter, using tags is an easy way to help users find your videos easily. Keywords will be especially valuable here, with single words being more effective that full sentences.

Thumbnail: this is a mistake that too many beginner YouTubers make, not using a custom thumbnail. While YouTube will supply you with thumbnails (3 of them, to be exact) once enough of your video has uploaded, they're hardly good ones, and will only be screenshots of your video. This means that they can be very unflattering. A customized thumbnail gives you the option of including whatever you want in your thumbnail, including text, a good image, and more. The only thing is that you have to verify your account before seeing the thumbnail option, which is not a hard thing to do. You can find this in settings.

Add to Playlists: having playlists on your channel is a good way to keep your channel organized, but it also helps with keeping your users engaged, keeping them watching your videos, rather than it auto playing to something else. Say you're a movie reviewer, and you organize your reviews based on the genre. That means someone who is really into that genre can watch each on in a row without having to bother clicking the next video. Many popular channels use this system, separating them based on everything from what their content is to their length to who made it.

Now, these are the basic settings that you can set. Now, a lot of YouTubers don't really take advantage of all of YouTube's advanced settings. I still think you should check them out, even if you don't find anything that you're interested in tinkering with. If there are certain settings that you'd want for all of your videos, you can set them to defaults in advanced settings.

In this section, you can do the following things:

Disable comments: I wouldn't honestly recommend this because I think that comments can be valuable to YouTubers. This is the most direct form of communication with your audience that you have. But there are situations that call for it. If there is a certain video that you don't want to get hate comments on, consider deactivating them.

Categories: YouTube has 18 different categories your video can fall into: Auto & Vehicles, Beauty & Fashion, Comedy, Education, Entertainment, Family Entertainment, Film & Animation, Food, Gaming, How-to & Style, Music, News & Politics, Nonprofits & Activism, People & Blogs, Pets & Animals, Science & Technology, Sports and Travel & Events. You can pick and choose which one you feel best suits your video. Make sure that whatever category you choose is accurate, as it will help people find you.

Content declaration: this is particularly important if you're going to participate in affiliate marketing. If your video has been sponsored by a company and you're getting paid to talk about them, this must be stated for legal purposes. But this isn't just because of legal reasons: there should always be transparency with an audience when they're watching you, as you're depending on them for views, subscribes, and thumbs up. If there is product placement, endorsement or sponsorship involved you must tell them. Telling them upfront will build an element of trust.

And done! Your video is officially live once it's finished processing! Congrats!

Now, if you're planning on sharing it to other social media networks (which I strongly recommend, and something I'll be talking about soon). Share it to your other social media channels. This is simple: you can either take the URL and directly copy and paste it, or you can use the share button. Another window will pop up, showing you your options where you can share your option. It will also give you a condensed think.

How To Grow YouTube

Of course, the next question is this: how can I grow in a way that's organic and sustainable, that will bring me subscribers who are loyal and watch my videos? Growing on YouTube can seem like a long, crazy, tenuous process that takes years and years. It doesn't necessarily have to be this way; here are some tips on how to speed up this process.

1) Consistency. Consistency, consistency, consistency. One thing that is the most important thing for your audience is that you're consistent with the content that you're bringing to the table, but not just that. You also have to be consistent with your schedule. As in, you always upload on the same day and at the same time. There are YouTubers who post consistently but on random days. This works, but not as well if you're on a schedule. This means that if you always post on Sunday, your subscribers know to look forward to Sunday. See what I mean?

2) Use other social media networks. Look in next chapter for more information on that exact subject!

3) Try keeping videos short and snappy, at least for the first few 10,000 subscribers or so. If you can sum things up in three minutes, do it. You can get into longer videos later when you have a good number of followers involved and interested.

4) Use keywords. Use keywords. Use keywords. That doesn't mean just rattling off whatever words come to mind when you're thinking of in your video description though. Make sure that it actually makes sense.

5) Put a trailer on your channel. Once you have a lot of interesting videos, or even if you just want to take the clips from future videos that you've filmed, put together a trailer for the front page of your channel that's less than 2 minutes long. You can put in at the front of your page and should be treated similarly to a YouTube channel. Introduce yourself and captivate potential subscribers. Ask them to like, comment, and subscribe. You could even ask them a question at the end of your video such as "what do you think"? This really ups your comment count.

6) Use call to actions in your videos. Do you know how every single YouTuber in the history of YouTube asks whoever's watching to subscribe? There's a reason why they do it; it actually works.

7) Engage with your audience. Reply to comments (including negative ones, if you dare). This shows you're paying attention to them. You should be especially paying attention to the ones that are always commenting and liking. Treat your followers well.

8) Collaborate. More on that in Chapter 6!

9) Subtitle and transcribe your videos in your native language, and if you can, any other languages you can. This not only opens up your videos for people who are hearing impaired but also shows up for your international audience.

10) Use annotations and end screens to promote other videos, the channel, or your website. Annotations are useful links that can be made in the creator's studio, basically just leading back to more

of your content. Use content that you think your followers will want to watch.

But, what if you don't want to do all this work? Maybe you just want to buy your subscribers and be done with it. That's what we're going to talk about next.

Buying Subscribers

Buying followers, or in this case, subscribers, is a popular tactic online to quickly grow your follower base. Be on any social media network for long enough and you'll likely be contacted by several of them, especially on Instagram. Now, YouTube isn't Instagram, but it's still an important topic to address. The people who will write to you, or the ads that you will see, pertaining to this very subject will claim that "this is the fastest, cheapest way to grow your base!" and that "this is the only way to do this! A shortcut to success!"

So, the question is; should you do it?

I would personally say no. And we'll get into that. But, first, I am going to acknowledge the fact that yes, it can be really tempting to take the easy way out. If you're going to invest into your channel, you may as well just buy followers and views, right? It's easy, fast, and generally affordable. No downsides! Not only that, but many big names in the YouTube are rumored to have done it, with even celebrities such as Beyoncé and Rihanna allegedly being guilty of this.

Not only that, but the whole business of buying/selling YouTube (and other social media networks) subscribers/followers/likes/ views is pretty lucrative. There are people pulling in $200,000 a year doing just that, just in case you ever choose to go that route. But buying subscribers has just a few problems, which in my opinion, should lead you to balk:

- YouTube is working on their bot detection capabilities, and they're only going to get better.
- YouTube's algorithm has begun to pay more attention to the behavior of the account rather than how many views the video has.
- It won't bring in money for you.

Basically, what this means is that if you buy fake subscribers, you risk the chance of your channel getting deleted, it may not help you attract new subscribers, and the worst part of all, the followers won't bring in new money for you, because they won't be rewatching your videos, and they won't be buying anything off of you because they're fake. They're not here to learn anything from you.

We all want to grow in the fastest way possible, and we all want to just make it easy on ourselves. After all, hard work, a lot of effort, and your time and money are going into it. You want to get the quickest results possible. But, there are better ways to grow your channel organically than just buying a bunch of fake followers, many of whom we've already run over in this book. You could also consider buying ads if you're really wanting to grow fast.

So, personally, I would balk away from buying followers, especially as YouTube gets smarter about catching accounts that use them. You don't want to build up an incredible, engaged base, and get banned just as things are starting to flow well.

How To Brainstorm Video Ideas

Any YouTuber has been there. You've started out, everything is going great, and after a few weeks or months or even years, the video ideas just stop coming to you. Maybe it's happening over time, or maybe it's just one day, you wake up, and realize you just can't think of anything. Regardless, it's annoying, and now you're stuck.

Creative block happens with any artist, and that's really what a YouTuber is in some way, an artist. You're creating content to be enjoyed by the masses, and you want to create good content. You're often writing, directing, and editing your own videos. So, you have to treat this like an artist would consider a block. Here are some tips on how to come with new video ideas, no matter what your niche is:

1) Use the search result method. This is a simple method that merely involves Google's habit of completing our sentences without asking. When you start to type something into the search bar, Google tries to finish your thought. Simply type in some keywords having to do with your niche, and you'll get some ideas. Not only that, but you'll know what people are looking for. Google's automated suggestions are based on what is looked up for a lot. So, people will already have been looking for your ideas.

2) Check out trends. No matter what your niche is, there will always be trends in whatever it is. Be sure to keep your ear to the ground as to what is happening in your community, and even try to keep up with what's happening in the larger community. This has two benefits. One, you'll be constantly be exposed to content in your

niche that might provide you with ideas, and two, by addressing the topics that are on trend in your videos means that you're showing your followers that you're paying attention. Win, win.

3) Search your comments. Once you have been on YouTube or any social media outlook for an amount of time, you're going to start getting comments. And, if your content is good, people will want to see more from you and will offer suggestions in the comments. Some of these ideas are actually really good, so be sure to make this a habit of combing through your comments. If you're not getting many comments, actually ask your followers for them. They probably have some really good ideas.

4) Ask the people around you. This is very similar to the above one, but if you have close friends or family who watch your videos, then consider asking them. This one is good for newer YouTubers who may not have that many comments.

5) Seek media different from yours. This means that if you review cars, you should check out beauty channels. Yes, I'm serious. Engaging and picking up media that is vastly different from yours will get different parts of your brain going, and will widen your worldview. One of the easiest ways to do this to go to a bookstore, a magazine stand, or even your local library, and seek out materials that are vastly different from yours. There may not be very many ideas for you at first glance, but you just might stumble across something really interesting.

6) Check out the other side. If you're a channel that posts a lot of videos about your opinions (reviews, political content) consider checking out other YouTubers and especially focus on the ones that you don't necessarily agree with. They may cover a topic that you want to cover, or you may want to argue against one of their videos.

7) Ask yourself: what do I want to say? This is the best way to make sure that you're sticking to your original ideas. What do you want to say about your channel? What message do you want to put forward? If you find that this by itself isn't working, try expanding what you want to say.

How to Record Compelling Videos

Finally, how do you create content that will keep your followers coming back for more? How do you keep them watching? How do you do this in a way that will not just keep them watching, but make them want to come back for more and watch more of it? Well, here are some tips.

1) Tell a story. If you're selling something, it's important to focus on the story, not the actual product. If you look at any real ad from the world of advertising, they focus on the emotional pull over the fact that they're selling. Remember the viewer, and pull at their emotional strings. The best way to do this is with a good story.

2) Be relevant. Make sure that every video falls in line with what you are as a channel and your channel. No matter how great the video is put together, it won't be good for your subscriber count if you're not on base. Make sure it's relevant not only to who you are, but who they are as well.

3) Give away information. Social currency is basically just information, something that people can share or use or something that makes them look or feel good.

4) Hook them in 3 seconds. Make it interesting in the first 3 seconds of your videos. This is when new viewers will decide whether or not they're going to watch it. Be description, use catchy titles and music, and have a great opening.

5) Be wary of the times. Right message, right person, right time. Pay attention to what's happening in the world, and embrace what people want and what they're looking for. Your subscribers will be paying attention to current events as well, so they may want to hear from you about certain topics.

And, that's it for posting and creating videos. From here on out, we're mostly going to be talking about how to actually make money on the platform, but first; we're going to talk about two things. Next, social media and how to utilize it to really grow your channel, and then collaborations, and how to make the most of them.

CHAPTER 5
Leveraging Other Social Media

If there is one way to think of the internet, it's similar to high school. And what does high school have? They have cliques. There are the cheerleaders, the jocks, the nerds, the art kids, the drama kids, and so on. That's just how high school works. They may be some crossover, but for the most part, people usually stick in their lane. They want to be surrounded by people that they know, and who they know to agree with them. We like to say that we have left high school behind, but just look at social media demographics and you know that it's not true.

When you've discovered what your niche is and who you're demographic is, aka who you're making the videos for, and once you've actually started uploading videos, you're going to need to find a way to reach more people in that demographic. This is why selecting the social media network that works for you is so important; different kinds of people are attracted to different kinds of places online.

YouTube is pretty universal. People from every walk of life, whether it's their gender to their sexuality to their religion to their families can have a place on YouTube. It's because of what makes YouTube different from other social media networks on the site; it's a search engine. YouTube is often listed among social media networks, but it's really not. Social media networks, like Facebook, Twitter, and Instagram were designed for the sole reason of maintaining social connections with other people. YouTube was designed for people to create and upload content.

And this is what works for the platform. The demographics of YouTube spans across the entire board. 96% of 18 to 24-year-olds use the platform, but it's not just them. That number is rising among the older generation too. Here is a list of all of the percentage of people, divided by age group, who use YouTube regularly:

25 to 34-year-olds: 95%
35 to 44year-olds: 90%
45 to 54-year-olds: 85%
55 to 64-year-olds: 79%
65 to 75-year-olds: 66%
75+-year-olds: 51%

As you can see, that's a huge group of people who are on the platform. So, finding a demographic on YouTube shouldn't be a huge issue. But, that's not what this chapter is about. This chapter is about where else can you go online to find people with whom your content is aimed at. This is why using other social media channels will help elevate your brand. But this chapter isn't just about finding a social media network that works for you; we're also going to talk about how you can use them (briefly). I would definitely recommend that once this is all over, go out and do research on your chosen social media network. How you approach this could mean the difference between your channel succeeding or failing.

Now, let's get into it. Below, you'll find information on 4 of the biggest social media networks on the planet, plus some quick facts on what to know how each platform works.

Facebook is the one social media platform you really can't ignore. It's the third most visited website in the world and the top most downloaded app for mobile. It's the King of social media, whether you like it or not, and their recent issues with privacy have done nothing to slow it down. It has over 3 billion users worldwide, a third of the population, and 2 and a half billion of these users use it regularly.

This means that if your content is something that appeals to a wide audience, you probably will want to have a Facebook page. This goes without saying. But, Facebook seems to be dying slowly with the younger demographics. Teens and young adults just aren't interested in the platform, and while it still used by their generation, the trend seems to be dying fast. So, if you do have a product that appeals to both the younger and the older generation, you may want to consider having a Facebook account along with something like Instagram or Snapchat, both of which are incredibly popular with the younger generation.

So, here are their age demographics:

18 to 24 years olds: 15%
25 to 34 years olds: 26%
35 to 44 years old: 20%
45 to 54 years olds: 16%
55 to 64 years olds: 13%
65+ years olds: 10%

As for gender:

54% of the platform is women
46% of the platform is men

And here are some other stats:

- 85% of Facebook's daily users are from outside North America.
- About 80% of daily internet users use Facebook.
- 82% of college graduates use Facebook.
- The country with the most amount of Facebook users is not the USA, which has 210 million users. It's India, with 270 million.
- 75% of urban residents are on Facebook, with 67% of suburban residents and 58% of rural residents.

Here are some tips on how to use it:

- Post 1 - 3 times per day. Any more time and you're going to lose your likes.
- Engage and reply back to comments.
- Post behind the scene videos from your shoots; videos and photos get more engagement.
- Ask your followers a lot of questions and engage them with your posts.

Facebook is one of these platforms you really can't ignore, but you can get away with it if you don't want to. While it's definitely a platform that's worth looking into, some people just don't like it, and that's OK.

Instagram is easily one of the hottest websites online, with it just hitting it's 1 billion user mark in 2019. Instagram is the place to go if your content is very visual, or if you're selling products. Instagram is built all around the pictures, so if your content is very engaging and pretty to look at, this is the place to go. After all, you're making videos, your content should already be engaging.

Instagram is also very useful for anyone who wants to sell things. Instagram is all about selling, with influencers making thousands of dollars off a single pretty picture. This is because if people follow others for two reasons: they're personal friends of them, or they want that lifestyle. Instagram is all about showing off what you have, and people tend to like things that they can't have. So, if you can show off your products in an appealing way that really shows off the lifestyle, then Instagram is perfect for you. It's also a great place for vlogs and lifestyle brands.

Let's break down some of the age demographics:

18 to 24 years olds: 39%
25 to 34 years olds: 32%
35 to 44 years old: 15%
45 to 54 years olds: 8%
55 to 64 years olds: 3%
65+ years olds: 2%

As for gender:

50% of the platform is women.
50% of the platform is men.

Instagram is pretty even when it comes to their gender, but you cannot deny that among millennials, it is still hugely popular. Over half of the platform is people under the age of 35, and all of the features only make these numbers keep skyrocketing. Instagram is owned by the company Facebook, so the two platforms work well together for anyone who is looking for fluidity.

Not only that but here are some other stats:

- Out of 1 billion monthly active users, over half of them use the platform daily.
- The average Instagram post gets 4 times more engagement than the average Facebook post, but they spend about the same amount of time, 53 minutes per day.
- 1 in 3 Instagram users have directly used the platform to buy products. 83% of them say they discover new services and products on Instagram.
- 50% of Instagrammers follow online businesses and brands.

To use Instagram, follow these tips:

- Post at least 1 to 3 times per day. Anymore and you'll annoy your followers into not following you unless you're a big time celebrity.
- Use stories. Stories, which was ripped right off of Snapchat, is a great way to get more personal with your followers on top of all of the put together pictures on your feed. Using stories about 3 to 8 times per day is golden, and there are plenty of features that make them fun.
- Use hashtags. Hashtags are one of the easiest ways that people can find you on Instagram. Use them. If you don't want to put them in your main photo, you can instead comment on your

picture yourself with all 30 of them. There's no difference in the amount of attention.

- Share your Instagram photos to Twitter, Facebook, and Tumblr (if you have them).
- Edit your photos, but don't use the one inside Instagram. The photos edited there tend to look a bit cheap. Instead, invest in a photo editing app like VSCO or Snapseed. Both of these apps are available on iOS and Google Play Store and are popular with Instagram users.

These tips are easy to follow and should gain you a lot of followers. The most important thing to remember that on Instagram is that engagement is really key. As long as you encourage engagement, you should be golden.

Twitter is all about the "now". Basically, if something is happening right at this very moment, Twitter is the place to go. This is why it's a huge place for things like current events and news. It's also the place where social media marketing got its roots, believe it or not. On Twitter, someone can contact their favorite businesses, content creator, or brand directly, without any barriers. This is why it's huge for businesses, and is the place where the majority of people go when they have something to say directly to a company.

In terms of what kind of people hang out on Twitter and use the platform a lot, this section is all about these things that you should know.

By age, the stats go as follows:

18 to 20 years olds: 4%
21 to 24 years olds: 7%
25 to 34 years olds: 43%
35 to 44 years old: 28%
45 to 54 years olds: 12%
55 to 64 years olds: 3%
65+ years olds: 1%

Teens aged below 18 cannot be counted on the platform. Keep that in mind.

In terms of gender:

70% of the platform is female
30% of the platform is male

Here are some other stats that might solidify your choice:

- Twitter has a huge international base, with 80% of its users based outside of the USA. The three countries with the higher user count (other than the USA) are Brazil, Japan, and Mexico.
- Almost half, about 46% of their users are on the platform daily.
- A third of Americans aged 18 to 29 years old, about 36% of them, use Twitter.

Here's how to use twitter to help grow your YouTube channel:

- Tweet anywhere from 3 to 6 times a day. Just continually updating your followers about your day, from how a video shoot is going, to how writing a script, to asking them questions, anything goes.
- Engage with your followers. Reply to them. Twitter is the perfect place where users can reach you and talk to you directly, so use it that way.
- Use all their features. You can run polls on Twitter, and make lists. Use them both.
- Engage with other creators. Twitter isn't just a great place for your fans to be reaching you, it's also a great place for you to reach your favorite YouTubers. Do it! You may get some collaborations out of it.

Twitter is the perfect customer service website, and if you want to engage directly with your followers, plus if your niche is in that demographic, go for it. It's perfect for you.

Snapchat is the place to be if you're trying to appeal to teens. That's basically it. I'm not going to talk too much about what the age demographics are too much in this, but if you're trying to appeal to teens (or anyone under 25) Snapchat is the place to be. Over 70% of people under 30 use the platform for some reason or another, and it's not very common with anyone over that age.

Snapchat is at its core a messaging service. Known for its "snaps", picture messages that disappear after usually about 10 to 15 seconds, it now has about 180 million users, and the majority of them are under 30 (easily about 70%). It's more popular with women, but the gender specifics are very even, with about 60% of women using the platform, while 40% of men. Here are some other stats:

- 69% of 13 to 17 year olds use Snapchat, while 68% of 18 to 29 year olds.
- The average Snapchat user visits about 25 times a day, spending about 40 minutes on the platform.
- It's more popular with higher income adults, with 30% of adults with an income of $75,000 per year using it. In contrast, only 23% of adults with an income of less than $30,000 per year use it.

To use Snapchat, follow these tips:

- Post to your story often.
- Use all of their features (gifs, stickers, etc.).
- Hold a Q & A session.
- Show a lot of behind-the-scenes shots.
- Do announcements and special offers.
- Don't be too perfect and put together. This is a big one. Snapchat stories are a lot more personal than other platforms like Instagram or Facebook, so you need to be more personal. It's what your followers expect. This means blurry videos, no makeup pictures, stuff like that. Just be personal.

I know what you're thinking, this isn't nearly the amount of advice you got for the other social media platforms, but that's really the point. Snapchat is very simple in how it works, and very straightforward. It's all about taking your followers through your day, so just bring them through your day. Your imperfect, messy day.

Now, using at least one or two of these social media will really help bring attention to your channel in a good way. There is a whole group of people on these platforms that have never heard of your channel that you can appeal too. Plus, you'll make money faster. Win, win.

CHAPTER 6
Guide To Collaboration

Collaboration. What is collaboration?

Collaboration is the act of working together with another YouTuber, ideally one who is also in your niche. It's a technique used by a ton of YouTubers online, and you'll often see them doing it on their channels. It's beneficial to everyone, a tit for tat idea so to speak. It's easily one of the best ways to build your YouTube channel and subscriber list.

Collaborating is not just a way to build subscribers. It's also an easy way to stay connected to other YouTubers on the platform. By doing collaborations with other YouTubers that your followers subscribe to and enjoy, you're showing that you're paying attention. Even if you just do a collaboration with a YouTuber that nobody has ever heard of (it's the internet, it's a big place), you still show that you're a part of your community. It shows you live outside of your own little bubble of the internet.

The basic fact is, collaboration is a good thing to get into the habit of doing on your channel. In this chapter, we're going to discuss not only all the reasons you should be doing YouTuber collaboration, but also how to get one done in a way that will be smooth for you, and how to find people to collaborate with.

Why Collaboration Works Well

Why should you collaborate with other YouTubers? A lot of people get into YouTubing because they want to be alone, because they don't want to be talking and communicating with other people. To be completely fair, you probably could build your YouTube channel without collaboration and only ever communicating with your followers through a camera and a laptop, but I would advise against it. Collaboration is hugely beneficial for everyone involved. Let's just count a few of the ways.

- You reach their subscriber base. This is an obvious one, and one of the biggest reasons why YouTubers started up collaborations in the first place. When you appear on someone else's channel, or when they appear on yours, you are immediately exposed to an entirely new group of followers. If you're working with someone in your niche and who has the same audience as you, these people are very likely to be potential subscribers for you. This is easily the most basic reason why you should be collaboration; you can build up your base hugely this way.

- It shakes things up. It's something different for your current base to watch. It's something that's fresh and offbeat. Collaboration usually opens the doors for you to do something different. It's not just your head anymore. It offers you a lot of different ways to approach things.

- It helps creativity. This is similar to the last reason, but it's still important. Collaboration is all about that; collaboration. This means that you're working together with someone, and they may not think the same way you do. They may challenge you to see something differently. This can be a great thing for your channel. You may come up with some video ideas that you never would've thought of alone, and this can inspire you in general for your channel.

- It helps you build relationships. It's really important to be an active part of your community on the internet, especially if you're trying to get people to pay attention to you. Hanging out on the forums, responding to comments and questions, these things are great, but actually working with other people shows that you're paying attention to your community. Whether they're up and comers or people who have posted more than 5,000 videos, working with other people gives this impression that you're open to building these relationships. They can just be working relationships if you wish, but the internet is great at bringing people together if nothing else. You'll get along really well with a lot of these people, and you might find yourself with good friends, who you will want to work with again and again.

- It shows you care. Not just about views and subscribers, but about your base. Scroll through your comments enough times, and you'll find that there probably are a few requests for a collaboration or a few "you remind me of *insert YouTuber's name here*". Giving the people what they want shows that you're actually paying attention to what they're saying, and you value their opinion. This is never a bad thing.

- It's fun. It can be a lot of fun collaborating with another YouTuber. There, I said it. It's actually a blast. You're talking with somebody else who you already know is interested in the same things you are, so you already have an entire base of what you can talk about. You'll walk away with more ideas than what you came with, and you're getting creatively stimulated. It may be a little different at first, especially if you're used to working alone, but it can be a lot of fun.

Next up, we're going to talk about two things; what kind of collaborations you can do, and how to make them as smooth (and fun) as possible for you. There's a bit of a science to it.

What Kind of Collaboration?

Similar to the fact that there are about 600 types of YouTube video, there are probably about 600 types of collaboration as well. Collaboration comes in all shapes and sizes, and similar to choosing the type of YouTube videos you'll make, it really depends on what you're capable of and what your niche happens to be. But, here are some general ideas that will work for pretty much everybody.

Guest Appearances: simply just appearing on each other's channels and in each other's videos, doing a challenge or something else, is an easy way to do this. This works best if you live close to the person in your area, or if you're visiting them or vice versa.

Do a video together, and split it in half: do one video together, and divide it so one half is on your channel, and the other half is on the other channel. Just remember to include a strong call-to-action at the end, and plan who gets each half before so you can film accordingly.

Upload their video to your channel (and vice versa). If you don't live to each other, and traveling isn't an option for you right now, you have to get creative. This is a great way to bring attention to your channel and is similar to guest writing on someone's blog. Just make sure it's in your niche.

Just exchange shout-outs. Not all collaborations are videos. Some of them are just simply communicating online through Twitter or Instagram in front of your followers. Just mention each other and link to each other's pages, along with something positive or a mention of how it's helped you. You could even create a response video if you want!

Now, there are some ideas. Now, I bet your next question is; how can I make this process easy for me? Well, I've got you covered in this guide below.

Guide to Collaboration

In this part, we're going to talk about how you can make this process as easy and as simple as you can, without going overboard.

First up, find someone to collaborate with. The easiest way to collaborate with someone is to find someone who compliments you and has the same, or very similar, niche as you. The easiest way to find someone is in the search bar. Using the search filters will help tremendously. You can find people there based on their content, their subscriber base, the length of their video, and more. This may take some research and some hard work, but it also might not. It really depends. Here are some tips on what to look for;

- Someone who is around the same age. Different age groups tend to not have the same audience. There are definitely exceptions to this rule, but a 22 year old probably won't have the same opinions and audiences as a 45 year old. Of course, this doesn't apply to everyone, there are exceptions to every rule, and just finding someone whose content compliments yours should do the trick.
- Check their subscriber numbers. If you have 150 subscribers and the other person has about 250 thousand, I'm sorry, but they're not likely going to work with you. It'd be nice, and if you could swing that (like if you know the YouTuber personally), go for it. But, stick to people who have the same subscriber numbers, you'll have a much higher chance of getting a yes and actually getting things done.
- Check to be sure that they're committed. Some people get into YouTube, and they don't realize just how much of a massive undertaking it is. They just don't take it seriously. If you work with these people, you're taking on the risk that they won't take you seriously either. Only work with people who clearly have a posting schedule and are engaged on their channel. Really scope them out.
- Have your expectations set. Before you even reach out, you should know exactly what you expect of your collaboration partner, from when you're posting to how much work you want to do to how much promotion each of you will be doing on social media. Have all of these details ready, and communicate them clearly. There is no such thing as too many details and communication in collaboration, trust me.
- When you're first starting out, don't put all your eggs in one basket. Don't just prepare to collaborate with one person. If you can, reach out to multiple people. Things go wrong, and it's never a bad thing to have a few projects at once working for you.

Now that you've picked someone or a few, now it's time to reach out. Here's how you do that:

- Subscribe and comment on their videos. Bring their attention to you, but not in a spammy way. Don't bring attention to your content (yet) and actually watch their videos. Compliment it in a sincere way. You shouldn't be working with someone whose content you like anyway, so this shouldn't be too hard. Once you have started up a genuine connection, and show interest
- Make your expectations clear. Remember these expectations you laid out before you even reached out? Now is the time to put them forward. Likely, the person you're working with will have their own expectations.

Now is the time brainstorming your ideas. Bring some of your own to the table, or just meet up, either in person if you live close enough or over video chat (distance really isn't an issue when it's collaborations, so don't let yourself be limited by that). You can brainstorm together. Here's how to brainstorm productively;

- The best idea always wins. Don't get too attached personally to your idea, as it will probably change and evolve over time. That's what happens when you collaborate with someone. You don't have full creative control, and they're going to want to get their half in too. Be open to changes or compromises.
- Create a plan. This means a plan in what gets done at what time, how often you'll be promoting each other on social media, and who will do what. Creating a schedule and sticking to it will keep everything running smoothly.
- Put something out on social media right away (if it's OK with the person you're collaborating with). Tease a collaboration on your separate social media pages, even just a tagged picture of the two of you. This will give your followers hints of what they can expect, and you could even ask them outright what content they want to see from the two of you.
- Put your best foot forward, and work hard. This could lead to more collaborations in the future, not just with this person, but any other person who sees your channel. This is all about building your relationships and showing off a bit. Don't do a mediocre job, or your collaborate partner won't want to work with you again, or anyone else. You need to impress them and their audience, some of whom may be other YouTubers you can work with, after all.

Now, all you have to do is bring together your ideas, make a few videos, and voila! You have a collaboration! Now, as you make the video and when you upload it, do the following:

- Put the links to their channel in your description box, and talk about their content in the actual video. If you're doing a video on their channel as well, be sure to link to that video as well, plus a description.
- Include an email address on where other people can reach you. When you're open to collaborations, it's important to actually tell people. This is why making it easy for people to actually contact you is an easy way to find more people to work with.

Well, I'm pretty sure that covers all about collaborations. Actually, we've covered pretty much everything content wise now. Now it's time to talk about what we all came here for; *money.*

CHAPTER 7
Money

I know what you're thinking: finally. Finally, we're at the "how to make money" part of all of this. You're finally going to be able to quit your boring day job and go right into making videos and content that you love. But, I've kind of got news for you.

It's not that easy.

Not that at any time in this book I made it out to be like it was easy. Being a YouTuber is hard work, there are long hours, and you do a lot of your work alone. For some people, that's not an ideal situation. Honestly, when YouTube is hailed as a get rich quick scheme, where all you have to do is upload a few videos and wash the cash deposit itself into your bank account, I want to roll my eyes. Nothing that is valuable is done with just a few quick videos, and any successful YouTuber, no matter how successful, will tell you that.

Before you make money, there's a lot of time, dedication, and effort you have to put it, but it's totally worth it in the end. But, it can be a long road with very little reward, so first, let's go over the rules of making money on YouTube:

1) Understand that it may take a while. And until it does happen, you have to stop focusing on money. Don't think about making money, and just think about how your videos are as a channel. Do you like them? Do you not like them? What's wrong with them? What do you like about them? How can you make them better? You need to pay attention and finetune your craft before you can make real money off of something.
2) Understand that 50 active subscribers are better over 1,000,000 inactive ones. It's rarely about the subscriber, or even view count when it comes to making money, believe it or not. So, don't get wrapped up in subscriber count, it's not nearly as important. It's only an ego boost.
3) Understand your craft, and stick to it. Once you have your niche, your strategy, and your schedule down, follow that like you would the bible. Fine tuning your craft and making sure you're putting out good content is the most important thing.
4) Understand that this is your job. This means being professional. This means that you have to treat it like you would any job that's

114

9 to 5. Actually, spoiler alert, a lot of YouTubers actually work much longer hours than that. But, treating this like you would any other job will really help keep your head where it's supposed to be. This also means that you can't start treating the internet like a playground; it's a workspace.

5) Understand your brand. I know that we've already talked a lot about the brand in this book, but it's important. Especially when it comes to making money. You shouldn't ever do something that if off brand, regardless of how much money you stand to make from it. You run the risk of losing a lot of your following this way, as if they see you doing things that have nothing to do with your brand, they'll assume that you're just after their money. You really don't want that.

And there you have it; these are the rules of making money off of YouTube. While these are definitely not the official, YouTube rules (we'll get into these next chapter when we're talking about monetization). They're still good to have on hand.

Now, the real question is, how long will it take for me to make money on YouTube? And the answer? Well...

How Long Will it Take Me to Make Money?

Compared to the old days, making money on YouTube is a lot more difficult than it used to be. There are a few reasons for that, but it mostly comes down to three; the competition, the number of views, and YouTube's policy.

We've already talked a lot about just how insane the competition is on YouTube, so we don't need to go over that again. But it is crazy, and that is something to keep in mind. But rather than let that deter you, let it inspire you to make sure that every piece of content you put out there is absolutely amazing and incredible. If you need to stand out in a crowd of a million people, make sure you're doing something that makes you stand out. By doing this, this is how you'll get subscribers and views.

Subscribers and views really come out of putting quality content that people are interested in out there. That's literally it. Once you have gotten enough views and subscribers, you should be able to use them to make money. This shouldn't take too long as long as you're being consistent.

Finally, YouTube's new policy. This policy, at the time of writing a book, is only about a year old and caused a huge amount of uproar when it first came out. It affected not only new YouTubers but older ones as well. What's the policy?

To monetize your channel, you need at least 1,000 subscribers and 4,000 hours of watch time, all done in the span of about 12 months. There a few reasons for this change (before it didn't matter), but one thing that seemed to really inspire it was the infamous Logan Paul video that showed him finding a dead body in the suicide forest in Japan. Other things that may have influenced it was advertisers complaining that their ads were being played on videos that put forward racist or homophobic content, something that they as a company didn't want to be associated with.

This is the big reason why it's so important to really hammer home for subscribers and views that first year. It can be a little intense and can take some getting used to, but if you want to make money with monetization, it's important. Of course, there are other ways to make money on YouTube that don't involve monetization, and we'll get into that now.

How To Make Money on YouTube

Now, there are so many different ways to make money through YouTube that you would need about 800 pages to get through all of them. There are so many cool and creative ways that people have found a way to make money online, and you really have to hand it to them. I doubt that when YouTube started off, they thought that one day there'd be people making millions every month just off of posting videos of their day to day lives. It's kind of crazy, no matter how you think about it.

But, anyway, when it comes to making money, you really just have to be creative. I can give you these options, yes, and we're going to devote a chapter to each of them, but it's up to you. In each individual chapter, we're going to get into how you can into it, the easiest ways to get into it, and more. Let's get started.

Monetization: this is the one that people generally think of when they think of a YouTuber making money off of the platform. It's also generally the one that makes people the least amount of money. Advertisers have gotten notoriously picky about what kind of content they want their videos to be on, and not only that but rates have been going down. But, that doesn't mean that it's still not an option to try out for you and that you shouldn't be doing it. In fact, it means exactly the opposite.

Affiliate Marketing: this is a way that you can take advertising directly into your own hands. You choose which products or services you speak of on your channel. It could even be your own! But, this can also erode trust with potential and current subscribers, so be sure that you never find yourself being paid to say you like something. If you're being paid to say you like something, and a subscriber goes out and buys that thing and it's not very good, the person who gets the heat will be you. Not the company that made the product, but you for suggesting it. You want to establish a level of trust with your followers, and just saying you like something for money is one of the easiest ways to lose that.

Selling: if you want to sell on YouTube, the first thing you should know is that you need to do two things; you need to be able to sell a product, and you need to do it a way that's personal and not too sales pitchy. You can either sell products that you believe in, or you can sell your own. There are plenty of YouTubers online who sell their own merchandise, some of them just simple T-shirts and mugs. This one takes a bit more investing than the other four on here, but if you can find a need for something, why not sell it?

Fan Funding: there is no limit to what project you can do, as long as you have enough money to do so. Before doing this, you usually had to go to big scale producers to convince them to give you money for projects, but now, thanks to the internet and the cameras in our phones, anyone can do this. Not only that but if your project is good enough, you can get other people to help foot the bill for you. If you can get enough people to believe in your channel and your content, using a program like Patreon or Kickstarter is a perfectly valid option.

There are, of course, plenty of ways to make money on YouTube. This is only the basic, average list and pretty much every big YouTuber out there has pretty much everything on this list.

Personally, I would recommend starting off with one or two of them, and as you get more organized and used to the process, then you move up into doing more. Don't overdo it or you just won't get anything done. Crashing and burning is not how you want to start off your YouTube career.

Which ones you choose to do is really all up to you, and what your channel is. Different channels will warrant different types of money. For example, if you're a makeup reviewing channel, affiliate marketing is probably where you'll aim. If you're doing skits on YouTube, Fan Funding is probably the way to go. It all depends on you.

So, now we're going to talk about each of these different forms of money making, and you can pick and choose which one you want to do.

CHAPTER 8
Becoming A Youtube Partner

When more and more YouTubers started pulling in thousands, or in some cases millions and billions, of views online, YouTube realized they needed to do something about it. These YouTubers were bringing people to their website, and as a result, to their advertisers. And that's when they came up with their partnership program. It was a way to make sure that the YouTubers were getting money for what they were doing, encouraging them to keep creating and posting on the platform. It's simple, and it's absolutely up to you as to whether or not you want to participate in it.

It works like this: you create and publish videos onto your channel. Your subscribers view them, and each time that someone views one of your videos and sees the ads, you get paid. For every click, you earn revenue. However, how much you earn depends on a variety of things, from the type of ad that the viewer sees or how they respond to it. For example, if a short commercial appears at the start of your video and the viewer chooses to skip it, you will not earn anything on that ad. Not only that, but even to just earn a few dollars requires thousands or tens of thousands of views every month. How does this work and how can you get into it?

These are the questions we're seeking to answer in this chapter.

Becoming a YouTube partner used to be a lot easier than it is now. In 2018, their program eligibility requirements were updated. This was mostly thanks to the fact that advertisers were complaining over their ads being shown over inappropriate videos. While any YouTuber can apply for the partnership program, but you have to meet these requirements to be accepted into it.

- Everything must be original.
- Your channel has 1,000 subscribers, 4,000 watch hours in the last 12 months, that shows it is still growing.
- A linked AdSense account (look ahead)

You can check your watch hours in the Analytics tab in the Creator's studio, so you know what is working for your channel and what isn't. When you apply, all of your channel activity is reviewed so they can be sure you meet the guidelines. This process could take a few weeks, and

YouTube will let you know when it's done. If you want to check the status of your application, go to Creator's Studio - Channel - Monetization.

Whether or not somebody chooses to become a YouTube partner is optional, and it's all about what you want for your channel. Let's take a look at some of the pros and the cons of being a YouTube channel. Knowing them will help you make your decision.

Becoming A YouTube Partner: Pros and Cons

I like to start with the positive side of things first, and there are a lot of them when it comes to joining the YouTube program, so here are the pros.

Pros

1) You own your own content. When you upload to YouTube and you're not a partner, they can use your content however they like. When you're a partner, you own all the copyrights and distribution rights to ALL of their uploaded content, no exceptions. This means that you can upload on other websites, not just YouTube.

2) It does make you money. While it may not make you as much as other streams will, ad revenue will bring in some extra cash. There are new features being added to help make you more money as well, such as different kinds of advertising.

3) It's all automated. When you become a YouTube partner, Google takes your channel and handles all of the advertising. It pairs you with advertisers, chooses what ads will appear, and tracks all of the traffic on it. Then, it will pay you accordingly, with you doing very little work. You don't have to go out looking for them.

4) You get more exposure. As a partner, YouTube wants to make sure that you're getting as many views as possible. This will put your content at the top of video searches pertaining to it, and there are no restrictions as to where your content will be delivered.

5) More page customization. As a YouTube partner, you'll be able to customize your page with colors and more. You can choose colors to match your brand.

6) More control. YouTube partners have more control over their content when compared to channels that aren't partnered.

7) Lots of other features. YouTube is constantly adding more to the program, as more and more ways to make money for the platform

pop up. YouTube wants to make sure they're nurturing their relationship with their YouTubers, so they're willing to listen and want to work together. There's no telling what features they'll be adding next.

Of course, not everything is good in the world, not even in the world of YouTube. There are some not so great things about the YouTube partnership program. Let's take a look.

Cons

1) All your content must be 100% original. That, or you need the permission of the creator to use it. YouTube has a policy that if their algorithm even picks up a 2 second clip on videos that aren't yours you won't get a cent of that revenue. Everything that you post if you're a YouTube partner must be yours and yours alone, no exceptions.

2) Language and location restrictions. If you're not a resident in certain countries, you cannot become a YouTube partner. The only countries eligible are from Australia, Brazil, Canada, France, Germany, Ireland, Japan, Spain, Great Britain, New Zealand, and of course the United States. Keep in mind that if you aren't in one of these countries, it probably wouldn't be a bad idea, considering that it'll be expanding to new countries all the time. Early bird gets the worm.

3) Strict rules to follow. If there is one group that has to follow YouTube's rules more than the rest of them, it's YouTube partners. YouTube partners must remain in good standing with the website, and run the risk of suspension or even losing their channel if something happens.

It's hard to say whether or not it's worth it to become a YouTube partner. After all, it's up to you and how you want to run your channel. It also depends on the kind of channel you want to be. If you plan on publishing nothing but original content, I would say apply.

But one benefit of it is that it's totally optional. You can choose whether or not you take part in it. Of course, it does take some hard work, considering the amount of effort that goes into getting 1,000 subscribers and 4,000 viewing hours. Even so, it will still take a lot of time and hard work to earn anything substantial. Most YouTubers make only about 1 dollar for every thousand views. This varies YouTuber to YouTuber, but regardless, you're going to be earning peanuts at first. Here are where you should be putting all your focus in if getting approved for the partnership program is your goal:

1. Create content that is yours and yours alone, but also high quality. There are plenty of YouTubers out there who are at the top of their game now who claim that how they got there was through experimentation. Well, most of these YouTubers who started out when the average YouTuber was putting on bad content. This meant that viewers really didn't have many choices as to where they were going. This is not the same now, with high quality content being cranked out along with. While experimentation is good at the beginning a bit, I won't ever tell someone not to make sure that every video isn't high quality. This doesn't mean you need to know how to use the best editing programs and have the best cameras. This means do the best you can do every time that you post a video and make sure that you did the best every single time. People notice the quality and hard work, and YouTube is not an exception to that rule.

2. Stick with your niche. For the first few months/years, you're going to have to stay in your niche if you're really focused on building your subscriber base. They're going to be coming to you for a certain type of content that you promise, and if you don't deliver, they're going to be disappointed. Consistency with your niche, plus as to what time you post, will help build subscribers.

3. Engage with your audience. Remind your audience to subscribe to every single video. Remember, your audience likely actually want you to keep making content. So, they want you to make money off of it, maybe not directly. This is why programs such as Patreon work so well because people want their favorite creators to keep going. So, reply to comments, remind them to subscribe, and ask questions, either in the videos or in the comments.

4. Follow all the strategies in this book. A lot of what you've read here is stuff that you've already read in this book. But, this is because it really is all that simple. You just need to keep following the formula. YouTube isn't an art; it's a science, and the quicker that you understand that the faster you will make money.

How To Apply For YouTube Partnership Program

Once you have gotten your 1,000 subscribers and 4,000 viewing hours, now it's time to apply for the program.

First, you're going to need an AdSense account. An AdSense account is a program run by Google. It allows people in their network to serve text, video, image, video, or other interactive ads on their websites, as long as it's a Google based content website. One of these websites is YouTube. You can choose the types of ads you want to run, where and when you want your ad to appear, and eventually, if you become big enough, advertisers will actually start bidding on your videos, similar to an auction. This means you're making more money.

To create an AdSense account, follow the following steps:

1) Go to google.com/AdSense/start.
2) Click the green sign up now button.
3) Enter the URL of your YouTube channel. Using your YouTube channel, you can then click continue in... after you enter your URL. This will go faster then.
4) From there, you can choose whether you'd like AdSense to send help. They will send you tips on performance that is tailored to you, and a lot of beginner YouTubers (and creators online) find it very helpful.
5) Review the terms and conditions to make sure that you're not getting a surprise later.
6) Congratulations, now you have an AdSense account!

Now all you have to do is apply for the YouTube Partnership Program. After applying, this may take a few weeks, and there are no guarantees that you're going to be accepted. But no worries, you can just try again!

1) Sign into YouTube.
2) In the top right corner, select your account icon. Scroll down to the creator studio.
3) When the creator studio opens, head to the left sidebar. Select channel, then Status and features.
4) Under monetization, then click enable.
5) Follow the on-screen steps, which will guide you through the entire process.

Whether or not you choose to enter the YouTube Partnership Program, keep in mind that you probably won't be able to make all your income just from this. You probably won't even make that much, at least at first. Even the most successful YouTubers, most of their income doesn't come from this.

A few years ago, this may have been the case, but since YouTube's crackdown on who can get monetization, that's no longer what's happening. YouTube advertisers have gotten notorious about submitting complaints about where their ads appear, so that means that your videos may not even get approved. This is all based on their content.

But, there are other ways to make money on YouTube. AdSense is not your ride or die way. So let's get into some of them. Next chapter: Affiliate Marketing.

CHAPTER 9
Affiliate Marketing

The concept behind affiliate marketing is that you basically can just make money at any time throughout the day, no matter what time it is, and you can even sleep making money. Sounds nice, right?

Affiliate marketing is often used by companies to help drive up their sales and will bring you large amounts of revenue if you do it correctly. This means that both the company and the person doing the marketing wins in this situation.

While you may think that it's really hard to get into it, that's just not the case. The stats are in, and there is plenty of affiliate marketing opportunities for everyone.

- 81% of brands regularly use affiliate marketing when they're putting a new product out in the world. This number will only get higher as more and more brands become aware that this is an option. Every year, the increase in the amount of spending done by brands for affiliate marketing goes up about 10%.
- 16% of all online orders made are because of affiliate marketing, with content marketing generating three times more than more traditional methods of advertising.

We've pretty much all seen affiliate marketing. It's when a company pays someone, usually a celebrity in the olden days, and talk about how much they like the product. Every time a Kardashian posts a coupon code online, they're getting a slice of the cash generated from each of these coupon use.

The actual definition of affiliate marketing is this: the process by which an affiliate (you) earns a commission for marketing another company's, brand's, business's, or person's products. Basically, you promote the product and get paid for it. The sales are tracked using coupon codes or special links called "affiliate links" that lead you from one website to another.

Here's the step by step breakdown of the process:

1) You show an ad or link for whatever product it is on your website, talk about it in your video, you post on other social media about it, etc.
2) The customer clicks on the link.
3) Customer is sent to the store.
4) The customer makes a purchase.
5) The network takes note of the purchase.
6) The purchase is confirmed by the company/brand/business/person.
7) The transaction is credited to you.
8) You get paid your commission.

These steps may seem really complicated, but they're really not. Most of the time, you're not even doing that much work. Basically, it comes down to three separate groups:

You (the Affiliate)
The Product Creator/Seller
The Consumer

To make sure that you're successful, you need to understand the relationship between these three groups of people:

The Product Creator/Seller

This person is a business. That's it. They're looking to sell something and make money from it. It can be anything, a physical object like household cleaning supplies or a brand new cell phone, or a service, like music lessons or a course on speaking French. There isn't much you can't buy on the internet these days. The seller may not be involved in the marketing process, but they could be as well.

The Affiliate

This will be you. Your job is to promote the product and persuade your subscribers that this is a great product and they need it in their lives. You need to convince them to purchase it. You won't make any money otherwise. We'll talk more about the rules of affiliate marketing in a bit, but one of the big ones is that you don't choose products that don't fall in with your niche.

The Consumer

These are the people that you need. These are the people who will drive all of your income. You can have the best product in the world, the best deals, but if nobody buys anything, you won't make anything. So, nurturing this relationship is critical. We'll get into more of this in a bit, but it's important to remember.

Affiliate marketing is a draw because it seems to be really easy. It's quick, costs very little money, but it's also one of these things that do require some grind at the beginning of your time doing it. You may not make money for months.

To be fair, there are several ways an affiliate marketer to make money. In most cases, affiliate marketers only get paid in pay per sale. This is when you get a percentage of the money made off the product after the consumer actually makes a purchase through the affiliate marketer's strategies. This means that you actually have to get someone to buy the product before you get paid.

There are two other methods, but you'll have a hard time using them if you're just starting out. These are "pay per click" and "pay per lead".

Pay per click is simply if you can get someone to click on a link, then you get paid. You're paid based on the increase of web traffic from your link, and the more web traffic you can drum up, the more you get paid. This is obviously the most ideal one because it's a lot easier to get someone to just simply click on a link rather than actually buys something. But, offers like these are rare, unless you're a celebrity or someone with 10 million subscribers.

The third way that affiliate marketers work is pay per lead. Pay per lead is a bit more complex than the other two we've mentioned. This one is based on how far you can get a potential viewer to go. How many links can you get them to click, can you get them to enter a certain code, all of these things. You have to get someone to go onto another website to complete an act of some kind. It will depend from brand to brand, but examples include subscribing to a newsletter, downloading software, or signing a petition. It really all depends.

And that is pretty much basically what affiliate marketing is.

YouTube is the perfect place to get started affiliate marketing. There are plenty of YouTubers who take a part of it. Spend enough time on the platform and eventually, you're going to find YouTubers talking about services and products from other parts of the internet. It comes with the territory of YouTube now.

Once you have built up a large enough following, you can start finding people to work with. Let's start first by looking at how YouTube cannot just help you get into it, but what requirements you need to look for when you do find products that you want to talk about.

The Rules of Affiliate Marketing

1) Must always fall into your niche. Why would you promote a product that you aren't sure your followers would actually be interested in? This means that if you get offered to become a marketer for a hair products company and you're a channel who focuses on health and fitness, your followers aren't following you for the tips on the latest beauty products. No. They want things like new protein powders and the most advanced workout gear available. That's what they want to see sponsoring your videos. So, if you're going to market to anyone, market to them. They're the ones who are going to be clicking. Of course, there are some niches that are so diverse they don't really have to worry about this (think comedy skits or business advice), but what they choose to market on their channel should also cater to a large audience (coffee, office supplies, etc.).

2) Always be products that you actually believe in. Too many marketers make this mistake where they choose to put their voice behind a product that they don't actually believe in. This means they don't actually use it, or they haven't even touched it, or they know that it's not a good product. This is a huge mistake, as it ruins the trust between you and your subscribers. Your monetary gain depends on their support, remember? Bonus points if you can find a company that you already love that's willing to work with you.

3) Do your homework. If it's a new brand, do your homework on it. Yes, on the surface they may match you perfectly but underneath it all. Maybe the product looks good on the surface but actually isn't that great once you have taken it around for a few spins. Be sure to actually test out what they're selling before you sign anything, and ask for a free trial of a few days every time (at least).

4) Pay attention to new products that are coming out. Always stay on top of the new products that you may want to support. This goes hand in hand in making sure that you've also got the latest news on your own niche. If there is a company that you've worked with, or you want to work with, that's coming out with new

features, you want to be aware so you can offer your services up front.

Now, to get into affiliate marketing, it's not as hard as most people think it is. People often assume that you need 100,000 subscribers to get started, but you really don't. The easiest way to get into affiliate marketing is to join an affiliate program. Don't know what that is? Keep reading.

Affiliate Marketing Programs

So, for those who don't know, affiliate marketing programs are basically just an easy way for brands looking for YouTubers and bloggers and other content creators to work with. Many YouTubers are already signed up for large affiliate marketing programs like Amazon's one (which we'll be talking about), but I have great news for you: there is no limit to how many affiliate programs that you can sign up. There are literally hundreds, and most YouTubers don't realize just how much money they could be making if they just did a little research. Don't be one of them.

Here are some of the best affiliate programs available online as of 2019. These are catered to a certain user base, and different programs will have different kinds of offers. This means that you probably won't fit with every affiliate program on this list, and it's all about what works for you. Some of them just won't have offers that are in the same niche as your channel. But, I did my best to cover all the bases. But, even if I missed it, there are plenty of other websites online. You just may have to do some digging.

Movani

If you're a channel who focuses on photography, cinematography, or anything really art or movie related, this one's for you. Their affiliate program is incredibly attractive, as they start their margins at 40% (for every purchase, you get 40% of the profit), and they're well known and raved about. Even if you're not a channel about art or photography or videography, they do have products that aren't necessarily hard to sell. There are plenty of people who are looking to break into the YouTube game themselves, and Movani's products can help them do this.

Nintendo Creators Program

Yes, gamers, your dreams have been answered. Nintendo has an affiliate program. This was created after YouTube gamers used Nintendo games on the platform. Basically, when you use Nintendo games in your videos, Nintendo receives a cut of any ads you get, and you get some of that. Pretty sweet, right? You have a choice between registering your entire channel or just a couple of videos, and you can get 60% to 70% of each cut.

PointsPrizes

An easy, basic platform, this works by you including referral links at the top of your video descriptions that are relevant to your audience. This is one of these channels that run off of traffic rather than actual purchases. All you have to direct them over to whatever website it is, and they pay much more than other affiliate programs (up to 10 times the amount). They're also not interested in changing your content.

Sigma Beauty

Hands up for all the beauty gurus! Basically, this one works by you signing up for the program, receiving a special affiliate code, and reading their instructions. Sigma would rather you use all of their brushes by name, and including all the links in your about section on your profile, as well as your description box. This seems like a lot, but it can earn you a lot of money. Especially since the amount all depends on the amount that you sell.

Amazon

The king of the internet, Amazon is usually the first program any YouTuber signs up for. It's easy, free to join, and there isn't much of a sign-up or approval process. You basically just choose whichever products you want to advertise, and you can earn up to 10% in fees. Most YouTubers choose to put up links for their camera gear or any item they're using in their videos, as they can vouch for the products without even having to outright mention it.

Shopify

This little known e-commerce platform is a treasure trove for YouTubers. How Shopify works is that you spread the word on your channel, and encourage others to sign up for it. There are reports that you can earn almost $60 for every user that signs up for your own link! Plus, there is around the clock support, with links to blogs, tutorials, and more. This will help you really understand the platform and able to adequately explain it to your audience.

Here are some other ideas on how to find brands that you want to work with:

- Follow others' examples. If there is a lot of YouTubers promoting one thing on YouTube at any time, you can bet that there is probably a brand behind it that wants more to work with. When a business first launches, they're working to get the word out there as quickly as possible. If you may be able to help with that, jump on it right away.
- Reach out yourself. Now, I'm not saying that Coca-Cola will want to work with you if you just give them a call (I mean if you can swing it, go for it). But, if there is a brand that you really enjoy, such as a local business or a course that you enjoyed, see if they're interested in working with you as business partners. They may sponsor one or two of your videos in exchange for you talking about them in the videos.

How To Start Making Money

Now that you've found a way to actually get affiliation deals, now it's time to talk about something else: how to get people to actually click on the links in the first place. Thankfully, there are some tricks to this that will make people more likely to tap it, and get you some cash.

- Know the product inside and out. You should really know exactly what the product is before you start selling it anyway, but if you can provide a demonstration on your channel, that's huge. By listing all the products features and showing your fans how to use it, it shows that you've done your research and actually care about what product you're showing your subscribers.
- Be honest. Never just be paid to say I like a product. We've gone over this before, but it's super important. This will 100% destroy the trust you've already established with your subscribers.
- Tell a story. If the product has a personal story that will resonate with your audience, share it. If you can find a product that answers a problem that you wish you had the answer to in the past that also fits your niche, that's the perfect fit for you.
- Be likable. This goes without saying, but to be a YouTuber you do have to be likable on some level or another. But, if you're likable to your fans and able to make them feel like a friend and relate to them, they're more likely to buy from you and help you out. This also goes for selling and fan funding as well.

131

- Treat it like you would sales. Anyone who is or has been in the sales industry, or the customer service industry, understands this. Sales really is a science, and only a select few people can do it for a long time. This means you have to make sure to keep smiling, always understand that some people just may not buy it, and some months will be slower than others. It's a slow process, but you'll get there.

The concept of affiliate marketing is pretty great. You basically just go to sleep and wake up with money coming in. But, it can be a long time before that starts to happen for you, and take some really hard work. But it is worth it and is a great way to make some money while talking about what you love. Seriously, you get to post 5- to 20-minute videos talking about a topic you love, and you only have to include a 2-minute pitch on a product you probably like anyway? That's a great deal.

Anyway, now it's time to talk not about selling other people's products, but selling your own. The next chapter, we're going to talk about merch, and how eventually, it could easily have a huge earning potential for your channel. Read on.

CHAPTER 10
Selling

Maybe you've got a product to sell. Maybe that's your whole reason for starting a channel, is because of that product, whatever it is. Having a product on YouTube that you believe in and want to sell is great, but if it's your own products it's even better. There are plenty of YouTubers out there who use YouTube to sell things, whether it's through affiliate marketing or their own products. While the last chapter was all about affiliate marketing, this one is going to be about the products that you actually create yourself.

Here's the thing, to really sell on YouTube, you need to have a product you can 100% get behind. If you read our chapter on affiliate marketing, you should know that you should never sell a product on your channel that you wouldn't use yourself. It reflects badly on your viewers. This goes double when it's your own products that you're selling. If you tell your followers how great this product is and it turns out to be a dud, you'll lose customers at an alarming rate and the sense of trust. People talk on the internet, remember that.

I would say that if you really want to sell on YouTube, you need to show that you know your stuff. For example, if you're trying to sell makeup, you need to show that you know everything about makeup. If you're trying to sell a course on speaking Japanese, you need to show that you can speak it fluently. If you're trying to give travel tips, you need to show yourself traveling and visiting a lot of different places. You need to be able to prove that you know your stuff without too much issue.

People will only buy from people who have succeeded in what they do. This is one of the reasons why blogging is so popular. If you're a cooking blog, and your blog is full of photos showing that you know what you're doing through the beautiful pictures of delicious meals and helpful tips on how to make someone else's life easier in the kitchen, they're more likely to buy from you. If you recommend it and you show that you know your stuff, and you're making your own products on top of that, people will buy from you.

We already talked a bit in the affiliate marketing chapter about how important it is to be likable when you're selling, but it's doubly important when it's your products. You also have to be transparent and honest. One of the most popular ways people sell things on YouTube is when they review other companies' products in an honest and transparent way. This doesn't mean they bash the product for no reason. Quite the opposite, actually. They give reviews in a fair review. This shows likeability and the fact that you are going to be transparent about your own products. You show your value up front.

Another option on selling on YouTube is to just sell merchandise having to do with your channel. Merch is a popular way to make money on YouTube, with some YouTubers literally making millions of dollars every year just on selling T-shirts. While I'm not saying you're going to make that much, you will definitely make a bit more money this way. This is especially popular and a good idea if you're a vlogger or personality YouTuber of some kind.

Merchandise Ideas

Did you know that Logan Paul made an estimated 5 million dollars just from his merchandise? No matter how much the internet hates the guy, you have to hand it to him. While Logan Paul excessively talks up his merch, you don't have to do this. Just simply add a store in your video (YouTube lets YouTube partners do this), and make a point to mention your products somewhere in your description. Even include it in your comments, if you dare.

Here are a ton of different ideas for merch. Even just picking up one or two of them can bring in some cold hard cash. Not only that, but a lot of these items are meant to be taken out in public, meaning that you'll get paid for someone to advertise for you. That may be a bad way to put this, but it works.

1) T-shirts: Do you have a cool slogan? A funny saying that you repeat all the time? A great logo? All of these things sound perfect on a T-shirt. Fun fact, did you know the reason why a lot of singers sell T-shirts is that it's an easy way to get the word out there? I mean, think about it, how many times have you seen a band T-shirt on someone, asked about it, and went home to look it up? Yeah, it happens.

2) Stickers. Stickers are perfect for kids. They're cheap to make, cheap to buy, and you often see children and teenagers putting them on their school supplies. This is one reason a lot of YouTubers, particularly whose content is aimed at children, invest in them and sell them. But, that doesn't mean that just because your content is aimed for adults, that means that you can't sell them. Adults love stickers too, after all!

3) Backpacks: similar to T-shirts, backpacks are another great way to get the word out while making money doing so. These are perfect for kids especially, as they use backpacks for school, so be sure that they come in a variety of sizes and colors. But you will probably have more success with children. Also, if they're high quality, that's just a bonus. Nobody likes a backpack that breaks after two months, so people will be less likely to buy from you again.

4) Tote Bags: if you're running a channel that's all about being environmentally conscious, this one's for you. More and more people are turning to use tote bags in place of plastic bags, which means that more people as investing in them. This is a great opportunity for you whether or not your channel is based around living a green lifestyle.

5) Stationery Set: we may not write letters anymore, but people still love cute or cool looking stationary. Even just 20 sheets made up with neat looking designs will get some sellers. If you're an art channel or something along these lines, this is a perfect idea for you.

6) Subscription Box: literally any channel could do this. It's where you put together a box around your niche. For example, if you're an art channel you could do art supplies. Or if you're a movie channel you could do movie merch. Just have a mixture of items every month (or just one surprise item) that's worth about the same amount of money. Any mix of items is great.

7) Cell phone accessories: who doesn't have a cellphone in today's world? And who doesn't love decorating up their phone with little pieces of personality? Things like phone cases are a cheap and easy way for fans to support you.

8) Journal: writing may be going out of style, but cute notebooks are still very much in. Whether they're big notebooks meant for taking notes in class or a small daily planner, these do sell really well. They're also useful, so people actually have a need for them in the day to day life, making them more likely to sell.

9) Stuffed animals: again, stuffed animals are much more aimed at children than anyone else, but there are plenty of adults out there who will invest in them. Just one or two limited-time-offered stuffed animals can also be used as collectibles later on.

10) Perfumes: making a good perfume often takes a lot of time, energy, and money, so be warned this way take a while. However, there are plenty of celebrities out there who have perfumes attached to their name, some of them not so great, some of them fabulous. Regardless, this is not for everyone.

11) Autographed items. If you're a channel that's doing a lot of hauls or you go to conventions to get things signed, selling it to people online is a great way to make some extra cash on the sign. There are people who specifically go to conventions to meet film and TV actors and writers for this specific purpose.

12) Hair ties. Small, but sweet. If your audience is largely female, this is a cheap and easy way to bring in some income.

13) Watches/Clocks: people may be using their phones to tell time now, but watches can still be a fun and funky way to spice up an outfit. Since they're mostly used as accessories, make sure that they look good.

14) Jewelry: earrings, necklaces, bracelets, or rings, all of them are a great addition to your store.

15) Makeup/Toiletry Bags: this is one of those things that is sold by a lot of makeup artists, and there aren't too many people on this planet who don't need a toiletry bag. The bigger and nicely colored, the better.

16) Socks: socks are one of these gifts that everybody hated getting at Christmas when they were kids but now, not so much. Now we all wish we had more.

17) Mugs and Travel Mugs: we all have that one friend who collects mugs like they are priceless treasures, right? I mean, I'm not the only one with that friend? Mugs are a perfect little gift for a friend, and relatively cheap to get made. You can add funny cartoons, little sayings, and more. Bonus points if you choose to get the ones that change color or pattern when hot water is added to them.

18) Slippers: everybody loves slippers, right? Perfect for lounging around the house in PJs watching YouTube videos, which is exactly what you want your subscribers to be doing. Be sure to offer them in a variety of colors and have a little fun with them. They could be classified as gifts for friends.

19) Hoodies: yet another thing that people love and an easy way to advertise. Who loses here?

20) Pins and badges: a cute thing to stick on your purse, your bag, your jacket, whatever you want. Either way, apparently pins are back, and you often see kids sewing badges onto their backpacks.

21) Lanyard/Keychains: who doesn't have keys to carry around? Even kids who have no keys love keychains. Keep them in your channel colors and keep a couple of ones with fun patterns. Keychains done in your channel logo or something else that relates to it are cute too.

22) Pillows: either a couch cushion or pillows meant for sleeping on (yes there is a difference), this can be a fun addition to your store.

23) Calendar: a calendar is a staple in many households, and many people go out to find them at the beginning of every new year. Put together a bunch of fun images and maybe some quotes from your channel, match them somewhat to the month (or not, it's your choice), and have fun!

Either way, a lot of the ways you can sell things on YouTube also apply to affiliate marketing. Make sure to follow these tips for selling:

- Mention it in your videos. Even if you're not talking about your product in that specific video, it's never a bad idea to mention the fact that yes, you do have a store in your videos.
- Put your links to your website or where they can buy the products in your description. This goes hand in hand with the last tip mentioned.
- Offer coupons. Who doesn't love a good deal? Be sure to also show the deal on other places, like you Instagram or Twitter, if you choose to. But, if it's an exclusive deal only to those who watch your video, advertise the fact that there may be a deal on another network. This will draw people to your videos.
- Show followers how to use the product. A video showing how the product works, how to use it correctly, what the packaging looks like, with a run-through of all the products features will help with sales. Bonus points if you use the product casually in your videos all the time, not just that video.
- Always be honest. It's OK to fluff up the truth a bit, but don't lie outright. Be honest about where your product is manufactured, what's in it, everything. It shows authenticity and transparency and means that more people will be likely to trust you.

Basically, now that we've got affiliate marketing and selling your own products out of the way, now it's time to talk about another form of making cash online that will work for anybody with truly great content: fan funding.

CHAPTER 11
Fan Funding

For anyone who remembers the old days of YouTube, it was considered absolutely the worst thing in the world to ask your subscribers for money. It was seen as cheap, lazy, and entitled. Well, these days have changed, and with services such as Patreon, and Kickstarter, it's only become easier for fans to help out their favorite creators online.

While there are way too many people out there who think that artists should do what they do for no cost, there are some decent people out there that realize that creators are people who need to eat as well. There are plenty of YouTubers, and other online creators such as artists and writers, who get funding through Patreon and Kickstarter so they can reach their goals and provide higher quality content.

People want more content from their favorite creators for a simple reason; they want more. They like it. They understand that it takes a lot of energy and time to make and that if they want more, the artist needs to be able to devote more time and energy to it. Let's say you're doing a movie and TV show analysis channel. Well, to do this, you have to watch the movies and TV shows, which can take hours depending on what it is, take notes, write the script, and edit the video together. This could be up to 100 hours' worth of work.

Fans know this. They know it takes time and energy. And if they want more, they're going to have to pay for it. This is where fan-funding comes in.

Fan-funding is great if your idea doesn't use 100% original material (look at things like movie reviews or music video covers), or if you just have a project that you're passionate about that just isn't going to make much money (comedy skits or other short films). There have been plenty of extremely successful short films that have raised thousands of dollars on Kickstarter, or Patreon. In A Heartbeat, an animated short film from university students, got $14,000 when they only needed $3,000.

Now, I'm not saying that you're going to get $14,000, but it can happen. People want to pay for good quality art, and these programs are a way to do it. In this chapter, we're going to go over not only all the ways that you can raise money but the different places online you can get it. We're also going to talk about how you can thank your fans when they do donate.

First, let's start off with the obvious: How To Raise Money.

How To Raise Money Online

Now, to be clear, Kickstarter and Patreon both work a little bit different. Patreon is more for people who want to donate to their favorite creators every month. Kickstarter, on the other hand, is more for one time projects. Let's say you're a short film writer who wants to go bigger. You're not satisfied with how low quality your films are and would like to buy some better equipment so you can put out higher quality. So, you'd probably go on Kickstarter. There, you pitch your idea to your fanbase, show them the link, set a goal, and hope that the money rolls in. On Patreon, it's much more of a month to month basis, with the same amount of people giving you money every month. But, it can be a one-time thing, just to be clear.

First, because it's the more popular one when it comes to YouTube, we're going to go over Patreon. Mostly because of how popular it is, and it's much more steady income than Kickstarter. Let's Roll.

Guide to Patreon

Patreon is the perfect place for monthly income from people who love to watch your content, and who want to see more of it. It could be as low as $5. Some creators have been known to pull in over a thousand dollars per month, meaning that this is a full time job for them. This is because they've done a lot of the things outlined in this list below, and if you follow these tips, you could too.

1) Build your fan base first. To really be successful at Patreon, you're going to need to have content that speaks for you already. People aren't going to invest in you unless they see you can actually do the work. This means putting in the work and the time to really connect with your fans, putting in a whole lot of effort to make sure that your videos are the best they can be, and giving people something that they want to give money to. There is no such thing as a person who just scrolls through Patreon looking for somebody to give their money to. That's a total myth. But, a person who loves a creator and wants better content does. Keep in mind that you don't need a lot of subscribers to do this. Even if you could get 50 subscribers to donate $2, that's $100 dollars!

2) Look to other Patreon examples. There is no shame in copying other people's work in this situation. Check out the other examples of what people are doing, probably some of your favorite creators. Take note of what they all have in common, and really look to see what you like and don't like. There will be potential investors who share these opinions and will donate to your campaign based on that. Patreon is still relatively new, but people are using it. Learn from their mistakes.

3) Be upfront and clear in your introductory. When you create a Patreon account, you get a Patreon clip, basically a three minute video explaining what you do. Make sure that potential Patreon supporters know exactly what they'll be getting when they donate to your fund. Be passionate and sincere in when you pitch to them, and approach it the way you would approach investors. Be passionate, direct, and sincere. Get them pumped up for your content.

4) Let your followers know what they'll be getting with goals. You can set a goal by telling your followers "if I can raise this much money, I'll do this...". Remember this; Patreon donations are literally money that comes out of the pockets of people who want certain content from you. That means communicating with them, giving the options, and more. Setting goals mean showing your viewers what they stand to gain when they donate. When you're first starting off, I would start with just one or two goals.

5) Use the reward tier system. When people donate to you, there should be some sort of reward. However, on Patreon, you can create tiers. Meaning, that the more money someone donates, the more rewards they get. These rewards can be anything, from getting access to videos of your recorded bloopers, to participating in special group discussions, to being able to get content earlier than other supporters. Higher tier rewards may not get as much attention as the $1 to $2 ones, but some people will jump at the chance to get special treatment. Do a lot of different levels, as this encourages other people to donate.

6) Promote it. Remember to tweet about your Patreon, mention it at the end of all your videos, and keep a link of it in your Instagram. Just make sure it's all over your social media feeds, so people know to support you. Just be sure to remind your fans, so they know that they can support you. Don't just mention it once.

7) Keep it unique. Remember, the more unique your content is, the more likely it is going to go viral. It's the same thing with your Patreon account. The better the rewards, the better content you're offering, the better the Patreon trailer, the better you will do.
8) Keep shipping costs in mind. If some of your rewards are physical items (like something from your store, perhaps?), then consider the cost of shipping. You don't want to blow all the money that people have given you to create good content on sending out T-shirts and mugs. It gets even more expensive if some of your backers are from foreign countries. Keeping physical items to envelop size will help lower the costs tremendously if you really want to have a personal item.
9) Don't forget about your non-patrons. Look, the people who are donating money are amazing. They're incredible, actually. They love your content that you're offering for free so much that they're paying you to make more. But, there are probably still watchers who aren't paying. You don't know their situation. They could be young kids, people who just can't afford it, or people who aren't sold on your channel enough to pay for it just yet. Keep creating for them, and don't put all of your good content behind a paywall. Actually, I would say very little of your content should be behind a paywall; come up with creative little bonuses for your patrons rather than the content that your channel is known for.
10) Always remember to say thank you.

Good content doesn't just appear out of thin air. It really doesn't. And people who support artists and creators on Patreon understand this. But, it also takes a lot of work to make sure that people will actually support you, which is why it's so important to follow the tips outlined in this chapter.

Patreon is admittedly better for those who plan on creating content all the time. Who posts weekly. If you're not going to be one of these YouTubers (despite the fact that I would recommend that you don't), or if you want to just have a Patreon account with regular content while doing special content every once in a while, Kickstarter is another great place to go. Let's go.

Guide to Kickstarter

Now, Kickstarter is a bit more tricky. It requires a lot more planning, and because you have a limited amount of time to raise money. It's also better for if you have a special project that you've never done before coming up, something that is entirely new and fresh. So, follow these tips on how to create a successful Kickstarter Strategy.

1) Do research. When you post something to Kickstarter, you are literally competing with thousands of other projects, some that may be pretty similar to your own. While there are some crazy success stories out there where they raise double or triple the amount that they need, it probably won't be you. So, do some research. Look at the successful campaigns and see what has worked for them and what hasn't. Look under sections such as "popular" or "staff picks", as these are the best of the best. Check out the ones that are similar to your idea of the perfect campaign, and that will give you an idea of what your goals should be.

2) Know exactly what your goal is. How much do you need? What do you want to accomplish with it? Don't overextend. On Kickstarter, if you don't reach your goal, you literally get nothing, so it's better to have the most reasonable number you can muster. This is also another reason why it's important to have an audience that you can share this campaign with, as they will donate, thus bumping your campaign up a bit to get more recognition.

3) Consider rewards before you get started. Similar to Patreon, people want something in exchange for donating. Consider how much you can spend, and don't forget to consider mailing costs if necessary as well.

4) Make sure your pitch is really good. A good or bad pitch can be the difference between a successful campaign and an unsuccessful one. You're going to have to mention your goals, your rewards, and your project. You need to be specific, and I would definitely recommend creating a video. They're known to get more funding, and it shouldn't be too hard considering that you're a YouTuber, right? You want to get people excited about your upcoming project, whatever it is and show a lot of enthusiasm and passion.

5) Market, market, market. You can choose what is your deadline for when you need to get the money for it, but you do have limitations depending on the amount. Once you have gotten the project published, market it like a crazy person, whether it's on your channel or through other social media networks. You should also be encouraging your fans to bring their friends to it. You could even try pitching to other YouTubers that you know and who will support you.

6) Keep going. One of the biggest mistakes a lot of Kickstarter make is not keeping at it. This means letting your followers and friends know how it's going, updating on the progress and reminding them that it exists. Even add more rewards as time passes.

7) Patience. Just like with Patreon, some days the money will flow in smoothly, other days, not so much. You need to be creative, positive, and keep your head screwed on the right way. If it doesn't work out this time, try again in a few months. Keep spreading the word, and if your project speaks for itself, it will get there.

8) Be creative, and nothing ever goes as planned. As a YouTuber, you should be ready to try new and different things anyway. Raising money is no exception to that rule. Be ready to try a whole bunch of things you weren't ready to try before.

Remember, at the end of the day, people online, whether or not they follow you, really don't owe you anything. Your posting content on a website that is free for anyone to make an account on. They can watch your videos as much as they wish without paying a dime.

This goes without saying, but this is why you need to have a topic that you're passionate about. You won't be able to get people to care about whether or not you can make new content if you don't actually feel the same way about the content. People don't owe you anything, so you need to make them care. That's the basic rule of any fundraising. Good luck.

CHAPTER 12
Self

Being a YouTuber is hard work. It really is. There, I said it. I'm not one to really tiptoe around things. While a lot of YouTubers (and mainstream media, actually) tend to glamorize YouTubing as this easy thing to get into that requires very little work, that is far from the truth. To be a full-time YouTuber takes a lot of dedication, time and energy, and could eat up your life in a very literal sense.

The best word to describe a YouTuber's day to day life is compact. You have to know how to do so many different things, such as video editing, writing scripts, using a camera and it's gear correctly, how to appear on camera, relating to others, lighting, a thorough understanding of the internet, and more and more. It requires constant planning, sometimes months or even years in advance. You're often working 12 to 14 hour days, which can wear down on you fast.

There has been a lot of evidence that actually links YouTubers to things like depression and anxiety, and other mental health issues. This is because of how isolated they are, often working long hours at home and usually alone. This is why I included this chapter. This chapter is full of tips on how to navigate this issue, keeping yourself healthy while still putting enough time and energy into your videos that you're still making a good living.

First, we're going to go over what a typical day in the life looks for in a YouTuber.

A Day In The Life

Of course, this will differ greatly on a few things, such as the type of channel you run and what day of the week it is. This is just a basic idea of what you could be doing day to day. Now, to keep yourself sane, it's best to keep yourself on a steady schedule. This doesn't mean that you won't have days that run longer than usual. But, at least having a schedule will at least give you a goal to get going.

Start of the day:

Wake up, morning routine; breakfast, shower, get dressed, etc.
Scriptwriting, and/or Research

Preparing for filming (learning lines, researching locations, setting up collaborations)

Spending time on social media networks, replying to comments on your channel, checking the analytics

Get ready for filming (get in touch with whoever you're collaborating if you are, confirm locations, pull together your camera gear)

Meet up with your team (if you have one)

Begin Filming; promote new content and behind the scene photos on your social media channels during this period

Film and/or record all your content

Clean up

Edit; keep promoting as you're doing it

Check your social media accounts again; reply to comments

Edit again; watch through the video twice

Go to bed; don't post the video until you've gotten a good night sleep and you've taken some time away from it. It will help you catch mistakes that you didn't the night before.

Yeah. There are some YouTubers who do this all in one day, and many of them do it alone. You really don't want to get sucked into this, especially if you're working solo. I get it, you love your job, and you want to be successful at this, but if you really want to be successful, you'll understand that this isn't the answer. While grinding and consistency are important (we'll also be talking about that in this next chapter), it's also important to take care of yourself. Here are a few ways you can do that:

- Get human contact. If you're working alone, and even if you're one of these people who claim to dislike hanging out with other people, getting human contact from friends and family occasionally will help you out. It will keep you from getting too sucked into the world of YouTube. Even doing collaborations with people in person will dramatically help your mental health, as you're still working with other people. Just be sure that the friendship isn't just for the views, and is actually genuine.
- Eat healthily and get enough sleep. Taking care of yourself is essential if you really want to succeed in this career. Yes, you can eat cereal all day and give yourself only 6 hours of sleep every night, but if you want to be at your optimal level, a nutritious diet and 8 hours of sleep every night will really serve you better.
- Get fresh air. Get off that screen occasionally. One method a lot of YouTubers use is to take a walk around the block every 2 hours. This gets their brain working again and gives them some breathing room. There are other ways to do this, but just giving yourself a break is really important.

- Give yourself vacations and breaks. Once you've transitioned into being a full-time YouTuber, it's OK to take a few weeks out of the year where you literally disappear. Why not? Just give your subscribers some notice and keep writing down ideas for videos when you get them. This doesn't mean disappear for 5 weeks at a time. Bonus points if you can schedule your videos in advance so your followers are still getting new content while you're just laying on a beach somewhere.
- Don't be afraid to hire someone. Once you've reached a point where you're making a substantial amount of money, putting the editing work on someone else isn't a bad idea if editing isn't your strong suit. Or, if you want someone to do the camera work, or help you with writing. Whatever you feel you need help with. Of course, if you're not financially prepared to do this, this may not be for you.
- Don't get too caught up in views and subscribers. Views and subscribers are great. Actually, they're basically how you're going to be making your money. But they're not everything. It can be easy to get too obsessed with accomplishing the next batch of subscribers, the next batch of money makers. Instead of getting too caught up in the number of subscribers, choose to really focus on the content you're making. You're determined to make amazing content, not get a ton of subscribers. That should be your focus. And the most important part is that your value is not determined by how many followers you have. At the end of the day, they're just imaginary internet points. Literally.

Just remember to keep yourself healthy. Make time for yourself and your friends. Don't get caught in the trap of just obsessing over the next video. It's not going to serve you, or your content, well in the future.

The Importance of Grind and Consistency

So what's grind and what's consistency?

Grind is the determination you need. It's the spirit that you need to be able to get through every day, no matter how hard it is. It's what you need to wake up, put in your absolute hardest work, and go to bed every night to get up and do it all over again, even if things don't pay off for you. And with YouTube, they may not, at least not for a while. This is why it's important to keep trying and keep going. Yes, we'd all love it if our videos went viral overnight and made us a million dollars, but this probably won't happen. It can take years. This is why you need to grind.

Consistency, on the other hand, is keeping to the schedule. It's waking up every day and getting things checked off your checklist. It's about showing up for yourself because you know that if you're consistent with all these little steps, they'll add up to a huge step. And eventually, all you'll be taking are big steps, because of all these little steps you took at the beginning. Consistency is keeping yourself on track. It's about holding yourself up to the standards you've set for yourself, and nailing them every time. This section is all about how you can meet these standards on your YouTube channel and keeping yourself inspired, all with grinding constantly day in and day out.

1) Figure out your end goal with your channel. And by "end goal" I mean ask yourself; what would your perfect channel look like? You need to know exactly what you're aiming for, and where you want to get. You can do this really creatively, even making a vlog of yourself talking to yourself that you can watch back every few months. Be as descriptive as you can, and every time you find yourself getting unmotivated, watch that video. You could also write a letter to yourself or an essay. The choice is yours.

2) Break up everything into tiny steps. One of the best tips I got for getting things done, especially more self-done things like a YouTube channel, is to break up every single task into smaller tasks possible. Small milestones keep you motivated, as you see things adding up quickly as you get closer to your goal. Want to get your first 100 subscribers? Write down exactly what you need to do to accomplish that goal into tiny steps.

3) Understand why you're doing this. Why do you want to be a YouTuber? Do you want to spend all day talking about what you love? Do you want to communicate with people who love the same things you do? Do you want financial freedom? I would avoid being motivated by money alone, as it can get tedious after a while. This is why it's important to do a channel that you're going to want to wake up and think about every day.

4) Make friends with other YouTubers. One of the most valuable lessons I ever learned was "keep the company you want to be". That means, hang out with people you admire and want to be like, ones who will keep you inspired and grinding. They'll keep you going and inspired, and doing collaborations with them is a fun way to be held accountable for your actions. They'll be expecting new content from you, just as you expect content from them.

All in all, the most important thing to remember about being a YouTuber and hanging out online is remembering that it's a job and also remembering to give yourself a break. It's a business first and foremost and should be treated like one.

This means that it's not just about waking up at 2, spending an hour or so filming, then slapping together a video that lasts about 5 minutes. It's about carefully planning out your day and being motivated to get things done. It takes a lot of thick skin too, dealing with trolls on social media, which are running rampant.

I wish everyone luck in this career. But I also want them to be realistic. The best advice I can leave you with is this:

Don't. Focus. On. The. Money.

Focus on the content. Focus on making content that you want to make, that you want to see more of. Don't get trapped in this cycle of being worried about how many subscribers you're getting and obsessively refreshing your page.

Make the content you love, and you really can't go wrong. The money will follow, just as long as you work hard and are consistent. I wish you all the luck in the world.

CONCLUSION

Thank you so much for making it through to the end of this book. I hope it was informative and able to provide you with all of the tools you need for your making money on YouTube journey.

The next step is to start trying some of these techniques and find out what works best for you. Testing out what you can do is how you get things done and how you figure out what will work for you. It will take a lot of that at first, but eventually, you'll find a way.

 Lastly, if you enjoyed this book I ask that you please take the time to rate it on Amazon. Your honest review would be greatly appreciated. Thank you!

DESCRIPTION

So, you want to make money on YouTube?

When someone makes this decision to finally take control of their income and turn to this great platform, the next feeling is almost always panic. Then it's defeat. Why? Because most people just don't know how to make money on YouTube anymore. It's not like the old days where people would test out and experiment until finally, they'd stumble across it.

Nowadays, there is so much competition on YouTube that it's just better to get out ahead and have the information needed on hand. And that's where this book comes in. In this book, we're going to teach you exactly how you can make money on YouTube.

It's really easy to fall into the trap of just doing whatever. But this is not going to be how you make money. The lessons in this book include:

- A look into the history of YouTube, and the kind of person you need to be to be a YouTuber
- How to grow your subscriber base (and keep them)
- An in-depth explanation of a niche and how to find yours
- 4 different ways of bringing in income for your channel, including fan funding, affiliate marketing, and monetization
- A guide to the YouTube Partnership Program that nearly every big YouTuber is a part of
- How to get started with affiliate marketing and ideas how on how to incorporate it seamlessly into your channel
- How to start a Patreon Campaign
- How to get comfortable on YouTube with a look into what your day to day life will look like
- Why quality over quantity is so, so important in today's YouTube world

Keeping yourself informed is the first step to making a successful YouTube channel, and this book is going to take you through every step. It's a long road ahead, so you may as well have all the information that you're going to need. Actually, no, you should have all the information you need, hands down.

This book is the perfect guide for that first few months (or years) that it takes to establish your YouTube channel and start making money. These steps are easy to follow, and everything has been broken down as much as you can. Now, pick this book up, follow these steps, and watch the cash start to roll in!

MAKE MONEY BLOGGING

How to Start a Blog Fast and Build Your Own Online Business, Earn Passive Income and Make Money Online Working from Home

By
James Ericson

INTRODUCTION

Congratulations on purchasing *Make Money Blogging: How to Start a Blog Fast and Build Your Own Online Business, Earn Passive Income and Make Money Online Working from Home* and thank you for doing so. Let's face it, who wouldn't like to be making a bit more money than they already are? Money powers pretty much everything in the world. If you want to pay rent, buy dinner, or go to a baseball game, you're going to need money. So, it follows naturally that you need as much as possible if you want to be able to do whatever it is that you want.

That's how you wound up on this book. You've heard of affiliate marketing in one place or another and you're wanting to get the real skinny on how to get into it and how to get started with setting up affiliate marketing programs that will start making you a lot of extra money!

If you follow every instruction in this book really well (and you have a good niche), then you can find yourself making tons of money doing very little work. The most successful affiliate marketers make six figures doing only around two hours of work per day. Now, is this realistic to expect right away? Not at all, no. However, it's a possibility using this tactic, and that alone should tell you why this tactic is worth your time.

Over the course of this book, we're going to be discussing how you can start making money using affiliate marketing. We're going to be going over all of the key concepts such as picking your niche, identifying what you're wanting to do, reaching out to potential users, maintaining a consistent stream of high-quality content, and essentially just pumping out a fantastic product in very little work that will hopefully make you a fair amount of money.

Certain parts of the book will discuss your customer's mindset and how to really motivate people to visit your site often, as well as how to tap into people's emotions through mediums such as email so that they feel a connection to what you're making and feel more enticed to return. We're also going to be talking about the best way to keep up with all of these users that you gather so you have repeat business – which means more people making you money through affiliate marketing more often!

This is still a very new industry, and the chances of you making a little bit of money for yourself are fairly good if you have quality content.

153

The following chapters will discuss everything you need to know in order to turn your future blog into a money-making machine starting with an outline of what to expect from a passive income stream and how to get started successfully. Next, you will learn to choose a niche that will maximize your profits while minimizing your required effort. You will then learn all about creating the type of eye-catching blog that people are sure to be drawn to time and again.

From there you will learn the secrets to generating the type of content that people are actually interested in reading, as well as the many ways you can successfully grow your audience time and again. This will help mightily once you learn about the basics of how you will be turning a profit from blogging, affiliate marketing. You will learn about the ins and outs of affiliate marketing as well as starter strategies to try. You will also learn about the importance of email marketing when it comes to reliably turning a profit. Finally, you will find plenty of tips for success as well as common mistakes that new affiliate marketers make and how to avoid them once and for all.

With so many choices out there when it comes to consuming this type of content, it is appreciated that you've chosen this one. Plenty of care and effort went into ensuring it contains as many interesting and useful tidbits as possible, please enjoy!

CHAPTER 1
Getting Started With Passive Income

While it might seem ridiculous now, the fact of the matter is that as little as 30 years ago, a person could get a job with a company right out of college, and realistically expect to remain with that company for the entirety of their career. Unfortunately for the vast majority of working-age individuals, this is no longer the case which means it takes a lot more than company loyalty to ensure that you will eventually be able to retire while retaining the lifestyle to which you have become accustomed. This issue is then compounded even more as current estimates put the amount needed to retire successfully at somewhere north of $500,000.

What all this means is that unless your 9 to 5 pays extremely well, you are likely going to need to consider alternative avenues to ensure that you have the money you need, when the time comes for you to really need it. The easiest way to go about securing your financial future is via passive income streams. While you may have heard talk about passive income streams, it can be easy to be confused about just what exactly they entail as you could easily hear about them in numerous different contexts. This is because a passive income stream, as opposed to an active income stream like a 9 to 5 job, is any type of income stream whose dividends do not directly relate to the amount of time and energy they require.

What's more, a passive income stream rarely means that you have absolutely no work to do, it simply means that the amount of work and the amount of compensation are in no way similar to one another in the long run. What's more, knowing that you have some measure of financial security can also make whatever other active income tasks you need to accomplish much more manageable because they are no longer a matter of financial life or death that they once were.

When it comes to generating passive income online by using the methods outlined in the following chapters, the general cost should be relatively low. Outside of this, you will need time to commit to generating passive income in the future and the right mindset regarding your passive income goals.

Belief in what you are about to accomplish: When you are just looking into generating passive income streams for the first time, the idea may seem too good to be true. This is because society has taught you that the only "true" way to earn a living is to work long hours in return for modest pay and the first thing you must do is banish this type of thinking from your mind. Thinking that the passive income that you are working to develop is a pie in the sky idea means you won't commit with the drive necessary to make it a reality.

Decide how you will start: If you are working towards a long-term goal, doing everything yourself by putting in a few hours here and there for months, or even years, in order to get your passive income stream up and running might be a reasonable timetable. If you are interested in generating real results as soon as possible, it might be in your best interest to consider freelance content creators who can be found on freelance websites like UpWork.com instead. While the initial cost to create the passive income stream in the second scenario might be somewhat higher, it doesn't get more passive than having other people do all of the work for you.

Remain focused: Setting up a passive income stream, especially for the first time, will likely be a substantial undertaking that may well feel impossible at times. This is why it is important to remain focused and dedicated to the idea of getting out from underneath the shackles of active income in order to power through when the going gets tough. Likewise, there are going to be pitfalls and potential landmines that may be couched in good ideas or avenues towards success that seem as though they are worth pursuing. Nevertheless, you must power through if you ever hope to achieve success.

The right mental state: While at first, it might be hard to wrap your head around the idea that you can make money 24 hours a day, 365 days a year, it is important that you come around on the idea, not just as a neat theory, but as an indelible practice. This can be easier said than done, however, as modern society has likely trained you to view success as something that only comes after years and years of back-breaking work. This means that if you want to commit yourself fully to the practice, you are going to have to work on actively cultivate the type of mindset that believes having a successful passive income stream is not only something that is possible, it is something that is in reach right now.

If you find yourself having trouble getting into the passive income mindset, you might find it effective to start by having an honest and open conversation with yourself about your goals for the future and how passive income can help you meet them. You may find that by taking the potential passive income stream out of the realm of a pie in the sky possibility and plugging it into your actual plan for the future it becomes easier to truly accept as a realistic possibility.

From there you can then consider the types of passive income streams that could be the most effective for you based on your passions and proclivities. Choosing a passive income stream that you truly feel passionate about is another great way to get past any mental roadblocks you might have as to its overall success. This doesn't mean that you should blindly commit to the first passive income strategy you come across, as you should still be on the lookout for realistic flaws in any plan, it just means you shouldn't let societal prejudices get in the way of your potential success.

Set the right goals: Regardless of what you are trying to accomplish, setting clear goals for yourself will help to motivate you to actually follow through on them. When it comes to choosing the right goals, ensuring the ones you choose are SMART is always a good choice.

- Specific: SMART goals are specific which means they have clearly determined metrics by which you can judge their success or failure. Statistically speaking, a clear goal is going to be one you are more likely to finish as opposed to one that is vague. A specific goal should address who you can turn to for help when it comes to completing it, have a clear target that you are trying to achieve, including when you want to meet the goal, where you will go to complete it, why you are looking to achieve it and how you are going to go about doing so.

- Measurable: SMART goals are those which can be broken down into small, easily manageable chunks that can be tackled one piece at a time. A measurable goal should make it easy to determine when exactly you are headed off track so that you can self-correct as quickly as possible. Measuring your progress will make it easier for you to keep up the good work.

- Attainable: SMART Goals are always attainable. Ideal scenarios are nice, but including goals that have only a slim probability of materializing is doing little more than wasting your time. This is not say that complicated or difficult goals should be avoided, rather it is about realistically knowing your limits and when they can be expanded. Setting long-term goals can for you to grow in an attempt to reach them.

- Realistic: A realistic goal is one that you are both able and willing to strive for in the current climate. It doesn't matter if you would be able to accomplish the goal if another set of circumstances were true, focus on the here and now and work from there. Realistic goals are also those that are set at a level where it will require work to reach them while at the same time not requiring too much work that they seem forever out of reach. Realistic goals that require a moderate amount of effort from the team to achieve tend to create the most motivational force.

- Timely: Every good goal has a specific timetable that ensures it will be completed at a reasonable rate. This timetable is important, as without it the goal will never be looked at by anyone on the team with any real sense of urgency. An end date makes a goal tangible and ensures you can count on your team to make it a priority when it matters most.

CHAPTER 2
Choosing A Niche

The thing you need to understand is that you're going to be promoting people's products. That is your entire purpose. So, if you can find a way to make somebody's product sound good enough for people to click over and at least consider buying it, then you can probably make a fairly good amount of money off of affiliate marketing.

This is where two components come in: your niche and your platform. For the purposes of this book, your platform is going to be a blog. Your niche is something else entirely.

In order to get repeat traffic and get people constantly visiting, you're going to need to attract people with a certain interest. You'll have to pinpoint that interest and start making posts that are geared towards that specific interest. This is your niche: the area of interest that you decide to take advantage of and post about.

You can make several different blogs with several different niches but be aware that this will somewhat increase your workload. Start with one for now.

The best way to make a lot of money is for your niche to be something you care about enough to go back to every day. This is going to drive you to work on it and constantly produce content. If you don't care about your niche then it's going to show through in your posts. You can expect some amount of return, but they will almost certainly not be great. Bear that in mind as you go forward.

So, you've gotten to the point now that you want to start acting. The first thing that you're going to need to do is to pick your niche. There are two ways to go about doing this.

The first is the hardest: go off of your passions. If you do this, you're going to have to find innovative ways using products that affiliate companies offer, if they don't have any for your specific niche. However, this can pay off by you making really creative and potentially viral posts using things in unconventional ways that people will see as super intriguing. This is a good way to bring in a whole bunch of people.

In order to do this, you're going to need to be very crafty and keep an eye on what's available. Additionally, a lot of your income will be coming through other means mentioned in this book rather than affiliate marketing. However, it's an option worth considering because affiliate marketing can almost certainly play a part in a strategy like this one.

The second is the easiest, but you're playing chance in two respects. The second method is to simply see what products and avenues are available to you through affiliate marketing channels and then derive your niche from that. In some cases, this will intertwine with the first concept and you'll find something that you're both passionate about and that there are a fair number of products for which you can market. However, this won't always be the case.

In the event that you can't find something you're reasonably passionate about, simply try to find something that you're somewhat interested in or would like to learn more about. This will make it easier to research and find topics related to it that you're interested in.

However, sometimes you just won't be able to find anything that interests you. In these cases, you can still just go with whatever you think would do fairly well. Sometimes intuition can be a really important thing, and in these cases, you should just trust your intuition in trying to find a pertinent niche through affiliate marketing channels.

In some ways, this is the best way to start affiliate marketing if you want your focus to be solely affiliate marketing, or at least primarily so. This is because you'll know going into it what mechanisms and products you can try to take advantage of when trying to pull in customers and users.

The last and third most prominent way to figure out your niche is simply to use keywords in order to learn what topics are hot right now. This might give you the most instantaneous benefit, but you will inevitably find it rather difficult to carry this out for a long period of time because trends are constantly changing. You'll most likely find success using this method in the short run (if you can write some great articles and take advantage of available affiliate marketing opportunities) but you'll find it difficult to maintain that same level of success in the long run.

That's not to say that your site when using this method will ever be worthless. Quite the opposite, you're fairly likely to make a decent amount off of this even after the bubble bursts on whatever trend you're taking advantage of. However, it is worth bearing in mind that this is not a great tactic to use when you're trying to make a great-quality and long-lasting site. You may find yourself having difficulties coming up with a good topic down the line, especially if your given trend is particularly niche.

If you do decide to take this avenue, however, all you'll have to do is get access to popular keywords and figure out what's trending. The easiest way to do this is probably to take advantage of Google Trends. Simply Google "google trends hot trends" and the page you're looking for should be relatively easy to find. This will tell you the most trending topics of the day every hour or so. It's generally the top 20.

However, this can be rather unwieldy as it won't exactly tell you the sort of information you're wanting to write a book about. After all, these are just the most trending searches for the last day or so, and they generally on very specific people and events rather than topics you can easily write a book about.

Narrow down your search

Find the right target: Once you have a number of potentially profitable niches to consider, the next thing you will want to do in order to cull them down to the best ones possible is to consider what type of potential customers you are interested in targeting. Finding your target audience can be done in several different ways, starting with consider your own demographic and considering if people like you would be interested in your product or service.

Like with the niche itself, it's important to focus on a specific segment of the purchasing population as each target group is going to have very different likes and dislikes. For example, if you go too broad with your category you may land on men, but a student who isn't yet old enough to drink is going to have dramatically different priorities than a 40-year-old family man. If you decide to go to broad on your target audience you will only end up creating content that doesn't really appeal to anyone.

Understand the problems that they face: Once you have a specific demographic in mind, the next thing that you are going to want to spend some time thinking about the problems that the demographic faces on a regular basis. Additionally, you are going to want to consider the aspirations and desires that they have and the issues that might confront them when it comes to making their dreams a reality. Once you have done some brainstorming, the next thing you will want to do is to head back to Google and plug in the words you have come up with to see what the general online space regarding them looks like. If the problems you come up with don't see many results then it isn't really a problem your target audience is concerned with.

Consider the potential for profit: After you have landed on multiple different problems that you know your target audience needs to solve, you will then need to consider if there are products out there that this group would be interested in paying for in order to solve them. This is an especially important step as there is no point in creating advertising content if your target audience is unlikely to bite on the solutions you are peddling. If you like the audience you have chosen, then it is best to focus on items that are well within their price range, though not so cheap that they would constitute an impulse buy. This will ensure they don't spend too long thinking about each decision, while at the same time ensuring they still seek some guidance.

To ensure that people are buying what you are considering selling, you can head to Adwords.Google.com and look at the keyword planner tool. This will allow you to view search results as they are filtered by keyword as a means of determining how frequently they come in search results in general. It will also show you the breakdown of the timeline of the searches, allowing you to determine if the products you are considering selling are on the rise or on the way out of the public consciousness.

Look more closely: Outside of understanding the particular problem a specific group of individuals is having, it is important to understand exactly what this group wants when it comes to solving a problem. As an example, if you are targeting people who are in the market for a soulmate, you will need to understand both what that specifically means to them as well as how they approach love in general and the tools which they help them to succeed.

In order to ensure this part of the process works out as planned, you are going to want to go as deep into the details of the target audience as possible. You will need to learn how they think, but you will also want to pick up the type of slag that they use, the lingo they have for the products they use regularly and any other language they might use to describe their desires in relation to your chosen niche. The more you know about the market, the more you can use that knowledge to create the type of advertising that speaks to them directly.

With these details in mind, you will then want to visit numerous different existing sites that are doing what you are considering doing to determine what the demand for this type of information currently is. While visiting the competition, it is important to keep an eye out for those that have active advertising beyond Google AdSense as this is a sign that they are popular enough to attract outside advertisers as well. This is a strong sign that there is money to be made from the community you are considering targeting.

Consider the options: While even the least active sub-niche imaginable has at least a few merchants who cater to it, those who are looking to build their first niche marketing site should like to start out in a market with a bit more variety. Your goal for multiple affiliate programs to already be in place, which will ideally allow you to set up multiple compatible compensation agreements per site.

Decide if you like what you see: At this point, you should have a pretty good idea of what it is going to take to cater to the niche and the target audience you have identified, all that's left is to determine if you have what it takes to go the distance. First, you need to consider if you can stand to deal with the type of people you have uncovered on a frequent basis. Don't forget, you are going to be interacting with these individuals daily if all goes according to plan, which means if you don't like what you see then you are better off going back to the drawing board.

In addition to being able to deal with the niche that you have chosen, you are also going to want to ensure that you have the ability to keep the content you will be creating fresh. In order to be successful, you are going to want to be able to do more than just create random stray bits of content, you are going to need to create an entire story around what you are doing and make it believable to those who are going to be in the easiest position to call you out if you are faking it.

Look at the industry as a whole: Just because a given niche currently has what appears to be a thriving audience base doesn't mean that you are going to want to jump in right away without some additional research. This is because it is entirely possible that the niche you have chosen has already peaked in popularity so that despite your best efforts, it is extremely likely that there will be fewer and fewer customers to be interested in your content as time goes on.

The trend tool from Google is extremely useful in this instance as it shows how often a keyword was searched in a given month. Specifically, in this instance, you are going to want to target niches where the number of searches each month is always on the rise as opposed to the niches where the biggest surge of search popularity has already peaked. While the number of searches for a topic that has already peaked might be acceptable now, you will only see decreasing returns if you put your efforts towards it moving forward.

CHAPTER 3
Creating Your Blog

So you've chosen a niche or sub-niche that you are interested in moving forward with. Now, we're on to the next big part: setting up your blog. This is where the magic happens.

The blog is not going to be the be-all end-all of your online identity. Chances are that if you end up having a successful couple affiliate marketing sites, a lot of your engagements are going to happen through social media and email and your blogs are only going to serve as a place to store your content as well as a portal to things such as your dropshipping store, should you decide to do something involving dropshipping.

However, it's still the foundation of everything else that you're going to be doing, so you need for it to be very strong. I'm going to write this chapter as if you've never set up a blog or a website before. If you have some prior experience with web development or hosting then you may not entirely need this chapter, but it's still worth giving it a read as a refresher or just in case there are some things that you missed before.

Getting started
What's in a name: The first thing that you're going to need for your blog is a name. Your name should evoke your niche, as well as the identity that you're wanting to portray. Take all of this into account when deciding on a name, because it's the cornerstone of everything that your site represents. A good or bad brand name can seriously make the difference between a site that people talk about and a site that nobody remembers. Keep this in mind as you go forward.

When you're deciding on a name, you might consider the imagery or basic components of your niche. For example, if you were trying to start a website about the Paleo diet, you might call your site "Caveman Eats" or "Rock Solid Eating". This is going to give your browsers and users a distinct and memorable name that correlates directly to what you do. Your name is your opportunity for you to tell the world what you're about, so take as much time as you can in order to make sure that it's a good one. There's no reason that you should be losing traffic because of a bad name; this is one of the simplest parts of the whole process, but it's also one of the most vital parts.

Find a domain: Once you've decided on a name, you need to work on getting a domain. If you're following this book's instructions and setting everything up through WordPress, then this isn't a huge deal to buy individually because WordPress offers to buy your domain for you. However, at the same time, it's important that you check to see if the domain is available in the first place, especially for a decent price. Many domain names are already taken and this is an unfortunate fact. Sometimes you have an absolutely amazing idea for a name but the domain name which would correlate to it is already taken. In these cases, you're probably going to have to change the name of your brand. This is why it's important to consider this from the very beginning!

Setting up your site

Once you've settled on a domain name, it's time that you start to actually set your site up.

The best way to do this is to go via WordPress, at least if you're not very tech-savvy. If you have the know-how to set up your own blog and your own hosting, then, by all means, go for it. If you don't, however, you're almost certainly going to want to use a package like WordPress because it offers a fair amount of customization, plus if you set your site up as a WordPress blog then you can get fairly good deals on hosting and domain names by using WordPress services. In other words, it really simplifies the whole process where it may otherwise be pretty difficult.

Again, this book is going to tell you how to set up a site through WordPress. If you're wanting to just create a site that will attract visitors and be very usable, there is absolutely nothing wrong with using WordPress as the platform of choice. It's a highly reputable service that will make it super easy for you to create new blog posts whenever you want, and you also have a relative amount of freedom in the way that things are set up and styled. The only way your site's design could be more open-ended was if you took the time to design it yourself.

The trade-off is that WordPress is a little less cost-effective than just setting up your own blog platform, domain, and hosting if you have the knowledge of how to do so already. Setting up a site on WordPress with a year of hosting costs somewhere around one hundred dollars. Meanwhile, setting up your own hosting and domain could cost somewhere around fifty dollars (depending on what domain name you're specifically trying to use – some are costlier than others). However, if you're completely ignorant to technology and setting up websites, this could take you a few hours to get the hang of, even if you're using an open-source platform. What it really ends up being about is how much your time matters to you.

In essence, using the second method, you can get the best of both worlds: WordPress will let you download their template and set it up on your own server for free, so you could feasibly set everything up for yourself and still get the ease of use that WordPress enables you toward.

However, if you don't want to get your hands dirty with the domain and hosting, then using WordPress for everything offers a very simple and very user-friendly manner for you to get the bloat of designing a website out of the way and get to the part that counts: putting your content up for the world to see and getting your name out there so that you start to have a visitor stream. So, with all of that said, we're now going to dive into the actual process of setting up a site through WordPress and then setting up your own domain.

Consider hosting: With a domain name in hand, the next thing that you will need to do is to choose a website to host your site along with all the potential traffic that you will be bringing in as without a host your site won't actually be visible to those suffering the net. While there are plenty of hosts available offering a wide variety of different services, you don't need to worry about anything too complicated at the moment and can settle for something like HostGator.com which will host your site for less than $5 per month.

All you need to do is to follow the on-screen instructions and enter the domain name you have chosen when prompted to do so. At the end of the process, you will be given a username and password which you are going to want to keep on hand for the next step in the process.

Activate WordPress: Host Gator offers users the ability to install WordPress with just a single click, to do so, you will need to log into cPanel with the username and password that was generated in the previous step. From there all you need to do is find the page heading titled Services and Software, find the WordPress option and enter the information that is asked of you, domain name, title of the site and your name. Choosing the install now option will create your site in WordPress and create a new username and password that you can use to enter the backend of your WordPress site specifically as well as post content on the fly. This username and password should be automatically sent to your email address.

Login: Once your nameserver is properly pointing at your WordPress site, you can now log in to the backend of your site by typing the address to your site followed by /wp-admin. This will take you to the WordPress login site and allow you to log in with the username and password that were generated when you installed WordPress.

Logging in on this screen will take you to the WordPress Dashboard which offers up many options, some of which will be discussed below. The first thing you may want to do is to set a password that is easier to remember. To do so you start by looking to the right side of the screen and finding the option to edit your profile. This will take you to a page where you can enter lots of different information, for now, find the box for a password, type your new password and select the option to update your profile.

At this point, you should also take the opportunity to poke around on the Dashboard somewhat and determine what all of the primary functions are. Tasks you can complete include, manipulating plugins, adding categories and pages, creating posts and changing the theme which you should consider doing next.

Setup up your WordPress domain: Essentially, the first thing that you're going to want to do is set your site up on WordPress's domain. This will let you tweak everything and see how you like it all before you even invest in your own domain and hosting. This is entirely free and you should have no problems doing it without spending a cent.

Go to the WordPress website and try to create a new account. Enter all of the relevant information, such as your name, email address, and the name of your site, then you should be off.

Visit your site: Once you've set up your site, you'll arrive on the homepage of your new WordPress blog. This is your command station. You can click around a bit and see everything that there is to see.

WordPress has some really neat features that can help you to steer your posts to be even better and to help you produce quality content all of the time. You're going to want to take advantage of things such as the analytics features that are available to you, which allow you to see which posts of yours are faring the best and things of that nature.

Choose a theme: Once you have your blog set up, try to pick out a theme that you think fits the style of your site really well. Eventually, you're going to want your very own theme (especially if you care about your niche and you're trying to have just one or two primary affiliate marketing sites) and you'll either have to learn CSS or contact a designer to create it, but for right now, there are a lot of different custom themes available that are super easy to apply.

You should also Google WordPress themes and see what kind of things you can find on the internet. Sometimes, independent designers will create amazing WordPress themes that they can't get sponsored by WordPress, or you simply won't see them in the design and appearance panel, so it's important that you take some time to explore all of the alternatives out there.

Eventually, you'll come upon a theme that you really like. WordPress makes it relatively easy to change themes. If you're wanting to use a custom theme, you're going to have to either have the off-site version of WordPress or WordPress Premium, which we'll be discussing here momentarily.

Focus on user interactions: At this point in your development, you want to really start to consider how your user is going to interact with the site. User interaction is what will drive your site forward and is almost as important as the quality of the content itself, though not quite. Consider how you're wanting your user to get around. Think about everything that you're wanting on your site and think about what you can do in order to start serving each and every purpose.

If it takes more than three clicks to get anywhere on your site, then you've got a really poorly designed site. Using something like WordPress doesn't automatically exempt you from the perils of having a poorly designed site, so it's something you need to take into account from the get-go as you work on your site.

You may even get out a pen and paper and try drawing a site map. Start at your homepage, then branch out to every other thing that you want on your site. Going back to the Paleo diet idea, if you're serving up news and recipes and anecdotes about the Paleo diet, then your site's navigation should consist of "Home", "Recipes", "News", and "Life Updates". Then, think ahead as to whether these will have further links. For example, recipes would probably need to be subdivided further than just "recipes"; for instance, you'll likely want a section to do with breakfast recipes, a section to do with lunch recipes, a section to do with dinner recipes, and a section containing snacks and desserts. Therefore, the Recipes part of your navigation bar should likely have a dropdown menu that lets you select Breakfast, Lunch, Dinner, or Snacks and Desserts.

You don't have to get extremely deep into the theory of web development at this point, and you really won't ever need to – the chances are, in fact, that for most niches, your site won't need to be terribly involved. There'll be no reason for it to be. However, it's also worth taking the time to think ahead about how your users can most efficiently get around the site and get the information that they're wanting because this will make a huge difference as to whether people decide to use your site regularly or not.

Make it pop

Posts and pages: WordPress is fantastic because it provides a really expressive canvas. You're going to want to be able to do an assortment of different things on your site, whether they're drop shipping, setting up a landing page with a JavaScript pop-up that asks people to join your mailing list, and so on. The fantastic thing about WordPress is that there's a lot of built-in functionality for whatever it is that you're really wanting to do.

These sorts of posts will be the foundation of all of your affiliate marketing work. Everything that you'll be doing is going to be propelled off of these posts. We'll talk more about how to write a proper post in the coming chapters because there's a lot more that goes into it than you might think. For right now, just get the hang of posting and try messing around with your posts so that you feel comfortable with them.

At this point, you're probably discovering another thing that makes WordPress really practical: they have a WYSIWYG editor, or a What You See is What You Get editor, which means that pretty much what you put inside of the text box for your post will be what the post ends up looking like. This may not seem like a big deal but if you've ever fumbled around with things like HTML, then you know how much of a blessing this feature can really be!

So, once you've gotten the handle of posting, you can work with adding pages to your site. There's a relatively easy interface for doing so in your admin panel. WordPress can be a tad bit clunky to navigate at first, but you'll start to get the hang of it after a while. Pages, in the context of WordPress development, are dedicated to offering static single-purpose pages that allow you to convey certain amounts of information consistently. That's a lot of technical mumbo jumbo that basically means that pages aren't blog posts. Pages are, however, great places to put stuff such as your "about me" information or any information that you feel

170

comfortable putting out about your brand. You can also use these as throughways for other information, such as your social media or contact info.

Anyway, now that you know the purposes of both posts and pages – pages are intended to give static information where posts are intended to be, well, blog posts – you can now move on to setting up your navigation bar. For most simple sites, you're just going to need your primary blog as well as an about page. You can change exactly what's on your navigation bar in the admin panel of your WordPress site and, conveniently, you can also link to specific locations within your WordPress site. This will make it really, really easy for you to set up pages on your site and then link to them seamlessly.

Focus on navigation: There's no reason to clutter your navigation bar, but also keep your pages somewhat clean. If you're about to add something to your site, one good rule of design is always to consider whether it really needs to be there. If it doesn't, then consider scrapping that idea altogether. Again, you're trying to keep the focus on your blog posts, because those will be where you're doing all of your affiliate marketing work. Everything else will be essentially an afterthought. That's not to say that you need to be lax about your site's design – your site's design conveys everything about it, and you should take care to be sure your users have a great experience. However, don't put extra things that aren't needed. Knowing what doesn't need to be there is equally as important in design as knowing what does need to be there.

Once you have a decent idea of how you want your site laid out and how your navigational bar will be laid out, in addition to maybe having a bit of a "skeleton" running on it, you're probably going to want to get going with setting up your own domain and hosting.

Fortunately, if you're acting through WordPress, they make this really simple. Until now, you've been using a site on the WordPress domain (sitename.wordpress.com). This is fine if you're just a hobbyist looking to share your posts with friends and family, but if you're wanting to have some kind of enterprise or brand identity, you're going to want to move away from this by setting up your own domain. There are a couple of really good reasons for this.

The first has to do with brand identity. You want to convey to people that you're a professional and that, moreover, you know what you're doing. By setting up your own domain name, you convey that sense of authority that you need to in order for people to feel like they're going to the right place for their information. There are some cases, of course, where this may not really be as necessary of a component – for example, if you're running a very lax cooking blog - but you'll still want to have your own domain name for a flurry of other reasons!

The most prominent other reason that you'll want to have your own domain is search engine ranking. The simple fact is that by having your domain name, search engines will look at you in a better light than they would otherwise. You really need to take full advantage of search engines because they'll be a massive component in pulling vital traffic. We'll talk more about how you can show up higher in the search engines a little bit later, but the key point is that you really need all the help you can get when you're trying to run an affiliate marketing blog just because more views means more money. By having your own domain name, you give yourself a certain air of authenticity that makes search engines see you as a more reliable source. When search engines see you as a reliable source, they're a lot more likely to link people to you than an alternative when push comes to shove and somebody needs info on the best paleo breakfast recipes or the best vacuum cleaners under $500. Search engine ranking matters, so you're going to need a domain.

As previously discussed, WordPress makes it really simple to get your own domain. When you upgrade to WordPress Premium, they'll give you the option to buy your own domain, as well as upgrade the perks that you get by using their hosting services. By combining the two, you can build up an extremely stable site on a really reliable hosting service with a pretty cheap domain name. Getting a domain name through WordPress, for example, can be much cheaper than getting the same domain name through a popular route such as GoDaddy. In the end, the two are functionally pretty much the same as well – after all, the domain name is just the address where computers can find your files on the internet. Because of this, using WordPress domain names is a pretty safe bet.

Once you've gone through the process of signing up for WordPress Premium, you're pretty much over the hump in terms of setting up your site. Hopefully, by now, you've had ample time to get comfortable with WordPress and how everything works. In the next chapter, we're going to build on all of this information and start talking about how you can start writing extremely great content in order to pull people in and keep them there!

Fix your URLs: When it comes to ensuring your SEO is top-notch, one often overlooked step is to ensure your URLs for all of your pages are descriptive, rather than automatically generated. To get started, you will want to choose the Settings option from the navigation menu before then choosing the option for Permalinks, followed by the URL structure. The resulting menu will have numerous different options to choose from, even allowing you to create your own if desired. Depending on the number of posts you create each day, as well as your overall naming conventions, using the post name in the URL might be sufficient, otherwise, you might want to consider either the month and the name or the day and the name instead.

With the right types of URLs showing, you will want to ensure that each new post is picked up by search engines separately. To start, you will want to ensure your RSS feed is active, to do so, go back to the navigation bar and choose the option for Reading settings. Choosing the RSS option will then allow you to determine how many of your posts show up on your RSS feed and if the show the full content of the post in the RSS feed (not recommended). Once your RSS feed is broadcasting each post will then be indexed separately by the search engines.

CHAPTER 4
Generating Content

Some people are natural writers and some people aren't. The key to having a great affiliate marketing blog honestly comes down to knowing which of these applies to you – and it's not always the easiest thing to know.

Approximately 27 million pieces of content are generated and put out into the world on a *daily* basis. This means that if you want to go on attracting potential customers and keep the users you have coming back for more, then you need to do something to stick out from the crowd. Custom content that targets not just your target audience but also the unique demographics of the users that you have already attracted is crucial to your website being not just an additional resource but a prime online destination. If you want to ensure your content marketing is effective in the long-term, then stepping up your game is key.

There's always a way to improve, though, so don't be afraid to admit that you have certain things you really need to improve on. Additionally, while some people are skilled writers, some people are not. Moreover, some people just want to avoid getting their hands dirty and want to make affiliate marketing as passive of a process as possible. For these people, another alternative exists: outsourcing the blog posts.

This may not seem like a terribly great idea, and that's true: if you don't know what you're doing or you outsource to the wrong people, then you may end up with messily written posts that in the end are not very great. However, there are numerous different companies out there that would love for you to consider letting their staff take a crack at your blog posts. There's also a huge number of freelancers out there who are looking for short easy work to hold them over between jobs, and you'd see success with these people as well.

Granted, sometimes – especially if you intend to outsource a lot – you want to have a personal on-going relationship with your freelance partner. In this case, you may want to post to Upwork or Freelancer. Both make it relatively easy to find native English speakers who will accept really negotiable rates in return for some sort of consistent work.

What should you be paying your freelancers? It can really vary, but for most lower-end freelancers (which will be fine for your purposes), the going rate is generally around one to two cents per word. Some charge even more but, as I said, in the lower end this doesn't happen very often. It shouldn't be hard to justify to yourself how much you're wanting to spend on a freelancer if you're not great at making content for yourself and they produce quality content. In the end, you'll hopefully develop a long and stable relationship with a consistent freelance partner who is willing to write you whatever post you want for your particular niche.

Custom content improves social media interaction: With so many different social media options readily available, it can be difficult to improve your social media presence in an oversaturated market. Making your content readily available across the spectrum is a good start, but it is just that, a start. Studies show that the most reliable way to increase the members of your target audience who share your content is to give them more interesting content to share, which is where custom content comes into play. As such, when it is done properly custom content can do more than just keep existing potential customers interested, it can help to generate new leads as well.

Custom content helps to support and guide existing users: Creating custom content can ultimately save you time in the long run when it comes to helping out customers with questions, complaints, and concerns. Instead of having to answer the same question via email a dozen or more times a week, creating custom content to do so in a well thought out and easily shareable fashion will not only save you time but make it seem as though you care about your customers' time as well.

Generating content
That raises the question, how do you know what to write about? Whether you're writing for yourself or having somebody else do it for you, you're going to need to be coming up with different topics rather often. After all, you'll have to post every week or so at least, or you'll fail to get return visitors due to inactivity. There are some ways around this (we'll talk about these later), but still, people want to follow pages that actually do things, not pages that just release content every two weeks or every month or so.

How do you know what you're going to need to write about next? Well, there are three different ways.

Consider potential products: The first is to look at products available to you or try to do something new with a product that you've already worked with. This is how you can guarantee a somewhat constant stream of creativity using existing affiliate marketing opportunities. The thing to remember about this is that not all affiliate marketing deals will last forever, so be sure that you have a somewhat stable deal on whatever product that you're intending to use, or else this might not benefit you so much in the long-term when your deal falls through. (Unless it's a genuinely good idea that will pull you traffic, anyway!)

It's not a generally good idea to base a post entirely around a product for reasons that we'll discuss later, but by incorporating products into your posts, you may very well hit a creative well and be able to get a few posts out of even a single product. Try to work with the opportunities that you have to the very best of your ability so that you can always take full advantage of the possibilities before you.

Focus on niche topics: The second is to look at keywords and recent trends in your niche to see what is, well, trending. Responding to trends can be a great way to generate quality content that will bring in an influx of sudden hits. A good example of this would be that in food and drink, there recently has been a focus on the use of activated charcoal for perceived health benefits. By recognizing that this trend exists and acting on it, you'd be potentially riding a wave that will bring a lot of people in.

Try to do this in such a way that you end up creating a worthwhile post in the end. Analyze trends to the best of your ability and then create the best thing that you possibly can using them and you're almost certain to see an influx of users that are there as a result of that trend specifically, especially if you're on about your search engine ranking, which is something we'll be discussing in this chapter.

Listen to your gut: The third is to simply act off of your inspiration. Generally, people's intuitions are pretty good. When you have to work for a creative work, it generally doesn't turn out as great as those which come naturally, and in the end, this is a creative work. If you're inspired to write about something (or inspired to see what somebody else has to say about something) then this could just be an option for you; take the time to jot the idea down and maybe write a few things about it. Get your thoughts on paper and then make something happen, then write a blog post about making that thing happen. This is the number one way to make quality posts. The best results come when your inspirations are the result of a product that you can market.

Stick to a schedule: These are the primary ways to determine what to write. If the first and the third ever fail you and you find yourself totally and absolutely creatively exhausted, you can just try for the second one

176

and analyze trends and piggyback off of those trends for one post or another.

The key to all of this posting and writing is that you are doing so on a schedule. It doesn't have to be every single day, but it does have to be regularly – once or twice per week is more than enough for people to know that you mean business and that they can come to you for all the information they need. Better yet, it builds a subconscious rapport with them, which means that they're a lot more likely to convert some clicks for whatever products you're marketing. In the end, this means money in your pocket!

Planning: Before sitting down to write, you must make sure you have collected all the material you need. Do not think that planning is a waste of time because preparing yourself in advance can save you a lot of time in the drafting phase. For starters, you are going to want to choose a topic that genuinely interests you, or at least holds your interest throughout the process of creation. This shouldn't be too difficult if you have chosen a niche that appeals to you, but if you are working in a niche you are ambivalent about then ensuring that you are at least somewhat interested in the content is key as a lack of enthusiasm is sure to show through in your writing in a way that your readers are sure to pick up on.

While the blog posts that you put together regarding products you are trying to market are going to be more straightforward, they are still going to require research in order to make them as appealing to the masses as possible. The non-sales related posts that you create should be as well researched and planned out as any you would find on a non-affiliate marketing blog, as they are going to be what keeps people coming back for more. The higher the quality of your content, the more likely your regular readers are to come to trust you. That trust is an extremely valuable commodity as it can be traded directly for sales.

Finally, it is important to arrange your content in such a way that it comes out swinging right from the very start, which means choosing an effective title. An effective title serves to capture readers' attention but should be no longer than 65 characters as otherwise it will be truncated in search results. Many of them will only read the title and the introduction of your article. This is why the first part of a blog article must be so strong. You can engage readers in many ways: tell a story, show solidarity with their problem or present a fact or interesting data. The early part should then go on to describe the purpose of the article and how you will deal with the problem that your readers are trying to solve.

Maximize SEO

The last big key to getting users with the content of your blog posts themselves is that you pay attention to search engine optimization, also called SEO. This is a very dense topic and you could write a huge book on this topic all by itself. However, there are a few basics to keep in mind when you're wanting to work with SEO.

First, what is SEO? We've already discussed it, in brief, earlier in this chapter. SEO is essentially the process by which you can boost your site's rankings in the search engines. Using SEO, you'll be able to push your site to the top of the search rankings and essentially make yourself a force in whatever it is that you're doing. Many of the general practices that will be discussed in this book will work towards your search engine optimization – for example, social media presence and advertising, which will be discussed in the following chapter – but there are some other factors.

All of SEO is based around trust. The internet is filled with useless or bad information or the same information that people have already seen before a million times. Your goal, in creating a website, is to be filtered out through all of this drivel and show that your site is worth something. In essence, your site must be considered not drivel by the search engines.

There are a few ways that you can take advantage of this and make your site far more likely to show up higher in internet searches.

Keyword usage: The first is keyword usage. What search engines do when they rank their sites is they have a robot called a spider crawl across web pages, scan their content, see how good it is (this is parsed algorithmically and allows them to determine whether you're actually putting out new information or if it's just more of the same again) and how trustworthy your site is. It will also see how many "hot button words" you're using.

If you want your site to show up higher in the search rankings, take some time to learn about keyword usage and keyword study. Essentially, there are some words that will cause your site to be more likely to show up in general searches because these words connect to an overarching topic. These keywords are taken out of their original context and pieced together in order to get a vague idea of what the page is about. If you use enough of these, your site is more likely to show up when people do a search for that key concept.

Linking: The second is linking. Search engines care a lot about how trustworthy your site is, but there's no clear referendum on how a site's trustworthiness is necessarily dictated. However, being linked to by other sites – as well as linking within your own site to other places on it – will increase your site's trustworthiness and make it come across as a more trustworthy site to the engine crawlers.

Basically, they will see that your site has been linked multiple times and think oh if it's been linked here, it must be somewhat reliable. Try, also, to have your site referenced by other major sites within the same niche if at all possible – this will come somewhat naturally if you're producing good and creative content because people will want to see it. This will drive your search engine ranking up (because already-reputable sites have linked to you), and it will serve the dual purpose of bringing new faces to your site that previously may not have discovered you.

In the end, your rankings on search engines are based off of your trustworthiness and your overall traffic. If your site is deemed high-traffic and trustworthy, you will become one of the top results for your particular niche. If it isn't deemed high-traffic and trustworthy, then you may fall to the wayside or not find yourself climbing.

Don't worry, a lot of the advice given in this book will actually serve the purpose of intuitively and organically raising your search engine rank, which will lead to you being discovered by even more people and making even more money off of your affiliate marketing attempts.

In the end, you want people to find your site and look at everything that you've got to offer. The key to doing that is through your posts. Integrate keywords and links to your own site in your posts, as well as links to other reputable sites, and you'll find yourself quickly growing as a reputable and trustworthy source. You'll find your rank growing, too. This will cause your traffic to grow exponentially.

All of this can be done just by putting more work into the posts that you're making and taking a concerted effort in order to make quality posts that people want to read (or paying somebody with experience in SEO and your particular niche to do so for you.)

Keep blogging: It is important to keep up the blog on a regular basis (taking weekends off is fine) and really commit to it in the long term if you plan on starting it up at all. A regularly updated blog shows that you are serious about your website and about the topic that you are writing about. At the same time, a blog that is updated several times to start and then never again, or only sporadically, will make viewers assume that you don't update your website regularly or care about it that much at all. As such, if you do not think that you can commit to a steady output of blog content then you are likely going to be better off not starting a business blog in the first place.

Keep direct advertising content to a minimum: While every now and then if you get a particularly interesting new product in then, by all means, you can blog about it as long as you can come up with a reason for doing so besides the fact that it is a new item in your store. Especially early on, it is important to keep this type of content to a minimum, however, as it can be easy to turn new readers off if they feel as though all you are doing is plugging items that are in your store. A good rule is that one blog post in ten can contain content that is not purely informational, though your readers should never feel as though all they're reading is a hard sell.

Posts about products

Detailed product reviews: Depending on the goals of your content marketing strategy, reviewing products related to your niche or sub-niche is often one of the best ways to bring in new members of your target audience. A review of a product will naturally slip past the standard defenses that many people put up towards sales pitches while still containing virtually all of the same information of a good pitch without any of the traditional stigma that typically comes along with the process. Remember, a review can help customers avoid wasting their money on a shoddy product while a sales page is considered an especially pushy advertisement.

The easiest way to go about doing product reviews is to focus on a single product or group of products with an exceptionally critical eye. This means you are going to want to single out the various weaknesses of the product or product line as well as focusing on its strengths and what makes it unique. It is important to keep in mind that this type of content needs to come off as unbiased as possible otherwise the illusion will be ruined. This means it is important to intersperse positive reviews with negative ones to allow your target audience to come to the right conclusions about your review integrity.

Broad strokes reviews: Depending on the type of products that are relevant to your target audience, you may find an in-depth review of products to not only be difficult to write but relatively useless as well. Instead, you may want to focus on brief reviews that typically include just a single picture and a few hundred words outlining the product's bullet points before including an overall rating and links to purchase if relevant. These types of reviews are typically most effective with cheaper products which readers just want a little information on before making their purchasing decisions.

As an added bonus, these types of reviews often generate a higher rate of link click-throughs as users are more likely to click the link in question with the goal of finding out more information on the product. These posts are often going to include a round-up of like-minded products in each post and a ranking of the same from best to worst.

Create more visual content
When it comes to creating quality content that people are actually going to be interested in, quality visual content beats quality digital content nearly two to one. The reason that this is the case is actually two-fold, and it partly has to do with the fact that the adoption of smartphone technology means that people are always looking for content they can consume quickly, thus they are more likely to click on a cleverly constructed graph as opposed to the same information paragraph form. What's more, visual content has been proven to reach directly into the psyche of the audience in a way that has currently proven more visceral than text can match.

Proper visuals have also been proven to cause readers to pay closer attention to any related text, and also cause them to feel more engaged with whatever it is they are reading at the same time. This is why content that is full of interesting pictures is regularly shared three to one when compared to content without any pictures. With numbers like these, is it any wonder that content marketers who know their stuff when it comes to visual content often see their brand awareness shoot through the roof.

The long and the short of it is that images are required for engagement in the modern age which means you are going to need pictures to supplement any facts and figures you may feel the need to spread the word about. For most people, this is easier said than done, of course, and they will easily spend far too much money, time and energy in exchange for mediocre results. In order to ensure you end up with the best visual content possible, keep the following in mind:

Start with pictures: Regardless of how savvy you are when it comes to Photoshop, adding a few pictures to your content will help to separate it into more manageable chunks. In addition to making the layout look more professional, this is actually proven to increase the odds that readers will actually make it to the end of what you are saying. This strategy will also make it easier to consume your content while on the go which, as previously stated, is more and more important each day.

Consider YouTube: After you have your site up and running, creating a YouTube account to review the same products is an excellent way to double dips on the products you are already promoting. These videos are going to be shorter than your written reviews, typically only about two minutes, and should serve to highlight the best and worst features of the product in question. You will then want to be sure to include a link to the full review, as well as an affiliate link to ensure you are profiting from your YouTube page immediately.

With enough time and page views, you can become a YouTube Partner and generate additional income through impression-based ads there as well. While this might not seem like much, in reality, YouTube is the second biggest search engine in the world, directly behind Google. Additionally, YouTube gives preferential ranking to its partners, which will help your video reach a top-ranking spot.

When it comes to creating the types of video content that people are going to be interested in, your goal should be to remain as concise as possible without leaving out any major concerns that potential buyers might have. You should also try to inject a bit of a personal story surrounding the item, outlining a potential usage case as you go. The more details you can include within the time limit, the more effective your reviews will be.

CHAPTER 5
Growing Your Audience

First and foremost, it is important to understand that there is more to a successful affiliate marketing campaign than simply bringing the right type of people to your site. You may be interested in generating a higher rate of brand mentions, improving your social media mentions, improving your search engine ranking, improving your email newsletter metrics, generating sales leads or just improving your website traffic to generate additional advertising revenue. It doesn't matter what your goals are, you are going to need to track your results properly if you hope to gain any traction.

Luckily, there are metrics that can be used to track your goals, whatever it is that they might be. If you are looking to track the number of times your website is mentioned elsewhere, then you are actually looking to track a metric known as voice share which can be done with a free tool called Social Mentions which compares your overall mentions to others in the same niche. If you are looking to improve your search engine results, then there are plenty of SEO tools that can help you track your rank in real time.

Meanwhile, if you are looking to track your social media presence, conversion, website traffic or even how close you are to reaching your current goal then you track all of these metrics from the backend of your website. Regardless, you can't ever hope to improve your conversion rate without keeping a close eye on your metrics.

Audience profile: This is essentially a specific profile of who is in your audience, what defines them, what their motivations are, any opportunities you have to serve them, and what you can do to serve them better. Knowing this person specifically and doing all that you can to understand them ensures that you know exactly who you are talking to and how you should be talking to them in order to help them resonate better with you.

The best way to do this is to create an identity profile that outlines one specific person in your audience. This person should be the ideal character that defines who you are talking to, thus making them the "mascot" of your audience. For that reason, they do not need to be a real person. Instead, they can be a profile you create based on the summary of all of the information that you are learning through the audience.

Your profile needs to contain the following information:
- Age
- Gender
- Career
- Hobbies
- Location

You should also include anything relevant to what you are doing. For example, if you are creating a family-based brand, you would want to include information about the age range of the family, whether the parents are together or not, how many children they have, and anything else relevant to what you are aiming to do.

The more you detail your description of your ideal audience and understand who they are and why this makes them ideal for your brand, the easier it will be for you to identify how you can share with them. Be specific and include anything that you think will be relevant.

Ask for engagement: Asking for engagements on your posts is a great and straightforward way of increasing your engagement and following. Many blogs include some variation of "tag a friend who would love this!" or "who would you share this with?" then they will often end the caption with something like "follow us for more great content!" This encourages people to think about who they could share the post with, meaning that they end up commenting and sharing your content.

Some blogs will use this on almost every post, which is not necessarily a bad thing. It definitely increases engagement and following. However, it is important that you understand that customer relationships are often an important part of encouraging people to purchase from you. Make sure that you are posting additional content that encourages people to read and pay attention so that when you post a sale post, individuals are more likely to continue engaging with it. You do not want to condition your following to only engage when asked because this can result in them ignoring almost anything else you post. Creating genuine connections with your followers after asking for their engagement and follow is a great way to take full advantage of this feature and get maximum sales from your affiliate marketing campaign.

Giveaways: Giveaways are a phenomenal way to increase engagement and grow your dedicated follower. They allow you to share what your product or service is, encourage people to share you with their friends and to follow your page. You get incredible benefits from your giveaways. Giveaways can be costly because they do require you to give away a free product or service, but ultimately they are going to increase brand awareness and maximize your reach. When done right, a giveaway is ingenious.

The best way to facilitate a giveaway is to begin by choosing what it is that you want to give away. Pick something that will be attractive and well-liked by your audience and that will not cost you too much. Early on, it is ideal to give away something that is going to be smaller and more affordable for you. Your engagement when your following is already somewhat small will not be on par with someone who has an already large following, so choose accordingly. Be sure to factor in shipping costs if you are shipping it to the other person as a part of what this giveaway will cost you.

Once you have chosen, write a post that captures the product or highlights the benefits of the service. Then, in your headline, post something like this: "GIVEAWAY! Want to win this FREE product? Here's how! Tag a friend, like this post, like our page, and on the last day of this month, we will draw a lucky winner! Good luck!" It is important that you format the giveaway in a way that requires individuals to tag, like, and follow you because this is how you maximize your engagement and following through a giveaway.

Use apps to post your content: As a business owner, you are probably busy attending to your customers and business most of the day. You probably lack the time to develop and post content on social media on a regular basis. Just the knowledge that you have to develop content for each of your social media accounts can be daunting.

The good news is that you do not have to break your back developing fresh content every day. There are plenty of apps that can help with this. One of them is Muse Cam. This is an application that helps you to shoot great images on the iOS platform. The images can then be edited using advanced tools and other features.

You can also use an app known as Boomerang. This is an application that takes a series of great images in quick succession. The effect is to create a GIF-like image that you can then share on your various social media platforms. There are plenty of other tools that can actually schedule your social media content posting for an entire week or so. This saves you the time and effort of having to log onto each of your social media platforms in order to post and share content.

Learn from the competition: Pay attention to your competitors and learn from them. Studying your competitors is also a good way to identify your strengths and weaknesses. You can learn a great deal from your competitors, especially ways on how you can better improve your business.

Your competitors can also help you promote your business and draw more followers. In fact, it is not uncommon for bloggers to share one another's posts to their own network. This way, you get to tap a bigger audience. You do not have to fight against your competitors; you can work together.

It is very common for people online to support one another. If you have a blog, it is a good practice that you connect with other bloggers, especially those who are in the same niche. Do not think of them as your direct competitors, and you might be surprised just how friendly they can be.

Podcasts: Podcasts are essentially radio shows. These are a lot more common than you think, and they are produced with a very specific intention in mind. The idea of producing a podcast usually comes in tandem with the promotion of a product which needs to have constant engagement. Also, podcasts are used by individuals who seek to position themselves as experts in their field.

That being said, deciding to embark upon a podcast requires consistency. It requires you to have a regular and committed approach to producing content that your followers and subscribers will come to expect. Podcasts can be available on a number of platforms such as iTunes or Spotify. In general, they are free but do come with some type of advertising attached to them. Often, this advertisement is related to the creator's own business model. As such, the creators of the podcast might be pushing a book, a subscription service, and in the case with some YouTubers, they ask for donations via PayPal or Patreon.

Sharing: The most powerful endorsement you can get from your followers is having them share your content. When they share your content, you are getting a vote of confidence in your content. So, what does that mean? It means that as long as your content is useful and relevant, the chances of it becoming shared increase dramatically. So, rather than discouraging your content from being floated all around the web, make sure that you produce content specifically intended for sharing. After all, what could be better than free publicity?

Create the right call to action: A call to action tells your reader what to do. People who surf online are open to suggestions. In fact, just the fact that they search for information online shows that they are willing to listen or learn something. Using a call to action helps to direct your readers to what you want them to do next. It may lead to a sales page or a part of your blog that you want them to see.

A call to action is a good way to tell your readers the next content that you want them to read. Usually, it is placed at the end of an article with a hyperlink to the page where you want to take your readers. However, it should be noted that a call to action can also be made in the article itself. This will depend on your preference. The important thing is to clearly tell your readers what to do next. Take note that readers do not think so much. Do not expect them to analyze everything on your blog and know exactly to locate the next page that they should visit.

So, how do you write an effective call to action? A call to action has to be short and clear. Making it long will only confuse your readers. The suggested length is just around 1 or 2 sentences long. Be sure to provide a link that will direct your readers to the page where you want to take them.

Don't forget about the mobile audience: There are so many people who get their information from their phones and if you aren't meeting them there, you will miss out on a lot of revenue. Make sure that your website will work on most mobile phones so that you can reach your target audience.

You will find that many of the customers you are going to run into will also look at your pages through their mobile devices. This means that you need to take some time to make sure that any content you work with is going to work well on a phone as well. You don't want to put in all that effort on an amazing website and then find out that half or more of your viewers aren't even able to read through it at all.

The good news is that many of the websites that you use to help out with making your own website, such as WordPress, will have options that make it easier for you to optimize for mobile devices. This can make it easier for you to do the work, without having to come in with a lot of technical knowledge in the first place.

Becoming an authority
In many situations, the word expert and the word authority are often used interchangeably; this is not the case with online marketing, however, as being an authority is everything and being an expert is much worse than simply getting second place. In this case, an expert is

someone who knows a lot about a certain niche while an authority is the person that all of the experts agree is the first stop for information on a given niche. To put it another way, authorities aren't authorities because they say they are, they are authorities because when they make declarations in regard to their niche of choice, other people listen.

The benefits of being an authority in relation to a given niche, are much the same as any other authority figure when you speak everyone will listen. This is because those who know you are an authority will expect that you know what you are talking about in any given situation, after all, you must know best. It doesn't take much of an imagination to see how this can directly translate into additional sales when given the proper push. If you can reach the status of authority for your niche, then you will be able to set the tone for the entire niche as well as have a legion of loyal followers willing to defend everything you say.

When it comes to marketing for your online business or website, it is important to have a healthy social media presence as well as a firm grasp of the importance of SEO if you want to reach out and find new revenue streams. If you also spend time slowly building a reputation as an authority in a given niche, then you will be able to rest easy the revenue streams will come to you instead.

If it seems as though this explanation is giving niche authorities too much credit, take a moment and think of an authority in a given niche that you consider yourself a part of. Odds are you listen when that person renders judgment on something, and you likely follow along without doing the research required to form your own opinion.

Do your homework: The first step to writing content that will help you to see as though you are an authority in your niche is going to be difficult for some people and easy for others depending on their ability to get online and do the research that being an authority in a chosen niche requires. Put another way, you need to learn enough to know what it is you are talking about in any situation you might find yourself in regarding your niche.

Not to worry, this isn't something that is going to take you years to master as it is perfectly acceptable to focus on a single aspect of your niche to the exclusion of all others. Not only does this have the benefit of ensuring that you will actually get to use the information you are learning at a point in the near future, but it will also allow you to differentiate yourself from any other authorities in the niche without having to actively go head to head with them.

Once you do get to work, it is important to do more than simply becoming familiar with the Wikipedia page on the topic, it means going to the sources that you can find connected to that Wikipedia page and then tracking down their sources as well. You will then want to do this again, and again and again until you can honestly say that you have left no stone unturned. It will require lots of hard work and effort, though the results will certainly pay for themselves in the long run.

While you are working your way through this process you may also find it helpful to create a starter guide as if you were writing for someone who is completely unfamiliar with whatever part of your niche you are working at becoming an authority in. While putting together a study guide for a topic that you are not yet terribly familiar with might seem like a poor choice, the fact of the matter is that absorbing the complicated topics you are studying and breaking them down in such a way that anyone can understand will help take the content from something you've learned to something you can easily explain, which is what you will be spending a lot of time doing through your blog.

Consider your voice: Every writer has a unique voice, a one of a kind perspectives on the world that comes through in their word choice and their phrasing. In an extremely competitive online environment properly honing your tone can be the difference between being an authority and being just another faceless expert. You are what sets your content apart from any other, do everything you can to ensure it is unique and compelling as possible. If you aren't sure what the right voice for you is, consider the following.

The best place to start is by making a list of all the words that you feel other people would use to describe you. You should spend some time on each of these words and consider how you might make each as clear as possible when it comes to showcasing your personality in what you write. From there, you may be able to add in the written equivalent of any unique speech patterns that you have. These can be difficult to pick out for yourself, which means you are going to likely need some outside input for the best results. You can express these types of things including the sentence structure that you use, the way you separate your paragraphs, the length of your sentences and more. It is perfectly alright if you can't come up with much right now, the longer you keep at it, the more unique your writing will naturally become.

If you can't come up with much of a voice early on, it is important to let it develop naturally rather than forcing it. Having a forced voice will only limit your voice from developing naturally, and essentially paint you into a corner as if you change it once people have gotten used to it you will risk losing their trust.

Know your competition: Just as there are going to be major players in your niche that you did research on before committing to a specific goal, it is important to know who your competition is in the authority space surrounding your niche. Finding this person shouldn't be hard, all you need to do is search for your niche on Google and look for the names that come up most frequently. Once this is done, you will then need to decide if you would be better off trying to dethrone them or taking on a subsection of the niche instead. Regardless of how entrenched this other person is, there is always going to be room for another authority in a niche, you may just need to go above and beyond when it comes to determining just where that room actually is.

Write it down: While it might seem like you are putting the cart before the horse if you try and write a guide about your authoritative topic while you are still learning, the fact is that putting the things you have already learned together in a way that a beginner could successfully utilize them will allow you to make connections you would otherwise miss. Doing so will then leave you feeling even more comfortable with the topic in the long run and will also leave you with useful content that you will be able to use later on to reinforce the idea of your authority even more.

Additionally, the formatting you ultimately decide on can be used later on to generate outlines for content you will write in the future, saving you time in the long-term when you need to generate content for your goal of becoming an authority. When determining these details, it is crucial that you make sure you can explain everything you write in such a way that a person who is completely unfamiliar with the topic can understand it on a surface level. It doesn't matter how much you know about a topic if you can't explain it clearly you will never be an effective authority.

Become well-known: While it should be easy for your regular readers to think of you as a credible source of valuable information by this point, if you hope to clear the last hurdle to true authority you will need to branch out. Your goal in this phase should be to spread out throughout the niche so that wherever your subscribers and any other interested parties turn, they see your name and some useful content that you are talking about.

This means forums related to the niche in question, the blogs of other experts in the niche, popular social media gatherings related to the niche, anywhere you can attach your name, you should try and be there twice.

With enough exposure, your name will be directly associated with the niche by default through sheer force of will.

Additionally, when you post to these alternative venues, you will want to include your website as a part of your signature. By this point, you should be confident in the content you are generating which means you know you are generating useful information which means you want to ensure that the people who want to find more of your insight know how to do so easily and with as little hassle as possible.

During this period, none of the content you post should be designed with marketing or sales in mind, that part comes later. Instead, you should be focused exclusively on community outreach and building up your personal brand as much as possible through a grassroots movement devoted to how much of an authority you are. When working through this part of the process, you can certainly answer base level questions regarding your niche, but generally speaking, you will want to stick to high-level discussions whenever possible. Each post you create during this time should be seen as an opportunity to show off just how knowledgeable you are which means that you will need to go above and beyond what most members of the target audience are going to know by simply being associated with the niche. Only by taking the conversation in new directions will people remember your name after reading your post.

Create custom content in eBook form: eBooks occupy an interesting space in the custom content pantheon. They are inherently more evergreen than most other types of posts and yet they can easily be updated when they need to be. What's more, they are a great way to generate additional website income if you are considered an authority, or even an expert in your field and yet each copy costs you nothing which makes them the go-to when it comes to value adds as well. Additionally, they are readily available across all digital platforms but can easily be printed out with no change in formatting to give them even more legitimacy. Finally, they can be both inward and outward facing for target audiences and even be used internally to train staff on a wide variety of topics.

The most effective custom content eBooks group together a wide variety of information on a coherent theme and act as a "one-stop shop" when it comes to filling your target audience in on everything they need to know when it comes to a specific facet of your niche. If you haven't yet reached the level where your users consider your authority, there is no faster way to jump-start that assumption then with an eBook.

Even better, you don't even have to write it yourself. For under $200 you can visit UpWork.com or any similar site and hire a ghostwriter to write a 15,000-word book for less than $200 on any topic imaginable. After adding in a few personal touches from your site that converted users are sure to appreciate, you can then have it formatted and a cover created for around $10 if you use the crowdsourcing site Fiverr.com for your labor needs. Despite giving it away on a regular basis, if your content marketing campaign has been even the least bit successful you can easily recoup those costs by charging as little as $2 for what you have created. Overall, you can easily have an essentially free way to generate a nearly unlimited amount of custom content that also generates user goodwill as you can give it away with no cost to you.

CHAPTER 6
Affiliate Marketing Basics

The purpose of this chapter is to provide you with the foundation of what affiliate marketing is and how it functions. Most likely you already have an idea of what affiliate marketing is, and at the very least you have heard of it, but you are here because you want to know more about it. To begin, let us start with the bare-bones definition;

A commission is paid to an outside agency for promoting or selling another companies product.

There are two parties involved in this process; the one who creates the product, the merchant, and the one who promotes the product, the affiliate. The affiliate receives the commission they sell, similar to how a door to door salesman is paid or a call center representative. The product offered by the merchant does not have to be a tangible item, like clothing or a food product. It can also be a service, like a video tutorial. Finally, the merchant and the affiliate can be one entity. For example, you could be the one that makes the video tutorial and places it on a network for others to sell for you in exchange for a commission.

Another party involved in the process, although it is often overlooked, is the publisher. This is the intermediary that links the merchant to the affiliate. Their role is to provide the means for how the product will be promoted. The final party is the customer or client that purchases the product.

This is an attractive marketing concept because it makes all the parties involved happy
- The affiliate is happy because of the commission earned.
- The merchant is happy because of the product sold.
- The customer is happy because they have received a product they need or want.

How affiliate marketing works: The first step of the process is the merchant who creates a product. Once the product is created, they provide it on a website or affiliate network with a reference link attached to it. The purpose of the reference link is to let the merchant know which affiliate promoted the link successfully with a customer. This means that when an affiliate promotes the product through their publisher, the customer clicks on the link letting the merchant know from what affiliate the customer came from and who they need to pay the commission to.

The affiliate can promote the merchant's product in several different ways. One of the most effective forms of promotion includes writing through reviews. More information about this topic will be shared later in this book. The way an affiliate is paid a commission for their promotion includes cost per action, or CPA, and cost per order, or CPO. These payment forms are similar to cost per click, which is popular with online advertisements and pays the affiliate up to 50% of the product's price.

In conclusion, this beneficial marketing tactic is a commitment between a merchant and an affiliate. The affiliate provides the publisher, which is a website that shares the content. The website usually includes SEO and other services to help promote the product to the customers. When a customer clicks on the product link on the affiliate's website it alerts the merchant where the customer came from so the affiliate can be paid their commission.

Profiting from affiliate marketing

While the revenue for affiliate marketing swells into the millions, some people wonder how much really remains in the affiliate networks. These networks are a place where merchants and merchant's advertisers can list a product that needs affiliates. The sites connect affiliates and merchants and offer a platform to pay and track commissions. For example, when a merchant puts their product on an affiliate network they offer to pay the site a set amount per new customer. A portion of what they pay for that new customer is then paid to the affiliate through that site.

As an affiliate, one of the most important questions to ask is what the commission is for promoting a product from the affiliate network. The typical percentage is 30%; however, it can vary greatly for many different reasons. Two main reasons for this variability include the product's price and the demand for the product. If a product has a high demand already the commissions are lower because the affiliate will not have to work as hard to promote it. Commissions can be higher is an affiliate must work harder to drive customers to the product. Commissions typically do not go above 50%.

Typically payments are made to affiliates anywhere between 30 to 90 days after the bill for their services is received. This requires the affiliate to wait for the payments to be made. In addition, these payments are made after the merchant has paid the affiliate network. Very rarely do networks provide early commissions.

If a network can pay their affiliates earlier than their competitors it is typically an indication that that particular network is a good one. By advertising that they pay earlier than others the network seeks to attract and grow their number of affiliates. This competition benefits the affiliates greatly.

Affiliate networks typically only serve one niche but occasionally do diversify. To find a market that fits an affiliate's needs, research various networks to find one that is the most attractive for you. To find the best fit for a merchant's needs, gather information about the different networks by comparing different ones that are related to the product.

Affiliate networks

An affiliate does best if they seek out products that are marketed to wealthy customers and are of high quality. This tactic results in a higher commission and typically the merchant has more money invested in promoting the product through the affiliate. An affiliate can expect sales ad leads for these types of products to be invested in to increase the traffic. This approach is helpful for both seasoned and new affiliates. New affiliates need to also remember that they will make mistakes; however, having a higher payout can make it worth it to keep learning as you go.

Below is a list of various affiliate networks that currently market to the most in-demand niches. These are a good place to start your research. Amazon: An affiliate that sells products in the "consumer electronics" category is guaranteed 5% commission while they offer 10% on all other products. Using links or banners that connect to any page from Amazon can generate sales and commission.

- Awin: Traffic to an affiliates site can be monetized with very attractive products with this network. The network is performance-based and only pays out when the products sell.

- Clickbank: This is one of the most popular networks. It is user-friendly, making it simple to sign up, and can pay out high commissions. Sometimes the network offers commissions that are over 70% of the product! The products are mainly membership sites and e-books. Another attractive reason to choose this network is that an affiliate can take on an unlimited number of products.

- Coinbase: Cryptocurrency is a current hot item, and bitcoin has created a buying frenzy. This frenzy has opened up the opportunity for people to register on this network and make large sums of money for participating in bitcoin's affiliate marketing program, free of charge.

- Juiceadv: While this does restrict their affiliates to those that have successful sites that generate over 1,500 visits per day and an email list of over 25,000 subscribers, it does also offer a very attractive benefit. This network is a single source for a multitude of income streams. This variety can make an affiliate more diversified in their passive income.

- JVZoo: For affiliates looking for high-end products, this site is one of the most popular American affiliate networks. The price range is between $49 and $500. In addition, commissions are paid out early and regularly. The approval process for this network may take several weeks; however, once approved there are few limitations on how to use their products.

- Oaxmedia: While doing your research into different networks, this affiliate network offers you an incentive to visit and register quickly by giving you a registration bonus of $25 Euros. Another incentive they offer is the guarantee of the highest "effective cost per thousand," or eCFT, for its members.

- Spoutable: This network offers larger profit opportunity than other competition, like AdSense. It is easy to register, use, and monetize.

- Tradedoubler: This international network is very popular for a variety of reasons. One of the reasons is the variety of niches it offers. With over 19 choices, the affiliate base has reached over 140,000. An affiliate has practically an unlimited number of products to choose from.

Common compensation models

There are several different ways that, as an affiliate, you can work with companies or merchants to help sell their products. When it comes to choosing a product or products to market, you will find the best results with products that are naturally of interest to the types of individuals who are already drawn to your site. This is what is known as your niche and taking it into consideration when you plan out your affiliate marketing strategy is sure to lead to better results overall.

PPL: With the pay per lead model, you don't actually sell anything directly. Rather, you convince your followers to provide their personal information to a company for their personal use. The profit here typically ranges between $2 and $20 depending on the amount of information that is generated per lead. This type of affiliate marketing agreement is typically found with service providers of varying types including internet service providers and smartphone companies.

PPS: Pay per sale affiliate marketing is the most common type available and is offered through Amazon.com on practically any item you are interested in shilling for. To start, you simply sign up with Amazon as an affiliate and you are then provided unique links to the items you request. Then, for every time an item is sold through your link, you receive a small percentage of the profits. While this may make you think that big ticket items are the way to go, quantity is typically going to override quality in this instance.

PPC: The pay per click model doesn't require you to actively strive to sell products, it simply requires that you have a website that is visited regularly. You then sell ad space on your site and are paid a few cents every time someone clicks on one of the ads regardless of whether or not a sale is then generated. The starting rate for this type of affiliate marketing is typically just 1 or 2 cents per click but if you build your website into something that gets thousands of visits each day then the payout can increase substantially.

PPI: Pay per impression is the type of affiliate model that ensures you have to do the least amount of work overall. All you need to do is post the advertisement on your site and every 1,000 times some views it, you will receive a small amount of compensation. While this option is never going to be anyone's first choice when it comes to making money off of their website, if you are already enjoying a reasonable monthly number of visitors then it could certainly provide a reasonable ancillary income stream. When setting up a PPI or PPC it is important to not overload your site with ads as this is sure to drive down pageviews. Remember, moderation is key.

CHAPTER 7
Affiliate Marketing Strategies To Try

Retaining your audience in the long-term

There's a pretty good chance that if you don't have a good company infrastructure set up, you're going to have a situation somewhat like this: you have a lot of users coming through, but for some reason or another, you can't quit turning them over. There could be multiple reasons why, but people just aren't sticking around. If this is the case, you really have to think for a second about why this is happening.

Chances are, you either don't have quality content (they come through, are unimpressed, and decide to never come back) or you don't have a way set up for them to actually keep up with you. There are a few different ways that you can set this up, but if you're wanting consistent traffic, this is something that you're really going to have to take into account with your site, because the entire idea hinges upon the notion that you can have people not only come but come consistently.

So how can you set up that infrastructure? There are two primary ways, and they're both extremely simple.

The first is obvious: mailing lists. You need to have a mailing list set up. If you're using WordPress, there are numerous tools in place to help you do exactly this (and do it quite efficiently at that!). Search around for something that will let you easily compile a list of users that you can send a mass email to with ease.

Once you have that mechanism in place, you then have to ask yourself: how am I going to get people to sign up for the mailing list? There are a lot of different routes that you can take for this specific purpose, but the most obvious is to simply ask them. Some people make it a lot more complicated, and we'll get into that in just a second, but there's absolutely no harm in straightforwardly having a box to the side of the webpage where people can enter their email address and sign up for the mailing list.

This is an easy way for your users to keep in touch with you and keep up to date on your most pertinent posts, so if they like your site, there's no chance that they'll miss out on your posts.

However, there are a few other options you can take. It's pretty easy to set up scripts that will "gate" content if people don't join your mailing list. This is a good way to turn people away from your site, but if you set the floor high enough – maybe 10 posts before people are asked to sign up – then you can avoid ostracizing people who aren't interested and get the email addresses of the people who are. Moreover, you can do something simple like set up a pop-up box that will ask people to enter their email address and join the mailing list, with an obvious way to leave the box and continue browsing if they choose to do so. This shouldn't upset too many people, as most users understand that mailing lists can be one of the most efficient and important ways for an enterprising entrepreneur to keep up with their customers.

It's really easy to think that mailing lists are outdated or deprecated, but this couldn't be further from the truth. Most people check their email at least once per day, so setting up a mailing list can be a good way to ensure that you're within a day's reach of anybody on it.

The other super important option for keeping up with users is arguably as important – if not more important – than a mailing list in this day and age. That's social media. Social media is an important cornerstone for any business these days because it allows users to follow you and allows you to actively engage with them.

Social media also offers something that email doesn't very easily: the ability to share posts that you like. So, this means that if you get a decent following on social media and make a really popular post, you could quickly see your following skyrocket, potentially even exponentially, and that would mean a lot of good things for you.

The most essential social media for any company or brand to have is Facebook. Pretty much everybody uses Facebook and having an active Facebook page is absolutely essential. Do whatever you can in order to build your Facebook fan base. Your posts aren't always going to get a ton of traction, but any traction and any traffic matters... plus, if you make a really good post, you're going to see a lot of traffic come from it naturally. That's just how it works with social media.

You're also going to want to consider getting Twitter and Instagram. These aren't quite as popular as Facebook and are more geared towards people in the 16 to 30 crowd, so if your niche aims at people who are older, then you may not have as much success on these. However, having a popular following on these networks can make a lot of difference for you as a company if you follow through with it appropriately and make a lot of posts.

Finally, you're going to want to set up a Snapchat. Snapchat is potentially one of the best marketing platforms because unlike other forms of social media, where only a portion of your followers can see your content without specifically going to your page, a story on Snapchat is visible to all of your followers. If you have a particularly visually appealing niche, Snapchat can be a great way to show people what you're up to and what's up next on your blog. This extra traffic and these return users will, in turn, lead to a big return on your affiliate marketing products.

Additionally, if you get big enough, there's a chance you'll personally get companies asking for you to review or promote their products. Companies care about people with niches, and you could get a lot of perks for having a big social media following beyond just the extra traffic you'll get flowing to your affiliate marketing referrals.

These are the two most important methods for keeping up with your users and are, in turn, really the ones that you most need to know. Bear these in mind and you'll see your search ranking grow leaps and bounds, alongside your credibility and – yes – the amount of money you make from your affiliate marketing referrals!

Videos
If you are here, you may be asking yourself, "How do I make a good marketing video?" unfortunately, the answer is not simple and requires a lot of attention to detail. You need to create a compelling video that showcases the company and the product being promoted. There are a lot of moving parts. Below are recommendations on how to use videos to drive customers to purchase the promoted product, and with practice, you should see high conversions.

1. Don't just make one video: Having a constant presence is important in this fast-paced world. Short, new videos being constantly circulated keep your brand fresh in people's minds and allow one bad mistake to "disappear" in the sea of your other great promotion videos.

2. Change up the content: Offering a variety of messages allow you to reach more people. This is especially important if the customer is global. Choosing to focus a video on the brand, the service, the promoted product, and other topics allow you to offer something that is of importance to almost everyone in any culture.

3. Help customers with their search: Internet users are searching for something when they put in keywords into the search fields of YouTube. This site is an actual search engine, but the rules of SEO do not apply to videos here. For this reason, you need to learn how to create a video that users can find easily.

4. Tailor to the audience: While having a variety of content within the videos is important, having a variety of channels for this content is not a good strategy. Instead, have one or two channels with strong content in the videos. The content should focus on the target audience's lifestyle and needs at all times.

5. Create a recognizable and visible brand image: In the video, tags, metadata, and description your brand needs to be visible. This constant visibility is important for user recognition. Having the brand present in all these places makes sure that the brand can be seen even when not viewed through the YouTube channel.

6. Stay social on social media: Tweeting, posting, and sharing the company's videos on the common social media platforms allow you to reach total visibility. Visibility and promotion often start on one of these platforms.

These basic suggestions should give you a starting point on how to approach creating a video for marketing purposes. But what should be highlighted in those videos exactly? Below are some suggestions on content:

- Show off your skills: Highlighting the skills you bring to the table builds credibility for your customers and shows that you have what it takes to be successful in your industry. This should show your skill set but also a relevant example of those skills in action in your video.

- Cover it all: You only have 3 t 04 minutes to connect with your customer through your video so use that time to give as much information as possible and answer their questions. Consider offering a "FAQ" type video for first-time customers or visitors to help answer many of the common questions that arise. The goal is to answer every potential concern so the customer feels confident in your company and the promoted product.

- Make it personal: Relationships are the most important part of doing business. This is one feature that sets successful businesses apart from their competition. To establish these relationships, it is important that your video has a relatable and friendly face. Show the areas you do business in, key employees, your personal office and other people and spaces that will help the customer feel more connected to you personally. These little details can make a huge difference in the customer's purchase choice.

- Spend money on telling a memorable story: Funny and thrilling videos that have exciting storylines can establish brand identity and recognition quickly. This process does require a significant investment behind the screen, such as screenwriting and video director. If this is not in the budget, consider trying to spice up a topic like the history of your company so it is more fun and relatable than a traditional documentary. Consider re-enactments or video snippets from previous years to have a fun story.

Now that you have decided on the topic of your videos, you must develop a strategy for the promotion of these videos. This strategy does not include just the technical pieces.

Designing: The purpose of the video is to reach a specific and measurable goal. It is not an end result. This means the different video should be shared on different platforms and this means their design should vary for where they will be located.

"Video is not an end; it is a medium." This quote by Phil Nottingham, author of the article "Goal-driven approach," which is included at the end of this chapter, explains that the videos should have an objective that it is clearly guided by. A video should not be made just for the sake of making a video, despite how popular that current trend or story is at the time. A video should always be there to help promote the product and communicate information.

To accomplish this, you need to ask yourself questions like, "How can my video improve XYZ, an area in need of improvement, for my company?" or "Will this video draw X customer to our channel?" A big budget is helpful in creating successful marketing content; however, creativity that has a goal is more effective. A funny and well-crafted story is wonderful, but it does nothing if it does not have a beneficial purpose.

Decide what you want to get out of the video campaign. Think of things like converting traffic, building links, increasing shares, or creating a stronger brand awareness. Establishing the objective of the marketing strategy allows you to pinpoint a stronger video promotional strategy.

Traffic conversion: YouTube is not the end-all-be-all for video promotion. More and more companies are focusing on their own websites, creating video content on there to improve their various pages. Placing a video on a website can be more effective at driving traffic and improving conversions than a channel on YouTube. Videos on the website can include product reviews from customers or demonstrations on how to use a product.

You may be thinking now that you could do both; place the video on YouTube and on your website. Unfortunately, this is not a winning strategy. This is because you want to improve your search engine results standing with Google, the video on YouTube will not allow that to happen. In addition, the video on YouTube will drive people to YouTube first rather than your website. This cannibalizes your website traffic. There is a more intuitive method to get your video in both places successfully, which requires you to use a service like JWPlayer to customize the video code so that it is embedded differently on YouTube than it is on your website, despite them being the same visuals. By doing this extra step you can improve the search engine results page on Google.

Facebook Open Graph and schema.org offer a video transcription and accurate sitemap for videos that allows quality shortcuts of video to be used on websites. This means less data and pull on a customer's computer will be needed to view your website's video content.

Taking a video that is meant to be on a website's landing page and placing it on YouTube lowers its effectiveness. This is because the video is not viewed in a purchasing context but rather an educational or entertainment context. This means that the video that is designed for conversion needs to be placed in a location where the customer is ready to convert. YouTube is not a place for product videos, but it is a great location for stories, tutorials, or viral videos. If you list a video on YouTube, choose to classify them as "not listed" so they can be embedded and not visible in the results of searches.

Creating a video that works both on a website and YouTube takes skill and practice. An excellent example of a company doing this is Poo Pourri and their "Girl's Do Not Poop" campaign. It was funny, created a buzz, and was viral. It worked on both their website and YouTube.

Building links and increasing shares: When sharing the link to a video, be aware of where you are sending a customer. Sending them to YouTube means you are not sending them to your website. This drives people away from your site and lowers conversions. Other video hosting solutions can help increase shares by using exclusive videos on a company's website and having links directly to there. Do not sacrifice traffic for building links or increasing social shares.

Stronger brand awareness: Videos promoting products do better on various platforms. This is because they are dedicated to different niches. Three of the most popular places for video promotion include YouTube, Facebook, and Instagram. Choosing several platforms for promotion is good if you want to advertise a product or build a brand's reputation. This is because different target customers have a variety of browsing habits. Keep in mind that, while Facebook videos can be effective, it is wise to have it listed somewhere else because Facebook videos are not searchable at this time. Opt to also promote the video on YouTube to let customers find your video again.

Finally, can video be used for every message? Yes. Sometimes using another medium would result in information being lost or left out. Video allows you to use the closest form of promotion to personal contact. It is important to note that videos need to be used in conjunction with other mediums for a complete approach. In order to communicate well with customers, it is important to model their tone and language in the promotions. Messages should also be shared on relevant social sites and on other related blogs and websites. Messages should also contain a call to action that is appropriate for their targeted customer.

Tracking statistics: The strategy's objective is what determines the metrics used for determining the effectiveness. One constant strategy that is used is the viewing time offered in the Public loyalty report on YouTube. While the viewing time is good to know, because it indicates how much of the video a person watched before stopping it, the true indication of the effectiveness of the content are the comments left. Other tracking methods include relative and absolute audience loyalty.

The videos average quality is shown by relative audience loyalty. This identifies the video's capability to keep the viewer's focus while playing in comparison to other YouTube videos that are about the same length.

To go further into understanding at what point customers become more engaged or less engaged in the video you can use absolute loyalty. The percentage of total views can be tracked with this information. It shows exactly what happens when a customer begins watching your video and how many viewers leave after the initial 5 to 15 seconds.

Effectiveness tracking systems: The name of the strategy or the keywords search volume can be measured, but the challenge is that things listed as "not provided" for Google Analytics restricts you from knowing if the traffic is coming from keywords attached to the brand or the video. On the other hand, the "search query" report for Google Trends or Google Webmaster can also assist in tracking effectiveness for viral or large brand initiatives. Another way to check the effectiveness of keywords is to us an AdWords campaign to track opinions of keywords once the video is released to the public.

If you want to track video effectiveness outside the website it was published on, use a tool for social monitoring like Mention or Topsy. You can also use Google Alert to let you know when someone talks about the video or embeds it on their website.

For affiliate links within the videos, you can track the effectiveness by watching the correlated fluctuation in clicks through those links. Bit.ly is a service that can be input as part of a video description and tracks clicks. This service also allows you to add short links in the video descriptions with altered text to make it more appealing to the viewer.

In the video's description or comments you can insert links to help you use the YouTube Analytics report, or, if a website is linked, a Google Analytics code can be used and tracked.

CHAPTER 8
Email Marketing

While it may appear as though public opinion has turned when it comes to the general success rate of email marketing, the reality of the matter is that when done properly, email marketing is still one of the most powerful marketing tools in an online marketer's toolbox. The guiding reason behind this fact is the same that it has always been, it is successful because it appears more personal when it comes to a customer's private space (their inbox). As long as the email is sent with permission, studies show that email is the marketing channel that is most preferred by consumers nearly 2 to 1 over both mobile and social media marketing.

This means it is also still the most cost-effective way to reach potential customers bar none, with the Direct Marketing Association estimating that its return on investment is a staggering 4,000 percent. Email marketing is so effective for the cheap and easy way it allows you to reach consumers on the regular but it will only be so if you take the time to become an authority in your niche and provide useful content in your emails, outside of just a list of the latest deals. From there, the quality of the content will become more well-known and the number of subscribers will grow, ultimately leading to more sales as a result.

This doesn't mean that any type of email newsletter will ultimately lead to results as it is easy for any email from a business or website to be marked as spam regardless of how much useful information it may contain. This is why it is important to moderate your pitches and only include them as a part of a value exchange between yourself and your subscribers. The implied agreement is this, you promise not to send out a constant stream of newsletters and only include things that show you value your subscriber's limited time.

Building this trust is a difficult row to hoe as you will inherently start out at a disadvantage because your potential subscribers have all been burned before, guaranteed. This doesn't mean it is impossible, however, it just means that your emails need to include effective subject lines and have a distinctive voice while always provide information that the niche you target is sure to care about.

Getting started: To create an effective email marketing strategy, the first thing you are going to want to do is to determine just what your goals with email marketing are going to be. This will allow you to tailor your content in a way that generates the greatest amount of positive results in the shortest period of time. When it comes to generating goals, consider how much content you plan to create each week, how you will connect the email newsletter with sales, how you will attract new subscribers and how the email newsletter can tie into your broader marketing goals.

From there it is simply a matter of generating the right email newsletter list which can be easier said than done. The first thing you will need to do is create a new page on your site to link people who are interested in signing up for your email newsletter. There should be a link to this page from your blog as well as on the order confirmation page that every customer sees after they have completed their order, these are the most valuable customers you have as they have already bought products from you once which makes them more likely to do so again in the future.

When it comes to attracting new email subscribers, the best way to do so is to promise access to something with perceived value, say an eBook you had written, in exchange for signing up for your newsletter. It is important to not use underhanded tactics to get people to sign up for your newsletter or to gain their email address through other means and then send an unsolicited email. Either of these actions are only going to get your email marked as spam, they will never, ever get anyone to open them unsolicited.

Once you have a new subscriber, you will want to ensure they open the first email they receive from you by including the right subject line. The subject line is one of the only things that you can reliably assume your subscribers are going to see which makes it extremely important when it comes to influencing open rates. Surprisingly, studies show that the true determining factor as to whether an email will be opened is not the content of the subject line, but its length.

Create the right content: Once you have started successfully getting new email subscribers, you are going to want to ensure that you are producing content that for them to read. The rate at which you put out new email newsletters is up to you, though a good rule of thumb is to do so often enough that your readers, especially those who are paying customers, don't forget about you, which will make it easier to convince them to buy your new product when the time is right. When it comes to content you are going to want to always include a 90/10 split where 90 percent of the content is relevant based on the topic of your webinar and 10 percent is an advertisement for your products.

The content that you create for your email blast is a great way to further convince people that you are an expert in your field and creating new content will ensure that your newsletter open rates remain high. As long as you continue creating unique, worthwhile content that presents a persona that is one with the community in question, then you can expect your email newsletter email list to continue growing and when it comes time to sell new content you will see it begin to bear fruit.

Consider your email marketing strategy: Creating an effective email newsletter week after week and year after year can only happen if you take the time to create the right email marketing strategy for your company before you ever send out your first email. Doing this will require you to understand what email marketing means for you as well as your content marketing strategy as a whole and that it naturally means different things to different people. It is also important to be realistic when it comes to setting email marketing goals which is why you should create a list based on what your end goal is which will help you decide how you are going to generate the required content as well as what it is going to cost you.

Think about what email marketing means for you: To make things simple, this book considers email marketing as a type of communication-based on permission from your target audience that will allow you to increase customer retention and improve sales in the process. Permission is the key word here as without getting permission first, all you will be doing is generating additional spam that won't be doing anyone any good. As such, it is important to remain extremely vigilant when building your email list of willing participants instead of simply buying a bulk list from some semi-legal website.

Build the right email list: After you have a firm grasp on your current content marketing strategy's strengths and weaknesses, the next step is to consider how to build an email list full of willing participants. Hopefully, you have already collected some information on users you have successfully converted to customers; if not, you are going to need to start from scratch. Either way, the best course of action is to determine what information you need and how you will most likely get it.

While adding a function to your site that will allow people to sign up for your email list automatically is a logical starting point, you are also going to want to include the same option during the purchasing process as well. Adding the same functionality to kick in after a user has spent a predetermined amount of time on your site is also recommended.

Use an autoresponder properly: When setting up an autoresponder message, you will want to pick an average of 5 products that do not directly compete with one another but are still clearly related.

In addition to sending out a new unsolicited email every 4 days, you need to track the emails that you do send out and determine how many people opened each email and how many actually bought something because of it. As you gain more information to work off of you can more specifically target your emails to have a better success rate among your target audience.

When it comes to understanding what you can do to ensure that your autoresponder emails are opened, the first thing you will want to do is to send emails from your name directly. Assuming you have connected your name with your brand, opening an email from you should be akin to opening an email from anyone else your readers know. Outside of that, there are several important guidelines to consider to ensure readers keep opening your unsolicited emails for years to come.

Approximately 35 percent of your subscribers will open any email with the right subject line. This means your subject line should be short and sweet, no more than 10 words but no fewer than 6. The subject line should imply useful content related to the niche in question. This ensures you are at least including something you know your audience should, in theory, be interested in.

Add in obvious links: The purpose of your emails, or at least some of them, is to lead your customers back over to your affiliate link, your website, or even your product page. Without setting it up so that people will go back to the website that you want, you are not going to be able to convert them to be customers. The key to do this is pretty simple. You just need to learn how to capitalize on each time when you think that the customer may feel compelled to click. You don't want to overdo this, but make sure that there are at least a few links along the way.

Honestly, your customer is probably not going to make it to the end of your email, no matter how great it is, especially if this ends up being a long email. Their attention span is going to be incredibly short and you don't want to end up placing the affiliate link only at the end just to have them miss it because they never made it to the end of the email. Placing the link throughout the email (some experts recommend doing it every paragraph but concentrate on placing it anywhere that it makes sense), can make it easier for your reader to click when it makes the most sense for them.

In addition, make sure that your user understands that they are looking at a link. You do not want to work so hard on the email and then have your customers go away from the email because they didn't see any links for them to click on. So, add the links into the email a few times and make sure that it is easy to see the links, and you will see some more conversions.

A call to action at the end of the email can be helpful as well. After you have provided the customer with some useful and valuable information, you can then add in a call to action, one that includes your affiliate link, for them to click on and check out the item and the solution to their problem. If you wrote some good copy in the email, it is going to be easier to convince them to make the purchase because they feel like they need it.

CHAPTER 9
Tips And Tricks

Think like your users

In the end, when you're doing affiliate marketing, you're trying to do one really simple thing: sell a product. The blogs are just a means by which to do that. However, there's a right and a wrong way to do things when you're trying to sell a product, and these are as true on the internet as anywhere else. In this chapter, I'm going to be giving you some valuable tidbits that I've collected which will help you to best market and sell your products.

Moreover, it makes them even less likely to return to your site, because they subconsciously feel like they're just going to have sales offers lobbed in their face. They're not wanting that. They're searching for something to buy related to your niche – they're looking to know more about it, first and foremost.

Keep that in mind: you aren't trying to sell them anything explicitly. You're offering them the opportunity to buy something, and if they don't take it, that's their choice.

So, with all of that in mind, let's say that you're the end user and you're looking for a site full of information about the Paleo diet. You're considering going on it, and you want to find a bunch of recipes and enough information to get started. So, you run a Google search and you see a result for "Rock Solid Eating". You think it's a clever title and you decide to check the site out.

What would you want to see, and – more importantly – what would you not want to see?

People are looking for very specific things when they go to a website. First, they scan it to see if it looks legitimate. People are not dumb, and they know what scam websites look like. Blank websites or websites without character do not strike them as legitimate, no matter how DIY you're trying to come off. You need to do what you can in order to establish both a professional image and a professional design for yourself.

We'll go on with this analogy in a second, but for right now, I need to mark a really important set of distinctions here: voice. The voice that you speak to your user in makes a really big difference. You can't switch voices all the time either. You need to find a voice and stick to it.

Anyway, now imagine that you're the end user again. You found this site, it looks professional, and you decide to dip into some posts and see what this Paleo thing is about. You start reading a recipe: would you as the end user trust your site at this point? Is everything about the site attractive enough to make you actually feel like you would want to follow the recipes that it describes? Does it make you feel like you're wanted there?

Now, imagine you're reading the recipe itself, and they're mentioning a product (the affiliate product) that helped them to complete it or the affiliate service that sent them the produce they used to make the recipe. What kind of phrasing would make you interested in picking up their product?

People who try to market things online make big mistakes because, too often, they sound like marketers. They don't sound lax, nor do they sound like they know what they're talking about; they just sound like guinea pigs pressing keys a thousand times trying to make a commission selling a product they don't believe in.

If you want to sell things to humans, then, believe it or not, you have to act like a human – a real human being, not somebody who types "ACT NOW!!!!!! And you'll get a FIFTY percent discount – this DEAL WON'T LAST LONG!!" trying to sell a product. That's not good, and though my example just now is hyperbole, there genuinely are internet marketers out there who completely fail because they just don't know how to market their products. That's a shame, and you need to be smarter than to let that happen to you.

Now imagine that you're the user again, and you've read a couple of recipes and you like what you see. You've decided to give the Paleo diet a go, and you want to follow this site and know when they post new things. What can you do to make it as easy as possible for a user to keep up with you? Do you post your Facebook, YouTube, and other social media links very clearly on the header so that they can find it and get to those channels readily?

These are all factors that you need to consider when you're working on your site. If your site isn't really straightforward for the end users, then your site is not really worth anything at all. You have got to get into the head of the people who will be using your site so that you can make intelligent design choices.

With that, we've now reached the end of the book. The takeaway from this chapter needs to be that you carefully consider everything about your user's experience. It's really not complicated to be a good marketer, all that you have to do is think about how you would want to be taken into the site if you were just a common user.

Investing money is a requirement for an affiliate to make money. Buying traffic is a way for an affiliate to drive up the volume and to scale business. Traffic is driven to a website landing page, a website, link, or advertorial of a campaign for the affiliate is the goal. To generate and but this traffic, you may be wondering where to go. There are several different places you can go to that offer different types of potential customers. Your niche requires a specific audience, so it is important to choose a source that will provide you with the right people and context to look at your promotion.

AdWords: Keywords are words readers look for most often in search engines. This means that they have shown interest in a certain topic. This particular resource was one of the firsts to let affiliates reach about 70% of the search traffic globally. There are several tools offered which allows you to choose the right one for your campaign. There are some drawbacks, such as the strict rules regarding certain affiliate links and the expensive costs associated with certain keywords or subjects.

Bing: Bing.com is a search engine that offers Bing Ads for affiliates to advertise through. It does not generate as much traffic as AdWords, but it is not as strict and less expensive.

7Search: This advertising network allows you to promote a variety of vertical search engines including mobile capabilities. Other sites associated with 7search include bestsearch.com, finditquick.com, kijji.com, Kijiji.ca, and the freedistionary.com.

Social media: Social media is the advertising spot of choice right now. This platform allows you to contact and engage large amounts of people quickly. It also allows you to develop an interest in a product easily. This low-cost option capitalizes on the impulsive sharing of content from the users who pass on information they think is valuable to their community.

Facebook: Facebook Ads are one of the most popular resources for traffic. There is a large customer base, a variety of promotional options, and latitude for creativity and personalization. You can set goals anywhere from generating website clicks and image or video post sponsorships to generating leads, downloads of an app, or optimizing conversions. This resource allows you to identify your target audience regarding social media interests and behaviors and create a method for tracking and growing a base of audience members. To use this, you will need a free Facebook account and purchase traffic for little investment. Facebook does have rules regarding niches of a sexual nature and other topics, like cryptocurrency.

YouTube: This is the most used video-sharing platform currently. The collaboration with AdWords allows you to promote your video on YouTube by showing your promotion before or during a video or in the search results within YouTube. Influencers are the main users of this resource, but many businesses have seen success using this resource by increasing traffic and sales. It is a great resource for those that wish to increase profits using video marketing.

Twitter: Branding is what the Twitter platform is mainly used for currently. The streams of potential users that a brand targets can include images from Twitter advertising easily. There is a high cost associated with this ease and if you are looking mainly for conversion, it may not be the best platform for you. It is also a challenge because there is limited opportunity for writing information to a potential customer. It is a growing influence, so it is worth looking into and trying.

LinkedIn: If you are targeting B2B conversions, this is an advertising platform for you. It is an attractive resource because it is one of the few platforms that is aimed at almost solely professionals in various fields. LinkedIn ads offer the ability to pay for clicks and views with visibility on a variety of devices. Prices can be considered high but because of its specificity, it can be a good generator.

Instagram: One of the newer social resources, this platform is already gaining traction as one of the most used traffic resources. You can generate clicks, promote app downloads, or interact with posts thanks to the integration with Facebook ads. This audience is typically young, and influencers are the ones that drive their purchase decisions. The ads are visible on mobile apps for Android and iOS devices.

Pinterest: A women-frequented site, this resource most successfully promotes clothing, furniture, and kitchen items. Sponsored pins are a method of promotion you can purchase. These are images with links attached to them that show up in the feeds or searches of targeted audiences or based on specific keywords.

Writing rules for success

These rules are here to shorten the learning curve and bring on your first sale earlier. Dedicating the months of preparation and dedication is important to the success of your blog. This requires more than just exciting concepts for articles. Commitment, preparation, and attention are all required consistently and cannot be neglected.

There is immense competition, with new content hitting the web every day. The good news is that not all of these will stay long or sell anything. Low traffic will kill off some of the competition within only a few months. Following set guidelines and utilizing good strategies to develop, monitor, and keep up your blog will improve your opportunity for success. By having an established blog that lasts a longer amount of time, you develop a reputation and potentially open the opportunity for consulting on blogging subjects. The following guidelines are here to help set you up for success. They are here to help you steer clear of common mistakes and risks almost every blogger face.

Make a great first impression: It matters. This means that the content is not enough. You need to have an attractive layout with good graphics to partner with the expert content. Choose a good theme that can showcase the site's content in a functional and an easy-to-navigate manner. Free templates from web hosting companies are nice to begin, it is important to decide if the template will allow you the ability to work with your demands. Decide if it is flexible enough to handle things like regular updates or has the ability to work with plugins and widgets. A function is critical to the theme and template. It needs to work with the latest version of WordPress.

Graphics are constantly improving for blogs. If you need to use a premade theme, consider opting for a premium one. These often have more functions and offer many demos. These demos are there to assist in developing strong graphics for the site. Sometimes these are already created and can be added to your site easily.

Graphics partner is content: It is essential. This can be considered the heart of the blog; the thing that keeps it all going. Return traffic is a result of your content that is accurate, readable, and informative. A true mark of credibility is when a reader chooses to use your blog as a reference for information. Sometimes the authors get too caught up in the graphics and lack the attention to the content. Sometimes they get lazy and copy content. If a blog or website is caught plagiarizing content, they will receive a penalty. It is not worth it, no matter how exciting a topic is. Having useful and original content will grow your readership and improve your SEO. Search engines will list articles with over 1,500 words higher, especially when this detailed content is produced regularly on your site.

Organization leads to success: Making your blog easy to navigate for your readers is important. You can use a tool like WordPress to help you be more efficient in this manner. The different features in WordPress that you can use to make it easier for your readers to browse topics without difficulty include:

Widgets: Layout your sidebar for your reader. Offer links with labels such as suggested reading or most popular posts. If you are offering a FAQ-type post, consider having it listed here.
Tags and categories: Topics that interest your readers can be easy to access with good categories and tags in place.

Lend your expertise to others: Guest blogging is a valuable tool for increasing you and your blog's credibility. It also drives more readers to your site. Reaching out to other bloggers that cover your niche and requesting to guest blog for them on a one time or consistent basis is an easy way to make your own blog successful. This method does require you to write in the manner of the other bloggers and requires that you pay extra close attention to your professionalism and grammar. Choosing guest blogging as one of the promotional strategies is often a wise choice.

Reply and engage: When a reader takes the time to comment on your article or asks you a question, take the time to respond to them. This interaction is crucial. The more you interact and respond, the more people will comment and reach out. Your readers will feel that you listen to them and that you notice them. Simply recognizing their concerns can sometimes rectify conflicts or mistakes. This also fosters trust and an increase in referrals. Your readers will then start driving traffic to your site for you. The comment section on your blog is also a mini-community. Use this area to grow and foster a strong community, which is essential for brand development.

Be social: Immediate and effective interaction with your readers is now possible thanks to social media. It is a valuable tool for a successful blogger. Developing social media accounts on popular networks helps establish a strong audience for your site, creating a loyal readership that comes back again and again. These sites also help you promote your blog to potential new readers. The concept of going "viral" means that content on social media is bounced quickly between large groups of users on sites. This can be powerful for brand development.

Help others help you: Having social media buttons on the bottom of your articles lets your readers share your content for you. This means that they are reaching to their circle and beyond on your behalf, potentially driving new readers to your site. Many host sites and themes offer this function, which means you will not have to install anything additional to get this on your site. If you do select a theme without this function, follow the guidelines from your host site to learn how to add them. You do not want to miss out on this opportunity!

Link building is nothing to scoff at: Connecting your articles to various other blogs or resources helps build a valuable network of allies. Driving traffic to another site typically facilitates them driving it back to you in return. Do this sparingly, only linking to real sites with valuable information. Providing too many links or links that lead to irrelevant topics can be harmful to your content and credibility.

Up your ranking on Google with SEO knowledge: In order to get free traffic to your site, you need to get high on Google's list. WordPress offers plugins to help optimize SEO with tools like Yoast SEO. To be successful at affiliate marketing, it is essential that you learn and understand SEO.

Quick and easy are good terms: This means that your site does not take a long time to load. You can do this by selecting a hosting provider that values loading time as well. SiteGround is an example of a hosting provider that is excellent for support and performance. W3 Total Cache is an example of another tool that has been developed to help sites remain quick. Also, remember to choose tools on your site that can accommodate large increases in traffic. You do not want your site crashing, as it gets flooded with visits after a successful post!

CHAPTER 10
Mistakes To Avoid

Not being careful of the scammers: There are a ton of people out there who are looking for ways to make money. They want to be able to quit their normal day job and just work from home on their own schedule. Because of all this desire, there are a lot of scammers out there who are more than willing to take your money, after giving some big promises, and then running away. There are a lot of great affiliate marketing companies out there to work with, but then there are a lot of scammers out there as well. If it sounds too good to be true, then it probably should.

If you are going through and the company is making big claims that you will be able to make thousands of dollars in a few weeks, then this is a sign that you should run away. If they say that you will only need to work for half an hour a day, or an hour a week, or some other silly claim like that, then it is time to look the other way as well. These companies are simply looking to part you with your money, and as soon as they have it, they will run away, and you will never be able to get ahold of them again.

In addition, reputable affiliate marketing companies are not going to ask you for any money to start. They may ask for a bank or PayPal account, but this is so they can pay you once you get some referrals on your link. If a company is asking for this information because they want to charge you, that is a big sign that they are fake, and you should look somewhere else.

Having only one source for affiliates: It is usually a good idea to have a few different locations online where you are promoting the products that you want to sell. If you just focus on a website or just on social media, then you are going to find that you are missing out on a lot of the customers you could be reaching. Many successful affiliate marketers are going to focus on at least two different options, and in the beginning, this may be all that you are able to handle because that is a ton of work.

Not maintaining a consistent brand: The fight isn't over just because you've gained a large number of followers. They can decide to stop reading your content at any time. That's why it's important to both peak interest and to keep that interest. To do this, you should stay true to the reasons these followers were inclined to follow your brand in the first place. Did they follow you because of the interesting infographics you posted? Then keep posting infographics. Keep feeding them the content they like, and they're much more likely to stick around.

You also want to post regularly. Whatever presence you have on social media should be dependable. This not only keeps their attention but again and again exposes them to your brand. The more familiar someone is with your brand, the more likely they are to become customers when they decide they need to have what you are selling. Post things that are closely related to your company's product or service. Share interesting things about your business and present them in interesting ways. Give them exclusive information, make your company seem transparent and honest.

Look for people talking about your brand. Do they have something positive to say about your company? Then Engage with the post and leave a comment expressing that you're happy you had a good experience. Do they have something negative to say? Then leave a comment inviting them to let you sort out whatever problem they have. Be honest about your mistakes and take great effort to correct them.

Denying a customer's problem is probably one of the worst things you can do for your brand. It makes your brand seem vain and close-minded. When someone communicates with a big company over social media and they get a response back, it often has the effect of making the customer appreciate the effort you expend for them. It makes them more likely to remember you and also more likely to engage again, which keeps their interest and ensures your content reaches them.

Not utilizing SEO correctly: SEO can be done on your own, or you can find sites that will do the SEO for free for you. One of the biggest benefits to this, of course, is that you will not have to worry about paying a dime for something that will help to increase traffic to your website. The downside is that you may not get the highest quality possible when it comes to your site. You may also not be able to get the most out of it or the same type of support that you would with typical SEO.

While paying for SEO may be an extra cost that you will have to consider when setting up your affiliate site, it is something that will be able to pay off for you in the long run. Even though it can cost a lot of money, you will have a higher quality SEO turnaround and your site will show up much better on the search engines. No SEO professional will be able to guarantee that your site will show up first, but someone who is good at it can make your site higher up on the ranking.

You will need to make the decision of whether or not you want to be prominent on the website. Do you want your affiliate site to be your face? If yes, you should consider the tone and the style of the site before you even begin putting it together so that you will be able to have yourself at the forefront of the site. It is a good idea to make sure that you are getting what you want out of the site and that it is truly working for you. You may also want to stay completely behind the scenes on your website which is also a great option for people who just want to use their site for affiliate marketing purposes. If this is the case, make your site more objective than it is personal.

Not using outreach and PR: This form of promotion is called "earned media" and it relies on you building quality relationships with people in the industry. You want to reach out to the media and bloggers and pitch the idea that they write about you. Whether you are writing to the media or to a blogger, you are going to first want to find out what the writer or reporter is interested in. Then, you can carefully generate pitches that are unique to the person you are writing to. You want to make sure that the pitch features something that they would find particularly interesting, without including everything you've ever created or accomplished in your life.

The majority of the time, the person you are pitching to will want something special in return for the exposure. The majority of the time the special something they would want might be early access to some form of important information, or another exclusive offer. Bloggers specifically may also be interested in receiving free goods or a special deal for their reader. Before you approach them, you want to make sure that you have reviewed any special submission guidelines they may have to ensure that your submission meets their guidelines and you are taken seriously.

It may feel uncomfortable directly reaching out to the media or to bloggers, but this is a great way to get your name out there in a major way. Some people may not be interested in writing about you or your business, but others likely will be, and this will give you a great advantage for marketing your business.

Not using the top SEO practices: Search engines are one of the best sources of gaining valuable, organic traffic of interested buyers. These people are actively seeking information related to your products and services, and as such are already halfway through the buying cycle. Your SEO practices should be top-notch to be found by those interested and relevant readers. Get into the habit of using H1, h2, and H3 (HTML tags). Ideally, the title tag should include a couple of relevant keywords.

Do not forget to include a meta title (which is nothing but the title appearing on your page in search results and not the actual page) of under 60 characters. The meta description (again the description of the page appearing in search engine results and not the actual page) should be below 160 characters. It should succinctly yet compellingly convey what the page is about, so readers have a good idea what to expect.

This practice also makes it simpler for search engines to locate matching content among millions of other pages and improve user experience by displaying the most relevant results. Include keywords naturally and wherever relevant to your posts. Do not create spammy, keyword stuffed articles in the hope of boosting your SEO. Few things affect your search engine optimization efforts as forced, excessive and irrelevant keywords. Affiliate farm blogs are heavily looked down upon by Google, and your site runs the risk of being permanently banned by Google.

Use long tail keywords, especially if you have a very narrow and focused sub-niche that interests a select group of audience. This practice will you access to audience/users who are already interested in buying or looking for exactly what you are offering. For example, if you are an affiliate to range for kitchen appliances, instead of simply including keywords such as "Belgian Waffle Maker XYZ", you can say "the best or cheapest price for Belgian Waffle Maker XYZ" or "comparison of Belgian Waffle Maker XYZ with other Waffle Maker models" or "buy Belgian Waffle Maker at the best price."

Common Marketing Mentality Mistakes
- "Marketing is puzzling and totally unpredictable" - There are many, MANY marketers that come into the game with the idea that online marketing is a puzzling type of mystical game that they just cannot quite grasp. They like to think that some people have more of a "magic touch" than they do. But the truth is, marketing, if done correctly, is highly predictable and easy to control
- "Marketing just isn't the right fit for my business" _ The individuals who think this way have probably had a few goes around the block, having little marketing success. Due to this, they have become accustomed to the idea that marketing must not be a thing their business would benefit from, which is far from the truth. They have to realize that to grow their revenue, they

must be able to successfully leverage marketing to their advantage.

- "I just suck at marketing" – And then there are some business people that shoot themselves in the foot with negativity before they even get started. Even the ones that have marketing down to science had to at some point learn, grow and improve. If we find the right guidance and learn how to acquire knowledge gracefully from our past mistakes, this can make anyone a very valuable marketer. You just have to stick with it! Patience is key!

- Success is never permanent, and failure is never fatal. This is a good quote to live by as a marketer, entrepreneur, etc. We eat, breathe and live from the mistakes we make, making learning curves constantly to stand behind in regard to our business no matter what that business might be.

CONCLUSION

Thanks for making it through to the end of *Make Money Blogging: How to Start a Blog Fast and Build Your Own Online Business, Earn Passive Income and Make Money Online Working from Home*, let's hope it was informative and able to provide you with all of the tools you need to achieve your goals, whatever it is that they may be. Just because you've finished this book doesn't mean there is nothing left to learn on the topic, and expanding your horizons is the only way to find the mastery you seek.

Now that you have made it to the end of this book, you hopefully have an understanding of how to get started with your blog, as well as a strategy or two, or three, that you are anxious to try for the first time. Before you go ahead and start giving it your all, however, it is important that you have realistic expectations as to the level of success you should expect in the near future.

While it is perfectly true that some people experience serious success right out of the gate, it is an unfortunate fact of life that they are the exception rather than the rule. What this means is that you should expect to experience something of a learning curve, especially when you are first figuring out what works for you. This is perfectly normal, however, and if you persevere you will come out the other side better because of it. Instead of getting your hopes up to an unrealistic degree, you should think of your time spent building your affiliate marketing empire as a marathon rather than a sprint which means that slow and steady wins the race every single time.

The next step is to really take the initiative to set up your affiliate marketing blog. It can be a fair amount to get started, roughly a one to two-hundred-dollar investment, but if you follow the steps outlined in this book you should see a return at least of the money that you invested.

Remember: this is not a terribly difficult affair. All that you have to do is define a niche for yourself and then work on setting up your blog. You need to decide whether or not you're comfortable writing your own blog posts; if you're not, you need to work on setting up a working relationship with a freelancer on Freelancer or Upwork. You're going to need a fair amount of posts for people to be interested.

I suppose that the biggest thing to take home about all of this is that it's not just a one-and-done. You can't just set everything up and then leave it if you want to make a lot of money off of affiliate marketing. It's going to be a long and ongoing journey, but if you carry it out as I've written, you'll see fairly good returns, most likely. There aren't very many reasons that you wouldn't.

At the end of the day, though, just because you may spend less time working and more time making money on this, you're still going to have to put in some work. This isn't the sort of thing where you can just let it go entirely and slack off. Even outsourcing the work isn't a fantastic idea unless you get a really fantastic deal, because you're most likely going to not have as much of a personal connection to the blog posts as if you do them yourselves. This can limit the quality because only you know your own vision.

You're going to have to put in hours to get your site set up, to get it looking like people should trust you, and to get all of the stops in place so that people like your site and are willing to go to it. That's not even including the time that you'll have to put in setting up social media and marketing on those channels. Plus, if you add in setting up a worthwhile YouTube account or dropshipping system, it will be very much time investment.

However, the end goal is that you will end up only spending roughly two hours per day if that working, again not including time to make and edit videos if you should do YouTube. Meanwhile, the returns that the average affiliate marketers get when they put out this much work can be upwards of a thousand dollars per month, and many even make enough to live off of it – some very comfortably.

If you put out the work, you will almost certainly get results. The thing is that people look for reasons to like things, most of the time. If you make good content, people will like it. The hardest part is getting it out in front of people. Hopefully, you've gotten enough out of this book that you can probably get it to everybody that you'd like to get it out in front of.

Remember, your goal, in the end, is to market products. But there are a lot of ways to make money through your blog; build your affiliate marketing empire using your blog as the base, then build up from there incorporating everything that you can in order to promote the products you're wanting to.

Finally, if you found this book useful in any way, a review on Amazon is always appreciated!

DESCRIPTION

The sad truth is that the traditional means of working, whereby the average person would work for 40 or 50 years with the same company and then receive a pension for all of their hard work, is dead and buried. These days most employees are lucky if they get health insurance, much less some type of guarantee their job will be around in another five or ten years. As such, those who are really looking for a way to achieve financial stability in the long-term need to look elsewhere if they hope to be successful. If you are looking to do more than survive in the new economy, you are looking to thrive, then *Make Money Blogging: How to Start a Blog Fast and Build Your Own Online Business, Earn Passive Income and Make Money Online Working from Home* is the book you have been waiting for.

Inside you will find everything you need to know in order to turn your future blog into a money-making machine starting with an outline of what to expect from a passive income stream and how to get started successfully. Next, you will learn to choose a niche that will maximize your profits while minimizing your required effort. You will then learn all about creating the type of eye-catching blog that people are sure to be drawn to time and again.

From there you will learn the secrets to generating the type of content that people are actually interested in reading, as well as the many ways you can successfully grow your audience time and again. This will help mightily once you learn about the basics of how you will be turning a profit from blogging, affiliate marketing. You will learn about the ins and outs of affiliate marketing as well as starter strategies to try. You will also learn about the importance of email marketing when it comes to reliably turning a profit. Finally, you will find plenty of tips for success as well as common mistakes that new affiliate marketers make and how to avoid them once and for all.

So, what are you waiting for? Take control of your financial future and buy this book today!

MAKE MONEY WITH FACEBOOK ADVERTISING

Learn How to Make $300+ Per Day Online With Facebook Marketing and Make Passive Income in Less Than 24 Hours

By
James Ericson

INTRODUCTION

Congratulations on taking the first steps toward mastering Facebook advertising and boosting your profits!

Social media represents an unprecedented opportunity for business. The problem is, most business owners don't know how to utilize it. And that's a shame because advertising and marketing on social media can help grow your business and find new customers rapidly.

In this book, we're going to teach you how to use Facebook to laser target prospects that you can turn into buying customers or high paying clients. If you're a noob now, by the time you finish this book, you'll understand how to utilize Facebook to make your business explode within 24 hours – at low cost.

We'll explore:

- What is Social Media Marketing? In this chapter, we'll review the various social media marketing outlets, and discuss what makes social media different from traditional media.
- Why Facebook Advertising. This chapter introduces you to an overview of Facebook advertising, giving you a taste as to why Facebook is head and shoulders above the rest when it comes to a powerful marketing platform.
- Getting started on Facebook. In this chapter, we will learn how to create a Facebook Page and then work on our first Facebook Ad campaign.
- Targeting Customers. In this chapter, we will go into detail on the different ways that you can target Facebook users.
- Audience Insights. Next, we explore a powerful tool that is built into Facebook that lets you research your ad demographics. This includes basic things like age and gender but also drills down into page likes and more that will help you understand your customers.
- Facebook Pixel. What is Facebook Pixel? Find out in this chapter and learn how you can use it to collect data on people that visit and use your website.
- Introduction to Facebook Ads Manager. In this chapter, we go into more detail on the Facebook Ads Manager.
- Analyzing Results. Proper analysis of the results of your campaigns will help you determine which ones to keep, which ones need refinement, and which ones to trash.

228

- Traffic vs. Page Likes. In this chapter, we help you understand the differences between these two campaigns that can drive traffic to your business.
- Lookalike Audiences. Perhaps the most powerful tool in internet marketing. Learn what they are, how to use them, and how to profit from them.
- Creative Media Types. In this chapter, we'll go into detail to learn the various creative types that you can use in your advertisements.
- Boosted and Promoted Posts. Learn how to advertise specific postings from your Facebook page.
- Common Mistakes Made by Newbies. We go over common mistakes made by beginners that we've identified.
- Facebook Business Manager. Learn about the Facebook Business Manager and how it can help with the administrative tasks related to Facebook advertising.

By the time you finish this book, you will have a solid handle on the fundamental principles behind Facebook advertising and what it takes to use it to grow your business and take it to the next level.

There are many books on Facebook advertising on the market. We'd like to thank you for choosing this one and we sincerely hope that you will find it informative and that you'll gain some actionable tips from it!

CHAPTER 1
What Is Social Media Marketing?

Everywhere you turn, these days you're hearing about social media. Whether it's the President or some Hollywood star tweeting, or the latest news about Facebook, it seems like everyone is on it and everyone is obsessing over it.

Why is marketing on social media important? And in particular, why is it important for business?

Let's look at some of the reasons:

- Everyone is on social media, and they're spending more time on it.
- It's become the primary way to communicate with friends or family, especially about products or the news.
- Social media actually allows you to incorporate multiple types of *creative* media into one or more posts. By this, we mean incorporating text, video, and audio together, or using them separately.
- Unlike television or radio, social media can give you global exposure – or you can fine tune to the most local exposure imaginable.
- It works for any interest or type of business – from promoting video games to beauty shops to real estate.
- It's easy to find customers who already want your product or service.

Social media can even be exploited for free by business, but the reality of that is it takes time. If you want to use social media for free then you'd have to spend months and months – maybe more than a year – working hours each day to build up an audience. We're not going to say that can't work, but chances are you're looking to build your business and find new prospects *today*. The good news is that it's entirely possible because you can start running ads on multiple platforms and do it instantly – at very low cost.

While running ads on television or radio on a local basis could cost you thousands or tens of thousands of dollars, advertising on social media can cost you as little as $3 a day. On a per prospect basis, you can acquire prospects for a few cents.

Of course, that is if you know the tricks of the trade.

But it doesn't end there. Using traditional media, if you want to go national, it would literally require an advertising and marketing budget in the millions of dollars. And then trying to advertise worldwide? *Forget about it.*

Not so with social media.

With social media, not only can you easily target any and all locations in the United States, you can advertise *anywhere* on planet earth. OK let's say virtually anywhere, there might be one or two exceptions. But if Facebook, YouTube or Twitter is operating in that country – you can advertise there.

And the good thing is that the prices will be the same or cheaper.

Just think about that for a moment – a few decades ago to run a nationwide TV ad you had to spend millions. You had to hire a fancy ad agency to make the video for you and edit it. Then you had to arrange for placements with major TV or cable networks that would cost millions for a 30-second ad.

Fast forward to today, and you can make your own video on your computer in a couple of hours, and then run it worldwide for a few dollars.

Stunning isn't it?

Well, maybe your business isn't looking for global customers. You might be an attorney or a real estate agent looking for local folks in your proximity. The good news is that social media works like gangbusters for you too! As we'll see, you can laser target prospects at dirt cheap prices, making it easy as could be to get new, paying customers.

Now even though we are talking about paid advertising, the ubiquitous sharing and interactive features of social media will play a big role in your campaigns. That is huge, and something entirely new for business. Sure, in the old days someone could see a commercial or product they liked and they might mention it to their friends. But the reach was limited and mentioning a funny commercial to someone you know is hardly the same as actually letting them *see* it for themselves. Today, you can post an advertisement on social media – and people who find it useful, funny, or enjoyable can share it with their friends. And then they share it with their friends...and pretty soon it "goes viral" and get far more views than you actually paid for.

So what are all the major social media networks? You probably know them already, but just in case you don't let's review them

- Facebook: This is the biggie and the topic of this book. Facebook essentially launched the social media revolution. Even though Facebook wasn't the first (remember MySpace?), Facebook turned social media from a side curiosity for young people into a *must-have* tool that connects friends, family, and people that shared interests or hobbies. Worldwide, not everyone is on Facebook, but globally Facebook has 2.32 *billion* monthly active users. Every day, 1.52 billion people log into Facebook at least once.
- Twitter: Twitter has enabled people to communicate with the public on an instant and unprecedented scale. Twitter is smaller and more concentrated in the United States, Canada, Europe, and Australia, but with 321 million users in 2019, it still has a major impact. News organizations constantly monitor Twitter and use them in articles to share opinions. You'd be surprised, while they mostly focus on public figures, when a post by an unknown person goes viral it can show up on leading news publications too.
- YouTube: YouTube, the video engine, has 1.3 billion users. It's estimated that 5 billion videos are watched on YouTube every single day and that 300 hours of video footage are uploaded to the site every minute. In our estimation, YouTube ranks second only to Facebook as a platform to reach customers (and in the English speaking countries, it's probably on equal footing), and you can use YouTube and Facebook in conjunction with each other to extend your reach.
- Instagram: This company is based on image sharing and it sprung to life as a result of the incorporation of cameras into smartphones. As soon as people were able to take pictures anywhere and anytime, they wanted to share them with the world. The good news for you is that Instagram was acquired by Facebook and so you can advertise on both simultaneously.
- Pinterest: Another image sharing site.
- Stumble Upon: A site that can be used to share articles.
- Gab: A lesser known message site that works like Twitter.
- Vimeo: Another video uploading site.
- Daily Motion: A video sharing website like YouTube.

- Linked In: The social network where people post their resumes and make professional connections. Growing in importance, but not the focus of this book.

In our opinion, while you can spend time going crazy trying to learn about and target every social media network out there, the only two you really need to worry about our Facebook and YouTube. Twitter is actually losing users. It was reported that between January 2018 and January 2019, it's active user base actually declined by 9 million, or about 2%. Secondly advertising on Twitter isn't as powerful as advertising on Facebook. It's harder to target by interest or make your ads as compelling to view. And since Facebook and YouTube are going to give you complete coverage of your audience, it's more productive to focus on those rather than trying to hit everything.

Hopefully, we've convinced you that social media marketing is a very useful tool for business. Now let's take a look at Facebook specifically.

CHAPTER 2
Why Facebook Advertising

We've gone over the stats – billions of people are using Facebook every month, and more than a billion are getting on it daily. In fact, a large fraction of people are getting on it multiple times a day. Whether people are on their desktop computer or out with their smartphone, little dings keep bringing Facebook messages posted by their friends to their attention – and drawing them back to the site.

Whether that's a good thing or not for society at large we'll leave to the experts. As business marketers – our only concern is getting our message out to where the people are, and doing it at the lowest possible cost. And Facebook is the ideal platform for that.

Let's have a look at some of the reasons why you would specifically want to use Facebook for your advertising campaigns.

Laser Targeting

Facebook lets you do an unprecedented amount of laser targeting of prospects. By being able to "zoom in" on who your prospects are, you can give yourself an automatic edge before your marketing campaigns even begin. In the old days, you had to make an advertisement for radio or television, and throw them out for the entire world to see. Maybe only 3% of the demo in your city is interested in your product or service, but there was no way to target them using rich media as a television ad. You had to spend money on targeting everyone. Now it was possible to target people with specific needs and interests by say using direct mail or advertising in magazines, but that kind of advertising isn't nearly as effective as having a video show up on their Facebook feed.

Let's look at some of the ways you can target Facebook users:

- Location: You can target by location as broadly or as targeted as you like. For example, you could run an advertisement that targets users in the United States, Canada, Australia, New Zealand, and Great Britain. Or, you could target users within one mile of a specific street corner in Portland, Oregon.
- Interest: One of the things Facebook has done is catalog people's interests. Whether it's bowling, playing casino games on their iPhone, learning how to code software or invest in real estate, people build up a profile of their interests by liking pages and joining groups. Facebook lets you target ads by interests.

- Similar Products: Often, those page likes are for other products that might be similar to yours. Sell a basketball game for the iPhone? You can target people who've liked pages related to basketball and those who have downloaded other basketball games from the App Store. That's just one example – it works for any product or service.
- Age: Depending on your product or service, you can target people of any age from 13 and up.
- Gender: You can run ads targeted toward males, or females, or all.
- Employer: Some companies have a presence on Facebook, and you can target people who have indicated they work there.
- School: Some people have noted what university they attended, making it possible to do some targeting here.

Later, when we look at audience insights we will explore the ability to laser target your audience in more detail.

Lookalike Audiences

The *lookalike* audience is one of the most powerful features of Facebook advertising. The way this works is that you can get an audience of customers that have purchased some product or responded to an ad for a certain product. Then Facebook will analyze it to find out the characteristics of that group of people. We don't know how it works behind the scenes, but they do it. For example, if you are making an advertisement to sell bankruptcy services for your law office, you can have Facebook analyze an audience of people who have previously responded to advertisements for bankruptcy services, and then create a lookalike audience. You can then create an advertisement that targets that audience.

Why do that?

Because the lookalike audience is going to be super responsive – and so it's going to drive down the costs of acquiring new prospects.

So how do you get lookalike audiences? Well, they aren't free. You can either obtain them from someone else, or you can build them yourself. The fastest way is to either approach people with a prospect list or a broker and buy the list. It should have an email address and first and last name. Alternatively, you can build one yourself. The list should have at least 1,000 prospects but 5,000 is a very good number. The way you will build one yourself is to run ads basically cold until you've gotten 1,000+ people to respond to the ad. Then on your second run, you can build your ad around the lookalike audience that Facebook creates based on the prospects you gathered from the initial ad. The costs associated with your second ad will be much lower.

Think of lookalike audiences as cloning previous customers!

Facebook is Dirt Cheap

We've talked about the expenses of marketing with traditional media. They can run anywhere from a few bucks for a classified ad in a newspaper all the way up to millions of dollars for a TV spot. The great thing about Facebook is that you can advertise for dirt cheap! Of course, you have to know what you are doing. If you are spending $20 a day advertising and not getting results, you may as well gather a pile of cash and light it on fire. But luckily after you read this book you'll be armed with the knowledge you need to make ads that work at low cost.

You can literally start running ads on Facebook for as little as $2.50 per day.

We can see the benefits by looking at the cost to reach 1,000 people using different types of media:

- Newspaper: $32
- Magazine: $20
- Radio: $8
- Cable TV: $7
- Google Adwords: $2.75
- Facebook: $0.25

Now, the thing is – you can't approach a radio station and say "I'd like to run an advertisement that will reach 1,000 people. Here is my check for $8". If you run an ad on the radio – you must target the entire audience. Which is one reason that the traditional methods of advertising are so expensive?

Of course, costs are going to vary. Every time that you launch a Facebook advertising campaign, it's not going to come in at the $0.25 cents per 1,000 people range. But there is no doubt that it's going to be cheaper than traditional advertising methods and even Google Adwords, which quite frankly has grown a lot more expensive over the years. Also while you can't control the number of people reached using Radio or TV, with Facebook that's actually something that you'll be able to tune.

You are in Control

Facebook ads are under your direct control at all times. You can turn them on and off at will, so run ads when it's most relevant. You can also kill campaigns that don't work quickly. Imagine if you had spent $10,000 on a magazine ad in the old days. You'd probably have to wait 2-3 months before it even ran. Then you'd have to sit back and see how it worked out. If the ad was a dud, you were out of luck.

With Facebook, you can run an advertisement for a day, and then kill it if it didn't generate any prospects. Then you can make adjustments and have a new ad up in running in a few minutes. With that magazine ad, you'd have to make tweaks and wait another 2 months – while spending another $10,000. In today's fast-paced electronic world that kind of delay would be fatal to a new business.

Global Reach

Earlier we mentioned that you can use Facebook for laser targeting. So maybe you only want to advertise to people that live in the Orange County region near Los Angeles. You can do that with Facebook. But if instead, you want to advertise to people in North America, Europe, and China, you can do that too. Or you can even run ads worldwide. Whatever you choose, Facebook makes it easy.

Even better, it's very easy to target ads by location. If you need to, you can have specific ad creatives that are targeted to each of your primary geos. Try and imagine how many millions of dollars it would cost to run a global television advertising campaign. On Facebook, you reach a worldwide audience for a few dollars a day and a few clicks of the mouse.

Your Customers are on Facebook

OK, we won't keep harping on this – but more than two billion people are on Facebook. In the United States and Canada, it's fair to say *everyone* is on Facebook. It doesn't matter what product or service you sell – your customers *are* on Facebook. This isn't even debatable. Even if you are targeting seniors – while the share of the demo on Facebook will be lower – there are still large numbers of them using Facebook that you can reach.

Retargeting and Return Visitors

One thing that Facebook lets you do is advertise to people that have visited your site but not converted into customers. If they visited the site they do have some interest. You can warm them into buyers at low cost using Facebook advertising.

The Power of the Pixel

The Facebook Pixel might be second only to lookalike audiences when it comes to powerful advertising tools. The Pixel is a bit of code that you can add to your web pages that will track what your users are doing. Imagine being able to assemble a database of users who visited your website, added something to a shopping cart, and then left the site without actually placing an order. Then since everything is integrated, you can run a quick Facebook ad campaign to bring them back to your site to complete the order. Of course, it's not going to work with everyone, but it's going to boost your sales, that much we can say for sure.

If you don't have your own personally managed website and are using a third party tool like Drupal, Wix, or Wordpress, the good news is that Facebook has you covered here too. These companies have become partners of Facebook and installation of the pixel can be done practically automatically. It even works with Shopify.

If working with code seems too complicated for you, Facebook makes it easy to get the code to a developer that you specify so that they can integrate it into your website for you.

Media Creatives

You can target Facebook users with video, slideshows, single images, or carousels that mix video and images together. Multiple creative types mean more ways to create ads and do A/B testing to find out what really works with your customer base. If you don't have your own images, Facebook provides stock images that you can use in ads. Slide shows are a low tech way to up the game for your single image creatives, and carousels allow you to mix various single image and video creatives together into a single ad. They also have a "video creation kit". If you don't have a video available, you can upload or select still images that Facebook will use to create a video with some special effects that make it look professionally produced.

Interactivity

Facebook ads operate like regular posts. So the viewer can comment, like the post, share it, or post a reaction. The ability to have an interaction with the ad is a major advantage – and obviously not something you could do with a TV, radio or magazine ad. You can even respond to comments people leave if you like and you might find people who are commenting getting into their own discussions. Imagine having the ability to directly answer a question someone leaves on your advertisement, in near real time.

Customer Feedback

To run ads on Facebook, you will need to have a Facebook page. This will provide you with a free customer center that you can use to communicate directly with prospects as if you were their Facebook friend. It will also give you a ready to use site where customers can give you feedback or file complaints and request help. You can also speak directly to your customers when doing research, asking them to offer their opinions on changes you're going to make or new products you're thinking about bringing to market. Keep it active and keep it engaged.

Sharing

We just mentioned that people can share your ad – so if you have a good ad it could even "go viral". That can mean a whole lot of eyeballs on your advertisements free of charge. Even if it doesn't, some people are going to share your ad which means your ad will get in front of more people – and the customers are doing the work for you.

Well, that does it for our list of reasons you should advertise on Facebook. Hopefully, you're convinced! There are probably many more reasons but we think these are sufficient.

CHAPTER 3
Getting Started On Facebook

In this chapter, we'll learn about some basics you need to set up in order to take full advantage of the Facebook advertising platform. We'll begin by looking at Facebook pages, basic ad setup, types of campaigns, and budgeting.

Facebook Pages

A Facebook page is basically a web page that you set up on Facebook. It's free to set up and provides a platform you can use to "share" information. Like everything else on Facebook, it has a stream where you can add posts. It also has an About page and you can upload photos and buttons. The buttons can be used to set up interactivity with your users, such as prompting them to sign-up for an email list. In short, a Facebook page is like another Facebook profile, but for your business.

In order to set up a Facebook page, you need to have a Facebook profile for yourself. Don't worry though, Facebook keeps the pages you create separation from your personal profile. None of your friends and family will see the Facebook page unless you invite them to it. You may, or may not, want to invite your Facebook friends to like the page. That will depend on your specific situation and the product or service you're offering. Conversely, visitors to your page can't link it back to your personal profile, unless you want to explicitly reveal that information.

A Facebook page is required to run advertisements on Facebook. As we'll see, when you create a Facebook ad it's going to ask you which Facebook page you're linking the ad too. You can have one or multiple Facebook pages, and they can all be for different products, businesses, or personalities. The personalities can be "pen names" if that suits your purpose.

Besides being required to launch a Facebook ad, a Facebook page provides many advantages on its own. When someone likes your Facebook page, it shows up on their feed. So friends and family will see that the person has liked the page, and those who have similar interests might decide to visit your page as well.

Moreover, once someone has liked your page, it's as if your business has become a "friend" on Facebook. Think about how Facebook operates. When someone becomes your "friend", every time they post something on Facebook it shows up on your feed. If you have the mobile app with notifications turned on, these posts will ding your phone and show up like text message alerts on your screen.

A Facebook page operates in the same way. Every time you post on a Facebook page, the post will show up in the feeds of people who have liked the page. Relevant content will draw eyeballs from their friends, who may be drawn to like your page or to share it with others. This can start a snowball effect that could become viral, but at the very least will give you extra exposure even if it doesn't become one of the world's most popular postings.

Facebook pages can be used in conjunction not only with advertisements but to establish a wide internet presence. We suggest that you also set up two other avenues where you can post content and link them all together:

- Start a blog
- Start a YouTube channel

This provides a way to start backlinking and widening your presence online. For example, the following technique will be very helpful for promoting your business without spending extra money.

- Write a blog post
- Post the blog article to your Facebook page

An even better approach would be:

- Create a short video relevant to some problems your product or service solves.
- Post it on YouTube. In the video description, place a link to your Facebook page, and a link to your blog.
- Now write an article on your blog about the topic. It can be very short, but be sure to include your YouTube video in the post, with a link at the end of your article to the video.
- Then go to your Facebook page, and create new post linking to your blog article.

These techniques will help boost your blog and YouTube channels, and vice versa – attracting more traffic to your Facebook page. Backlinking will help drive some organic traffic over time.

We suggest doing this at least three times per week. The more you post, the more traffic you're going to get over time, but if you are focusing on paid Facebook traffic then you don't need to break your back using organic methods. The key to building and keeping a good customer base, however, is continually providing them with some useful content. This also helps build trust in the marketplace and establishes you as an authority figure in your niche, which will help make your advertising campaigns more successful.

A central approach to making this work is knowing what keywords to target. Jump on Google and search for "Google Keyword Planner". You can use this tool to find keywords that people are searching for related to your business. Then you can build a series of articles based on the keyword.

Let's suppose that we are an attorney offering bankruptcy services. Looking at Google Keyword Planner, we can identify several relevant keywords/phrases that we can use to write blog posts, make short videos about, and post both to our Facebook page:

- Filing bankruptcy chapter 7
- Bankruptcy attorney
- Bankruptcy lawyer
- Debt consolidation programs
- How to get out of debt
- When to declare bankruptcy
- Filing chapter 13
- Bankruptcy attorney near me
- Bankruptcy information

And on and on. For each phrase, you should use the phrase in the title, two or three times in the article (or in the case of YouTube, the video description), and in the tags on the blog post and YouTube video. After you've posted your video and/or blog post to your Facebook page, you can also post related content from others on your Facebook page, and use that as an excuse to link back to your article.

Prepping for Running Ads
What you don't want to do, is have users show up at your Facebook page when you start running ads and have nothing on it. Even if you're starting from scratch, you want it to look like there is an established online presence. With that in mind, you should aim to put at least ten posts on your Facebook page before you run the first advertisement that is uniquely yours. Don't start posting content from others until you've started building up a base of people who have liked your page. It's better if you keep your content original rather than posting other people's content. And while outsourcing is a possibility, it's also a risk. At least, in

the beginning, you want to be the one posting on the Facebook page so it will sound more genuine and also not like someone who speaks English as a second language wrote a post based on researching Wikipedia.

Aside: Starting a Blog

By far the easiest way to start a blog is to register with wordpress.com. You can take the free route or get a domain name. The point of the blog isn't to make money, its to provide substantial uniquely created content to add to your Facebook page. It's very easy to use and you don't have to bother with installing WordPress on a website. If you don't want to use wordpress.com, you can get a website on BlueHost or GoDaddy and then install Wordpress there fairly easily, but you might have to pay for a decent looking theme for the blog if you go that route.

Outsourcing Content

Some readers will be comfortable making their own content. But if you aren't or simply don't have time, you can outsource content creation at a low cost. The main site to use for this is Fiverr. You can find people who will write articles or make videos for you for a few bucks. Also, if you're not a good speaker on camera, Fiverr has plenty of voice professionals that you can hire for low prices. They can just read a script for you and put it in an audio file that can be overlaid on a video in a program like iMovie.

For video or written content, you can simply provide a sketch of what you want to be included in the content and tell them what keywords you are targeting. Many are SEO experts so will know how to write your articles so that they are well on search engines and get some organic traffic.

How to Create Your Facebook Page

Now let's go through the steps required to create the Facebook page. You're going to need two images, one for a profile picture and one for the "cover photo" which appears at the top of the page.

- Open up Facebook.com.
- On the left side, look for *Explore.*
- Click on *Pages.*
- This will open a new page showing pages you've liked.
- In the upper right, click on the *Create Page.*
- There are two choices, *Business or Brand* and *Community or Public Figure.*
- Choose the page type most appropriate for your situation – for authors, the public figure might be more appropriate for example.
- If you select Business or Brand, you'll be asked to name the page. You'll probably want to think of a name for your page ahead of time.

- You will also be asked to select a category. Start typing and a drop-down list will open. Select the category that most closely fits your business.
- If prompted enter information like your address. You can elect to hide the address from being displayed on the page.
- Next, upload a profile picture. A 200 x 200 px size image is good.
- Finally, you'll be asked for the cover photo. The exact dimensions aren't important but it should be about 2.6 times as wide as high, and at least 820 pixels wide. The exact size displayed on desktop computers is 820 x 312. Keep in mind that the cover photo is displayed as 640 x 320 on smartphones, so you might want the most relevant content in the middle of the image.

Once you complete these steps, your page is now up and running and you're reading to post. Be sure to bookmark it so you can access it quickly. Once it's up and running, you can edit the About page and start making posts. It works exactly like the Facebook you're used to so this is easy to manage. You can even post job openings here, and create an ad directly from the page.

How to Create Your First Ad

Now let's create our first ad. Since you've just created a Facebook page, one of the first ads you'll want to run on Facebook is a page likes campaign. We want to start building a fan base for our business. So before you go forward to this step, follow our previous advice and put at least ten postings on your Facebook page with relevant content related to your product or service. When we run our ad, we want people to see a page that has relevant content.

To create ads, you will go to the Ads Manager page:

https://business.facebook.com/adsmanager/

The page will have a list of campaigns you've created (obviously blank the first time you visit the page) along with the following tabs:

- Account Overview
- Opportunities
- Campaigns
- Ad sets for one campaign
- Ads for 1 campaign

The levels of the tree are a little bit confusing to new users, we will discuss these in more detail in the chapter on the Ads Manager. For now, draw your attention to the green *Create* button on the left side of the screen. This is what we use to create new campaigns.

When you click Create, You will see three broad categories:

- Awareness
- Consideration
- Conversion

Under Awareness, the options are:

- Brand Awareness
- Reach

For Consideration, we have:

- Traffic
- Engagement
- App Installs
- Video Views
- Lead Generation
- Messages

Finally, under Conversion we have:

- Conversions
- Catalog Sales
- Store Traffic

Seeing all these choices, it can be daunting to know what kind of campaign you need to run (unless you have a mobile app business, and are running an App Installs campaign). Here are some basic rules.

Traffic is simply a campaign that directs people who see your advertisement to a specific website. In particular, you use traffic to drive traffic *outside* of Facebook.

If you have a Shopify store or are selling on Amazon, then your most relevant advertisements might be:

- Catalog Sales
- · Store Traffic

If you have a brand you just want to make people aware of – maybe you sell barbecue sauce that's for sale in the grocery store, then brand awareness or reach might be the type of campaign that you should run.

If you're looking to build an email list of prospects, then Lead Generation or Traffic will work for you.

For our purposes right now, *Engagement*, which is located under *Consideration*, is the type of campaign we want to use. An Engagement campaign can be used for the following three purposes:

- Post Engagement: If you're interested in driving traffic to a specific post you've made on Facebook, then this is the option you should select.
- Page Likes: This is the type of campaign we will use in this example. It will get people engaged with the Facebook page you created and hopefully, garner a large number of page likes so that you'll be connected on Facebook with your prospects.
- Finally, there are events.

Click on the Page Likes button that you see on your screen in the middle. Now edit the Campaign Name field to give it a meaningful name. The default is engagement, we can change it to something like "Pagename(that you created) Page Likes".

If you want to create an A/B test – you can turn this switch on. But we'll leave it off for now. Finally, you can create multiple ad sets within a campaign. Each ad set has its own budget settings, but you can turn to Optimize budget across ad sets to spread the budget across the multiple ad sets (if you create more than one) and have it optimize the spending.

Frankly, I prefer to do things manually, in the sense of setting up individual campaigns and test them against each other rather than using the built-in A/B testing and optimization. Doing it manually is actually pretty simple, and you can turn off and delete campaigns that don't work. So we'll select Page Likes and click on *Continue* at the bottom of the page. The next page that opens on our screen is where we select the page that we want to advertise, you will see this at the very top where it says Page☐Facebook Page☐Select Page. Just click open the drop-down list and you'll see the page you created there.

Next, we will see the *Audience* section. We aren't going to worry about this right now until we've reviewed *Audience Insights*. But you can create an audience of targeted prospects here, or used a previously saved audience. However, as we'll see in a minute, even without selecting an audience or having one ready, we can laser target our prospects.

The next section is your Locations. If you click to open the drop-down list, it gives you the following options:

- Everyone in this location
- People who live in this location (the default)
- People recently in this location
- People traveling in this location

The last option is a really interesting one – great to use if you have a tourist related business. For example, if you have a bed and breakfast, you could run advertisements in your area targeting people who are traveling.

Next, it has a default location setup. If you are in the United States, that is what it will have there (and ditto for your country if you live outside the United States). If desired, you can add multiple countries to the list. Simply click on *Include* and start typing the name of the country, city, or state that you want to include. You can also exclude locations using this entry.

If you want to zoom in on a precise location and advertise within a certain radius, use this method. When you click on the Include input box, you will notice that a map appears below it. You can pan around the map and click the + button to zoom in. Then, click *drop pin* once with your mouse, and click once on the location on the map you want. The default radius is 10 miles (or km). If you click that open, a slider bar will open that you can use to adjust the radius from the pin location where you want your advertisement to be displayed. The range is 1 to 50 miles.

If you've entered a location you decide you don't want, simply hover your mouse over the location in the list and click on the X button on the far right to delete it.

For our example, we entered California for our location, so the add will target people who live in California.

Next, we find general demographic information: Age, Gender, and Language. Select these as appropriate for your target audience. Keep in mind that you can have different advertisements for the same product or service that target males, or females, and/or different age groups.

The next section is *Detailed Targeting.* This is a very important section for your first advertisement. This is where you specify various interests or associations of people that are important or relevant to your product or service. Click the box where it says *Add demographics, interests, or behaviors.* Then simply start typing something relevant.

For example, if we want to target a specific demographic, say U.S. Latinos, you can type in *Hispanic.* You will see multiple options popup, including primary language spoken. For the sake of example, let's say we are a California bankruptcy attorney who wants to target English speaking Hispanics that are interested in getting bankruptcy assistance. First, we click on *Hispanic (U.S. – English dominant).*

You can select as many special interests as you want. Generally, we recommend adding at least five, but it's good to add up to twenty. For our example, we select *Bankruptcy, Consumer Debt, Dave Ramsey,* and *Legal Services.* If you're not familiar with him, Dave Ramsey is a radio personality. We selected Dave Ramsey because he is a personal finance advisor, and people often call his show when they are massively in debt. By targeting people who've visited the Dave Ramsey Facebook page, we might find some prospects who are interested in hiring a bankruptcy attorney.

At the bottom, you have an option to save the audience. If you've made your selections and think you'll want to use them with other advertisements you create, it's a good idea to save the audience.

Next, we come to *Placements.* When you're just starting, we recommend using Automatic Placements. This also works well when you're experienced, because you'll want to test your ads on different placements and then after some testing, you can run the ads for a bit and see which placement's don't work. It's easy to remove them by unchecking the box.

To do that click on Edit Placements. The options you'll see are:

- Facebook
- Instagram
- Audience Network
- Messenger

Within each, there are several subcategories. For Facebook we have:

- Feeds
- Instant Articles

- In-stream videos
- Right column
- Suggested videos
- Marketplace
- Stories

Unless you see your ad is a complete dud on specific items, you'll want to take all placements you're eligible for.

For Instagram, it's a different story. Some ads that work on Facebook won't work on Instagram. One reason is it's simply a platform with a different use, it's based on sharing images. Your product or service may or may not work there. Also, Instagram tends to be skewed toward a younger audience. If you are targeting people aged 18-29, then Instagram might be relevant. If you are targeting people 35+, it's probably not relevant. For Instagram, you can target feed or stories. Stories are short 10-15 second video clips, so an ad can be useful for stories – but that isn't as important as to whether or not your customer base is likely to be on Instagram. Also, people on Instagram probably aren't interested in seeing a video about bankruptcy on their stories, but someone on Facebook will be open to seeing it on their newsfeed. For our example, since we don't think bankruptcy attorney is a good topic to advertise for Instagram, we will deselect it, so that the impressions can be used for Facebook instead of wasting them on Instagram.

Next, we come to the Facebook audience network. This is an off-Facebook advertising option. It's an advertising network in mobile apps. If you are advertising a game or an app, then it's going to be relevant. It's not relevant for a lot of products and services, and can't be used for Page Likes – so we will deselect it.

Finally, you can have ads that show up in people's Facebook Messenger. However, this option isn't available for Page Likes, so we'll deselect it.

Scrolling down you will see that you can select options for mobile devices, operating systems, and whether or not someone is connected to WiFi. Generally, you can ignore these unless you have a mobile app that requires a certain version of iOS. If you have a product you want people to buy on the spot after looking at the ad, it's probably best to turn on the WiFi box. This will ensure that people are either at home or in a location where they are in a position to purchase, rather than running around just glancing at their phone.

Budgeting

Next, we come to the budget. Budget can be set as Daily, or for Lifetime. Usually, you will use the Daily. Facebook provides a suggested budget – however, we are going to ignore it. We'll see why later. For Page Likes, the suggested budget is $25. However, we're going to enter $5 for the daily budget. You can even start at $3.

The reason is that we are going to use the following approach:

- Test
- Scale-up

So for now, set a very low budget. We're going to run the ad and see what happens.

You can run the ad continuously (the default option) or specify that it runs for a specific date range. Either is fine, but don't worry about selecting run continuously, because you can turn ads on and off on the fly from the Ads Manager.

For Bid Strategy, you can use the Lowest Cost, or select a bid cap. For the Lowest Cost, Facebook will try to optimize your campaign. Sometimes this works, sometimes it doesn't. It depends on many factors including how well your audience is targeted. Bid cap can work sometimes as well. You specify the maximum you want to pay. Keep in mind this is not going to be something that works exactly – the system will try to find buyers that it can bid your ad to at that cost. Sometimes it will beat your bid cap but sometimes it will only come close. Also, bid cap campaigns can run pretty slowly compared to the Lowest Cost. It's hard to say ahead of time.

The best thing to do is try both – but for now, select the Lowest Cost. Later we will explain how you can duplicate a campaign. So you can create the Lowest Cost campaign, duplicate it, and then change the Bid Strategy in the copy to bid cap. However note that Facebook suggests a very high bid cap for page likes at $5. You could be getting your page likes for under a dollar. You don't have to take their suggestion, however. Set whatever bid cap you prefer and see how it works.

The last relevant item on this page is when you'll be charged – you can select impressions or per page like. Impressions are probably better but this is something you'll probably want to test in real time.

Finally, click continue so we can set the ad up and enter our creatives.

Next, you'll see *Format* where you can select one of the available options. These may vary depending on the campaign type that you've selected. Generally speaking, the options include:

- Single Image
- Slide show, or a set of images
- Video
- Carousel, where you can mix images and video together

Video is the most effective, but if you don't have a video an image only ad can still work pretty well. Facebook has also recently added some canned "videos" that you can create using image and text that are actually quite nice.

You can upload video and images from your computer, or you can use stock images supplied by Facebook. You have the options of creating six different ads using different images in your campaign.

Scrolling down, you'll have the chance to enter a text message and headline that will appear on the ad (headlines aren't used on Page Like campaigns, however, it displays the name of the page for the headline). You will also be able to preview the appearance of the ad for different placements.

If the ad is designed for traffic to an off-Facebook website, you'll be able to enter the URL of your web page here.

For different campaigns, you will also be able to select the message of the button displayed in the ad. For Page likes there is only a "thumbs up" and no button, but if you run a traffic ad you can select "Learn More" for example, or for app installs you can select "Play Game" or "Install Now". Each choice provides more options for testing to see what works best in your situation.

Finally, scroll down and select "Confirm". Once you do that, the waiting period begins.

What's Next
Facebook will review your ad campaign. Please note that lately because of some scrutiny by government regulators, they are being a little pickier and taking longer to review ads. Be patient, your ad should be up and running soon after submission.

After you've run the campaign, that is just the beginning. Once someone likes your Facebook page, every time you post on it they see it on their feed. So you're going to want to keep generating content on your blog and YouTube and routinely post it to your Facebook page, at least 2-3 times per week. This will keep your prospects interested and actively engaged, and prompt them to share your posts and get you some organic prospects free of charge.

Ad Rejections
Sometimes Facebook will reject an ad. In these situations, it's best to work with the reviewers rather than try arguing. The first step is to carefully review the reasons that they give for disapproving the campaign. To give a specific example, recently I was advertising a diet product and a training course for starting an online business. Both were rejected.

The reason given for the diet ad was that the ad asked a question about weight loss. While it's ridiculous, Facebook said that asking the question was an invasion of privacy. I could have tried arguing, but instead, I reworked the question into a statement that was more indirect. They approved the ad.

The second campaign ran into trouble because Facebook didn't really understand what the training was about. They said that ads promoting "get rich quick schemes" and MLM or work from home were not allowed. So before resubmitting the ad, which drove traffic to a website, I put in an explicit disclaimer on the website that it was not a "get rich quick" method. I had also mentioned that you would work from home running an internet business in the ad but removed that text. Then I wrote the Facebook review team and pointed them to this disclaimer, and then also explained that the training was not an MLM scheme and why. I also made it clear I had removed the work from home reference, to show I was paying attention to what they were telling me. About an hour later the ad campaign was approved.

So if your advertisement is rejected, take a few minutes to review Facebook's ad policies and then write a calm and concise letter to the review team explaining why your ad campaign is compliant with their policies. If you have to make some adjustments to the ad text or your video/image, do so and let them know that you've made changes to bring the ad into compliance.

Remember – it's their platform and they make the rules, and our ability to advertise on their platform is a privilege, not a right. So the review team is "always right", even if they are being ridiculous.

Summary

So now we've found out how to create a Facebook ad with an associated Facebook page. Remember that you are going to need a Facebook page, period, for all your advertising activities. Also remember that to get the most out of your campaigns, follow these steps:

- Create a blog. It doesn't have to be fancy, but just a place where you can park period content. But to launch post at least 7-10 articles. They don't have to be long, we're just creating them for the purpose of being able to put linked content on the Facebook page.
- Create a YouTube channel for your business, and upload 1-3 videos (tip-install VidIQ to your browser, it's free and gives you a lot of insight on YouTube including what keywords others are using).
- If you are not the creative type, Spend $50 to have freelancers on Fiverr write articles and make videos for you.
- At this point, create your Facebook page. Create ten individual posts for each article and video you created in the first two steps to give your page some content.
- Run your Facebook ad campaign for page likes.
- After you start building a following, keep posting material on the Facebook page, about 3 times per week.

CHAPTER 4
Targeting And A/B Testing

In the last chapter, we went through the steps required to set up your first ad. As part of that process, we touched on targeting. In this chapter, we're going to explore utilizing targeting in conjunction with testing. Although people usually say "A/B Testing" for our purposes it will really be A/Z testing and maybe beyond, depending on how many factors you want to vary.

The goal is to drive advertising costs down by increasing conversion rates. Facebook is really good for advertising, so you can just throw ads up and if they are reasonably targeted they are going to get page likes, web traffic, opt-ins or app installs, whatever the case may be in your particular set of goals. However, there is a huge difference in advertising budgets when you're talking about paying $1 to get someone to visit your web page versus paying $0.19.

For the purposes of targeting, we can break down several parts of the ad campaign that we need to look at.

Location
The first targeting strategy is the location. In one of my ad campaigns, I advertise a slot machine game that I made for the iPhone. These have international popularity, however, you make more money in some locations ("geos" in the lingo of global advertising) than in others. Another factor is that different cultures are going to respond to advertisements in different ways.

So it would be foolish to throw up a global campaign with the same ad creative, bid, and daily budget.

In my case, breaking down ads by location in the following way was the best approach. In other words – I would create ad campaigns for these locations, and then they would be varied in some way tailored to the local market:

- The United States and Canada
- Australia and New Zealand
- Hong Kong
- Japan
- United Kingdom

- Western Europe
- Mexico

So I'd need seven campaigns, not just one campaign, to advertise my game. Location may or may not impact your product or service. Let's suppose you're a real estate agent in Phoenix. You could advertise in Phoenix hoping to find clients to come to look at your house.

Or – you could advertise in Phoenix, in the entire state of Arizona, and also nationwide. The first step in designing an ad campaign might be to look up the top five states that provide immigration to Arizona. I'm not going to actually do it for the book, but you might find that the states were something like California, New York, Pennsylvania, Texas, and Ohio.

This suggests that we might want to run ads in those states as well. At first, it's going to be a little bit rough. But here are some things you could consider if you were setting up these campaigns.

First, you create a campaign and set the location targeting to the state of New York. Then under interests, you add the following:

- Arizona
- Moving company
- Real estate broker
- Real estate
- Coldwell Banker
- Century 21

Notice that by tying these interests together, we might be able to put together an audience made up of people living in New York who may be interested in buying a home in Arizona.

On your first run, it's going to be a little rough. Kind of like throwing darts in the ocean. However, over time you're going to start picking up interested customers. And the important thing about this –while those prospects are important too – is creating a database of characteristics of people responding to the ad. You can then use this to create a lookalike audience. We discuss that in detail in chapter 9, for now, we just need to note that this is something you can build up with the data.

Without actually running these ad campaigns it's hard to know if creating separate campaigns for all five states is really necessary, and that might make the demo too small. This is something that is going to vary considerably depending on your product or service and target demo. So in this case, we might instead create just three campaigns:

- Phoenix metro
- Arizona statewide
- Out of state targeting NY, CA, OH, etc.

I'd be inclined to limit my out of state targeting to the top five states, however. Advertising in Utah or Colorado if hardly anyone moves from those states to Arizona would be wasting effort and advertising funds.

Basic Demographics

The next thing to look at for targeted ads is age, gender, and language (if applicable). The reality is that different age groups and genders respond differently to advertising pitches. Also, younger people (under the age of 30) are more likely than other age groups to be on Instagram. If your product or service targets people under the age of 30, you might want to create a separate campaign for that age group, so that you can create one for older demographics that leaves Instagram out. If you are advertising beauty products, you probably don't want to waste time and money showing the ads to males.

It may be that you don't need to break out ad campaigns to specifically target these base demos. But if you feel a need to do so, you will need to create campaigns broken down by each group PLUS the location breakdowns above, if you made them. So using our previous example, we could create ad sets in the following way:

- Phoenix Metro, males
- Phoenix Metro, females
- Arizona statewide, males
- Arizona statewide, females
- Out of state, males
- Out of state, females

If you were selling a home, then the 13-29 age group probably isn't relevant. So you'd probably want to set your age to be at least 30 in this case. If you were advertising apartment rentals, then you'd be more likely to advertise to 18-29-year-olds and block people 35 and older instead.

On the other hand, if you were marketing a video game, then including the younger demographic would be more important. Note that Facebook may have certain restrictions for advertising to those under the age of 18.

That can come off as exploitative, so I'd advise in not doing it unless you have a product specifically targeted at that age group.

Placements
Depending on your main target demo, you might look at placements as well. We've mentioned several times that Instagram may not be suitable for many types of ad campaigns. Another thing to consider is placement on mobile devices. Now it's true that millions of people over the age of 65 are using iPhones and iPads, but it's also true that someone 65+ is less likely than a young person to be doing so. Suppose that your real estate business was specifically targeted at retirees. Do you want to be showing all your impressions on iPhones? Maybe not – so in that case, it might be better to select Desktop for your selection of devices.

Of course, you should always let the market speak to you. So we've created this theory that people aged 65+ are not going to be on mobile very much and are more likely to respond to an ad targeted only at the desktop. The only way to really know is to run two campaigns. One that targets all devices, and one that specifically targets the desktop. Then the data will tell us if we need to make this distinction. We might even find that our hypothesis is false and that we actually need to advertise to people 65+ on mobile devices.

Budget Settings
When it comes to budget settings, there is only one area that we will look at for A/B testing. This is "Lowest Cost" (according to Facebook) and Bid Cap. You'll want to set up one campaign for each. For the Lowest Cost, there isn't anything to do other than let it run. For bid cap, we might experiment with our choice of cap. Remember that you should probably just ignore the suggestion that Facebook gives you. My suggestion is put in the price that you want to pay. If you run the campaign and it doesn't get any results or show enough impressions, then slowly raise the bid. Start with your ideal price.

Using the example of app installs, I know from experience that 85 cents are a workable price in the United States. However, if I were setting up a brand new campaign, I'd start off low – say 55 cents – and see how it worked out. Assuming that it started off really slow, each day I would raise the bid 10 cents. By the end of the first week, the campaign should be in a situation where it's doing well at a price that is far more acceptable than that proposed by Facebook.

Here are the rules of thumb to follow:

- Never accept the suggested bid cap that Facebook gives you.
- Start low, and don't expect results immediately.
- Slowly raise the bid, about 10 cents per day (you can even try 5 cents per day)
- When the ad is delivering a level of results you want, then leave the bid cap alone and start raising your daily budget.

Creative Types

When discussing ad creatives, there are two ways that you can vary the ad for targeting. These are:

- Creative types
- The actual creatives themselves

The first choice for creative types is whether or not we are going to use a static image or a video. Using a static image certainly works – however, the trend is definitely toward video. It's not very hard to make a good video. You might make a video of yourself just using the webcam making a pitch for some offer. Or you could make a slideshow on Keynote or Powerpoint and record it with narration. If you are not up to making your own videos, hire someone on Fiverr to make a video for you at low cost.

But if the video is out of the question, you can go with an image.

The ideal situation is to do more A/B testing. Create an advertising campaign that uses an image, and then create one that has a video. Then run them for a week and compare results.

Now, of course, you can see that the deeper we get, the more reasons there are to do A/B testing. Are you going to stop at one video? Hopefully, you don't have that constraint – but if you do we hope you are able to launch your campaign anyway. However, in the ideal case, you're definitely going to want to be able to test multiple videos in your ad campaigns. You should have at least three different videos to test. But the more the better.

You are also going to want to test them against the other breakdowns you've used. It might be more productive to have different videos that target males, and females for example. Or maybe if you're targeting by age group you'll have different videos for major age breakdowns. At least 18-29 versus 35+.

Using our real estate example, you can see that you're probably going to be running a totally different advertisement that targets people already living in the Phoenix metropolitan area as opposed to out of state residents. And when targeting out of state residents, you might need a different ad that targets someone moving from New York as opposed to someone moving from California. For someone moving from New York, you might want to be emphasizing the weather, and how it rarely if ever snows in Arizona. But that really isn't much of a selling point for someone coming from California, so for them, you might emphasize the lower cost of living, less pollution, and maybe less traffic. The specifics here aren't important, what is important is that you start thinking about how to develop advertising creatives that address the special needs of your different targets.

Headlines and Text

By now, your head may be spinning. We've already built up a pretty large number of ways that ad campaigns can and should be varied. Now we have two more – testing headlines and text.

The first thing is to look at the text. You can add a significant amount of text, so don't feel you have to restrict it to just a couple of lines. You don't want to overwhelm the prospect with the ad, it's just a vehicle to get them on your pages or captured as a lead. But you can write as much text as you believe is necessary.

Remember that Facebook is *interactive*. For that reason, one thing I like to do is make the ads in such a way as to encourage interaction. The more you do that, you start getting comments and the increased engagement leads to more shares, helping get you free traffic and publicity.

A simple way to do that is to ask a question. For an ad I might create for my slot machine game, I might say:

How would it feel to win 10 million bonus coins?

The type of question you ask will depend on the target demographic. Yes, I know there are some stereotypes but there is some truth to them too. Women, on average, are going to respond more to questions that ask about emotions and feelings. It turns out that players of slot machine games are around 60-65% female, and so I tailor my ads with that in mind. But asking the question is likely to get some people viewing the ad to post a response.

Your prompt doesn't have to be a question. It can be a statement that helps someone visualize something.

For the Arizona ad, we could make an ad targeting people moving from New York making a statement such as:

Imagine enjoying snow free moderate winters.

If the person viewing the ad is thinking of moving from upstate New York to the southwest, this statement is going to immediately trigger an interest – and help them visualize themselves enjoying January in 65 degree sunny temperatures.

Another copywriting technique that people use is a phrase that implies some type of unknown secret is being revealed that will solve a problem someone is having. This should be followed by a statement of benefits and a time within which the people can meet their goal. It should also include the word "guaranteed".

For example:

Discover the new low carb diet guaranteed to make you lose 14 pounds in the first two weeks, sleep better, and have more energy than you've had in years.

Notice that we've implied that a secret is being revealed by using the word "Discover". Then we give three specific results – lose 14 pounds, sleep better, and have more energy. This information is provided with a specific time frame of two weeks.

There is less room for the headline, so I keep my questions or longer ad copy in the text section, and try to make my headlines impactful and short. The headline should take on a more mundane but important role of giving a clear description of what you're offering or the type of business. Examples of headlines:

- New Slot Machine Game on iOS
- Bankruptcy Attorney with 20 Years Experience
- Custom Designed Handbags for Women

Now we aren't done. You're not going to come up with one clever statement or question – you're going to try coming up with five. And then we are going to A/B test all of them.

Carrying out you're A/B testing
After you've figured out all the variations you can test, then it's time to run your campaigns. You should probably have about 20 variations that

you have to build into 20 different ad campaigns. Although Facebook lets you create multiple ad sets within a campaign and so on, I find it easier to just create the first campaign and then duplicate it so that I can see everything from the main screen. But you can do what works for you.

After you create your campaign, you will see it listed on the Ads Manager. Hover your mouse over it and you will see a *Duplicate* option. Click on it and Facebook will make a Duplicate for you. Open it up and give the campaign of the clone a new meaningful name. For example, if our first campaign was called Real Estate – Phoenix Metro, we would create a duplicate and then name it Real Estate – New York.

After you've given it a name that identifies what you're varying, then edit the campaign to put your variation in. In this case, we'd go to Location and change it from Phoenix to the state of New York, and then we'd go to the Engagement/Creative Section to make changes that are appropriate for the testing.

The program you should follow goes like this:

1. Create your 20 clones and set all the variations you want to test.
2. Set your daily budgets low – you can try $3-5.
3. Let the campaigns run for at a minimum of 3 days. Five days is best.
4. At the end of five days, analyze your campaigns.

After five days, you'll want to weigh the following items:

- The number of results per campaign.
- Total money spent.
- Cost per result.
- Click through rate and other factors might also be important, but the top three are the most important.

For the real estate ads, we should have created a few ads that target New York residents looking to move. They might vary by text or video creative. Some will perform, some will not.

- Turn off all ads that don't perform.
- Any ad that has a cost per result of more than $1 after five days should be shut down.
- Any ad that isn't getting more than 5 results per day should be shut down.

If you started with 20 ads, you can probably whittle it down to 5-8 ads by the end of the week. So now you have ad campaigns that should be able to work for you. At the low budgets, we've set they probably aren't bringing in nearly as many prospects as you'd like. So the next step is to start ramping up budgets:

- Increase your budget slowly – about 15% per day.
- Leave it set for at least 24 hours before raising again.
- Keep raising it until you're getting the number of impressions and results that you're seeking.

This procedure works. If you're brand new, it might take a few rounds to make it work but if you follow it over time you'll be an expert at getting low-cost prospects for your business.

CHAPTER 5
Audience Insights

In this chapter, we are going to discuss an important research tool that you can use to create various "audiences" to target with your ad campaigns. Facebook calls its *Audience Insights*. To find it, click on *Ads Manager* in the upper left corner of the window. Then you should see the following options:

- Ads Manager
- Analytics
- Audience Insights

Click on Audience Insights and a new screen should open. The first thing you are going to see though is a little popup window that has two choices:

- Everyone on Facebook
- People connected to your page

After you've been running ads for a while, you may want to select *People Connected to your page*. However, that isn't going to be useful at the beginning. You will need to collect a significant amount of data before Facebook can show you that information. So for now, we'll start with Everyone on Facebook.

Location
The page is divided into three major sections. First, call your attention to the left sidebar. This is a toolset you can use to filter out your demographics. It's not all that different from the filtering options that we've seen when creating our first advertisement. At the very top of the left sidebar, you will see a *Locations* tab. The default selection is going to be your home country, for me, it says the United States. If you hover your mouse above the input box but below the default location you will see that you can switch to exclusion targeting – if that is useful. The default setting is inclusion, so when it shows the United States it shows all people living in the United States.

If you click on the Exclude option, this will open up a popup window. So for example, I could start with the United States, and then exclude California if I chose to do so.

Just to the right of Location, you will notice that it gives audience size and age and gender demographics. Just for fun, try deleting the United States or your home country and see how the data changes. When you have the United States selected, for example, you will see:

- Audience size 200-260 million active people
- 54% women, 46% men

If you delete the United States, you'll see the global data:

- Now it changes to more than 1 Billion active people
- The demographic has shifted, now it's 57% men, and 43% women

So you can see that demographics may vary considerably from country to country. If you are doing advertising internationally this could be a very important piece of information.

Age and Gender
Returning to the left sidebar, the next thing we find below location is Age and Gender. You can select a specific age range, gender, or some combination thereof. There are many ways in which you will find this helpful as we'll see, but on a gross level, it will give you a measure of your market size (for example how many women aged 35+ are on Facebook).

You can also target by moving your mouse over the graphics in the center of the page. Facebook has broken down age and gender demographics into the key marketing groups. This information will tell you what percentage of Facebook users are in each group. Something interesting to note for example – is that the percentage of women on Facebook in the United States breaks down with about the same number aged 18-24 and 65+ - at 14% and 13%, respectively.

Before we look at more items on the left sidebar, let's take a look at the center of the screen. Facebook has broken down the demographics in the following additional ways:

- Relationship status
- Education level
- Job title

So for example, we find that 53% of women in the United States who are active Facebook users are married, and 62% of them have attended college. If you zoom in on the 45-54 age group by clicking on the bar in the Age/Gender chart area, you find that 69% are married and 60% have attended college. In contrast, among those aged 25-34 only 42% are married but 67% have attended college. These bits of information may be useful for your business activities.

You can scroll down to the bottom and look at Job Title for some more interesting information. It will tell you what percentage of the selected demographic has what job title, and how that compares to the overall Facebook audience.

For example, for females aged 35-44 living in the United States, we find that 12% work in "community and social services" which compares to 7% working in this field for the Facebook audience at large. If you switch to men on Facebook aged 35-44 who live in the United States, you'll see that 4% work in the community and social services. This illustrates how you might analyze the characteristics of audiences to better target your advertising.

You can also select different cities to see how the demographics change. So using our previous example in the last chapter where we considered real estate advertising for Phoenix and reaching out of state, we might check the demographics of people in the different areas first, to get ideas about how we are going to target our advertising and what creatives we would consider using.

Interests
Now, return to the left sidebar and click on the Interest textbox. This actually works in a similar fashion to browsing interests when you create an ad campaign. When you first click on it, if you don't type anything in it will populate with a large number of categories that you can browse to see if they are of any relevance.

There are two ways you can explore interests to create audiences. You can do the browsing method and select among the given categories. These include:

- Business and Industry: You could use this to try and target people that worked in specific occupations. Examples – Banking or engineering.
- Entertainment: Includes a wide variety of entertainment categories. For example, you can select games and then pick out people that like to play board games, or people that like casino games. You can also select other options such as movies, TV, live events.

- Family and Relationships: Has multiple important categories. Including Motherhood, Dating, Family, Friendship, etc. Suppose you had a book on dating – you could use this to target your demographic.
- Fitness and Wellness: In this section, you'll find different physical activities listed, like weight training or yoga.
- Hobbies and Activities: Covers a wide range, from an interest in various kinds of pets to political activities.
- Shopping and Fashion: Includes Beauty, Clothing, Fashion Accessories, Shopping, and Toys.
- Sports and Outdoors: Includes outdoor recreation with subcategories and various sports activities.
- Technology: Last but not least people obsessed with their electronic gadgets, or maybe people that work on them.

Note that many of the listings include lots of subcategories. From this listing, you can see that you can drill down quite a bit into many different characteristics that will help you target your advertising. For example, you could write a book on the PE or Professional Engineering exam, and then advertise it to engineers aged 25-44 in the United States (younger engineers will be less likely to already be PE's).

As we demonstrated when creating our first ad campaign, you aren't limited to these categories. You can drill down even more by simply typing in words or phrases that might be relevant. For example, if we were targeting people interested in "Dating", we could use the browsing capability to select that. However, if you type "Dating" in the input box you see a lot more options pop up:

- Online dating service
- Speed dating
- Interracial dating
- Etc.

What approach should you use? Both of course! So select Dating from browse, and then type in dating and select the relevant interests. If we had an eBook we wanted to market to people interested in online, interracial dating, you can see that we could readily target them.

People Connected to Your Page
Just below the Interest section on the left side, we see an option to select either people connected to one of our Facebook pages or People Not Connected to one of our Facebook Pages. If you are just starting you're not going to have enough data for this, but once you build up a few thousand prospects you'll be able to utilize it. Well, of course, you can use

people NOT connected to your Facebook page now because you probably don't have many that ARE connected.

So why utilize this? You don't want Facebook to be showing your ads to people who've already seen them and then opted in by liking your page already. So even if you only have a few users, you might want to select your page for People Not Connected to your Facebook page.

Advanced

Now let's take a look at the Advanced section, which is just below the Page option. This section covers the following areas:

- Language
- Relationship status
- Education
- Work
- Market Segments
- Parents
- Politics (US)
- Life Events

Each of these has multiple subcategories. For example, you can use it to drill down to people who report being single, employed in healthcare and medical services, who are bilingual Hispanic females.

WOW!

Hope that makes your head spin. Remember where we began – talking about throwing up a TV ad that would show your video to everyone living in your hometown – and it would cost you a fortune.

Now for a few dollars, you can drill down big time.

Page Likes

Now return to the top of the page, and look at the tabs that run across the top of the middle section. Click on *Page Likes*.

This section is going to give you some ideas about what your targeted demographic is doing on Facebook in regard to what kinds of pages they are visiting and giving likes to. This information can be utilized to help tailor your messaging.

At the top, you'll see a listing of top categories. For my example, I selected women 25+ who play card games and work as engineers. When I look at categories, some of the items I see are Dollar General, Betty Crocker, Pillsbury, and IKEA. All the items listed in this section are linked, so you can click on them to examine the page in question.

Below this list, you'll see a ranked list of page likes. In my case, the top-ranked page is Screaming Owl. I have no idea what that is so had to open the link to see it's a boutique shop. Other items listed include Big Lots, Toys "R" Us, and Dollar General.

You can change up your demographic to see how the page likes change. Simply switching to men – the boutique shop gets replaced by AR Armor, which is a shop that sells body armor! The second page listed is Alien Gear Holsters – which sells gun holsters.

On the far right, you will see column labeled *Affinity*. This will tell you how much more a given page is liked by your target demographic as compared to the general Facebook audience. For example, the 500 Armor page has an affinity of 55x. That means that the target demo I've selected is 55 times more likely to like the page than the general Facebook audience. It will also give you the total number of likes.

Reverse Engineering
Hopefully, so far we've illustrated how you can use Audience Insights to help you target your audience. But it also should get the wheels turning in your mind. You can reverse engineer and then *develop new products* to target different audiences – by looking at what they are already interested in. The power of the tools Facebook provides advertisers are frankly overwhelming. Knowing that men who are engineers (and a few other characteristics I selected).

Location
Now let's return to the tabs at the top of the page. If you click on the Location tab, you're going to see a listing of the top locations for your targeted demographic. This can be viewed as top cities, top countries, and top languages. For each location, you can hover your mouse over the bar and it will tell you the percentage of your Facebook audience that is in that location, and how that compares to the overall Facebook audience. For my current selections, I find that my top location is Los Angeles. Surprisingly the numbers match up exactly – the proportion of users in Los Angeles in my target demo is the same as the proportion of overall Facebook users in Los Angeles. On the other hand, 1% of the target demo lives in Manhattan, as compared to 2% of all Facebook users.

Activity

Now let's click on the final tab, which is Activity. This tells us what sorts of things related to marketing and promotion the audience is engaged in – such as page likes, Ads clicked or comments posted. Below this, you will find device usage. We can actually use this to check the hypothesis I raised earlier. Remember I suggested that maybe people aged 65+ are more likely, perhaps far more likely to be using desktop computers. To find out for sure, I can filter the Facebook audience for ages 65+ here on Audience insights and then check the Activity tab. I find that:

- 54% are mobile only
- 33% are using mobile + desktop
- 12% are desktop only

Frankly, I find this a bit shocking – so the older people have gone a long way toward adopting mobile – and only a small minority are using Facebook on desktop only. So my assumption was totally wrong.

The lesson here is this – use Audience Insights to check any assumptions you make before creating your ads. Just for fun, let's bring up the 35-44 demographic. Here we find that:

- 69% are mobile only
- 29% are using mobile + desktop
- 3% are desktop only

So while the younger crowd is more oriented toward using mobile for Facebook than the 65+ group, the difference really isn't relevant since the proportion of those ages 65+ using only desktop computers for Facebook are a small minority.

Saving the Audience

Now that you've done all this hard work to put research into developing a useful audience and finding out what they're into, you're going to want to save it rather than just tossing it aside. To do this, go to the very top of the page where you'll see the following options:

- Create New
- Open
- Save
- More (includes Save As... and Take Tour)

Once you save an audience, then you can use it when you create new ad campaigns.

Creating an Advertisement

Now, you can return to the ads manager and create new ad campaigns that use your audience once you save it. However, you should notice that the green Create Ad button is found on the Audience Insights page. So you can go through the research steps and create your audience, save it, and then click on Create Ad and build your new ad campaign right there. So nice of Facebook to make it convenient to spend more money on their platform!

CHAPTER 6
Facebook Pixel

Now we approach the mysterious topic of the Facebook Pixel! We'll find out what the Facebook Pixel is when you want to use, why you want to use it, and if you're going to use it at all.

In short, the Facebook Pixel is an analytics tool you can use to track the behavior of your prospects and customers on your website. It can be used to track their behavior and to determine whether or not you're targeting the right people with your ads. You will also be able to determine if Facebook is really helping your website traffic when you've got traffic coming to the site from multiple sources. The "Pixel" is just a small bit of code that will connect your website to your Facebook ads account. The Facebook Pixel, once installed, can then be "triggered" when people using your website take various actions, like signing up on a form or buying a product.

The pixel will collect a wide range of data, including page headers, IP addresses, and button clicks.

Furthermore, you can create ads that target different actions taken by users on your website. For example, some people might visit your website without actually making a purchase. The Facebook pixel can be used to target those near converting customers who are interested but didn't buy. Maybe they didn't buy because the price is too high for them, so you could run an ad campaign targeting that group offering a coupon code for a reduced price.

You can even target people that engage in actions like watching a video – and maybe they don't finish watching the entire video. Gathering the user data from the pixel you can create an ad campaign reminding them to finish the video.

Another application of the Facebook Pixel is using it to target people who've purchased. Maybe you want to offer them an upsell option. Using the pixel data you can run a campaign offering the upsell.

Facebook provides a complete listing of "standard events" that can be used with the pixel. These include Add to Cart, Add payment information, Contact, Lead/Form Submission, and several others. You can view the entire listing here:

If you're using Facebook to drive mobile app installs, then you're not going to be thinking about the Facebook pixel at all. To run ads for app installs, you'll need to have integrated the Facebook SDK in your app, and that will essentially play the role of the Facebook pixel for you in that context.

OK so now let's turn our attention to the cases when you might not need to use it. For ads generating page likes – you don't need to worry about it because you're working inside Facebook. For all other ads, however, the Facebook pixel might be important.

First a caveat – you are not required to use a Facebook Pixel. However, if you don't use it, then you're going to miss out on a lot of information that it can collect. It just depends on your situation.

Let's take a couple of examples where you might be driving traffic outside Facebook but you don't really need to use the Facebook pixel. The first case we'll consider is email marketing. If you aren't familiar with email marketing, what this involves is driving traffic to a "landing page" which you use to entice people to give you their email address. Typically you'll offer them some kind of freebie in exchange for the email address. If you are marketing says a course on ketogenic dieting, then you can offer them a short ten-page cookbook with ketogenic compliant recipes in exchange for the email address. To do this, you add a landing page to your website or use some kind of page builder that can be linked up to an email list provider like Aweber. The landing page will have a small amount of copy together with a form for people to fill out to get their gift. Once they give you their email address, then you can start sending them emails to sell them on your product.

To do this type of promotion, you will create a Facebook ad campaign and select Traffic, and you'll give the landing page URL as the destination page for the campaign. So when a user clicks after viewing your ad then it will take them right to the landing page where they can sign up to join your email list or simply ignore you.

OK so why wouldn't you want to use the Facebook Pixel in this case? The answer is you don't really need it. All the information you need for this type of campaign is going to be contained both at Facebook and at your email list provider. The two pieces of information of interest for us here would be the number of clicks from our ad campaign, and the number of people who sign up once they hit the landing page. So for the time period that you're running your campaign, you will collect a given number of email addresses that are reported in Aweber or Mail Chimp say, and then you can compare that to the number of clicks your Facebook ad generates. Then you can determine the number of people who visited the page and the number who converted into leads.

So far what we're saying is you don't need a Facebook pixel to gauge the success or failure of your ad campaign. However, there may be cases when running a lead generation campaign like this that you will want to use the Facebook pixel.

The scenario which was described above works fine provided that Facebook is the only ad campaign that you're running. Suppose that instead you're running a lead generation campaign but advertising simultaneously on Facebook, Bing, and YouTube. Then you might have a problem. Maybe you're getting a good amount of organic traffic. In either case, when people start signing up for your email list, you won't know where they came from – so you won't have an idea as to whether or not the Facebook ad campaign was a complete waste of time.

So if you're a beginner and you don't want to dive into the Facebook Pixel right away – and that's fairly understandable since it seems complex – provided that you are not running a bunch of simultaneous campaigns on other networks, you may be able to get away with it, at least for a while.

However, if you want to find out what activity on your website is being driven by Facebook, then installing the Facebook pixel is a very good idea.

Another example where the Facebook Pixel will be useful is for an e-commerce site. The Facebook Pixel can not only help you determine where people visiting your site are coming from and hence whether or not the Facebook ad campaigns are working out for you, but you can detail the activity of people once they get on your site. For example, you can determine whether someone:

- Jumped on your site without adding any products to the shopping cart.
- If they added a product to the shopping cart, then left your site without closing the sale.
- If they entered the payment method and other info, and either bought or didn't buy.
- Product searches.

- Actual purchases.

This can help you determine whether or not advertising on Facebook is something that's worth doing for you. However, I take the position that advertising on Facebook is always worth doing. If it's not working out for you, what you need to do is revisit your ad targeting and make adjustments.

Creating the Pixel
You can open the Ads manager to create your Facebook Pixel. This is accessed from the Ads Manager drop-down list in the upper left corner. Click it open and select "All Tools". You will find "Pixels" under the events manager in the third column on the right-hand side.

Facebook has recently updated the page, so at the time of writing it says "welcome to the new Pixels Page". In the middle of the page, there is a green button that says "Create Pixel". Click on it.

A dialog will open that will give you three options.

- Connect to a Partner Platform (formerly the vague 'tag manager')
- Manually Install the Code Yourself.
- Email instructions to a developer.

The third option is pretty self-explanatory. If you have a developer that manages your website, then you can have Facebook email them the code with instructions and they can install it on your website for you.

Connect to a Partner Platform
A partner platform is some kind of website you're using that has worked with Facebook to help integrate Pixels. For example, several e-commerce platforms have integrated with Facebook to allow you to do this. Some of these include Shopify, WooCommerce, 3dCart, and Ticketmaster. Several site development tools can be integrated with the Facebook pixel used as a partner platform. These include Wordpress, Weebly, Wix, Drupal, and Squarespace.

If you are utilizing Leadpages for email lead generation, then you can use the Connect to a Partner Platform method to integrate your signup forms.

The specific instructions on how to integrate the Facebook pixel will vary by partner. If you are using one of the partners, you can look it up on the Facebook help page listed here:

https://business.facebook.com/business/help/1179210765468894

Click on the link for your partner and it will give you instructions. If yours is not listed then you can access the help for your given platform.

Let's take a look at a couple of examples to see what's involved. First, we'll check WordPress since so many people use the platform for their websites. For WordPress, the Facebook Pixel is built as a WordPress plugin. So you simply download the zip file, and then open up your WordPress Dashboard and go to install and activate the plugin just like you would any other plugin. Now that was pretty simple, right?

For many of the other partners, you will open the Events Manager which is found from the Facebook Ads Manager drop-down menu (this is how you will do most of them). When you open it up, you will see a menu on the left-hand side. Click on Partner Integrations. Then a series of buttons will be displayed in the middle of your screen where you can select the appropriate partner for your situation.

For example, if you have a Shopify account, then you can connect it inside the Facebook Events Manager by clicking the blue Connect Account button.

On your own website
Integrating the Facebook Pixel on your own website isn't really that difficult, but of course, you should seek out developer assistance if you shy away from techie activities. If you are OK with doing it yourself, you can follow the instructions on this page:

https://business.facebook.com/business/help/952192354843755

CHAPTER 7
Introduction To Facebook Ads Manager

In this chapter, we will dive into the Facebook ads manager, which is the "dashboard" for your ad campaigns. The Facebook ads manager can be accessed on this web page:

https://business.facebook.com/adsmanager/

When you open the page, you'll see your ad campaigns listed in a series of rows on the left-hand side. You can click on an ad campaign on the list to View Charts, Edit, or Duplicate. To the right, you will see three tabs: Campaign, Ad Sets, Ads. Facebook has a three-level system.

- The campaign is a top-level
- A campaign can include one or more ad sets
- Each ad set can contain one or more ads

I like keeping things simple so always work at the campaign level. However, if you'd like to add multiple ad variations to one ad set and/or multiple ad sets to each of your campaigns, you can organize things that way. To view the ad sets for a single campaign, select it in the campaigns tab, and this will open the ad sets tab. Here you can duplicate an ad set. If you click on an ad set in the adsets listing, it will move to the ads tab and show you a listing of ads for that ad set. Here you can create new ads within the ad set. Charts can be viewed for campaigns and ad sets. You can also duplicate ads, edit, or view charts for them if you select the ads tab without selecting the ad sets tab.

To understand the different levels, we can start by opening up one campaign. When you do this the editor will slide open from the right-hand side. At the top level, you see the ad campaign. The campaign consists of the following information:

- Campaign Name
- Objective (i.e. page likes, app installs)
- Campaign spending limit (optional)
- Campaign budget optimization (optional)

At the ad set level, you see most of the details that you use to set up your ads. This includes:

- Associated Facebook page
- Budget and Schedule
- Audience (Location, Demographics, Interests)
- Optimization and Delivery

Now let's look at the lowest level, the ad level. This includes:

- Identity (Facebook page used with the ad)
- Creative
- Text and headline
- Call to action (if applicable)

You can duplicate ads within an adset and then use different creatives or test different headlines and text to gauge performance.

Charts

Charts can be viewed to determine performance at the campaign level, ad set level, and ad level.

The charts are divided as follows. At the top, there are three tabs: Performance, Demographics, and Placement. Performance shows a graph with the time of results and cost per result. Demographics produces a bar chart showing age and gender breakdowns, with results and cost per result for every demographic slice. Finally, on the far right, we can look at placements. This shows reach, results, and amount spent for each of the major placements (Facebook, Instagram, Messenger).

Data in the Ads Manager

In addition to the charts, you can review tables of data in the ad manager. There is a long list of columns moving across the page left to right. You can see how many impressions your ad has, what the click-through rate is, the reach (number of people the ad was shown to), the results (page like, app install, etc.). If you look toward the right-hand side, there are two options labeled Columns and Breakdown. You can use Columns to specify what columns you want to be displayed on the screen. Breakdown lets you look at a large variety of data. For example, you can break it down by time frame, day, week, month, etc. You can look at delivery information, which will show you the data by age groups, time of day, gender, device, and so forth. Action will show you conversion device, and other information.

Reports

The last button on the right is Reports. You can have Facebook generate up to 25 different reports for your data. When you generate a report, it will open on screen where you can view the data. You can download it (for example as an Excel Spreadsheet or CSV file) or save it on Facebook.

Opportunities
Recently, Facebook also added another tab called "Opportunities' where you can find tips and other information.

CHAPTER 8
Analyzing Results

The key to having success with Facebook ads lies with analyzing the results, making adjustments, and killing ads when they are not working. Secondly, you will want to ramp up the campaigns that are working. We have already discussed the general procedure but let's outline it again here.

Begin by identifying variations that you want to look at targeting. You can start with a general advertisement and go from there. In fact, you should include a general advertisement in your campaign in case the variations you imagine that might be required really aren't valuable. Using the example of a slot machine game, at the beginning of the book we mentioned that slot machines are popular in multiple countries such as the United States, Canada, Australia, Hong Kong, Japan, and the United Kingdom. At first glance, you might think that different ads need to be set up for say Japan and the United States. And sometimes this is true, but it's not always true. Sometimes you can hit on an ad creative that just works. The only way to find out is to test, test, and test.

Continuing with the slot example, we can make a single ad with our favorite video creative and then simply show it across the board. Then we can set up ad campaigns for each individual country and then run those alongside it. At the week's end, we compare results. If there is no distinct advantage to specialized ads, we can kill them. If they perform worse, we definitely kill them.

The specialized ads might work in some cases but not in others. So maybe the same ad works in Japan and the United States, but it doesn't work in Hong Kong. In that case, then you'll want to work on tailoring an ad specifically for Hong Kong.

There may be other reasons to keep your campaigns separate, but for the most part, Facebook will let you break out reports that will let you break down things by location or gender. However, one reason that you may want to keep locations separate even though they may perform the same with the same interest targeting and ad creatives is that costs are different in different countries. This also means that rewards are different in different countries. You can take this same lesson to the bank for different states and cities in the United States too.

Let's have a look at it. The cost per acquisition may be about the same if you're running the same exact ad across multiple locations. But the rewards might be different. For example, in mobile games, you earn money through ads that you show inside your game and through in-app coin purchases. Some locations might tend toward more coin purchases than others. Japan is better than Hong Kong, and the United States is where the money is (relatively speaking). However, advertisers pay different rates based on the country. They may pay a lot more in the United States than they do in say Hong Kong or France. That means that the cost of acquisition needs to be lower in those countries.

Two things you need to look at to see if your campaigns are working are:

- Cost of acquisition of a new customer
- The average lifetime value of a user

So if I have a mobile game and the cost of acquisition of a customer is $0.90 and that customer will generate $2.50 in revenue, then that is a winning proposition. However, bundling locations in ad campaigns can cause problems. For example, in the United States, an average user might cost $0.95 to acquire, but they might on average bring in $4 in earnings. In Hong Kong, they might cost $0.85, but only bring in $1.25 in revenue.

The same thing might be in play for our real estate ad. You might easily acquire prospects from New York who are interested in moving to Arizona, maybe as easily as you're getting from people in California. But California is a lot closer, so in reality, it's a lot easier to make the move. So over time, you might find that you're making a lot more revenue from California residents but only occasional sales from New York residents. The sales from New York still add to your bottom line, so you don't necessarily want to cut them out. But maybe an approach you will take is keeping the campaigns separate and running a campaign aimed at NY residents that has a much smaller daily budget.

Testing Your Campaigns
So to review, you'll need to figure out what variations you're going to run on your campaigns. It can be varying demos, interests, or just changing up creatives. The goal is to throw everything out there and then find out what works and what doesn't.

You can find out what works by running the campaigns for a week with very small budgets. In my opinion, below $3 per day is too small, but $10 a day is too large. The more you spend the more information you're going to get, but about $5 a day for a week should get you enough information to determine if a particular video or ad copy is working for you.

Data to Check on Ads Manager
You can determine whether an ad is working for you just by looking at a few parameters. The main ones to check are:

- Amount spent
- Impressions
- Clicks (or installs or page likes)
- Cost per result

You will want to know the click-through rate as well. This is simply clicks/impressions * 100. You can compare click-through rates between various ad campaigns and determine which ones are working and which ones are not working as far as generating the response to go to your site or page, to take that initial step of taking action.

Of course cost per result is an important parameter. If you are in a new business, and you really don't know the lifetime value of a customer, then you're not really going to be sure if a given cost per result is acceptable or not, however, what you can do is compare across ad campaigns to see what's working.

Now if you go to the Columns button and select Delivery, you can get the cost per 1,000 impressions of the ad. It's important to compare this cost across campaigns as well. However, note that one impression doesn't mean one person. The number of people is given by Reach. Some people might get more than one impression for whatever reason.

Another parameter to look at is Columns ☐Engagement. This will let you see the cost per click. Targeting and Creative will bring many of these measures together in a single display, showing you the cost per result, cost per 1,000 impressions, click through rate, and cost per click.

Even if you set up all your ads with the same exact budget – and that is what you should do – you might find some ads get a lot more impressions than others. This might happen because of demographic choices or interests that you've selected. If an ad is really sluggish with impressions, that is telling you that you will need to open it up a bit – possibly widening the demographics, location, or adding more interests (or reducing the interests).

Killing Your Ads

After the five-day period is up, it's time to kill all the ads that are not working. Simply shut them off. This can be done by toggling the button on the far left of the listing. Keep in mind that you can turn things off at every level. So if you have multiple ad sets and ads, be mindful of what you are really shutting off.

Next Steps

The next step is the ramp-up phase. This can work in two ways, the first is mandatory. To ramp up, begin increasing your daily budget. Never increase by more than 15% per day. So we will go like this – assuming that the trial period was set to $5 Daily Budget.

- Day 1: $5,75
- Day 2: $6.61
- Day 3: $7.60
- Day 4: $8.74
- Day 5: $10.05

How high you go after this depends on how many ads your running and what kind of daily budget you can absorb. However, if you're after a large number of prospects a $10 budget probably won't cut it, and you'll need to keep increasing until you get to $40 and above.

A word of warning about budget increases. For some reason, the Facebook system seems to respond better to gradual budget increases. So you aren't going to want to move from $5 to $40 or $100 in one shot. You will probably find it doesn't work. Take it gradually – soon enough you'll be at your spending goal.

Issues with bid caps

Bid caps can work in a funny way. You might find – but this depends on a huge number of factors so maybe you won't – that setting a bid cap you hardly get any traffic. In one test I did, using app installs where bid cap is replaced by an equivalent cost per install – I set a low price of 75 cents. Not much happened. I kept raising the daily budget.

It finally worked – but I had to set the daily budget at $400.

That might sound scary – it isn't. At $400 the campaign was still proceeding at its glacial pace. It opened it up enough so it brought in 20-30 installs per day, and I was happy to have them at that low cost per install.

This may happen to you or it may not, since there are so many factors that will influence how many impressions a given ad campaign is going to get. However, you can test the high budget if you are running into something like that which just isn't doing anything. Just keep a very close eye on it so that you can shut off the campaign if it starts spending in an out of control fashion.

Cloning

Years ago cloning showed much promise when Dolly the sheep was born. We haven't been overrun with clones, but the good news is you can clone your Facebook ad campaigns. They don't call it cloning, they call it duplicate. It's a tool that can come in handy to ramp things up.

Suppose you have a campaign with a daily budget of $20 and you want to spend $100 a day, and that campaign is working really well. Instead of gradually raising the budget, you can make five copies of it and run them simultaneously. That will help you get from there to here a lot faster. It's a technique that has worked for me many times.

CHAPTER 9
Traffic Vs. Page Likes

If you're new to Facebook advertising then you might find the types of ad campaigns a little fuzzy. We can generate traffic in a lot of different ways, you can use a lead generation campaign for example. Or you can simply use a traffic campaign that sends people to your lead generation site. Those kinds of distinctions aren't really important but the other two differ from page likes. Why would you want to use one and not the other?

Page Likes Advantages and Disadvantages
We've been through some of the advantages, but let's review them here. When you run a campaign for page likes, it's not a one-time thing. It's a connection that you're making to the client. This brings up an important point:

Use your Facebook page.

As the marketer, you don't want to just set up a Facebook page and leave it sitting there. Every time that you post on the Facebook page – it's going to show up on the feeds of people that liked your page.

In a sense, a page like is sort of like an email list. Way back when, in the early days of the internet, web marketing worked like this:

- Set up a one-page sales letter with an order button.
- Run a Google AdWords campaign that sent it traffic.

Unfortunately, two things happened. The first was Google got on its high horse and decided that it didn't like those kinds of sales pages. It wanted content, and it saw those pages as basically content free. To Google, they were evil sales pitches taking advantage of people.

Also, people began to get more skeptical. So a single sales page wasn't working as well as it had in the past.

These two developments were the birth of email marketing. The new strategy was this:

- Create a content-based website, so that Google would not "slap" you. It might include 20 pages of articles.

- Create an opt-in form on your website. People would sign up for an email newsletter in exchange for a free gift of some kind.
- Then you send the prospects a series of automated emails, giving them occasional offers to buy.

After this, things evolved again with the "landing page", which is a web page devoted to nothing more than collecting someone's email address in exchange for some kind of free gift.

Now fast forward to Facebook taking over the world. With a Facebook page, you essentially have a similar kind of setup. The Facebook page is acting as an email list, in giving you a way to communicate directly to your prospects and doing it on a regular basis.

Of course, there is no auto-responder. So you're going to have to keep your Facebook page live by routinely posting on it. When doing so you might want to occasionally slip in opportunities to buy products. If you're selling digital products, you can include a link to your sales page in a Facebook posting. You can occasionally hard sell it, but be careful with this, you don't want people to unlike your page – so only do that sparingly.

So in short, Facebook page likes to build up a customer or prospect database that you're in regular communication with. So what are the downsides?

The problem with this setup is that it's all too easy to like a posting on Facebook. So some person is scrolling through their feed, and they see your ad. Maybe it has a video they check out and they think it's cool – so they click on the like button.

But it really didn't mean all that much to them.

A large fraction of your page likes is going to be from people who aren't all that serious about spending money on your product or service. So you're going to have to get a lot of likes in order to start generating money from it. Until then, it might amount to a mere popularity contest.

Let's not get too down with this talk – having a Facebook page and getting page likes is still very useful. But don't rely on it.

Which brings us to traffic. You have a website up for whatever reason. Maybe you're selling t-shirts. Maybe you're an attorney with an informational site. Either way, your ultimate goal is getting customers on your website, not interacting with them on Facebook.

One way you can do this of course – is to post links to your site on the Facebook page. Earlier we recommended having a blog. You can integrate it with your main site, and many providers like Shopify already have a blog built-in. So you can post articles on your main site and then post them to the Facebook page.

Traffic Campaigns

However, this should work in concert with a traffic campaign. There are a couple of ways to drive traffic. Using the attorney example, you could explicitly advertise for bankruptcy services in your Facebook ad, and make it clear that clicking on the link would take a person to a page where they could contact you or sign-up on a form to be contacted.

If you are selling a digital product, then you can use Facebook advertising in roughly the same way you'd use Google AdWords. That is, the goal would be to take them to a landing page where they sign up for your email newsletter. I know, that is kind of a drag, you might have been hoping the Facebook page would help you get away from all that tedious stuff. The bottom line though is that email marketing is still the go-to technique for generating leads.

You can also do cold traffic, say to your t-shirt sight. That should be simple enough, you can have a good ad which shows the t-shirt with a sales offer. Better yet, use a carousel ad that mixes up videos of models wearing your t-shirts together with still shots of the shirt. When they click on the ad, they go right to your Shopify listing for the shirt.

Cold traffic is as risky as it ever was. However, Facebook works a lot better than using say Bing or Google Adwords, because you can show them the product in a 2-minute video before they click the link to visit your website.

Traffic vs. Page Likes

So when it comes down to it, which method is better? Chances are you're going to want to do both. While a lot of prospects that you're going to acquire from page likes are not going to be all that serious – liking a page doesn't take as much effort as signing up for emails, and your email prospects have to confirm their subscription, that second step weeds out a lot of people – the reality is a lot of people signing up for email newsletters aren't all that serious either. Think about how many promotional emails you probably get in your own inbox. How many of those do you bother opening? Probably a small fraction of them.

The best approach to marketing is to use as many avenues that you can. Page likes can be had for dirt cheap prices. So you may as well build up an audience with them. And since the old methods still work, you should also utilize traffic campaigns.

CHAPTER 10
Lookalike Audiences

So far we've seen many powerful features that are available to Facebook advertisers. You can target by age, by location, by gender, by occupation, by interest, and so forth. Now we come to the most powerful of all – the lookalike audience. The lookalike audience is the nuclear bomb of advertising.

Lookalike audiences can be developed in one of two ways. Or maybe we should say they can be had in one of two ways. You can buy or obtain the data you need for a lookalike audience from a broker or from someone who markets a related product or service – in the event, they are willing to sell or share it. In this case, you will upload the data to your Facebook account. Facebook is going to ask you about it, and what you should do is be honest and tell them that it's from a partner.

The data itself is not the lookalike audience. What the data will do is help Facebook create an entirely new list of customers that are Basically the same as the people in the data you provide. Although we view ourselves as thoughtful, independent, and smart actors, the scary thing is if we share a lot of characteristics we're going to buy the same stuff. Robotically. If you're doing marketing – take advantage of it!

Facebook probably has secret formulas, and we don't know what their secret sauce is. However, there are a few things we can look at that Facebook uses to create the lookalike audience:

- Age distribution
- Percent of males and females
- Device usage
- Income distribution
- Locations
- Occupations
- Page likes
- Interests

So if we're selling Chevy trucks and just starting out, we might contact the dealer on the other side of town and ask him for a database of his customers. In the old days he might have told us to get lost, but today you can assure him that you're not actually going to contact a single customer on his list. You just want to find out how old they are, and what pages they liked on Facebook.

We don't know how that would really work out, but let's say that the dealer agrees to sell you a list of 5,000 people for $250. All he is going to provide you is their name and email address.

It doesn't sound like much – but that's all Facebook needs to get to work. When you upload the data, Facebook is going to use its system and all the data it has collected over the years to compile a list of customers – that didn't buy from your dealer on the other edge of town – but who are similar in every respect. That is your lookalike audience.

When you advertise to a lookalike audience, that is as if you have optimized your ad campaigns by running them for the past 6 months. You'll find that the performance of ads that use a lookalike audience outstrip those that don't by a massive margin. These will be your highest value customers.

You don't have to buy or borrow a database of people to create a lookalike audience. You can also create them from the data that you're generating in your own ad campaigns. You can use people who've liked your Facebook page to create a Lookalike audience. Although that will be your data alone, it takes time. From my experience, I'd recommend 5,000 people to create a good lookalike audience. You need to reach a certain threshold in order to be able to get enough data on demographics etc. in order to create a new list of similar people that will be responsive.

Another way you can create your own lookalike audience is to generate an email list using traffic campaigns. If you've had an online presence, you might already have one. So if you've been advertising your Chevy trucks online outside Facebook for years until now, and you've collected thousands of names and email addresses on your signup form, then you already have a base list of people with characteristics that are going to be associated with people who are interested in buying Chevy trucks. You can upload that list to Facebook and have it go to work to create an audience that you can then hit with Facebook ads. Some services, like Mail Chimp, have been set up so that you can simply import directly from Mail Chimp to Facebook.

Conversion rates using lookalike audiences can be astoundingly good, which means that the cost per result will be remarkably cheap. On a recent campaign using lookalike audiences I was able to get my cost of acquisition of new customers down to less than 20 cents.

That seems like it's almost back to the old days on Google in 2003 when you could advertise for pennies on the dollar.

Approaching Others for Data
Believe it or not, you may be able to get other people to share their data. You can put together a nice email explaining what you're interested in and ask if they are willing to share it. You can also try asking them if they will sell it. Most people are going to ignore you, that is a fact of life in a situation like this. But you're probably going to get lucky a few times and dig up people that are willing to give you some data or sell it to you. In your email, you might explain that a Facebook lookalike audience will not actually use their customers, and you can sign an agreement specifying that you won't contact their customers via the provided email (unless the customer happens to come to you some other way, of course). Since Facebook is taking the data and generating a new set of people from it (and the generated audience is a much larger size), you're not really using the customers themselves.

If you're willing to spend money, then you can search on the web for data brokers that can supply you with names and email addresses of people that have bought certain products. Just be careful if taking this approach as you're going to want to make sure you get recent and updated lists and not emails from ten years ago.

Uploading Your Data
Go to the Facebook Ads Manager drop-down menu. Select All Tools, and then click on Audiences. This will bring up a new screen showing any saved audiences you already have. In the upper left, there is a blue button labeled "Create Audience". Click on this button. You will see three options. These are Custom Audience, Lookalike Audience, and Saved Audience. Select Lookalike audience.

This will open a new window. You will specify the audience source, Audience location, and Audience size. To use data you have for upload, you click on Create New Source. There are two options:

- Custom Audience
- Custom Audience with LTV

We will explore the first option in the next section. In this section, we will select the Custom Audience with LTV.

This will open a new screen which will say Create a Data File Custom Audience with LTV. The top of the screen will show you information about creating a file that you can use to create a lookalike audience. It will say "Prepare a File with your Customer Data". It will also show the fields that are acceptable. The minimum that you need are:

- First Name
- Last Name
- Email address

This data is used to match up the people with their Facebook accounts. The data can be in an Excel spreadsheet but the first column on the left-hand side of your file must contain an integer that identifies the customer by row number. In other words, your file should have some structure like this:

1   Jane Doe jane.doe@gmail.com
2   Patrick Jones p.jones@swag.com
3   Betty Boop betty@boop.com

Column 1 is the number, column 2 is the first name, column 3 is the last name, and column 4 is an email address. A broker will know how to set this up properly for you. Upload your file and name the audience. You will have to specify some more information including location and audience size. Audience size is given as a percentage, I opt for 10%.

Other Sources
When you start off creating a custom audience, you will see two options, we explored custom audience with LTV in the last section. Now we will look at the plain custom audience. What this does is create a lookalike audience based on people that have visited your Facebook page or interacted with you some way on Facebook. Facebook sources that can be used are:

- Video
- Lead form
- Instant experience
- Instagram business profile
- Facebook page (now called "Events")

If you've been running video ad campaigns on Facebook, then you can select Video, which will pull up all the people who watched the video and then create a lookalike audience from them. Let's take a look at the video option.

The first thing that comes up is "Engagement". What this is about is how engaged were the people with your video. You can select the number of seconds they actually watched or a percentage. You probably don't want to create a lookalike audience from people that watched your video for just 3 seconds and left. A better metric might be picking people that watched it at least 50% of the way through – that demonstrates they had some significant interest in your offer even if they didn't follow through all the way to a sale. If you have multiple videos then you'll have to select the particular video you want to use.

Second, you need to select "In the Past" which gives a time frame in the number of days back that you want to use. In other words, if someone watched the video in the last 90 days, put 90 in the box. The default is the past year so it opens with 365 days.

Then name your audience and create it. Depending on how much data you have, i.e. how many people have watched the video since you posted it – it can take a few minutes for Facebook to crunch the data. When it's done it will give you two options:

- Create an ad using the audience
- Expand the audience

You'll want to expand the audience. This is a new set of people that Facebook gathers that match the people that watched your video in as many characteristics as possible. This brings up a new screen where you can set your parameters. These are similar to those used with an uploaded data set. The first thing is to specify one or more locations to use to generate the audience.

Then, use the sliding bar to pick an audience size. For the United States, if you set the bar at 5, it creates an audience with 10.7 million people. The values on the sliding bar indicate percentages of the population for your selected location. You can select a percentage between 1% and 10%.

Now you can save the audience, and it will be available when you create your next ad campaign. When you're in the audience section, use "Saved Audiences" to find and select it.

Page Likes
You can also use page likes to generate a lookalike audience. The steps are similar but let's quickly have a look. This time when you create your custom audience, select *Events*. Facebook will bring up a new screen

which will ask you to select a Facebook page from the drop-down list (if you only have one page, that's what will be there). Make sure that you select People that have engaged from the drop-down list above the Facebook page, and then set the number of days that you want to use for the metric. From here on out, the instructions are the same.

The impact of the Lookalike audience

To get an understanding of what this is about let's roll back to advertising from scratch. To make it even worse, let's say you don't even do targeting. When you run your ad, Facebook is going to show it to everyone on Facebook (well, a small subset of them every day). As you might imagine most people aren't interested in your ad, so you get a lot of wasted impressions and wasted money.

As time goes on, the system optimizes, so it starts finding people that have an interest in your product, and then it can begin targeting others that are similar as it learns what their characteristics are. This, of course, can take some time to work right, and it's not going to go as well because Facebook doesn't have that much data at first.

Now let's consider what happens when you upload a Facebook audience. Suppose for the sake of an example that you're again targeting people that live in the Northeastern United States that want to move to Arizona. So far in our discussion of this type of ad, we have been talking about randomly finding them. What if instead, you were able to obtain a list of people that actually did move from the northeast to Phoenix.

These people are probably going to have a lot of surprising things in common. They may be a similar age, marital status, wealth, education level. Maybe most of them will come from a subset of occupations. Of course, most will be retired but we may still find out their occupation when they were still working. In addition, these people have been spending time on Facebook and leaving a trail of likes.

And so we buy a database of these people that have already moved from New York, Maine, Pennsylvania, Delaware, Connecticut, New Jersey, Rhode Island and Massachusetts to Arizona. We upload it to Facebook and then it cranks out an audience of millions of people who have the same characteristics. Including many of the same likes and so on in their Facebook history.

Now we can run ads targeting this new subset of people that Facebook has found for us. It won't be any surprise to learn that the ads that target

293

these people are going to be far more effective than the ads that start cold. In fact, they are going to work like gangbusters!

Conversion rates are going to go through the roof. With that happening the cost to acquire new leads will plummet. You're going to have customers lining out the door wanting to buy a house in Phoenix from you (well provided it's in the right neighborhood).

As we said, lookalike audiences are the nuclear bomb of online advertising. Nobody else has anything as powerful as this.

CHAPTER 11
Creative Media Types

An ad campaign on Facebook has three vital elements that will help it drive traffic to your site or create page likes. These are the headline used for the ad, the text used in the ad, and the creative. As we've seen the creative can be a video, an image, a slide show, or what's called a carousel. Any type of creative can works as long as it's relevant and engaging. After all, a neutral photo is better than a bad video that drives people away. Let's take a look at the different creative types in more detail.

Single Image
This is the simplest kind of ad. Depending on what product or service that your offering, a single image can actually be quite relevant and engaging. For example, if you are selling t-shirts, you can have a picture of a nice looking young woman wearing the t-shirt in the image.

Facebook offers stock images that you can use if you are in a situation where you don't have anything you can use. These can still work too, although having your own creatives is a better path.

The ideal size for an image is a square that is 1080 x 1080. Remember that most people who are using Facebook are going to be doing it on a mobile device, so having a square image is better. If you don't have a square image, use the built-in cropping tools that Facebook has on the ad campaign creation page to make sure your image looks the way you want it to look when it displays on a mobile phone. You can use smaller images, but this is advertising – so you don't want to use something that might end up displaying with a blurry or pixelated appearance. If you don't have one of adequate size then you might want to simply use a stock image.

If you will be targeting your ads on Instagram as well as on Facebook, then you can use a different image for the Instagram ad. An Instagram ad is required to be at least 500 x 262 pixels in size.

Facebook allows you to create up to six ads using images for split testing. You can do this on the fly when you're creating the ad. Simply follow the instructions to upload or select all six images.

Video Creation Kit
For those who don't have any videos readily available, Facebook has introduced a very interesting option that research has shown is

surprisingly effective. It's called Video Creation Kit and what it does is create a video from a series of still images and text that you enter. Video ads tend to have better conversion rates, so if you're looking at only being able to upload still images – you should strongly consider using the Video Creation Kit. As Facebook tells it, the tool lets you "create a Single video ad when you don't have a video".

There are two options that you can use for your template. You can opt to have a square video, or you can use a vertical template. Vertical videos are becoming a new rage since everyone is spending so much of their time on their mobile phones. In particular, if you are looking at advertising on Instagram then a vertical template might be of interest.

After you've decided whether to use square or vertical style template, there are options to choose between themes. Since the video creation kit is fairly new, there aren't very many options. But if Facebook decides to keep the video creation kit, we can expect that over time the options will be greatly expanded. Right now there are two general categories – Holiday and Standard. When you select the one you want, you'll see a small number of available templates.

For Standard, you'll see "Promote a Product", "Drive Product Delivery", and " Sell Multiple Products". How well these are tailored to their stated purpose is really hard to say, but they all produce nice flowing videos that come complete with interesting effects guaranteed to keep people's attention. The number of images used and video duration varies. These tend to be pretty short videos, which can be useful these days because so many people are developing short attention spans.

First, let's have a look at "Promote a Product". This option requires 2-5 images, and the video lasts 6 seconds. That is a flash in the pan – but for an advertisement to people with short attention spans it's probably a winner.

Next, we have "Drive Product Delivery". This one supposedly will "Inspire people to explore and shop by showing what makes your product unique". Playing around with the template I am not sure how it actually meets this fluffy goal – but it does make a nice video that can probably drive conversions. It requires 1-6 images and lasts 15 seconds.

Finally, there is "Sell Multiple Products" which has 4-7 images.

All three options make nice flowing video streams with some pretty cool effects. Especially if you are targeting a younger audience, you might consider these as potential tools even if you've got your own videos.

Slideshow

Facebook has other options if you're stuck with still images. One of these that comes to immediate use is an old-fashioned slideshow. This is an alternative to the video creation kit that can in a sense turn your ad created with still images into a "video". You can use 3-10 images to create the slideshow, which can last up to 15 seconds. Images that you use for the slideshow should have an aspect ratio of 16 x 9.

The slideshow will play in a loop when the ad is on the consumer's screen. Since you can include up to 10 images, you can include multiple marketing messages to help close the prospect.

Video

Now we arrive at the old gold standard- video. As YouTube is showing with its massive daily views, video remains at the top in the media world. You have more flexibility with video including putting up really long ads. For an advertisement that only runs on Facebook, a video can be up to 240 minutes in length. A video must be MP4 or MOV format and can be a maximum of 4 GB in size.

Whether you want to essentially distribute an ad that is a full-length movie or not, probably not, that gives you a lot of room to put together a video where you can deliver the entire message you want rather than trying to cram something into 6-15 seconds.

On Instagram, however, smaller attention spans dominate as people swipe here and there, so videos can only be 120 seconds long for Instagram feeds. Instagram has a second option which is to place video ads on "stories", but these can only be up to 60 seconds in length. Additionally, the stories are better served with vertical ads.

In-stream videos can be up to 15 seconds in length.

If you have a game or app that you're advertising on the audience network, the videos can be up to 120 seconds in length, and they must be at least five seconds. Games have so-called rewarded videos where people watch ads in exchange for in-game coins, these can only be 60 seconds in length.

So what is the ideal length for a video? Honestly, it depends on what you're selling. On television, we've seen both short and long. The standard 30-second ad seems to work pretty well, it keeps people's attention without going overboard. For most applications having a 30-second ad is probably ideal. Even then many are going to find it running too long and they'll probably not finish watching the entire video. However, something else we know about television is that people sit and watch infomercial ads that last a half-hour. So if it's appropriate, you can run a longer ad. However, in that scenario, you'll want to try and catch people at home. If someone is out, they probably aren't going to watch a 30-minute video even if they are somewhere that they have a connection. They may decide they'll watch it later, but most people will forget about it. You can minimize the damage by requiring a WiFi connection for your ad to be displayed. With this, you'll be able to catch a lot of people at home, when they are more likely to watch the entire ad and buy your product.

IMPORTANT: You're going to want to have a video with some screen time that has no text on the screen. Facebook has a silly rule that you can't have text displayed in the image used as the thumbnail for your video.

Instant Experience
On mobile devices, a new option is available called "instant experience". Although the experience is limited to the screen on the mobile device, Facebook claims it's "immersive". What this represents is an ad that fills up the entire screen when the user interacts with it. The ad can include all creative types – so you can include video, carousel, slideshow, and single images.

Carousel
This is an interesting ad creative type. You can think of this as a kind of upgrade from a slide show. You can mix together multiple media items into the same ad – and you can include both video and single images. However, while a slide show plays automatically through the different scenes, a carousel requires the user to move through them. So they have to swipe through each one, and view or not view videos that you have included.

You can even add a slideshow into the carousel.

Another interesting feature of carousels is each card (the individual part with an image or a video) can have its own headline and text. That way, you can convey multiple messages that might be relevant to your product or service. The default setting is to have three cards but you can add more.

Facebook will adjust the way the carousel works. As the ad runs, it will analyze the performance of each card you've added to the carousel. Then it will move the highest performing cards to the front end so that users will see them first.

Headlines and Text

Of course, writing your copy is a vital part of the ad. The headline is bold text and doesn't have much room to display, so keep your headlines simple. You will want to put your most compelling copy in the text. This isn't a copywriting course, but some suggestions are:

- Ask questions to get users engaged.
- Ask a type of question that might prompt an emotional response.
- Use phrases that imply some kind of secret is being revealed. For example, start off with "Discover the hidden method that...", "Previously hidden secret reveals...". It seems silly, but these kinds of phrases work at getting people engaged.
- After your initial question or phrase, list 2-3 benefits of your product or service.
- It can help to put a time limit "good for the next 72 hours".

CHAPTER 12
Boosted And Promoted Posts

If you're running a Facebook page, then you have the option to promote individual posts from the page. There are a couple of ways to get more eyeballs on posts, the first way is called "Boosted post", and you can also do "promoted" posts.

Boosted Posts
You can access posts from the Facebook Ads Manager drop-down menu. Open it up and select "All Tools". Then select "Page Posts". A new screen will open showing all your posts in a list. A boosted post doesn't have to be one that already exists, you can create a new one here. However, we'll look at boosting an existing post.

Select the post you want to "boost" by clicking on it in the list. It will open the post with a blue button in the lower right corner that says "Boost Post". Doing this is essentially creating an advertisement that is going to target the individual post you select. As such, you can do targeting on the screen that opens to boost the post, such as setting your audience in the same way when you create a normal ad campaign.

You're also going to see options for daily budget and automatic placements. Boosted Post campaigns have a fixed duration however, so you should set your duration after setting the other parameters. You can also set options for a website and pixel if you're going to use this to drive traffic (the pixel can help you track conversions).

If you decide to create a new post to boost, it's going to open up a screen where you set the ad campaign parameters.

You also have the ability to boost certain posts from your Facebook page. If you are on your Facebook page on the post stream, then you will see the Boost Post option there. Once you click on it, then the same steps are followed.

Promoted Posts
A promoted post is not too different, this time you create a new ad campaign using the Ads Manager. For this type of campaign, select Engagement. We did this earlier for page likes, this time select "Post engagement". Then you'll select all your options for the ad campaign just like any other, and the post that you want to promote.

CHAPTER 13
Common Mistakes Made By Newbies

Creating Facebook ads is a fairly simple exercise, but following the analytics and learning about all the options and more advanced features like the Facebook Pixel can be daunting. That means it's easy to make mistakes. In this chapter, we will look into some of the more common mistakes that people make when creating ad campaigns on Facebook.

Failing to set clear goals
If you're a veteran of advertising and marketing who's just new to Facebook, this won't be a problem for you. But one area where Facebook is catching fire is with small businesses that haven't done much advertising before. These might be very small businesses, someone with a Shopify account, doing digital product marketing or affiliate marketing, or someone doing Amazon FBA or even Kindle books. If you lack experience in marketing and advertising you might be tempted to just throw some ads up to see what happens and then hope that everything is going to work out in the end. Of course, you can't get through life and have success if you're not planning some things out and that applies here as much as it does anywhere else. In fact, it might be more important when it comes to advertising because you're throwing money out there.

So let's look at some basic goals or maybe we can call them parameters that you should set before launching your ad campaigns.

- Figure out the average lifetime value of your customers. If you don't know this yet, then estimate it. In short, you want to figure out the amount of stuff they are going to buy from you and get an average value. This is an important parameter for any business.
- Next, using the average lifetime value, you want to set an upper limit on the amount you can spend to acquire a customer. If you're going to have a billion customers, then maybe you only want to make a penny in profit. But that isn't going to work for most of us. So get a comfortable margin, so that you can acquire enough customers and cover all your expenses while having some profit left over.
- Knowing the maximum cost of acquisition, now you have a solid benchmark for your ad campaigns. This will not be your goal specifically but will be the maximum cost per result that you will tolerate. Any campaign that fails to meet it must undergo

adjustments to see if it can enter profitability quickly, and if it fails to deliver, shut off the campaign.

- Next, you need to know how many prospects you want to drive to your various media platforms. Don't run a page likes campaign and "see how it goes". Set a specific goal – maybe its 100 likes per day. Now you know the other side of the puzzle – how many campaigns and how many results you need to run in order to meet that goal.
- It goes without saying that you should know what your total budget can be! So figure out how much you can spend on advertising per month. Of course, Facebook is dynamic, so this is an upper limit. You may be able to optimize your Facebook campaigns to beat the budget.

Giving up too early

It's important to understand that the advertising network is dynamic. So you can't run your ad for a day and then think that is all there is going to be to the results. The longer you run your ad, the better the results are going to be.

Of course, in today's world, it's all about instant gratification. You can be forgiven if you get frustrated if results don't pour in during the first few hours of your ad campaign. Many people give up far too soon, without letting their campaigns run for an adequate time span and making important adjustments. One way that you can look at Facebook ads is that they are a simple kind of artificial intelligence. And a system that is built around artificial intelligence is one that needs time to learn. It learns fast but be sure to give it adequate time to learn. Generally speaking, 3-5 days is a time span you should shoot for when testing out ads to see if they are going to work for you. One area in particular where you might see massive improvement is the cost per result in your ad campaigns. On the first day, you might be getting a lot of results but they might cost more than expected. So give it time to work itself out. If by the third day you're still not seeing reductions in costs, then you'll need to go in and make basic adjustments. Look at everything – can the headline and text be improved? Is your video really a good creative that will compel people to click? Do you have interests, and demographics well targeted?

Setting Initial Budgets to High

A common mistake that many people make is taking Facebook at their word. When you set your budget, Facebook comes up with recommended values. Don't be naïve – you don't want to start out with the Daily Budget they recommend on a campaign that hasn't been tested at all. If you start out with a $40 daily budget on a completely untested brand new ad campaign – especially if you're a beginner and you don't have a lookalike audience – you might end up spending yourself into oblivion pretty quickly.

After having advertised on Facebook for many years, it's not really clear to me how and why they come up with the recommended budgets that they use. In all the years that I've advertised, I've never once settled on the recommended daily budget. Most of the time I have multiple campaigns running with budgets half the recommended amount or a few campaigns with much higher budgets.

The best approach is to start with a very low budget ($3-5) as we've discussed previously. Then follow the standard benchmark of raising it 15% per day until you've got it where you want it to be as far as quantity and cost per result.

Not Having Enough Ads

I like to watch the show Shark Tank, and there is a Canadian software billionaire named Kevin on there most of the time who everyone thinks is grouchy (they always call him Mr. Wonderful). The guy is actually a first-rate businessman and you should read his books and watch his YouTube videos. One of the pithy lessons he always uses is to let the market speak to you. Facebook lets this happen in real time and does in spades!

On Facebook, you can throw up lots of ads with lots of variations. The more ads that you put up simultaneously, the more data you're going to collect and the faster you're going to find out what works best for you. By putting up multiple ads that all vary in some way, you're going to find out what works to get you prospects while driving down your cost of acquisition a lot faster than you will if you're only running one or two ads and then trying to tweak them to get them to work. Put in all the tweaks ahead of time and then watch what happens. Then immediately kill all the ads that exceed your cost of acquisition for a customer. You are going to need to do this over a long enough time period so that you're not killing anything off prematurely, so as we've suggested before running the campaigns for at least three days, and preferably five days.

When you're just beginning, you might be overwhelmed creating twenty ads at once and then trying to keep track of them all. In that case, start off with five or ten ads. Remember we are shooting low, so they are going to have at most $5 budgets during the test phase.

And give them enough time. One time I was advertising an affiliate product on Facebook. At first, nothing happened. I ran the ad for a day and a half and nothing. What I am talking about here is nobody would even click to go to my website – much less drive a sale. I was about to kill the ad and then clicks started coming in on a regular basis. Every hour when I went to check the ad, I had gotten 5-10 more visits to my website. Moral of the story – make sure it runs at a minimum of three days.

Another thing that Kevin says in his lectures is that business is war. You may not like to think in those terms but it's a 100% accurate statement. Of course, nobody is going to show up and burn your house down and kill your family, but they are trying to destroy your business. In the war for customers, Facebook advertisers who are adapting quickly and getting their message out rapidly to most people are the winners. You do that by having more ads than your competitors. Information from the market is like intelligence on the battlefield – think of your multiple test ads as spies that are out in the field collecting intelligence so that your business can be on the winning side.

Not Using Lookalike Audiences

The first time that I heard about Lookalike audiences I have to admit I got a bit of a headache and my eyes glazed over. Back then, I didn't understand Facebook the way I do now, and I just wanted to run my ads without having to worry about all this complicated stuff. But once you learn how lookalike audiences work, your eyes get wide open. It's akin to a religious conversion.

Actually using a lookalike audience will blow you away. You're going to see unbelievable conversion rates and costs of acquisition that are well below your requirements. At the present time, in my opinion, the ability to use lookalike audiences makes Facebook the undisputed leader in advertising.

Lookalike audiences are so important, it might be a make or break situation when it comes to Facebook ads. If you can't find someone to share a lookalike audience with you or sell you one, then it is going to be worth the time, money and effort to build your own data so that you have enough to create a lookalike audience.

When you take that approach, you set up a feedback loop of success. The first time around that you run your ads, Facebook will be really struggling and it may be slow to bring you the number of customers you want at a price that is acceptable. But it gets better over time. After you've assembled enough likes or video views or whatever you choose as your input for the lookalike audience, then you feed them to Facebook and it's going to develop a super audience for you that will convert like crazy in comparison to your original campaigns. There is no way that you can consider running your business on Facebook without having tried lookalike audiences. Go after those stellar conversion rates and low cost of results.

Not Doing Research

Research for your Facebook campaigns isn't going to start when you are creating ad campaigns. You need to do it before you get to that point. And you don't need to be relying 100% on Facebook either. If you can find out information about the kind of people that are interested in the product or service that you offer, and find it outside of Facebook, that is just as useful. Then when you come to Audience Insights which is going to be your primary research tool on Facebook, you'll have some inputs to start with that will make your research that much more effective.

Then when you get on Audience Insights you need to drill down on all the things we've talked about. That includes knowing what pages they've liked, and actually taking the time to go and look through those pages and the websites of the companies that made the page. You'll also need to know where they live, what their job is, and so on. Of course, you'll need to know basic demographics like age and gender.

Not Keeping Up Your Facebook Page

I've stressed this time and again throughout the book – you need to keep your Facebook page active. In the old days, when it became clear that you needed content to keep Google happy and customers interested, people were able to get by creating a "content website" that had 10-20 pages of text-based around important SEO keywords. Then you could leave the site alone and the SEO would pull in organic traffic. Of course, you could advertise too, but if you were not a blogger you didn't worry very much about adding new content.

Well, that strategy still can work. But it's not going to work on Facebook. The reason is it's an interactive platform. You need to be engaged. That means putting up regular posts on your Facebook page that will keep your prospects coming back for more, and sharing more material with their friends. The more sharing the better. Also if you're posting frequently, it won't seem like spam the time you send everyone a note saying "check out my book, it's only $27". But if you do that after never adding a new post since they liked your page, you'll lose a lot of your newfound Facebook friends.

Also, remember that everything works two ways. We talked earlier about how you can use blogs and YouTube to push content to the Facebook page. Facebook is a heavily trafficked site, so that means the converse can work for you-you can utilize the page to drive traffic to your blog or YouTube channel.

Also, look into the steps you can use to link your YouTube channel directly into your Facebook page. That way people can check out all your videos without having to leave Facebook.

Lack of a Strategy

Would you want to go into a war with a set of tactics, or a long term strategy with a clear winning goal in mind with an exit strategy? What about a football game? Is the best way to win a football game saying "pass a lot" or should you have a set of plays and a specific plan to deal with the opposing team? It seems to us that a strategy is better than just having a few tactics, even though tactics are important too.

Just tossing up Facebook ads and hoping for the best is a tactic. There is a chance that it will deliver results since Facebook is a great marketplace that lets you laser target your prospects. But doing that without an overall strategy isn't going to maximize your results. As we stated earlier before you launch your advertising campaigns you need to clearly lay out your goals and have a solid budget.

Ignoring Details

This book can't cover everything in the space allotted, so it's up to you to familiarize yourself with all the details in the Ads Manager. Ignoring some of the details can cost you unnecessary money that you don't need to spend. For example, on some of my mobile game campaigns, I began noticing that during the day downloads dropped a lot. The fact is that despite all the hype about people being addicted to their phones, they don't have time to download and play games during the middle of the day when they are busy at work. So would it make sense to be running my ads 24/7? Or should I run my ads when people are most likely to download them?

After you've run your campaigns for a few weeks, you'll need to take a deep dive into your data and ask yourself questions like these so that you can optimize campaigns. Too many beginners ignore all the details that Facebook makes available for them, and as a result, they fail to fully optimize their campaigns.

Being Afraid of Shutting Down Campaigns that Don't Deliver

We all get attached to things, even Facebook ads. If they are failing some people are going to have trouble letting go. It might seem like a personal failure when an ad you were sure would work failed to catch on. But this is business, and you shouldn't let emotions get in the way. Use a scientific approach and stick to the rules we've outlined for ending campaigns. Also keep in mind that times change, so you might develop some ads that run on all cylinders but then stop working all the time. Don't get attached to them and shut them down if they stop costing you money. There is no sense going down with a sinking ship.

Set Your Cost Targets

You need to know your marketing inside and out. That means knowing your cost per 1,000 impressions, and cost per click beside the cost per result. You need to be able to look at your campaigns in multiple ways to get a clear idea of what works and what doesn't.

Adapt to the ever-changing world of tech

Tech changes fast. It's easy to get lulled into sleep when something is working for you. We touched on that a little bit when we discussed the changes that web marketing went through when Google started paying attention to what was on people's websites. The thing about that situation is, that was not a one-time change. The technology companies are constantly changing how their algorithms work, or their terms of service. So it's important for you to keep up with what's going on and not fall asleep at the wheel.

Ad campaigns that you create this year may not be working in six months, because of some policy change that Facebook implements or changes in their algorithms. Spend time reading all their documentation, so you'll get wind of when things are changing or if they've altered their terms of service so that you can quickly move to make the changes you need to make.

Those who adapt to changes when they hit will be successful over the long term. It's no different than any other time in business, but the pace has accelerated. Those who fail to adapt will find themselves in a world of hurt that could be fatal to their business. It's even possible that at some point Facebook itself will become useless.

Getting the Right Placements

When you're just starting out, it's easy to not bother learning how things work under the hood and just accepting what Facebook gives you. That's true with Daily budgets and it's also true with placements. Facebook wants you to advertise far and wide, but that may not be in your best interests. So when they suggest automatic placements, you need to look into it first. Now keep in mind automatic placements may work for some people – but they may not work for others.

Placements can be important in determining what turns out to be a successful campaign and what doesn't. For various reasons, not all campaigns are suitable for running on all placements that Facebook offers. We've outlined a little bit about placements, for example, we talked about the relative skewing toward younger demographics on Instagram. That may help you or it may hurt you – but don't advertise on Instagram just because the system recommends it. If that is not your demographic, then don't waste time trying to get traffic there.

Far too many beginners simply go with Automatic placements when creating their ad campaigns. Don't make that mistake.

Using the Same Creatives

We've discussed this in other contexts. You should try running ads using different creatives. If possible, make multiple videos that you can test against one another. You can also test videos against slideshows or ads made with the video kit based on your static images. Then go with what works the best. If you follow major media on television, notice how they are constantly switching up ad content. Ads run for a while and then become stale.

Your ads are going to become stale too. So if you hit on a video that is really converting well, instead of relaxing by the pool you should be hard at work on your next video. Now a major media ad buy is going to show to the entire country over the course of a couple of months – you're reaching out to a far smaller subset of buyers on a daily basis. So your ads are not going to wear out as fast. However, you don't want to wait until they are done to start working on a replacement. Change out your videos or ad copy before your ads start declining or at least soon thereafter.

Not using Facebook Pixel

If you want to make people's eyes glaze over at a party, don't talk about physics, talk about computer coding. While the small band of devotees who are computer programmers love what they do, most people in the world are put off by computer code. In reality, it's a small thing, but when you start talking about the Facebook pixel people get put off. Maybe that's you too. But it's important to overcome your fear of the pixel. If it's too much for you, don't be embarrassed to seek out help. A developer will be happy to properly install it on your website. The Facebook pixel is one more tool in the Facebook arsenal and gives your marketing and advertising campaigns a power punch. Not using it is actually going to cost you money. In today's world information is power and the Facebook pixel is going to provide your business with large amounts of analytical information.

Failing to keep up with new technologies that Facebook may acquire

The acquisition of Instagram was a large move by Facebook. It's entirely possible that more acquisitions of that type will be made in the future. To have long term success, you should keep up with technology news and know what Facebook is doing. That way you won't be caught off guard when a new advertising platform shows up in placements.

The Seat of the Pants Approach

Many of the problems and mistakes we've been talking about actually belong in one category. Taking a seat of the pants approach to your business. Failing to set proper goals, failing to keep up with the changes at Facebook or the underlying technologies all add up to things that will keep your business from reaching its true potential.

CHAPTER 14
Facebook Business Manager

When starting out, you probably won't need it, but at some point, the Facebook Business manager will become important. In particular, if you're going to be using data for lookalike audiences obtained from outside sources, then you're going to need to migrate your ad account to Facebook business manager. The good news is that it's easy to do in a couple of steps and it doesn't cost you any money.

So what is it?

Facebook business manager arose out of the issue of Facebook users who were doing business activity being tied to a personal account. What Business Manager does is allow you to organize everything from your business activities in one central location. Some of the things that you can manage with the Facebook Business Manager include:

- Multiple ad accounts
- Facebook pages
- Multiple Facebook pixels
- Catalogs

It allows you to have this integration without sharing any of this information with your friends and coworkers. An issue that comes up is with business activities you may grow and need outside people to work with your Facebook ads account. Maybe they are developers that will need to access your Facebook pixel. Or maybe when you begin to grow you will hire someone to manage your Facebook pages or ad campaigns. You would probably like to do this without connecting them to your personal Facebook account. The Business Manager helps you do that.

When you set up the Facebook Business Manager, you will be able to invite others to your Facebook account to work on various aspects. Facebook has a routine signup process where you can enter basic information about your business. Once you sign up for Facebook Business Manager, the first thing that you'll want to do is add an account. You can invite people using the following roles:

- Employee access
- Admin access
- Finance analyst

- Finance editor

Chances are, of course, that you are going to be the one who has the role of admin access. When you add employees, they can see all the business info but can only work on tasks that you assign to them.

Another aspect of Facebook Business Manager is having a central location where you can manage multiple Facebook pages and profiles without having to switch between them. Pages can be assigned to different people with roles in your company if desired.

You can also add Facebook Ad Accounts to the Business Manager (so you can have more than one ad account).

Now let's say that you have not enrolled in Facebook Business Manager. There are some actions you can take in the course of running your advertising operation that may trigger a situation where you are required to join. One example of this is the use of an external data source of customers with LTV (long term value) that you are uploading for the purposes of creating a lookalike audience. If you upload this data it will automatically take you to create your Facebook Business Manager enrollment. The process is very quick and easy, taking only a minute.

If you have a product catalog, you can upload it to Facebook Business Manager. A catalog is a database that has information about all the products in your inventory (if you have any). Once you've uploaded the catalog, then its available throughout the entire Facebook platform, such as on Instagram.

The Business Manager also provides a centralized location where you can manage Facebook Pixels for use in your advertising campaigns.

The Facebook Business Manager solves a lot of problems that Facebook used to have because of the ties to personal accounts. Now with Facebook Business Manager, you can have an overarching Business portal associated with Facebook where you can manage all your assets associated with Facebook including your Facebook Ad accounts, Facebook Pages, Facebook Pixels, a Catalog if you have one, and also manage people that will be working on your business. You can create employees and have employees or contractors work on various limited aspects of your business operations such as managing Facebook Pixels or one or more Facebook Pages.

CONCLUSION

Thank you for taking the time to read this book! We hope that you've found it enjoyable and informative.

The first lesson we'd like you to take away from this book is that you've learned how powerful Facebook really is as an advertising platform. Second, you should be ready to utilize all of the tools that Facebook has made available so that you can run the most successful ad campaigns. That includes being familiar with audience insights and using it to the fullest extent possible to know who your prospects are and what they are interested in. How many times have you heard in marketing that you need to have a vision of your typical customer inside your head? Now you don't need to guess – Facebook can tell you who your typical customer is, down to the last detail. You also need to take our comments about lookalike audiences to heart. Having used lookalike audiences in real Facebook ad campaigns, I'm fully aware of their power and how they can act like a rocket in driving your business results. It can't be said enough that failing to understand and utilize lookalike audiences might be one of the top mistakes when it comes to Facebook advertising. Leaving lookalike audiences on the table is akin to leaving a pile of cash on the table. Sure you might get by without it, but you'd be a lot better off using the power that it provides.

The second thing we hope that you'll take away from this book is to go into action with a plan. Start by knowing two key facts about your business: how much it costs to get a customer and how much money you're going to make from that customer. Those are the two most important numbers that you'll ever know. Once you know those two numbers, you can accurately map out a marketing and advertising strategy and budget. Second, you'll be able to accurately forecast your growth potential and be able to meet targets by realistically increasing your ad budget with time.

The third key ingredient to success is to test, test, and test. Remember to start out with small budgets and test multiple variations against each other in real time. If you can run 30 $5 per day ad campaigns at the same time – do it and find out which ones work. Don't be afraid to flush any campaigns that fail to deliver the results you need. Change up your images, videos, headlines, and ad copy as needed and revisit your demographics and interests if things aren't working out.

Finally, we want to wish you the best of luck in your Facebook ad campaigns, and we hope that the advice we have provided in this book will help you grow your business in ways you've never dreamed of. To your success! Again, if you've found this book interesting, useful, and informative, please be sure to leave a review. Thanks for reading!

STOCK MARKET INVESTING FOR BEGINNERS

How to Make Money Investing in Stocks & Day Trading, Fundamentals to Successfully Become a Stock Market Pro and Make Passive Income in Less Than 24 Hours

By
James Ericson

INTRODUCTION

Congratulations on beginning your journey toward wealth and a secure retirement!

For those of us who have lived through the 2008 stock market crash and the Great Recession, many have become a little leery about stock market investing. And with good reason – the risk of collapse is real. However, the reality is the stock market still represents the best place to invest your money. There are several reasons:

- Over the long-term, the trend is always up.
- Returns on the stock market consistently beat those from other investments.
- Nobody who sticks it out and rides out the downturns has failed as an investor.

The long-term trend of the stock market is so consistent that it's practically a rule. That means if you're looking to grow your wealth and retirement funds, the stock market remains the best place to do so – and today, it's never been easier for the individual investor. In this book, we're going to explain what the stock market is and explore how to invest your money and what you can expect. We're going to cover the following topics in this book:

- An introduction to the stock market and investing
- Different types of investing
- Is the stock market worth it?
- Mutual funds
- Stocks in depth
- Stock investment strategies
- Exchange traded funds
- Common mistakes
- International investing
- Bonds and government securities
- Playing it safe with banking
- The investors' mindset
- Retirement vehicles
- Advanced investment techniques
- How to invest large sums of money

Let's get started with an introduction to the stock market.

CHAPTER 1
An Introduction To Markets And Investing

If you're reading this book, then you have at least some vague idea about what the stock market is. Maybe you have a 401k plan at work, and maybe you've even owned a few stocks. But to get the most out of investing, we can return to that old but true cliché – knowledge is power. If you really understand what the stock market is, then you'll be a better investor and get better results. In this chapter, we'll have a look behind the curtain to see what the stock market is all about and how it came to be. Let's begin by examining the idea of a corporation, a special kind of business that is common yet not very well understood by a lot of people.

What is a corporation

Everyone has a common sense notion of what a business is. It's an organization put together to sell a product or service and in the process make a profit. The corner mom & pop store and Walmart are both businesses, but one is small, and one is huge. Aside from the difference in size, many people don't really understand how they are different and similar. For example, the mom & pop store might be selling many of the same products that Walmart does. And yet, they might be organized very differently – aside from the obvious difference in size and revenues. Or they might even be organized in a similar fashion even though the similarities aren't immediately apparent.

The main concern here is the legal structure of the company. Please note that for the sake of simplicity, we will use definitions that exist in the United States, but other countries usually follow something fairly similar. There are several different ways that a company can be organized. Going from simple to complex these are:

- Sole proprietorship
- General partnership
- LLC (limited liability company)
- S-Corporation
- C- Corporation
- Public corporation

A sole proprietorship is often how businesses start. This is a small business set up by a single person. Often this type of business will remain a single person and is utilized for activities like consulting or doing jobs in the "gig" economy. Or it could take the form of the "mom & pop" store described above. With a business like this, the ownership is personal and so are the risks. The owner reports all expenses and profits on their personal tax return. For the operation of the business, they answer to nobody – but there is a downside. Setting up a business like this opens up the owner to liability risks. If something happens that gets the business in trouble, such as a customer slipping on some ice outside, and they slip and break their risk and decide to sue – the owner is personally liable. If the business goes bankrupt, the owner is responsible for the debts. If the owner does not have enough financial resources elsewhere to cover the debts, then the owner will also go bankrupt.

Of course, it's often the case that two or more people join up to form a small business. When people decide to set up a business like this casually but without any formal legal structure (other than contracts they agree to amongst themselves), it's not much different than a sole proprietorship as far as the legal structure. The business owners may agree to different shares of income and responsibility and set up a decision hierarchy in the business, but they will still handle taxes (and face liabilities) associated with the business on a personal level. In this case, just like we described above, if the business goes bankrupt or gets sued, then the owners are responsible for the debts.

Of course, many people who decide to start a business want to keep it separate from their personal activities, financially and legally. The simplest way to do this is to form a limited liability company or LLC. In this case, the owners are not personally liable for any debts or liabilities incurred by the business. However, this type of company operates as a "hybrid" model, and it retains many aspects of an ordinary sole proprietorship or partnership. An LLC has so-called "Flow through" taxation, meaning the profits from the business go to the owners in their respective shares and the owners pay taxes. The LLC doesn't pay tax. Taxes on profits are determined on the owners' individual tax returns, and they pay the tax. An LLC has to be formally created by filing forms and a small fee in the state where it's created. If the company gets in trouble by failing to pay its debts, for example, then the company rather than the individual owner is liable (assuming the company has everything in order, legally speaking). An LLC is a relatively simple arrangement while protecting the owners from losing everything to debt or lawsuits based on the activities of the company. It can have as few as one owner or multiple owners including corporations. While most types of businesses can form an LLC, banks and insurance companies cannot be LLCs.

Any of the foregoing businesses could have investors, but they do not have public investors. The only investment would be using private contractual arrangements.

The next level up is the corporation. A corporation is a step up from an LLC, and it's considered to be a "person" in legal matters. A corporation can do many things a person can do, such as own property, make contracts, take on debt, get sued or initiate lawsuits. A corporation can also be required to pay fines or be forced out of existence.

A single person can form a corporation, or multiple people (or even another corporation) can come together to create a corporation. A corporation is formed by applying to a state for a charter. A corporation can be a government entity, but for our purposes, we're interested in private corporations which can be for-profit or non-profit (formally designated as a not for profit).

Ownership of an ordinary business corporation is determined by stock (also described as equity). A share of stock is an ownership share of the business. We could form a small corporation between three people, John, Sally, and Trevor. As part of the formation of the corporation, it would issue shares of stock. When a corporation applies for a charter with the state, they must specify the number of shares that it will issue. For our example, let's say it issues 100,000 shares of stock. It can then issue them as it pleases, so let us say John gets 50,000 shares, Sally gets 30,000 shares, and Trevor gets the remaining 20,000 shares. That means that John is 50% owner of the company, with Sally and John owning 30% and 20% respectively. When the company makes a profit that is distributed John will get 50% of the profits. People who invest in a corporation receive certificates of stock showing their shares in the company.

These stockholders, or owners of the company, can meet and choose a board of directors for the corporation. Votes are proportional to shares of stock. So continuing our example, if the company agreed upon 10 votes, John's vote would count for five votes while Sally and Trevor would get 3 and 2 votes respectively. The directors choose the officers of the company and set their salaries and layout corporate duties.

In very small companies, the stockholders, board of directors, and officers are usually the same people or even one single person. In larger companies, the officers may also be stockholders or directors, but you can have outsiders be the board of directors, and they may hire people from the outside to be the officers of the company because they may bring in skills and talents that are useful. In that case, officers may hold little or even no stock in the company and be compensated by salary.

Small stockholders who play an active role can gain power by getting a large number of other stockholders to give them their vote on issues facing the corporation. When this is done, it's called "proxy."

Stocks are transferable. This allows the corporation to continue in existence even if people leave the ownership of the company. Returning to our example, suppose Sally is tired of the corporation, sees no future in it, and is tired of the bickering between John and Trevor. She can sell her shares of stock to a third party which we'll call Mary, who will assume Sally's 30% ownership share of the business. Sally and Mary, if this is a private corporation, can agree on a sales price that might be based on a 30% share of profit earned by the company over a given time period, or it could be based on perceived potential earnings if it's a new venture or the company has an asset that could have potential earnings in the future. An outright sale isn't the only possibility. John, for example, could decide to sell 20,000 of his 50,000 shares to a third party, which could be an outsider or he could sell them to one of the other investors (Sally or Trevor).

Like an LLC, if the corporation owes money, is fined, or gets in some other type of trouble, the owners are not in general liable in any way, and the debts belong to the corporation. Taxes are a different matter. Depending on the type of corporation (more on that in a minute) it will be liable for taxes and fees. The corporation will pay those and the stockholders are not personally liable for them, even for taxes on profits. Stockholders are only liable for profits that are distributed to them by the company. Those profits are treated differently and not as ordinary income; the way income would be considered for a sole proprietorship, partnership, or LLC.

There are different kinds of stocks. The most important type is called Common Stock. This type of stock is an ownership share in the corporation, the type we discussed above. A corporation may also issue preferred stock, which provides additional benefits over and above common stock. For example, preferred stockholders may have a prior claim on the assets of a company. So if the company dissolves, the preferred stockholders will be able to claim ownership of those assets before anyone else. They can also receive other benefits, such as payment of fixed dividends before others can receive them. Preferred stock comes with a price, however. For example, preferred stockholders may not have voting privileges.

So far we've discussed the structure of private companies. A private company is privately held. You can't just go invest in it unless you are asked to invest (for example the company is seeking capital from outsiders) or are in the inside circle (family, one of the founders, friends of the founders). Many private companies get quite large and are even worth billions of dollars.

A public company, in contrast, has stocks that are traded on a public exchange. The activities of the company and its structure are more closely regulated by government agencies. Any member of the public can in principle buy stock in the company. Public companies are governed by reporting requirements, which force them to file public reports detailing their profits, losses, and other activities. A public company traded on the stock exchange is required to file publicly available quarterly profit and loss reports called "form 10-Q". Form 10-Q reports can be accessed online via the EDGAR database maintained by the U.S. Securities and Exchange Commission (SEC). The link for this is:

https://www.sec.gov/edgar/searchedgar/companysearch.html

Public corporations must also file annual reports, which are called form 10-K, which give a detailed description of the company's performance for the previous year.

They can also access "public markets" (like stock exchanges) to raise capital, while private companies cannot.

A stock market or stock exchange is a public market that exists for the purpose of buying and selling of stocks in public corporations. Stock markets are a vital part of the economy, that is, when considering a healthy and growing capitalistic economy because they give a company access to large amounts of capital from the public. A publicly-traded company can raise a great deal more capital than a private company can, and while private companies can get quite large, publicly traded companies tend to be much larger.

What is a stock

Stock is the capital raised by a corporation through the issuance of *shares*. The stock or capital is divided up into equal parts or shares. Each share represents fractional ownership of the corporation. A private corporation can define the value of a share. For example, suppose the corporation has $100,000 in capital. It could issue 1,000 shares worth $100 each. If an investor buys five shares, they own $500 worth of stock, giving them a 0.5% ownership stake in the company. A *shareholder* is someone who owns shares of stock in the company.

For a publicly traded company, the value of a share is determined by the markets. The value of a share of stock in a publicly traded company fluctuates on a constant basis when the markets are open.

So, in a nutshell, when a company needs to raise money, it issues shares. The company can use the money raised for whatever purpose it deems fit, and it is not under obligation to pay the money back. Instead, the shares can be bought and sold to other individuals (or institutions) on the markets. The company may pay out proportions of its profits as dividends, but whether or not it pays dividends and how much is solely at the discretion of the company, and many modern corporations don't pay dividends.

Types of stock
We've already touched on the different types of stock.

Common stock is the basic type of stock. When "stock" is being discussed although the word "common" isn't used as a designation, it is most likely common stock to which people are referring. A share of common stock represents fractional ownership of the company. A share of common stock is also a claim on that proportion of profits, which are paid out as dividends, although not all publicly traded companies issue dividends. Owners of common stock get "variable" dividends, and this type of dividend is not guaranteed. The board of directors of a corporation can decide how much is paid out for dividends, and even if dividends are paid at all.

Preemptive rights refer to the right of a shareholder of common stock to a claim the issuance of new stock so that they can maintain their previous share of ownership. In other words, suppose that a company had 100 shares of stock and you owned 10% or 10 shares. If the company issued 100 more shares, your preemptive rights would give you the option of purchasing another 10 shares to maintain your 10% ownership stake when the company had expanded to 200 shares. Of course, you would have to *purchase* it, the new stock isn't given to you, but you're given first opportunity to take the new shares up to your current ownership percentage.

Common stock has a high rate of return when compared to other investments. However, if the company goes bankrupt and liquidates, the common shareholders are at the back of the line. Typically those who the company owes money to are paid in the following order: first creditors, then bondholders, then those who hold preferred shares of stock. Only after all of these have been paid would owners of shares of common stock be paid. Of course, this assumes that the company is even able to pay any of its debts.

While owners of common stock aren't guaranteed dividends and are the last in line when collecting on debts, they can easily be sold at a profit enabling capital gains. So for example, you might buy 100 shares for $100 in company A in one year, and then sell the shares for $250 a year later if the company has done well and the stock price has risen by $1.50 per share. The ability to earn these types of profits is why people invest in common stocks and why they form the basis of most retirement accounts (because they can gain value over time). Since the value of common stock can go down as well as up, it is called *volatile*.

Owners of common stock are able to vote for the board of directors. There is one vote awarded per share of stock. So if you buy 80,000 shares of stock in a corporation, you would have 80,000 votes.

As we mentioned above, *preferred stock* is a different class of stock that comes with some tradeoffs. Shares of preferred stock are not as volatile and lack voting rights; however, they come with two major benefits. First, a preferred stock gives you a guaranteed dividend payment. A corporation must pay a fixed dividend to shareholders of preferred stock over a fixed period of time. Another advantage of preferred stock is shareholders of preferred stock have a claim on the assets of the company. If the company goes bankrupt, after creditors and bondholders have been paid, if there is any leftover capital or assets then preferred shareholders have a claim on it before owners of common stock.

Two drawbacks of preferred stock are the following. The first is that generally preferred stock does not offer the same opportunity to take advantage of capital growth that common stock does. Second, shares of preferred stock are *callable*. This means that the company, at its own discretion, can purchase shares of preferred stock back from the shareholders. Generally, this is done at a favorable price. However, the company can take the shares back from you without prior notice, and you have no say in the matter.

Types of stock can also be further differentiated at more levels if the company so desires. The other levels may be given other powers, such as putting more voting power in with a certain class of stock. Typical definitions include Class A and Class B stocks. Class A shares have more voting rights than Class B shares. For example, a company could issue

Class A shares where one share had 10 votes while a share of Class B stock would have a single vote.

Remember that a company issues shares of stock which people then buy in the markets, and the company then uses the cash. The company may or may not buy the stock back, and it's certainly not under obligation to do so. People can trade it among themselves on the market, and if an investor wants to get out, they sell their stock to a third party. So what is a stock worth? It's worth what that third party is willing to pay for it. This is what drives the daily ups and downs of individual stock prices, and when all pooled together the values of the markets themselves. You would think that the value of a stock would be set by the profits the company was actually making, but human nature being what it is that is rarely if ever the case. The value of stocks is based on hopes, beliefs about what the company may make in the future (or fears of collapse) and demand for the stock on the markets.

A brief history of investing and stock markets
We often take modern life for granted, but where does all this come from? Why is there a New York Stock Exchange?

The formation of stock exchanges arose out of a basic human need in organized societies. Some people need money for their business or project. There are other people who have money sitting around they could give out –for a price. Financial markets bring these two groups of people together.

The origins of financial markets trace back to medieval trade fairs which began around the year 1000. These trade fairs brought merchants and buyers together to trade agricultural and manufactured products. These trade fairs became "free trade zones" that were exempt from the usual taxes and duties imposed by various governments of the time.

Eventually, some trade fairs became permanent rather than happening periodically as you normally think about a "fair." One of the first trade fairs to become permanent was in Antwerp, Belgium. By forming a permanent trade fair, the notion of financial centers began taking shape. Moreover, some people at the trade fairs only traded in money, lending it out or converting currencies.

Another important development occurred during the medieval era when a concept variously called *census* or *rente* was developed. In short, this allowed people to rent or buy property using loans. The person who wanted the property would be allowed to use it in exchange for regular payments. The word *gage* is an ancient word meaning *pledge*. It's at the root of the modern term mortgage. In medieval times, a live-gage worked essentially like a mortgage, the user of the property was able to make regular payments for a specified time period, after which they seized ownership of the property. This was a great help to property owners of the time, who could then turn their illiquid property assets into cash flows.

Something that is liquid is something that is readily turned into cash.

By the 13th century, the city of Venice was flourishing, and also getting itself into periodic wars. Wars cost money, and so the government found novel ways to raise cash for its exploits. This would lead to the birth of the concept of tradable debt.

Basically, the government would seize a portion of wealth from the rich people of Venice, with the promise to pay interest on it. The government retained the right to pay the principal back or not pay it back as it saw fit. These deals were known as prestiti, which simply means "loan" in Italian.

The breakthrough associated with prestiti was that they could be bought and sold or traded. The value in doing so was to either sell your prestiti to someone to raise cash or to attain a guaranteed income stream by purchasing one. Essentially it would be a guaranteed income for life in the regular payments from the government.

During the interim centuries prior to the American Revolution, finance went through some shaky times due to the autocratic nature of the royal government. Kings could simply refuse to pay loans back and in some cases even jailed people who they owed money too. As a result, people who loaned money to governments often charged insane interest rates, going as high as 80% and even 100%. This was done in order to hedge the possibility the government would never pay the loan back.

This began to change with the formation of the Dutch Republic, which was one of the first examples of a stable and relatively free society. The provinces and municipalities of the Dutch Republic began paying perpetual annuities in exchange for investments. Interest rates came more in line with modern values, around 3%. The rates were low because people were virtually guaranteed that they would receive the payments, unlike the case of the harsh kings and queens mentioned earlier.

It was in the Dutch Republic that the notion of a corporation that issued stock ownership was also born. This idea began with the exploration of the globe by the sea where ships would sail out to collect "bounty" that they brought home. These were obviously very high-risk ventures, and expensive to launch. No single merchant was able to raise funds necessary to launch a voyage on his own, and so the idea of pooling money together for a commercial venture was born.

When the ship returned home, if it safely made it back, then the profits would be split up in proportions determined by the initial investment each person made.

At first, these ventures were single events. Then, in 1609, the Dutch East India Company was formed with the intent of making it a permanent and perpetual enterprise. The company received a permanent charter from the government, and it formed itself as a "joint-stock company." In other words, it allowed individuals to buy stock in the company which would entail them to a share of the company's profits.

This set off a snowball effect that has been in operation ever since. A few years later, in 1613, the Amsterdam Stock Exchange was founded, and multiple companies were formed that followed this model. In 1792 the New York Stock Exchange was founded, and by the early 19th century businesses essentially took the form of modern corporations.

People often don't know it, but different types of financial instruments or securities are traded on stock markets. In the early years of the New York Stock Exchange, government securities or treasuries formed a large part of the trading. It wasn't until around 100 years later that the volume of traded stock began exceeding the volume of bond trading on the NYSE. If you are not sure what these terms mean, don't worry as we will describe them in detail later in the book.

The importance of stock market investing

Stock market investing is important for the company and for the individual, as well as for the economy as a whole. Corporations would never be able to raise the kind of cash they do without the existence of public, regulated markets. Without companies being able to raise that cash, the economy would be much smaller and would grow at slower rates. So while you could envision a capitalist type system without financial markets where people could invest in stocks, which would be a less dynamic and far smaller economic system.

Building wealth and securing your retirement

For the individual, while investment in stocks carries with it real risks, it's largely an opportunity to build wealth. For the smartest investors, it's an opportunity to build wealth to tap in the future and so represents security in retirement. While people aren't entirely conscious of it, this is how pension funds grow wealth to pay their bills, from the pension funds people used to take advantage of when retiring from a lifetime career at a single company to pension funds used to fund public service employees. The stock market also forms the basis of 401k plans, college savings plans, annuities, and individual retirement accounts. For those who are willing to assume a small level of risk and play it smart, they represent an excellent opportunity for building individual wealth and long-term security.

CHAPTER 2
Different Types Of Investing

In the previous chapter, we learned a little bit about what stocks are and got a bit of an idea of how modern stocks and stock markets came into existence. Now, let us look at some of the different ways you can invest your money in today's world.

Preferred and Common stock

We saw in the previous chapter that shares of stock are fractional ownership shares in a corporation. Remember, the term common stock is a "common sense" idea of stock. That is, you buy a share in the company; if the value of the shares goes up, you can sell it for a profit or capital gain. You have one vote for share. You may or not may receive dividends, at the discretion of the company. And if it goes belly up, you are last in line to get paid and in truth will probably lose your money.

Preferred shares of stock are a more guarded form of investment. They are a claim on dividends but have fewer or no voting rights. They don't provide a means of capital gain, but if the company goes under you're ahead of common stock owners in line to get paid.

Some special classes of stock, class A stock, have more voting rights than class B stocks. Not all companies issue class A and B stocks.

What is a bond?

If you've looked into investing, you've probably heard the phrase "stocks and bonds." So what is a bond?

In short, a bond is a loan, made by YOU.

When you invest in a bond, you lend the money to whoever issued the bond. A bond can be issued by a corporation, so you could buy bonds issued by Apple or IBM. Or a bond can be issued by a city or even the federal government. For example, the federal government may need to raise money to fight a war. Or a city government or municipality many need money to fix roads or build a new library.

Why would you lend these people money? Because they promise to pay it back, with interest.

Generally, bonds are considered a "safe" form of investment, especially when it comes to government-issued bonds. Of course, not everyone pays their loans back. And just like a person with bad credit, a bond issuer who is viewed as risky has to offer higher interest rates. For example, Apple would probably be considered very low risk. People would be confident Apple will pay the principal back, and so Apple could offer relatively low interest rates. Your cousin Joey, however, who has a construction business is in a different boat. If he offers bonds, he'd also have to pay a higher interest rate. That would cover the risk investors are facing when buying bonds from Joey. That is, Joey may not be able to pay the principal back.

The interest rate isn't completely determined by the risk of the issuer, however. Market conditions will also have a large impact. As time goes on, interest rates go up and down depending on how things are shaping up in the overall economy.

Second, how long a bond is held has a big influence on interest rates. If you got a bond for Joey's construction company, and it was just a couple of months when he promised to return the principle – Joey might get by offering a lower interest rate than he would if it was two years before he paid his loan back. This doesn't just apply to Joey – it applies to Apple and IBM too. If Apple or IBM offers a three-year or five-year bond, they will be able to pay lower interest rates than they would on a 20- or 30-year bond. Nobody knows how Apple or IBM will be doing that far down the road, even if they still exist.

The higher the risk, the higher the interest rate that must be paid.

Of course, if you buy a bond, you don't have to keep it. You can sell it to someone else.

Bond prices depend explicitly on interest rates. The interest rate doesn't set the price of the bond in a specific manner, but interest rates and bond prices move in opposite directions. But keep in mind that the interest rate on a bond that has already been issued by the company never changes.

So imagine that in 2019 Joey issues a bond for his construction company and you buy it. It's a ten-year bond you buy for $10,000, and the interest rate is 7%.

A few years later, Joey wants to issue new bonds to raise more cash. Suppose that market conditions have changed so that interest rates have gone down to 4%.

In that case, the new bonds being issued aren't as appealing as the bond you currently hold, which pays 7% interest. An investor might prefer the higher interest rate of your bond and offer to buy it. Since it pays a higher interest rate than bonds currently issued, you can sell it for a higher price. Say for the sake of example you could sell it for $12,000.

On the other hand, if the new bonds have a higher interest rate, say 10%, then your bond isn't worth as much as the new ones. Someone could invest in a $10,000 bond from Joey and get a 10% interest rate, so why would they give you $10,000 to take over your bond that pays 7% interest? Of course, they won't. So if you needed fast cash and tried selling it, you'd have to sell it for a lower price, say $7,500.

The rule for bonds is if interest rates rise, bond prices fall. If interest rates drop, bond prices rise. Remember in this case we are talking about bonds that have already been issued and the issue is what price they would fetch on the market.

Of course, you can simply hold the bond, and collect the interest. Holding a bond for the time agreed upon is called holding a bond to *maturity*. Over the time that you hold the bond, you collect the interest payments at the rate agreed upon when you invested in the bond. At maturity, you get the *face value* back. So a $10,000 bond was purchased, you get paid $10,000 back at maturity.

How are stocks different from bonds

Stocks and bonds are totally different. A bond is a loan that you make either to a company or a government entity. If you buy a bond from a corporation, you have simply lent money to the corporation. But you don't own a share of the corporation, and at the maturity date, they will pay you back.

- A share of stock is an ownership share in a company. With a bond, you have no ownership share.
- A bond is a loan to the company (or government). At maturity, the company (or government) will pay back the loan (your investment in the bond). When you buy a stock, the company keeps the money and can keep it forever.
- Bonds and stocks can be traded on the markets.
- The price of bonds is influenced by interest rates. When interest rates go up, the value of a bond on the secondary market goes down. If interest rates go down, the value of the bond goes up.
- Stocks are not influenced by interest rates at all. The price of a stock may be influenced by the state of the overall economy, by perceptions of the company's future worth, or by a favorable or unfavorable earnings report, among other factors.

- Stocks are considered a high-risk investment. You might lose everything if the economy or the company collapses. On the other hand, you might earn a large capital gain if the stock does well.
- Bonds are considered safer investments. If you don't trade on the secondary market and hold your bond to maturity, you will get fixed interest rate payments in the meantime on a regular basis. This makes bonds appealing to retirees, and in general, as investors get closer to retirement age, they move their investment portfolio more toward bonds.

In short, stocks and bonds are different investment vehicles. People don't usually invest in one or the other, but mix up their investments instead. If you are a risk taker, the more risk you're willing to handle, the more you're going to be invested in stocks. The more conservative you are, the more you're going to be invested in bonds which are considered more stable but with lower potential rewards.

Investing in government securities
Governments at all levels issue bonds in order to raise money. The U.S. federal government issues bonds that are called "treasuries." They come in short-term and longer-term varieties and pay different interest rates depending on the maturity date of the bond. You've probably heard of other types of bonds issued by the U.S. government such as savings bonds.

Any government can issue bonds, and frequently you will see bond questions on voting ballots. Local and state governments may issue bonds to borrow money in order to get certain projects done, such as building infrastructure. Bonds issued by cities are called municipal, or "muni" bonds and have been a safe investment as well as a tax shelter. As time goes on, however, government bonds aren't being considered as safe as they once were as cities and even states face the possibility of not being able to pay their debts.

What is a dividend
A dividend is a payout by a corporation of its profits. Dividends are not mandatory for common stock, and many companies don't pay dividends on common stock, but if you can find investments from solid companies that pay dividends, and can invest enough to make it worth it, then dividends can be equivalent to bonds in the sense of paying regular income. Unlike bonds and interest payments, however, dividends will routinely fluctuate.If the company earns more profits, then you will be paid more money in your dividends. If the company doesn't make profits, then you're out of luck. In contrast, if you invested in a bond from the company but they don't make profits, they still have to pay you the interest payment on the bond.

The Dow Jones Industrial Average

Now let us look at some common market definitions that you'll see routinely thrown around on the financial news. It's a good idea to know what they all mean. We'll start with the most famous index, which is the Dow Jones Industrial Average.

The Dow Jones Industrial Average is an index which tracks the movement of stock prices for the 30 largest publicly traded companies. It's called "industrial" because it was developed in the late 19th century when heavy industry dominated business and the markets. Today that isn't the case. Over time, the companies on the Dow Jones index change, as new growing companies knock off older companies that may be growing more slowly or even shrinking. The purpose of the index is to track the overall progress of the stock market rather than of the companies themselves.

It was created in 1896 by a man named Charles Dow, who founded the Wall Street Journal. The editorial board of the paper selected the companies added to the index. It's a price-weighted index. To see how it's calculated, we can make up a fake index of five companies. Here are the companies with their share prices:

- Acme Corporation: $50
- Beta Company: $20
- Charles Corporation: $100
- Delta Company: $10
- Excelsior: $80

To get the price-weighted index, first we sum the share prices:

$50 + $20 + $100 + $10 + $80 = $260

To get the price-weighted index, we divide by the number of companies:

Our index = $260/5 = 52

This gives stocks with higher prices greater influence over the index. So in our fictitious example, Charles Corporation and Excelsior will have the most influence on the value of the index. This has led to a great deal of criticism of the Dow Jones because suppose those 2 companies go up in stock price while the other three fall – the heavier weight given by the higher stock prices could make the index go up, even though the overall economy might be entering a downturn because most companies are seeing their stocks drop in price.

332

The number of shares the company has also don't enter in the calculation, another weakness that means it may not accurately reflect the market as a whole. A big criticism is that a small company that has a high stock price can have a big influence on the value of the index.

Despite these shortcomings, the Dow Jones Industrial Average (DJIA) continues to be a widely accepted indicator of the market's health, and its value is regularly reported. The companies on the DJIA are still selected by the editorial board of the Wall Street Journal.

What is the S & P 500?

The S&P 500 tracks the largest 500 companies in the market. Since it tracks far more companies, it's a broader measure of the market than the DJIA. Moreover, to address some of the concerns people have with the DJIA, the S&P 500 tracks market capitalization rather than just share price. That is, it tracks the total value of all shares the company has issued. This eliminates the problem of having a small company that can have an outsized influence on the index by having a high stock price. Influence on the index is directly proportional to the market cap of the company. So a company that had a market cap of $80 billion would be four times more influential on the index than a company with $20 billion in market capitalization. In order to be in the S&P 500, a stock must be traded on the New York Stock Exchange, NASDAQ, BATS, or the Investors exchange. It cannot be an over-the-counter or "pink sheet" stock (see next section).

Other Markets

No doubt you've heard of the New York Stock Exchange, but there are other trading markets as well. The NASDAQ primarily trades in electronics or technology companies, but recently merged with OMX ABO, which is located in Sweden. Since then it also offers trading in commodities and other types of investments including derivatives.

BATS is a new exchange that is all electronic based out of Kansas, of all places. It was founded in 2005 and has been plagued by some problems including a large fine by the SEC in 2014.

Finally, we come to "pink sheets," also known as over-the-counter stocks. These are stocks issued by public companies that don't meet SEC requirements to be on a major stock exchange like the New York Stock Exchange or NASDAQ. Pink Sheets or over-the-counter stocks are low-cost investments but are very high risk. They are often priced so low that they are known as "penny stocks." In the old days, these "over the counter" stocks were traded by writing on pink paper, but today they are traded electronically. When a company is traded over the counter, it is said to "go pink." Frankly, these are dangerous investments for most people.

They go pink because they may not want to release their earning statements publicly, or they may fail to meet SEC requirements. Regulators generally consider them "ultra-risky"; however, some pink sheet stocks may be good investments. For example, new companies funded primarily by venture capitalists might be pinks. But generally, they are high risk and if you want to sell it's going to be difficult to find a buyer. While they don't qualify for NYSE or other major exchanges, there are government ratings. OTCQX designates the best pink stocks. OTCQB is monitored by the feds, and this category includes young companies that have been dependent on venture capital funding. OTC or over-the-counter ones are the lowest of the pinks and considered dangerous investments. It's the policy of this book to stay away from penny stocks/pinks/over-the-counter.

Exchange traded funds, what are they?

An exchange-traded fund is basically what its name says it is. It's a fund, so it is a "basket of assets" or several stocks or investments bundled together. You can think of it as a pool of money has been put together from a large number of investors, and it is used to buy stocks and other investment assets. Exchange traded funds can be anything, real estate, or commodities. In most cases, they are diversified holdings, for example, tracking a stock market index like the S&P 500.

However, there are exchange-traded funds for virtually any kind of investment, including bonds and gold. They are exchange traded, meaning they work exactly like stocks, and are traded on stock markets like the New York Stock Exchange. Since they trade like stocks, you can buy and sell exchange-traded funds (often denoted by the initials ETF) like any other stock, on the fly.

Investing in real estate, gold, commodities

Investing in a company is a real investment. In other words, you're providing capital to real corporations offering valuable products and services to the economy. People invest in successful companies hoping for long-term growth. Companies create value with time. For example, Apple has much more value now than it had twenty years ago before it invented the iPhone, iPad, and iWatch.

Although people talk about "investing" in real estate, gold, or other commodities, they are really *speculating*. Basically, when you're speculating, you're hoping that someone will come along in the future and offer you more for something than what you paid for it. An ounce of gold today is an ounce of gold tomorrow, it doesn't have any more intrinsic value than it ever did.

Real estate can also be speculation. For decades, people believed that the value of real estate would always increase. We found out in 2007-08 that this was not true. Believing that real estate will always increase in value is magical thinking. It might work sometimes, but it is not going to work all the time. Like buying an ounce of gold and hoping someone will pay you more for it in the future, if you're hoping to flip houses or sell for big bucks later, you're speculating.

Real estate can be an investment. For example, you can acquire multiple properties that can be used as rentals. Once the properties are paid off over the decades, then they will provide a steady stream of income.

That said, investing in real estate is really beyond the scope of this book, and we don't really consider investing in gold to be an investment at all. So our focus will remain mostly on stocks and to a lesser extent on bonds.

What is a Mutual Fund?

Like an Exchange Traded Fund or ETF, a mutual fund is a diversified group of investments wrapped up in one package. You can find mutual funds that track many of the same securities that ETFs do. For example, you can invest in mutual funds that track the S&P 500. An example is the Vanguard 500 Index Fund. You can even buy mutual funds that track the *entire* stock market, not just the S&P 500.

How is a Mutual Fund different than an ETF?

Mutual funds sound a lot like ETFs. And they are – but there is one crucial difference. Mutual funds do not trade like stocks. So they are not traded on the fly throughout the trading day. Similar to an ETF, a mutual fund is a pool of money collected from large numbers of people to put together to invest. In short, a mutual fund is a portfolio, and you're buying a share of the portfolio. Typically a mutual fund will hold hundreds of securities. Mutual funds are controlled by professional money managers. Unlike an ETF, a mutual fund only trades once per day after the markets close. We will discuss them in more detail in a future chapter.

What is an IRA and Types of IRAs

An IRA is an Individual Retirement Account. This is a type of investment account that is government sponsored and tax-deferred in some way. You can hold a wide range of investments in an IRA, such as stocks, bonds, ETFs, and mutual funds. You can also hold metals and other commodities such as gold. A traditional IRA allows an investor to invest money on a tax-deferred basis into the IRA account, where it's allowed to grow (assuming the investments will grow...). When the individual retires and begins making withdrawals from the IRA, the money is taxed when it is pulled out of the account. Any capital gains made by the investments are not taxed until they are actually withdrawn. So it can be described as invest now, tax later.

A Roth IRA is funded with after-tax dollars and will be tax-free when the money is withdrawn during retirement.

A SIMPLE IRA is a type of retirement plan that can be offered by small businesses. The business qualifies by having 100 or fewer employees.

There is also another type of IRA called a Simplified Employee Pension or SEP. These can be used by people who are self-employed.

IRA's are a large topic, and we devote an entire chapter to the details.

A brief overview of money market funds, CDs, and Banking

Perhaps the simplest type of investment is simply putting your money in the bank. At the lowest level, you could put money in a savings account. In the old days – not that long ago – when interest rates were fairly significant it was actually a good idea to put some money into a savings account. A savings account is virtually risk-free in the modern world because they are insured by the federal government up to $250,000 per bank. So if the bank fails, the government will cover the loss up to $250,000.

Even better was to put money into a CD. A CD is a Certificate of Deposit, a type of investment sold by banks. Like a savings account, a CD is basically "money in the bank" that is considered a safe investment. Savings accounts have interest rates that fluctuate with the market, the interest rates on a CD are usually fixed, although variable interest rate CDs are available. Also, while a savings account can be held for as long as you like, a CD is a fixed time investment ranging from three months to five years. Like with bonds, the time that the investment in the CD ends is called *maturity*. If you withdraw the money before the maturity date, the bank will charge you a penalty. CDs are also covered up to $250,000 by FDIC insurance.

A money-market account is a specialized type of high-interest savings account.

The final instrument related to banks we'll discuss are money market funds. These are actually a type of mutual fund. This is a mutual fund that invests in securities with short term maturity dates of 13 months or less. Colloquially, a money market fund is an investment in cash. In reality, it's an investment in highly liquid instruments, which means instruments that are either cash or could be converted to cash very quickly. It invests in cash, cash equivalent securities, and debt. It can invest in CDs. It also invests in so-called "commercial paper," which is a short-term debt issued by corporations. Similarly, they invest in short-term debt held by corporations that is guaranteed by a bank. These kinds of investments are known as "banker's acceptances." A money market fund can also invest in U.S. federal government securities called Treasuries. Finally, a money market fund will invest in "repos" or Repurchase Agreements. What this means, is you temporarily buy something from someone and they agree to buy it back at a future date. In this case, the dealer of the repo is selling U.S. treasuries to raise short term cash.

What is an annuity, are they worth it?
An annuity can be thought of as a kind of self-funded pension or even self-directed social security payments, although annuities are run by private companies and not by the government.

There are two types of annuities, *deferred annuities,* and *income annuities*. With a deferred annuity, the investor invests a sum with the company and payments are deferred until the investor decides to take them out. They are regulated by the IRS, and there is a 10% penalty for taking withdrawals from a deferred annuity before the age of 59 ½. These types of investments are run by life insurance companies and usually involve a guarantee of principle.

Funds are deposited by the investor with the life insurance company, which holds the funds with an interest rate that may be fixed for up to 10 years. After that period is over, the insurance company can adjust the interest rate once per year. Unlike banking investments, they are not FDIC insured. The funds can be taken out as a lump-sum or as guaranteed monthly payments.

An income or immediate annuity immediately begins paying out a fixed monthly payment in exchange for your investment. So you could put in $100,000 and then have $500 monthly payments delivered to you immediately, for the rest of your life. You're guaranteed a fixed sum of money that will be paid the rest of your life in monthly installments, but you lose all access to the principle. Generally, annuities are not considered to be the best use of your investment dollars directed toward your retirement, but some people will find them appealing because they offer a level of security (but remember – as 2008 showed nothing is guaranteed in life). Fixed income annuities offer security because they aren't impacted by the volatility of the market and you'll be getting that monthly check forever. You can also get an annuity that includes a cost of living increase, but you'll have to pay additional costs.

The best advice regarding annuities is to first watch for hidden fees that the life insurance company can be used to gauge you. Second, while annuities might be a good idea to boost your social security by giving you a guaranteed monthly income when you're retired, don't invest all of your money into an annuity. Also, note that your children will not inherit any leftover principle.

Risk profiles for different classes of investments

Investments of different types can be ranked by risk, although there aren't any absolute rules. But we can give a basic risk rating to each of the major types of investments we've considered. It is important to realize that to a certain degree there is a relationship between risk and reward – often higher risk also means higher potential reward. For risk, we mean losing your principal.

- Federal Government bonds: Very safe
- Corporate bonds: Safe if not classified as "junk."
- Bank CDs: Safe, up to $250,000
- Savings accounts: Safe, up to $250,000
- Money Market Funds: Safe
- Municipal bonds: Very safe
- Mutual Funds: relatively safe
- ETFs: relatively safe
- Annuity: safe, however not necessarily very good return on your investment
- Individual stocks: can have elevated risk
- Penny stocks: Extreme risk
- Investment in private companies: Extreme risk

The actual risk profile may vary on how and when you invest, but the best advice to minimize risk is to avoid putting all of your eggs in one basket, as the old saying goes. For example, there is a big difference between someone who puts $200,000 in a savings account, $300,000 in a mutual fund, $100,000 in an annuity, and $50,000 in penny stocks and a person who puts $150,000 in penny stocks and $50,000 in exchange-traded funds. Obviously, the latter person is at a much higher risk. Different people have different amounts of risk they can tolerate. The bottom line is you can tolerate the risk if you're comfortable with losing all the money. If you've only got $250,000, then losing $200,000 of it too risky investments in penny stocks and private companies is a bad idea, but only putting $30,000 in those riskier investments, and maybe catching the next "sure thing" might be a risk worth taking.

In the following chapters, we will look at various types of investments in more detail.

CHAPTER 3
Is The Stock Market Worth It?

While the stock market beckons with dreams of riches and wealth, it also puts fear in potential investors with visions of huge losses. These fearful imaginings are backed with real historical experience, mainly by the crash in 1929 that initiated the Great Depression and by the 2008 Financial Crisis, where lots of people lost a lot of money.

However, a careful examination of the stock market shows that, in reality, these fears are unfounded. The historical record demonstrates that over the long-term, the stock market experiences growth. Those who hold out during downturns – and in fact increase their investments in stocks during downturns – turn out to be the winners.

Compound interest and how it works

Compound interest is one of the most fundamental financial concepts, and yet far too many in the general public are ignorant about this crucial topic. We don't want to get involved in the mathematics here, the purpose of this book isn't to give you a headache, so we'll just review the basic concept.

You know what interest does. If you save $100 in the bank, and interest is 6%, then you'll earn $6 over the course of a year. At the end of the year, you'll have $106!

If you're not very smart, you'll give yourself a series of high fives and withdraw the $6 and buy a pizza to celebrate. The following year, if you leave the $100 in there, and the interest rate remains the same, then you'll be able to get another pizza.

But by now you've figured out that there is a better way. What if at the end of each year we simply leave the $6 in the bank? At the end of the first year, rather than calculating interest on the $100 principal, now the interest will be calculated for the $106. At the end of the second year, we'd have a little more than $112 in the bank. We've earned interest on the interest. In other words, interest has *compounded.*

An even smarter thing to do would be to put another $100 in the bank every year. If you start with $100 and put in nothing but don't take any of the earned interest out, with 6% interest every year after ten years, you'll have a bit more than $179.

Now, suppose that we go ahead and put in the $100 every year. If we were stuffing it in our mattress, saving $100 per year for ten years would give us $1,000. On the other hand, if we put it in a savings account with 6% interest and don't pull any money out, after ten years, we'll have $1,576.25.

When we are talking about $100 investments, an extra $576.25 isn't something to sneeze at over a ten-year period. In short, we've increased our principal by almost 58%, as compared to the poor fool who stuffed money in his mattress.

A bank is a safe investment. But at the time of writing, interest rates are really low. Checking you might find something around 2.4%. Some CDs might go as high as 3.1% — not very impressive numbers.

Let's say that instead of $100, you were putting $1,000 a month into bank CDs for ten years with an interest rate of 3.1% with an initial investment of $12,000. At the end of ten years, you'd have a nice nest egg of $158,770.29. Congratulations! At least you didn't blow the money. Had the interest rate been 0%, then you'd only have $132,000. So the bank basically grew the money by a little more than 19%. Of course, there is inflation too. At the time of writing, the inflation rate is around 2.2-2.5%. It's a historically low inflation rate, but with interest rates that low it's eating away at the money. Your investment is slightly better than keeping up. That's a good thing – at least you have the cash on hand. But with an interest rate on CDs that is barely above inflation, you haven't increased your purchasing power at all.

What if you invested in the stock market instead? From 1926 to 2018, the S&P 500 averaged an annual growth rate of 10%. In that case, if you followed the same investment plan of starting with $12,000, putting in $1,000 a month for ten years, at the end of the ten-year period, you'd have $241,498.21. This time, you've grown your money by 83%, outstripping inflation by a huge margin. Of course this example is a little simplistic, the S&P 500 has major fluctuations, the 10% figure is an average and you might do better or worse over any given period (in fact, in recent years, it's been around 7.7%, but that is much better than the maximum of 3.1% you're likely to find at a bank). Even so, you should see that the example is quite dramatic and unless interest rates go much higher, investing in the bank isn't a great idea. That isn't to say that you shouldn't put *some* money in the bank – you should.

Values of stocks over time

Using a real example, suppose that you started with a $12,000 investment, and invested $1,000 in the S & P 500 every month for 20 years, starting in March 1999. How much money would you have in March of 2019?

The answer is $616,704.38. The total invested or *cost basis* is $252,000. The real annualized return was 7.887%.

Your cost basis tells you how much money you'd have if you just stuffed it in the mattress. Of course, due to inflation, you've actually lost some purchasing power in that case.

If we had invested in a savings account instead, with a 2.5% interest rate, after 20 years, we would have $333,862.29. That's $282,842.09 less than if you had put it in the S&P 500. Investing in stocks is a far better deal.

TIP: The S&P 500 is a great investment vehicle that gives you immediate diversity in the world's biggest companies. Look into a Vanguard fund or consider the SPDR Exchange Traded Fund that trades under the ticker SPY.

Case Study: What if you had invested in these three companies in 1985?

Some investments are better than others. That goes without saying. Unfortunately, one of the problems people have when investing is getting too excited and emotionally invested in one or a few companies. Then, they throw everything they have into that one company.

Let's suppose that in 1999 you invested $12,000 into the Coca Cola Company. Seems like a solid investment –after all people are always drinking coke even if they switch to the diet variety. For this example, we'll suppose that you put in the initial $12,000 but don't make any further investments, and we'll compare that and a couple of other companies including Apple (below).

In this case, after 20 years, we'd have $18,000. The annualized return for the Coca Cola Company over the period is 2.16%, and the total return is 53.3%. Basically, investing in Coca Cola in 1999 and leaving it there for 20 years would be the same as putting into a savings account at the bank.

Now let's say that instead, you invested in ExxonMobil. Sounds pretty solid right? We don't have very good electric cars yet, so nearly everyone is still buying gasoline. The same scenario – invest $12,000 in 1999 on the same day that you invested in Coca Cola.

By 2019, you've got $27,973.76 in ExxonMobil stock. That's quite an improvement over Coca Cola, where you only ended up with $18,000.

But for comparison, suppose you'd invested the money in the S&P 500, without adding any additional capital. In that case, you'd end up with $54,600.27, nearly double the cash. Is that an argument for diversity in your investments? Looks to be the case.

Let's check one more company. Randomly thinking of a large corporation, how about Amazon? Actually, it's not that random because we selected that to illustrate the potential payoff from picking a high-value IPO – whose true value may not really be apparent to everyone at the time.

Amazon's IPO took place in 1997, at $18 a share. Suppose that you had invested $10,000. Twenty years later it would be worth a staggering $4.8 million. That's a return of 48,197%.

Of course, most of us aren't that far-sighted, and we miss opportunities like that, or we make huge mistakes and believe something is an opportunity of that magnitude when it isn't. Amazon's biggest competitors at the time were the bookstores Barnes & Noble and Borders (Amazon had not diversified beyond books yet). Over the same 20-year period, an investment in Barnes & Noble would have only grown by 26%. Borders, which was huge in 1997, went out of business and doesn't even exist anymore. Such is the world of capitalism. The fact is it is pretty difficult to pick winners and losers ahead of time, even if something seems like a sure thing.

Case Study: Investment in the Russell 2000
The Russell 2000 is a London based fund which invests in 2,000 small cap companies. Between 1999-2019, the annualized return on this fund was 8.55% - which is a bit higher than the S&P 500 over the same period. Had you invested $12,000 in the Russell 2000 in 1999 and invested $1,000 a month for the following 20 years, you would have ended up with $695,595.88. That's even more than you would have gotten putting everything in the S&P 500.

Of course, we're doing an exercise of looking backward, but we don't know the future. So the key is to put a little bit in the Russell 2000 (or another index) and a little bit in the S&P 500.

Case Study: Apple
Over the past 10 years, Apple has had an annualized return of 29.68%. If you had simply invested $12,000 in 2009 and left it there, today you'd have $149,592, and that is without having added an additional single penny. Not as much as Amazon over 1997-2017, but not half-bad. Remember if we invested in Coca Cola over a 20-year period, putting in $12,000, we would have ended up with just $18,000.

Other Market Indices

There are many market indices, we've mainly focused on the S & P 500 index and the Dow Jones Industrial Average, but hopefully, our discussion of those two gave you an idea of what an index is. If you're taking an index based approach toward investing, then there are several to consider (there are so many we can't possibly list a significant fraction, but we'll list our favorites). First, there are many ways we can divide up companies to make an index.

- Business sector or industry. Technology, mining, healthcare and many more.
- Asset type (say bonds vs. stocks or gold)
- Capitalization. Large company or small company, or maybe midsized?
- Location, location, location. Invest in certain regions or countries (EU or Japan, Brazil or China).

- The most general types of indices are those that track various markets or groups sizes of companies by capitalization. Some of these are:

- Amex – the American stock exchange, which was the third largest stock exchange in the United States before being acquired. It was acquired by the NYSE in 2008 and is now known as the NYSE MKT.
- The Wilshire 5000 – also known as the total market index, is a measure of all stocks traded in the United States.
- The Russell 3000 – another index that is a measure of all stocks traded in the United States. Other Russell indices measure different sized companies.
- The NASDAQ 500 – top 500 companies traded on NASDAQ.
- The NYSE Composite – an index that measures the entire collection of stocks on the New York Stock Exchange.
- The Global DOW – an index based on the 150 largest companies worldwide, companies picked by the editorial staff of the Wall Street Journal.

What are the risks faced when investing in stocks

The greatest risk you face when investing in stocks is picking one or two favorites and losing your money. Many exciting IPOs end up duds, and it is pretty hard to pick which ones those are ahead of time. We used Amazon as an example. If you were around in 1997 were you really thinking of sinking your life savings into Amazon, which at the time was just an online bookstore? That would have been pretty prescient, frankly. At the time, to most people, Amazon looked fairly solid, but nobody would have seen the massive dominance it's achieved today. Most people probably would have made equal bets on the physical bookstores it was still competing with at the time.

Of course, Amazon, and more recently Apple or Google, represent double-edged swords. Your greatest risk is completely blowing your principal. However, another risk you face is missing opportunities.

Apple is a good example of an enticing middle ground. In 2009, it was pretty clear that Apple was about to ride a major wave. It didn't generate as much growth as Amazon did over the period 1997-2017, but it sure generated enough, and any half-aware investor should have seen the growth coming. You can be forgiven for missing Amazon in the days that it was a simple website, but you can't be forgiven for missing the iPhone.

Some people play it far too safe, sticking with a long-term company that is solid, yet not going anywhere. Those that play it too safe aren't going to grow the kind of retirement income they may need.

But more often than not, the risk people face losing a lot of money. This usually results from being impatient or falling in love with a single company. We will talk more about common mistakes in a future chapter.

Ways to mitigate your risks

We'll talk about mitigating risk in Chapter 6, *An overview of stock investment strategies*. But here are some general principles:

- Don't put all your eggs in one basket. Or even a couple of baskets (don't buy stocks in a small number of companies you hand pick).
- Do massive diversification. Don't just diversify with a few stocks, diversify using indexed funds. Also diversify using different types of securities (some in stocks, some in bonds, etc.)
- Stay away from supposed "investments" that are just speculation like gold and silver.
- Only invest measured amounts in companies you think are the next "sure thing."
- Don't sell when the market is crashing. You will probably lose money.

When to get in and when to get out

You should get in when prices are low. Yes, follow the old axiom of buy-low and sell-high. The only time to get out is to do so gradually when you're taking money out during your retirement. If you can live off dividends or interest from bond payments, then there isn't even a real reason to get out of the market.

What is a buying opportunity

There are types of buying opportunities:

- During a crash, when prices that are going to rebound in the future are going for low prices.
- During an IPO, but this takes some level of luck and guesswork.

Looking at recessions and bear markets as an opportunity

How many people do you know who bailed from the stock market in 2008, or constantly talk about it now? People have an impulse to flee toward safety, and this happens with stocks as much as anything else. At the first whiff of bad news, they dump their stocks and head to the perceived safety of gold or bank accounts.

Their loss is your gain. When multiple people sell all at once – a stock market crash ensues. These aren't times to join the lemmings running off the cliff; instead, these are times to look for investment opportunities. Here is the fact that history makes clear – the market may be crashing now, but it's going to rebound, and it is going to go back up. Much further up than it went before the crash. That means a stock market crash is an opportunity. When things start sliding south, especially when they're about to hit bottom or shortly thereafter, that is the time you should be buying stocks, not stuffing money into your mattress.

In 2009, just as the U.S. was coming out of the "Great Recession," one share of the S&P 500 was worth about $832, which was down from a high of around $1,400. Now, it's worth $2,834. The time period between January 2009 and May 2009 was a great time to buy because prices were bottoming out. Had you done so, you would have basically tripled your money in ten years. The people who "played it safe" by stuffing their mattress or bank account with cash are the ones who lost out.

CHAPTER 4
Mutual Funds In Depth

A mutual fund is a professionally managed group fund that invests in a diversity of assets. It seeks to balance risk and reward carefully, and it's not a get rich quick type scheme. The more careful an investor you are and the more you would prefer having a professional manage your money, the more likely you are to seek out a mutual fund. There are downsides, however. Having a fund be actively managed means it costs money to manage the fund – so you can pay fees that can significantly eat into your investments over time. Second, there isn't solid evidence that a professionally managed fund actually does better than a diverse portfolio that isn't managed by an expert.

If you hand pick stocks, then you're going to ride on a roller coaster, with your financial identity tied to the small number of stocks that you pick. It's going to require constant analysis and possibly making judgment calls on when to abandon stocks or pick new ones. You might be forced to "cut your losses" and hope for the best. In all cases, you're constantly trying to "beat the market."

For some people, that kind of scenario won't bother them. Some folks like to dive into stocks in detail and look at the parameters that define success, stagnation, or decline for a large corporation. For others, the heightened risk and required attention isn't something they're into. If you're the latter type of person, who either wants the lower risk or you simply want to utilize an invest-and-forget-it strategy, a mutual fund might be what you're looking for.

In a mutual fund, a pool of money is created to buy stocks and other types of investments. The fund is managed by a professional money manager who does the thinking for you. The money manager is a trained professional who knows how to create a balanced portfolio that pits the right amount of risk against the right amount of caution to develop an investment vehicle that should be profitable over time. Of course, not all money managers are created equal, and some funds will perform better than others.

A key strategy used in the creation of mutual funds is diversification. That is, rather than buying stock from one, two, or three companies; a mutual fund manager will buy stocks from a wide variety of companies. For example, you could invest in a Dow Jones index that bought shares in all

347

30 companies that make up the DJIA. Since the DJIA basically tracks overall stock market performance, if you invested in this fund, you'd basically have shares in all the companies, and your investment would track stock market performance. And what does the DJIA do over time? It goes up. So it's a much smarter investment than gambling on one or two or even three companies. Another thing to keep in mind is that over time, companies move into and out of the DJIA, and other indices like the S&P 500. Are you smart enough to know which ones will do so over the next ten years? Probably not – so having an index fund where someone else takes care of everything for you is probably better.

The simplest definition of a mutual fund is that it's a portfolio of stocks and bonds that are actively managed by a professional money manager.

There are some differences between investing in a mutual fund and investing in stocks:

• An investment in a mutual fund is a share of a portion of a large portfolio. It may only be stocks, but it might be some combination of stocks and bonds.
• While buying common stock gives you voting rights, you gain no such rights when buying shares of a mutual fund.
• Stocks are traded throughout the day, and the price fluctuates throughout the day. Mutual funds are only traded once, after market close.

Mutual funds can be *active*, that is the manager of the fund actively picks stocks to include in the fund and decides when to buy or sell individual stocks that make up the fund. It is unclear that actively managed funds provide a clear benefit to investors. Even for a trained professional, trying to handpick winners and losers in the stock market isn't all that easy. You have to pay fees for an active fund manager as well.

A *passive* fund is not actively managed by a person picking stocks or getting rid of stocks in the portfolio. When a fund is passive, it's going to be tied to some kind of index, such as the S & P 500.

It's best to visit the website of a large company like Vanguard or Fidelity and explore the different types of funds to find out what kinds are available.

Pooled investments can make sense on a lot of levels. Mutual funds utilize diversification as a central principle. That is, instead of buying stock in one or two companies, they buy stock in hundreds of companies. That way risk is diversified – if one or two companies fail to meet performance expectations and lose value, or they even go out of business, it doesn't have much impact on the mutual fund since it consists of hundreds of companies. Risk is diluted and spread out. Besides offering the diversification, mutual funds offer the ability to invest in a wide range of securities. So you could invest in stocks, bonds, money market funds, and gold for example. You could also explore investments overseas.

A pooled investment is also one that benefits from economies of scale. The fund manager is able to buy large numbers of shares at once, something most individual investors are not going to be able to do. Because of the ability to make large scale moves in the market, mutual funds may be able to avoid transaction fees that would add up from small moves in the market. They may also have access to IPOs and other special interest investments that individual investors may not have.

Mutual funds provide ease of investment while being relatively safe investments. They also often require only small monthly commitments, so it's not necessary to invest large sums of money all at once.

Many people regard the active management provided for many mutual funds as a disadvantage. For one, actively managed funds incur higher fees, since you've got to pay the salary of the person doing the managing. Other costs related to active management such as printing marketing materials and reports on the fund's performance can add up.

Another downside involving money is "cash drag." Mutual funds must keep a large pool of cash on hand so that they can buy securities. Since we are talking about large moves on the market, the amount of cash kept on hand could be substantial. That cash is kept on reserve and so isn't available for investing. When you invest in a mutual fund, some of your money will be contributed for this purpose, meaning you're going to get less actual investment for a given dollar you put in than you would get investing on your own.

One particular risk of mutual funds is known as "dilution." In short, this means doing too much diversification in search of safety. At some point, diversifying across too many stocks might result in a situation with minimal returns or stagnation.

How mutual funds work in detail

Let's start with the word mutual. The definition of mutual is "experience or done by two or more parties...held by two or more parties for the benefit of all parties involved". From this definition, we see the first aspect of mutual funds, which is a pool of money gathered from multiple investors into a single fund for the mutual benefit of all.

Fund simply means a sum of money saved for a particular purpose. In the case of a mutual fund, the fund is saved for the purpose of investing in stocks, bonds, and other assets.

A mutual fund has some investment objective in mind. For example, one fund might focus on aggressive growth (high earnings) while another might focus on stability and regular income (think – more bonds). The professional money manager who manages the fund will select the stocks, bonds, and other investments to put into the fund to meet its specific goals. Investments are spread across a wide variety of companies, incorporating multiple business types and sectors. This is done to spread your risk and hence reduce it. Not all stocks are going to move in the same direction, and not all industries or business sectors will move in the same direction. By investing widely across businesses, industries, and sectors, we average out the risk so that the entire fund is not put in danger by the collapse of one or a few companies or a downturn in a particular sector.

A mutual fund is divided into *units*. There is a cash value assigned to a unit based on the value of the underlying investment, so units are issued to each investor in proportion to the amount of money they put into the mutual fund. The value of each unit is called the *Net Asset Value* or NAV. This is the current market value of a single unit in the funds holding. So if the total value of the fund was $100,000, and there were 100 units in the fund, the NAV would be $1,000. Investors buy units in the fund priced at the NAV. So, the number of units an investor can buy depends on both the NAV and the amount invested. So if NAV is $20 and an investor puts in $20,000, then they own 1,000 units.

Of course, it's always changing as the holdings in the portfolio rise and fall with each trading day. An important thing to remember about mutual funds as opposed to trading individual stocks or ETFs is that they only trade once a day, after closing.

It's useful to know the NAV per unit for the mutual fund. This is given by the market value of the underlying securities minus the total recurring expenses, and then you divide this number by the total number of units in the fund. Note that the number of units in the fund may not be fixed – so we need to know the number of units on a particular date.

There are two very important factors associated with mutual funds – strategy and fees. Fees are so important that we discuss them separately in the next two sections.

Basically, a mutual fund will take one of four different strategies related to growth. A general rule is the more aggressive growth, the higher the risk.

1. Aggressive growth: This is a high risk/high reward type of fund. The types of companies that are used for a fund with an aggressive growth goal include newer companies in high tech, startups, or companies in emerging markets: more risk but more potential for bigger earnings.
2. Growth and income: A more conservative approach that focuses on large-cap U.S. companies ($10 billion or more). Moderate to low risk, considered stable investments.
3. Growth: This focuses on large U.S. based companies that are growing, but companies that are smaller than those in the growth and income type fund. These are medium to large sized companies (or mid-cap to large-cap) valued between $2 billion and $10 billion. They will tend to have higher returns than those in a growth and income fund but are less stable. They are subject to be more influenced by the economy at large and will move up and down with the economy.
4. International: This type of fund focuses on large companies outside the United States. It may be fairly stable, as it focuses on well-known international companies.

Although our discussion has focused on stocks, it's important to realize that a mutual fund can also invest in bonds, cash, and money market funds. So another way to look at it is the more growth-oriented the fund, the fewer bonds and cash investments that will be in the fund. A fund can be entirely weighted toward bonds and cash investments, set up for low risk and income.

If you decide to invest in mutual funds, you'll need to do some upfront investigation. Don't just jump in feet first with the first mutual fund that you find. Look at comparable options offered by different investment companies. You'll want to seek out a fund that closely aligns with your goals, although many advisors suggest investing in multiple funds, splitting your money evenly between the four general types outlined above. If you're getting closer to retirement and are more interested in protecting your principal, then you're going to want to opt for investing in low risk, income-oriented funds. No matter what you do, check the long-term history of the fund and compare it to important benchmarks like the S & P 500. Do you want a fund that doesn't perform as well as the S&P 500? What would be the point of that? You could just invest in the S&P 500. It's a good idea to take the performance period to be at least ten years. You don't want to get suckered into buying a fund that hasn't done all that well over the long-term but had a good run the last year or two.

Fees and costs associated with mutual funds

Since a mutual fund is *actively managed,* there are going to be costs associated with it. It costs money to have someone else set up your investments, buy and sell shares on your behalf each day, provide customer support, and produce shiny reports for you to look at. These are the operating costs of the mutual fund, and they aren't going to eat them – they are going to make you pay the operating costs. So an important part of investing in mutual funds is seeking out a mutual fund that has reasonable fees.

Avoiding hidden costs and letting them eat your gains

The type of expenses we listed in the last section fall into the category called ongoing fees, sometimes known as annual operating expenses. These are the basic costs of the fund manager running their business. These fees are bundled together into a fee called the expense ratio. The industry average is 0.64% and can range from 0.5% to 1.0%. Some funds have expense ratios as high as 2.0-2.5%. If you find a fund with a large expense ratio, then you need to find out why it's high and if the fund has certain benefits that offset the higher cost. If not, it's best to look into another fund because those expenses will eat into your earnings.

For example, suppose you invested $10,000. If the expense ratio was 0.68%, then your fee that you'd pay annually would be $68. On the other hand, if it was 2.5%, then the fee would be $250. That is a significant difference. Let's use a more realistic example, comparing two funds over the course of 20 years. We will set the initial investment at $100,000. Then, we'll add an additional $5,000 each year, and assume the fund has an average growth rate of 6%. Now, we'll have a fund A, which has an expense ratio of 0.64%, and fund B, which has an expense ratio of 2.5%. At the end of the 20-year period, the expenses/fees that you would have to pay to fund B would be $115,514 higher than the expenses/fees you'd pay toward fund A – a lot of missing money that you could have used for your retirement or pay a significant expense.

You can try an online calculator for yourself here:

https://www.nerdwallet.com/blog/investing/typical-mutual-fund-expense-ratios/

How the fund charges fees may add up to extra expenses as well.

There are other fees to be aware of:

- Transaction fees – these are one time fees that are incurred when the fund manager makes a change in your investments.
- Commission fee: Charged when buying shares.
- Redemption fee: Charged when selling shares.
- Exchange fee: Charged when taking shares in one mutual fund and putting them into another.
- Account service fees: charged when you'd invested a smaller amount of money than some cutoff set by the fund.

The bottom line: small differences in fees can add up to huge amounts of money over a 20- or 30-year period, significantly cutting into your investments. Choose wisely.

Passively Managed Funds

A passively managed fund will have far lower fees, with an expense ratio on the order of 0.2%. In a passively managed fund, your money is invested in some kind of index fund like the S&P 500.

How to invest in mutual funds

The best way to invest in a mutual fund is to contact one of the larger companies that sells them. You can visit any investment company, but consider Fidelity or Vanguard and contact them about investing. If you own an individual investment account, you can also buy mutual fund shares on your own.

Stocks vs. ETF vs. Mutual Funds – Which is Right for You?

If you want to play an active, and direct role in your investments, stocks are definitely where you want to be. If you're interested in the freedom that comes with stock trading, including being your own money manager, but want the built-in diversification that comes with mutual funds, then you might be an ETF type person. If you're more safety oriented, and would prefer having a professional managing your investment portfolio, then you might be in the market for a mutual fund.

CHAPTER 5
Stocks In Depth

In this chapter, we'll talk about stocks in a little more detail. So let's recall a little bit about what we already know. Stocks are shares of ownership in a company that are issued when the company needs to raise money. If a company issues 100 shares, then one share represents a one percent ownership stake in the company. The amount in dollars that the share is worth is based on the total worth of the company. A stock is a claim on all assets owned by the company as well as a claim on future earnings.

Let's start by examining a small business to get a good feel for the principles of stock ownership. Suppose that a small company has $20,000 in cash, but they need to raise $80,000 to keep operating and expand the business. They could go for a loan, but maybe they have bad credit or simply don't want to bother with a loan and have to pay interest. So instead, they decide to sell slices of ownership shares in the company, and they issue $80,000 in stock. They are broken down into eight shares of $10,000 each. So the company is valued at $100,000, and the current owner keeps two shares for herself, and so retains a 20% ownership interest in the company.

If Bob buys one share, then he has a 10% ownership in the company, and it costs him $10,000. But suppose Betty opts to buy two shares. That means she will have to pay $20,000 but will end up with a 20% ownership stake in the company. Bob will be entitled to 10% of future earnings, while Betty will be entitled to 20% of future earnings.

If the company grows, everyone is happy. Let's say that it doubles in size a year later and is now worth $200,000. Since it's doubled in value, a single share that was originally worth $10,000 is now worth $20,000. While Bob and Betty made 10% and 20% of the earnings for the company over the past year, they don't get anything else for their shares. Saying what the share is worth is only something in reality if the shares are traded, or bought and sold. Betty's two shares are now worth $40,000. She could sell them to Steve for $40,000 and make a nice profit on her initial $20,000 investment. But if Steve isn't willing to buy them, she has to sit on the shares until she can find a buyer.

A company that doubles in size in a year has a lot of appeal to people who go around investing in businesses, so let us say that Sam comes along and buys the entire business for $500,000. That means Sam will own everything the business currently owns, including the building computers, and any business assets such as inventory or product the company sells. Sam will also be buying all of the shares of the company.

In total, there were ten shares. So $500,000/10 = $50,000 is now the price of a single share. This makes Bob and Betty very happy. Bob invested $10,000, and now he gets $50,000 from Sam in exchange for his share of ownership. Betty, who invested $20,000, gets $100,000 for her two shares and makes a nice $80,000 profit on her initial investment. Of course, she also earns a visit from the tax man.

Another scenario could be that Sam doesn't buy all the shares, but maybe he convinces Bob and Betty to sell him their shares, even if no one else wants to sell. Unless there is some prior contractual arrangement preventing this (perhaps Steve could write into the contract that he has first option to buy back shares if someone wants out), Sam could still take a controlling interest by purchasing the three shares from Bob and Betty, at a price they agree on. Then, Steve would have to answer to Sam since Steve now has two shares and Sam has three shares.

Of course, a company could also have losses. Instead, if the company drops in worth $50,000, then each share is only worth $5,000, and the best Betty can hope for is to sell her two shares for $10,000. If the company goes bankrupt, shareholders like Betty have a claim on the company's assets like computers and inventory, but creditors will be paid first.

This example of a small business outlines the general principles of stock ownership, but for large, publicly traded companies things are a little bit different. A large company is going to issue literally millions of shares, not just ten or even a thousand. To become a publicly traded company, a private one will have to meet certain regulatory requirements set by the Securities and Exchange Commission or SEC and then will have an IPO or initial public offering, where members of the public can buy shares in the company on a major stock exchange. A large amount of money will also have to be paid out to an investment bank like Goldman Sachs which will handle the IPO for the company. The company would need other professionals including attorneys and underwriters. For example, the requirements for a company to go public on the NYSE that include:

- A pre-tax income of at least $10 million for the past three years, with a minimum of $2 million each of the last two years.

- To qualify for the NYSE, the company must have at least 400 shareholders that own 100 shares or more each, and a total of 1.1 million publicly traded shares.
- The company will have to file important documents like articles of incorporation.

Where to buy and sell individual stocks

These days the best places to buy stocks are with online brokerage companies. An easy one to use is Capital One, or you can try eTrade. Online brokerages are easy for you to use from their website to manage things yourself and charge lower fees.

There are two general types of orders you should be aware of: market orders, and limit orders.

A market order is an order placed that you want to buy the stock right now and at any price. There is no price guarantee with a market order, but of course, the price is going to be close or very close to the price you see when placing the order, but it is possible that the price will change by the time you click the button and it goes through. So let us say you see a stock that is $50 a share. You place a market order for two shares, but by the time it gets processed it is now $50.10 a share. Since it's a market order, it will go through no matter what once you've clicked the button, and so you'll pay $100.20 for the two shares, even though they were $50 when you decided to buy them.

Alternatively, you can place a limit order. A limit order tells the system you want to buy a stock, but you're only willing to pay a certain price for it. For a limit order, you set the price you're willing to pay, and you won't get the shares unless the price exactly matches your limit. Using the previous example, if you set the limit at $50, but the stock keeps going up by 10 cents every hour the rest of the day, then you won't ever get the shares. You can set a limit to expire at the end of the day, or have a GTC, which means good until you cancel the order, so your limit will be hanging out there until your shares are either purchased or when you cancel the order.

To get out you can to a market stop, which is the inverse of a market order. This tells the system you want out immediately so it will sell the shares at the soonest. However, the price could change after you place your sell order and you might lose a little bit per share.

A stop-loss applies if you've already placed a market or limit order, and you can specify that you would be out of a trade if the price hits a certain value (for example you'll sell if the price of the $50 stock drops to $49).

If it's a limit stop, your shares won't sell unless there is an exact match. A limit stop could be risky – suppose that the price dropped from $50 to $48 and keeps dropping to say $20 a share – then your shares would never sell if you had placed a limit stop of $49.

Differences between public trading and private company stock example

We used the example of a small business to illustrate the general principles of stock ownership, but besides the number of shares and volume of money involved, there are a few other differences. The first is that with a public company, as discussed earlier, there may be different classes of stock. If you own common stock, you will be able to take advantage of gains in share price, but you will be in the back of the line if the company goes under and its assets are sold in bankruptcy. Those with preferred stock and creditors will come before you will. Also, while a share of common stock gives you voting rights, your voting is amongst millions of others, and the weight of your vote is proportional to the number of shares you have, and you're only voting on the board of directors. In a small business, the stockholders might have a large say in how it operates. While some large publicly traded companies may pay dividends, many do not. So you won't have the opportunity to share in earnings that you might with a small, private company.

Key Items to Look At Evaluating a Stock

Now let us look at a few key elements of a company and its stock to look at when deciding when to invest or not.

- P/E Ratio: This is the price to earnings ratio. This is an indication of what other investors are willing to pay for a stock and whether the company is "hot." For example, a P/E ratio of 15 means that investors are paying $15 for every $1 the company earns. While this is an important indicator, it can also demonstrate hype as much as saying it's a good investment.
- Dividends: A dividend is a payout of a fraction of the company's profits. If you are looking to hold an asset for the long-term, then a stock that pays dividends is something to look for. A dividend is paid out regardless of the share price, usually paid out quarterly. You can reinvest your dividends or cash them out. Dividend per share is going to be small, and so, you'll have to acquire a large amount of money to earn a lot from dividends. Some people with large amounts of shares can live off cashing out the dividends.

Look at older big companies for dividends, and some pay 6%. The dividend payment might be a few cents or a dollar per share. The dividend yield is dividend payment/price per share *100, expressed as a percentage.

- Ask Price: the price you are asked to pay when you buy a stock. Can be slightly higher than the current value of a stock. The bid price is an offer amount to buy a stock. When the bid price and ask price match, the stock is traded.
- Beta: Measures how volatile a stock has been over the past five years. If Beta is greater than 1, that is a higher risk stock that has had a lot of volatility. If Beta is less than 1, it has lower risk and not as volatile.

Definitions

Making your way around the stock market as an investor requires you to know several definitions. Of course, we've gone over a lot of investment jargon already but here is a basic list that should help new investors:

- After-Hours trading: Takes place outside normal business hours when the exchanges are open.
- Bear market: Most stocks are declining in value. They are often associated with recessions.
- Big Board: The New York Stock Exchange.
- Bid Price: A price offered by a prospective buyer for a stock. If you place a limit order, the price you've offered is your bid price.
- Blue Chip Stock: A large, well-established company. Has operated over a long-term period of many years and has a large market-capitalization in the billions, even above $10 billion. However $5 billion is generally accepted as a cutoff for blue-chip stocks, is a leader in its market sector, at least a top three company. Often a "household name," a stock does not have to pay a dividend to be a blue chip stock, but a regular dividend —especially if the dividend payments are either stable or steadily rise with time – is a good sign of a blue-chip stock. Blue chips are companies that have been around a while and shown the ability to withstand the ups and downs of the market and the economy. However, there are no guarantees. Consider that General Motors, which had been around for a century, faced bankruptcy in 2008.
- Bull market: A time of economic expansion when most stocks are increasing in price.
- Call: An option to buy shares of a stock at a pre-arranged price. It's called an option because the buyer has the option to back out of the deal while securing the right to proceed with it if they want

to. This is an agreement between a buyer and seller that will take place at some future date to trade a specific stock. A call has a set price per share that has been agreed upon on the given date, and a premium is paid to the seller. The seller cannot back out, so if the stock price has gone up by the time the sale date arrives, the seller has to sell at the pre-arranged price even if it's lower than the price per share on the markets that day. However, a call indicates confidence that the stock price will increase in the future. In other words, a call buyer will benefit if they have agreed on price $x but the stock went up to some new value $(x +y) by the date of the sale when the buyer gets that stock for $x.

- Discount brokers: Online brokers that provide trading at discounted prices.
- Earnings per share: This is simply the amount the company earned over the past year divided by the number of shares.
- Index: A composite representing a group of stocks. For example, we've already discussed the Dow Jones Industrial Average, Russell 2000, and S & P 500.
- Margin: This refers to borrowing money to buy stocks. The money is borrowed from the broker. Your broker will have specific requirements for you to meet to be eligible to buy stocks on the margin.
- Put: A put option is an agreement to trade a stock on a future date like a call. The seller pays the buyer a premium. The seller can choose to sell or not, and if the seller chooses not to sell, they still have to pay the buyer the premium. The contract has an expiration date, but the seller can sell the stock to the buyer before the expiration date. Like a call, this has a prearranged stock price that is set even if the price on the market has changed by the sell date. Since the price is predetermined when the contract is agreed to, this indicates a lack of confidence about the future price of the stock.
- Portfolio: A collection of investments. It can be held by a single person or a company. Could refer to the assets held by a mutual fund.
- Quote: Current price of a stock.
- Short: With a short sale, the investor borrows a certain stock from a broker. Then, the investor sells the stock at the current price and gets the proceeds credited to their margin account (the account used for borrowing from the broker). Later, when the share price drops, the investor buys the same number of shares on the open market at the lower price. Then, they return the shares to the

broker whom they originally borrowed them from. The difference in price is pocketed by the short selling investors as profit. For example, suppose you borrow 100 shares of Acme stock from the broker. Then, you sell them on the market at the current price of $100 per share. You now have $10,000. After some time goes by, the price drops to $50 per share. Now, you buy back the 100 shares for $5,000. Now, you return the 100 shares to the broker. And aside from some fees, you've made a profit of $5,000.

- Ticker symbol: The abbreviation used to represent a given stock on the exchange, for example, APPL for Apple Inc. Also used for funds, SPY is an exchange-traded fund for the S&P 500.

Keep in mind that options trading (calls and puts) and short selling are advanced activities that carry major risk.

How to choose a good stock to invest in

Knowing what a good stock is, depends on what your goals are. If you are looking for high returns, then you might be more interested in companies that have had recent IPOs that are expected to have solid long-term growth. Of course, some older companies are also growing rapidly, like Netflix. If you're looking for long-term stability and income, you can select from older, stable companies and seek out those who pay dividends. Actually knowing what stocks to pick can be a risky activity and it is not recommended for most beginning investors. Some other tips:

- Undervalued Stocks: Price to earnings ratio can indicate a hot stock people are chasing, but if the P/E ratio is 15 or lower that could indicate a lower valued stock. The stock price is relatively low for the earnings the company is generating, indicating it's a buying opportunity.
- Revenue growth: Seek out companies that have demonstrated revenue growth, and beyond the immediate short term. There are a lot of day-to-day and month-to-month fluctuations, check revenues for the past 3-5 years to see trends.
- Use balance, just like a mutual fund might. Don't put everything into one stock. Build a larger portfolio of stocks across different sectors.
- Check the news reports on the company to find out what people think about it and what its future prospects are.
- Price alone isn't a reason to buy a stock. If a stock is cheap, that doesn't mean it will gain in the future; it might even lose more value.

- Have your selling criteria ahead of time and set in stone. Don't let emotions govern your decisions, sell when a stock stops performing at a level you've set ahead of time.

CHAPTER 6
An Overview Of Stock Investment Strategies

Now let's look at some basic stock market investing strategies.

Riding gains (and losses) with individual companies

Investors with a higher tolerance for risk can buy stocks in individual companies and build their own, customized portfolio. While people intellectually approach things by examining the data and financials, those inclined to this kind of investing are also letting emotions intrude. Buying individual stocks is often something that happens based on gut-level feelings that may or may not be correct.

If you are this kind of investor, and important strategy – one echoed everywhere – is to avoid the panic impulse when stocks suffer short term declines. If you are interested in building wealth and having wealth over the long-term then riding out the losses that will inevitably be experienced is an important part of your investment strategy. Of course, some individual companies may tank, and so, it is important to know when to let go as well.

Diversification

A lot of stock market investing is built around the concept of mitigating risk. For many people, too much risk puts them off. The oldest way to mitigate risk in the markets is to diversify your portfolio. Suppose that John has invested $100,000 in three stocks:

- Apple
- Facebook
- Google

His friend Mary, however, has invested $100,000 in the following way:

- An income-oriented mutual fund
- A real estate ETF
- The S & P 500
- The Russell 2000
- The Wilshire 5000
- An international fund
- Apple
- Google
- Facebook
- Ford Motor Company
- Wells Fargo Bank

- United Healthcare

If a scandal hits (privacy violation say) and the big tech firms begin suffering stock declines, John also suffers – big time. Mary has bought stock in those companies as well so takes some losses there – but she is also well protected. Mary has taken the time to not only invest in high tech, but to invest in autos, overseas companies, banking, and healthcare. In addition, she's also protected herself by investing in several index funds and some bonds in her income-oriented mutual fund. Mary is well positioned to ride out the storm, and the overall value of her portfolio might be impacted. The losses for Apple, Google, and Facebook might be offset by gains in her other investments.

John meanwhile, loses a lot of money and panics, selling his shares at a loss.

Dollar Cost Averaging

Dollar cost averaging is a strategy that takes emotion out of investing and averages out the inevitable ups and downs that the stock market will experience. The procedure can be summarized in two steps:

- Invest a fixed amount.
- Invest at regular intervals.

If you choose to do dollar cost averaging, then it's a rule you must follow. If the market starts dropping – or whatever – you never deviate from the rule. The point of the rule is to average out those ups and downs. So for example, if we decide we want to use a $1,000 investment to buy stocks using dollar cost averaging, we can pick a specific day of each month to buy stocks. For example:

- Buy stocks on the 10th of each month.
- Buy exactly $1,000 worth.

This procedure can work with any type of investing, but it probably works best with indexed funds. Later we will discuss ETFs or exchange-traded funds. There are ETFs available for all kinds of investments and indices, but for example, you can buy an ETF for the S&P 500. So a good dollar cost averaging strategy would be to buy $5,000 worth of shares in the S&P 500 month-in and month-out. Of course, we just made up the $1,000 figure; you can do this using any amount of money, as little as $100 per month or even less. The point is to make your investments in fixed amounts, at the same time.

Dollar cost averaging eliminates the short-term volatility of the markets. It's a long-term strategy to build wealth over time. If you are doing your investing through your employer, it's easy to set up a dollar cost averaging type investment strategy with your 401k by investing a set amount each month into indexed funds. You can also use it with your own mutual funds or exchange-traded funds. In fact, you can use it with your own stock portfolio if you choose to go that route.

Another way to do dollar cost averaging is to buy a set number of shares per month if you are managing your own investing. So, for example, suppose that you have the following portfolio:

- Apple
- Microsoft
- Google
- S&P 500 index fund
- Russell 2000 index fund

We could commit as an example, to each and every month purchase:

- Two shares of Apple
- Three shares of Microsoft
- One share of Google
- One share of S&P 500
- Two shares of Russell 2000

After doing this for a year, then you own 24 shares of Apple, 36 shares of Microsoft, 12 shares of Google, 12 shares of S&P 500, and 24 shares of the Russell 2000. Doing it this way, the short term ups and downs of individual stocks won't impact you.

Long-term investment strategies

In truth, we've already reviewed some basics of long-term investment strategies. The long-term investor is not concerned with the short term ups and downs of the markets, or what's in the news. Today's recession will be tomorrow's economic boom. If a company like Apple flops a product this month, or sales don't match "expectations," chances are Apple will still be around and profitable in five years. Unless there is a very, very major problem – you should ignore what they are babbling about on the news.

The long-term investor should utilize all the strategies discussed in this chapter and a few more.

- Build a diversified portfolio.

- Invest in a Blue Chip fund as part of your overall investment strategy, to form a stable core of your portfolio.
- Invest heavily in indexed funds.
- Seek out blue-chip stocks that pay dividends.
- Don't panic when there is a market downturn – ignore the impulse to sell off.
- When there is a market downturn, start buying.
- Use a strategy based on dollar cost averaging. You really shouldn't be *thinking* about your investing very much.
- Never let emotion get in the way of your investment decisions.
- Include other non-stock investments in your portfolio. These can include bonds, US Treasuries, and cash investments including putting some money in the bank. You can even include an annuity.

Buy low, sell high

It goes without saying, but you want to buy low and sell high, probably the oldest principle in business. In the stock market, you can narrow this a bit further – you should see market crashes as opportunities. When the market starts tanking many people have the impulse to sell and move into cash or bonds. Knowing the long-term history of the market, you should be willing to ride out short term fluctuations (and even major recessions are short term fluctuations). When everyone else is selling, you should take advantage of the lower prices to grab stocks at bargain prices.

A look at the Dow Jones Industrial Average over the long-term can help set some perspective.

https://upload.wikimedia.org/wikipedia/commons/c/c8/DJIA_histori cal_graph_to_jul11_%28log%29.svg

Notice that while there are some short term bumps, there is one trend – it's upwards. Even the Great Depression doesn't figure much in the long-term history of the stock market.

Buying low applies at all times for all investments – if you are doing indexed funds, a stock market decline is a great time to load up on them.

If you are trading individual stocks with the hopes of building shorter-term profits, then selling high is another part of your strategy. Although it's not a good idea to guess, people have a sense when a market is peaking. You can sell at a time when you've made an acceptable profit by selling your shares. The actual value is up to you.

Knowing when to buy and when to sell

Frankly, there is no good time to sell an indexed fund unless you are in retirement and need the cash or you have an emergency. You should hold them over the long-term.

For individual stocks, you might make the wrong bets. When you see a company failing to live up to the initial promises, or if they run into trouble like Theranos, it's a good idea to get out early. If a company, say a coal company, has done well in the past but is experiencing very slow growth or stagnation and there is no long-term future, you might want to swap that stock out for a company with growth potential.

CHAPTER 7
Exchange Traded Funds

Exchange traded funds are my favorite kind of investment. You'll see why in a second. So far, we've discussed mutual funds, which represent a lower risk, controlled type of investment. Mutual funds are diversified, and it is easy to invest in mutual funds using dollar cost averaging. But, they cost money, and you have little control, which you've handed over to a money manager. Also, mutual funds only trade once a day after the market closes.

Buying stocks gives you more direct control. Rather than having a money manager you have to pay to carry out his services, including making copies at the office, paying for phones and other incidentals you probably don't like paying for, with stocks you're the one doing the trading. This has some risks, but for those who want control over their investing, it has appeal. Also, you may like the flexibility of being able to buy and sell any time the markets are open. However, due to the buying power of a large group of individuals and a money manager who is working on the markets full-time, it's hard to get the kind of diversification and other benefits that you're going to get with mutual funds.

What if you could wave a magic wand and combine the best of mutual funds with the best of stocks? Well, it turns out that you can. The result is the exchange-traded fund. When you boil everything down to basics, and the exchange-traded fund is an unmanaged mutual fund that trades like a stock.

An ETF gives you automatic diversification – its biggest advantage. Even if you don't exclusively trade in ETFs, it's a good idea to have them as a significant portion of your portfolio.

Typically, an exchange-traded fund will track some kind of stock index. There are a wide array of exchange-traded funds; they also track bonds, real estate, cash, commodities, currencies, and baskets of assets. The price of ETFs changes throughout the day as they are traded on the major stock exchanges. So buying or selling an ETF is just like buying or selling a share of Apple or General Motors.

Like with mutual funds, you may see a lot of discussion of asset classes on websites for investment firms that have created ETFs. There are five asset classes:

1. Stocks
2. Bonds
3. Money market instruments (cash)
4. Commodities
5. Real estate

In contrast to mutual funds, in addition to being able to trade them in real time rather than waiting for an end of the day settlement, many ETFs have larger volumes than mutual funds. They also have lower fees, in some cases much lower. As a result, they are a very attractive option.

For the beginning investor, ETFs are highly recommended. It's a way to get in on your own and have some protection by utilizing the built-in diversity that ETFs have. You can buy ETFs using market orders through your own online brokerage if you know the ticker symbols of the funds you want to buy. They are a great way to do individualized dollar cost averaging. You can buy shares at regular intervals as part of your investment strategy.

To get an idea of what kinds of ETFs are available on the market, you can visit the *State Street Global Advisors SPDR* site. It's located here:

https://us.spdrs.com/en

The low-cost core is the first class of ETFs we will look at. These are divided into:

- U.S. Equities
- International Equities
- Fixed Income

If you click on U.S. equities, you will see that there are several funds that have different options for tracking major parts of the stock market. For example, they have three options available for tracking the S&P 500:

- Growth
- High-Dividend
- Value

If you look under the general category for U.S. equities (not the low-cost core), you will see that you can also simply track the S&P 500 using SPY. Our friends at State Street work like a mutual fund, in the sense that they've used a large sum of money to buy stocks in the 500 companies that make up the S&P 500. You can buy small shares of it. At the time of writing, the stock is priced at about $285 per share.

However, SPYG – the S&P 500 Growth fund – is only $37 a share (prices will vary, by the time you read this). The fund also tracks the S&P 500 index but gives you a low-cost way to get in the market. However, this fund is designed to tap companies in the S&P 500 that are believed to have the most growth potential. According to the website, they base this on the revenue growth, price to earnings ratio, and momentum of the companies chosen for the index.

You can also use SPDR ETFs to invest in preferred stock or commodities. GLD allows you to buy gold shares. NANR is a natural resources fund that you can use to invest in energy, metals, mining, and agriculture. You can also invest in bonds, loans, U.S. government treasuries, and overseas investing like China or Japan.

SPDR is not the only company out there. A recent arrival on the scene is a company called Robin Hood. This company has a mobile app that can be used to trade on your smartphone or tablet. One advantage of Robin Hood is that it's commission free. It also allows you to invest in options and even cryptocurrencies, as well as directly in stocks.

https://www.robinhood.com/

Vanguard, a very popular investment firm known for mutual funds, also offers several ETF options. Their S&P 500 indexed fund VOO is one of the most popular investment options.

Another one of the big players in the ETF world is iShares by BlackRock. They are offered in four asset classes:

- Equity (stocks)
- Fixed income (bonds)
- Real estate
- Commodity

You can also invest by region:

- United States
- Europe
- Asia/Pacific
- Global

Or by market:

- Developed
- Emerging

For example, iShares offers a fund which tracks the Russell 2000. According to the website, had you invested $10,000 when the fund was started in 2000, today you've had about $40,000. The fund invests in smaller publicly traded U.S. companies that have long-term growth potential. Like investing in an S&P 500 index, this fund will give you a chance to invest simultaneously in all companies that make up the index – in this case, the 2000 small-cap companies on the Russell 2000.

If you look at the expense ratios, you see where you can get big advantages over a mutual fund. Expense ratios on iShares go as low as 0.04, with most around 0.19-0.20.

Remember these funds trade like stocks – so you don't have to enroll at iShares to buy iShares funds. You just have to know what the tickers are, and you can sign up with any brokerage firm and buy the funds as part of your everyday trades.

Note that while we've often talked about the S&P 500, you can invest in exchange-traded funds that track all markets. For example, the PowerShares QQQ fund tracks the NASDAQ 100.

The Advantages and Disadvantages

Although it's hard to say that ETFs have disadvantages, if you are person who would rather hand over control to a money manager, then an ETF is not for you because trading and investing in exchange-traded funds requires your active and direct participation, and there is no expert who is going to pick the right funds for you.

However, due to the instant and automatic diversification that exists with these types of investments, they are fairly low risk as long as you follow some basic investment common sense. The flexibility is a major advantage, but you shouldn't abuse it. In other words, when you decide to invest in a fund unless there is some very serious compelling reason to get out – stay in that fund. ETFs represent an opportunity for solid, long-term investing.

How to utilize ETFs and Where to Invest

You invest in ETFs at your regular brokerage. You should use the websites of major funds to educate yourself about what funds are on offer and what the goals are of each fund. That way you can carefully select funds that meet your own investment goals.

You can also compare funds offered by one company versus another, to examine performance. Earlier, we mentioned that iShares offered a Russell 2000 fund. SPDR also offers a small-cap fund that tracks the 2000 smallest publicly traded companies in the United States. How do the two funds compare?

- The iShares fund is larger, with 282 million outstanding shares, compared to about 40 million for the SPDR SPSM fund.
- Both have a similar P/E ratio of about 16.
- The expense ratio of the SPDR SPSM fund is 0.05%. For the iShares fund, it is 0.19%.
- The price of a share of SPSM is about $30, at the time of writing the iShares fund is $154 per share.
- Year to date, the iShares fund is up 15.8%, the SPSM fund is up 17.3%.

You might ask why the funds track the same index but don't offer the exact same performance. The reason is that each company makes its own decisions on the weight given for investments. For example, we can look at the top ten holdings of each fund. For the iShares fund we have:

- ETSY
- TRADE DESK INC-CLASS A
- FIVE BELOW INC
- CREE INC
- HUBSPOT
- PLANET FITNESS INC. CLASS A
- CIENA CORP.
- PRIMERICA INC.
- ENTEGRIS INC.
- ARRAY BIOPHARMA INC.

For SPDR's SPSM fund the top ten holdings are:

- MR. COOPER GROUP INC.
- TRADE DESK INCORPORATED CLASS A
- PLANET FITNESS CLASS A
- VERSUM MATERIALS INC.
- CREE INC.
- MELLANOX TECHNOLOGIES LTD.

- ITT
- ARRAY BIOPHARMA INC.
- COUPA SOFTWARE INC.
- INSPERITY INC.

As you can see, while there is some overlap, the different funds have given different weights to different companies, and the top ten lists then turn out different. The difference isn't all that significant, but you may note that the SPDR fund has performed a little better on a YTD basis. Over the past five years, the five-year market price of the SPDR fund has grown 7.59%, in comparison to 4.46% for the iShares fund. So the SPDR fund hasn't just done better recently, it is done better for the past five years. That coupled with its lower costs (both the share price and expense ratio) make it a more attractive option in our view. But we aren't here to advocate for one or the other, but rather to give you an idea of how you might do your own analysis with these types of funds.

The lower share price of the SPDR fund will make it more accessible for those who are starting out with a lower budget or who don't want to risk large amounts of capital.

Super Diversification with ETFs

As we stated at the beginning and illustrated by looking at a couple of funds, ETFs provide automatic diversification, the same kind you get with mutual funds but without the costs, constraints, and hassles. If you want to build a solid, really diverse portfolio consider picking your favorite ETF company and buying into all of their funds over time, or a diverse subset of them. Since there are funds that invest in stocks, bonds, real estate, and commodities, it's pretty easy to build up a portfolio that meets your investment goals, whether you're playing it safe looking for an income-based portfolio or looking for aggressive growth or some balance in between.

ETFs versus Picking Stocks

ETFs trade like stocks, but they are not investments in individual companies.

Where did ETFs come from?

The history of exchange-traded funds traces its roots back through mutual funds. The first mutual fund was developed in 1774 by a Dutch merchant. At that time, he used pooled investing to allow people to invest in a closed-end fund. A closed-end fund has a pooled amount of capital that it raises through an IPO, and it's managed by a professional money manager. In modern times, closed-end funds are publicly traded funds themselves. From 1774 until modern times, mutual funds were the only game in town when it came to index funds.

The first attempt to launch an exchange-traded fund came in the United States in the late 1980s when there was a fund indexed to the S&P 500. However, a federal judge actually struck it down, saying the fund had to be traded in futures markets. This ruling kept the fund out of the reach of ordinary investors, but soon afterward the first true exchange-traded funds were brought to market.

In 1990, an exchange-traded fund was introduced on the Toronto stock exchange in Canada, which tracked 35 large Canadian companies. This was soon followed a few years later by the creation of the S&P 500 Trust, an ETF that was created by our friends the State Street Global Advisors SPDR. This fund caught fire and remains very popular today, and as we've seen, State Street has massively expanded the funds they have available with investing possibilities in virtually every asset class and market segment, both here in the United States and globally.

At first, ETFs were primarily used by institutional investors. However, their use quickly caught on, and financial advisors and individual investors became interested in using exchange-traded funds to invest. Between 2000 and 2010, the total amount invested in ETFs grew from $0.1 trillion to $1 trillion, and by 2017 that figure had grown to $3.4 trillion.

CHAPTER 8
Common Mistakes

Now let's explore some of the common mistakes made by beginning investors. Don't let yourself get caught up in them. There are plenty of books to buy and websites to read to educate yourself on the markets.

Not understanding the markets

Not understanding the markets is the first mistake newbies often make. Before you get out your wallet or bank card, make sure that you understand the basics before you start buying. That means having a good idea what all the index funds mean, some basic stock market jargon, and knowing the different ways you can buy stock. It's also important to understand the markets on another level. That is, you should understand the history of the markets and not be another naïve fool that panics every time the DJIA goes up and down. Don't listen to the press, they concoct theories about ups and downs in the markets that could have some connection to reality, but the fact is nobody knows. All too often you hear that the market is dropping and people are unloading shares because of some news report. Are you going to be that person who unloads your shares because of a news report? If you understand the markets, then you won't be. You'll be buying extra shares instead.

Not having clear investment goals

Let's get one thing out in front – the stock market is not a get rich quick scheme. So you're not going to make a few investments and then have a big house, two luxury sports cars and oodles of time to travel.

Investing is not a gambling casino; it's a place where you invest real money into real businesses. In order to achieve success, you need to have clear investment goals. This comes from two sides, from the investment side and the end game side. For example, on the investment side the kind of goals you need to come up with are:

- What is the minimum amount you will invest?
- How frequently are you going to invest? Don't do it on the fly; have a plan. Once a month? Every two weeks? Daily? It doesn't really matter in the details, but it is important to have a plan.
- Set monthly and annual goals for the amount you will invest.

Next, you should have a clear idea of what you want to invest in. Too many people just go around not thinking very far ahead and then hear about some hot new company, "buy gold" or "invest in crypto" and then jump on the bandwagon. Impulse is not something that is good to have as a part of your investment goal bag of goodies. Instead, get a clear idea of where you want to go:

- What business sectors do you want to invest in?
- Do you want growth, income, or some combination of both?
- How much capital are you willing to put at risk?
- Do you only want to invest in the United States, or expand globally?
- What about real estate, natural resources, and commodities?

Once you've figured all this out, write down how you want to weight each item. For example, suppose that Mary decides she wants to invest in the following areas:

- Healthcare
- Technology
- An index fund
- Bonds, but looking for high income

The next thing Mary needs to do is think about what percentage of her investments she wants to devote to each of these four items. Since Mary is looking for high income from bonds, she probably wants to invest in some junk bonds that pay high interest rates. Of course, "junk" bonds suggests they may default, so there is a bit of risk there. There is also some risk for technology stocks. These days technology is changing rapidly, and today's giants might be knocked off the top by some currently unknown upstart. With that in mind, though Facebook or Apple might look secure now, you really don't know if they are going to be secure and remain market leaders in ten years, due to the sector itself being so volatile and ripe for disruption. Healthcare faces other issues. It might seem sensible to invest in large health insurance companies or health-related companies, but what if the public votes in politicians that want to install Medicare for all? That might diminish or even eliminate health insurance companies. On the other hand, if the current system stays largely in place, then investments in big health-related companies like United Healthcare make good sense. So Mary is taking a bit of a risk there too.

Since Mary has three risky investment choices, she decides to put 50% of her investments into an index fund, and she chooses an S&P 500 ETF. She then breaks up the other 50% by putting 10% into the bond investments, and then 20% each into technology and healthcare. Mary wants some security that comes with a fund like an S&P 500 ETF but also enjoys looking at individual stocks and doing her own picking, so she decides to buy stock in individual companies for healthcare and technology.

The details of this little exercise aren't really important, and rather, we simply want to illustrate how Mary has developed and executed a plan to organize her investments to get what she wants out of them. Now, she has to settle on a monetary figure that she will invest, and how often she will invest. Suppose that Mary plans to put $500 at the end of each month. Now, Mary has planned her investment strategy, and as long as she sticks to her plan, she is likely to enjoy success.

Letting emotions rather than facts govern decisions

Emotions have a nasty way of injecting themselves into stock market investing. It's exciting and can be filled with fear if you're looking at losing your shirt. Of course, the real problem is that people overestimate the dangers. In particular, people take a short term outlook. So if they are in the midst of a crash as we were in 2008, people see the stock market dropping and think it's the end of the world. We hope that we convinced you in earlier chapters that this is not the case, and those who tough it out get the most rewards. Going into a panic and wanting to sell before you think the market is going to bottom out is a naïve and emotionally based approach. Markets never bottom out and stay there.

A second area where emotions rear their ugly heads is in picking stocks. People often pick stocks on feelings rather than facts. That is not a way to generate long-term success in the markets.

Patience is a virtue

The stock market, for the most part, really is a race between the tortoise and the hare. Once you realize that you're not going to find a get rich quick scheme and begin regular, methodical investing, your patience will begin to pay off. Over the long-term, those that are patient and stick to a strategy that incorporates diversity and dollar cost averaging are sure to achieve secure retirement and financial independence.

The gullibility of the next "sure thing."

This happens all the time, but a good recent example is Theranos. The company had a charismatic female CEO and made promises of a medical breakthrough that would help patients. However the claims made by the company were sky high, and if you read the patents – it's incredible some of them were granted with the science fiction like claims that they made – you would realize there was a lot of smoke and mirrors surrounding the company. Despite that many good people who had reached the top of their professions in politics or the military and business became so infatuated with the idea of a medical breakthrough that would "save lives" that they ignored the endless flashing of warning signals. In the end, Theranos was a bomb, and now, people are even facing prosecution.

Of course, that isn't to say that every novel idea is wrong. But you should apply two principles:

- Go into any investment with your eyes wide open. Be skeptical and don't ignore flashing warning signs. If the warning signs are flashing, there is a reason – and you should steer clear of the investment.
- If you do decide to invest in the next big thing – only invest a small portion of your overall capital. Remember all too often the next big thing fizzles. If you put all your money into something that ends up failing, you end up broke and back to square one. Don't be that person.

Falling in love with one company and failure to diversify
This mistake is closely related to the previous one, but can also take shape when we are talking about large, well-known companies. For example, as everyone knows, Apple has its so-called fanbois who love the company to the point of absurdity. It does have good products that sell of course, but when you love a company that much, it might cloud your investment decisions. Again, don't take it the wrong way – obviously, Apple has been a good investment decision for a lot of people – so it worked out. But it won't always work out, and as they say, nothing lasts forever. While we're confident Apple will be around for a very long time, it may not be as dominant in the future as it has been the past decade. And that lack of dominance means its stock will become lackluster. Not a loser, for sure, but it is not going to skyrocket like it did after the iPhone was released.

The point is you can invest in your favorite companies – hopefully, there isn't just one – but you're going to be far better off if that investment takes up a minority position in your portfolio. Remember that diversity is king. A suggestion would be to invest 20% in Apple and 80% in index funds.

Knowing when to let go
Sometimes you may have a favorite company, especially if it's a new and exciting one, and get so emotionally attached to it that you can't let go. That can be a huge mistake and cost a lot in losses if the company ends up going south. And that does happen from time to time. There are many companies at the time of writing – such as Tesla – that excite a lot of people with the possibilities, but the way Tesla is going to turn out is very uncertain. If you are really in love with the idea of electric cars and Tesla's style and potential – are you really going to be able to break from it if the promises don't materialize? If you see that after another year your investment isn't going anywhere, it might be time to move on. As with everything else, diversity helps. If you are a diversified, long-term

investor, then no single company – even if you're putting significant sums into Apple and Tesla – is going to destroy your overall portfolio.

Too much turnover –trading too often

Some people think they can game the market. The most extreme example are day traders. If you fail to hold any stocks, you can put yourself at risk of never making any progress. Or you might make some money – but end up having a lot less money than you would have made had you simply followed a buy and hold strategy.

Bad market timing

Bad market timing might be the worse offense. Again, individual investors often sit on the sidelines. Then, after years of the stock market going up and up, they finally decide to get in. Then, a recession hits. That is bad market timing. They might find themselves in a buy high sell low situation. Using a dollar cost averaging strategy can help you avoid this.

CHAPTER 9
International Investing

For those who are more ambitious, international investing beckons. There has never been a better time for international investing, as the old standby markets are still going strong – the United Kingdom, the EU, Canada, Australia, and Japan – there are also great opportunities in emerging markets. The emerging markets are beginning to enter a more mature phase, but there is still an enormous amount of room for massive growth in the coming decades. Also, newer emerging markets will be developing in countries that may not have been favorable in the past.

Is international investing for you

Who is international investing good for? Practically any investor. However, in general, if you are more comfortable with risk, you'll be better suited for international investing.

However, international investing is not entirely risky. Obviously, the world abounds with mature and safe markets outside the United States such as in Britain, Europe, and Japan.

For emerging markets, there are tools available that can also help you mitigate risk. The best way for investors, especially beginners, to get involved in investing in emerging markets is through mutual funds or exchange-traded funds.

The risks of international investing

One of the main risks encountered in international investing is liquidity risk. This is the risk that you can't convert a security into cash in a timely fashion. Or, you may not be able to convert a security into cash without incurring a loss.

Translated that means you might have a stock you want to sell in an international market, but you're unable to sell it as quickly as you'd like. That can mean either having to sell it at a loss or having to hold onto it when you need to get rid of it.

Many foreign markets will have lower trading volumes, and they may also not be open all day long in smaller markets. That makes selling stock more difficult.

A second risk you will face – if directly buying foreign stocks on foreign markets – is currency risk. In order to buy something overseas, you have to trade your U.S. dollars for the currency of the other country, and then buy the asset. Exchange rates between different currencies are fluctuating daily, and this can impact your investment decisions.

Currency volatility can impact the value of stocks in unforeseen ways. You don't know what the exchange rates are going to be three months, six months, or a year down the road. So directly investing in foreign markets carries added risk, in that you've got to worry not only about the performance of the stock – but also worry about currency volatility. This can be very difficult for beginning investors to deal with. Experienced investors will know how to hedge the currency risk, which is an investment used to mitigate the risk of currency fluctuations.

Another risk is that foreign markets might have higher transaction costs.

Lack of information can also be a risk for those investing in foreign markets, and it's another issue that can be very impactful for beginning investors. The United States and other countries like Great Britain have strictly enforced regulations that require companies to provide certain transparent information that will help investors make decisions that are in their best interests. Many emerging markets may not have the same level of transparency, and in some countries, a company prospectus may not even be available in English. If you don't know what you are doing, then you might not make the best decisions.

Another obvious problem is political and social stability. The world is not always at peace, and sometimes, governments fall apart, or wars happen. This can make investing risky. If there is a major collapse or a war you might not be able to unload your investments. And while things may seem fine at the time you make your investments, none of us can see the future, so the risk is always there.

Next, another risk you may face is legal remedies. If you get in trouble when dealing with a company in the United States, you have access to U.S. courts where you can seek redress or a settlement. If you're investing in a foreign country, you may lack access to the courts to be able to seek a remedy. Even if you do have access, it goes without saying that all court systems are not created equal.

Traditional overseas markets
By "traditional," we mean long-term developed markets. Overseas markets that might meet this definition include:

- Great Britain
- The European Union
- Australia and New Zealand

- Hong Kong
- South Korea
- Japan
- Canada

Investing in emerging markets

Emerging markets are far riskier for a whole host of reasons, from problematic court systems to political instability to liquidity problems. That said, many emerging markets offer the promise of high returns. Some emerging markets of interest include:

- China
- Brazil
- India
- Vietnam
- South Africa

How to invest in overseas markets

The first way to invest in overseas markets is actually to trade on the foreign markets themselves. Doing so will incur all of the risks that we discussed above. You may be able to find a broker who can help you proceed this way, but it is not recommended for beginning investors.

Seeking the advice of the United States government, we've identified the safest ways to invest in overseas markets. The most straightforward way is to seek out overseas companies that trade directly in U.S. stock markets. You can visit the New York Stock Exchange website where you can obtain lists of foreign companies that are traded on the NYSE, which gives you opportunities to invest in foreign companies with some reduction in risk directly. Doing it this way is quite different than trying to buy stocks on a foreign exchange. You can visit the site here:

https://www.nyse.com/listings/international-listings

According to the SEC, most foreign companies trade in the United States using a tool called the American Depository Receipt or ADR. An ADR allows you to purchase the representation of a share of foreign stock, and an ADR is priced at the price of the stock in its home market. ADRs that trade in the United States can be purchased through a broker.

The best way to invest overseas is...surprise – mutual funds and exchange-traded funds. There are many available funds that invest in foreign markets – but you have the professionals setting them up for you and taking care of the risks. You can invest right at home, completely shielded from many of the problems that foreign investing entails. Just like any other mutual fund or exchange-traded fund, you can invest in them as if they are a stock index or other type of fund.

Let's look at a few options. Since we prefer exchange-traded funds, we will look at those, but if you'd prefer a mutual fund, you will find similar funds you can invest in taking that route.

We will go back to State Street Global Advisors (SPDR), but you can find similar funds on your favorite exchange-traded fund website. The first thing we will note is that there are global funds for every available market. Better and larger markets tend to be singled out for investment, while others are grouped together into single funds. Individual countries you can target with a State Street ETF include:

- China
- United Kingdom
- Japan
- Hong Kong
- Germany
- Canada

You can also invest in the "Global DOW" index, which tracks 150 international companies (including top U.S. companies) that the Wall Street Journal and others have selected as the world's 150 top companies.

Other options include:

- Investing in Europe (a fund that invests in Europe as a whole)
- Asia/Pacific emerging markets
- Developed world
- International small cap

If you look at iShares, you can find more targeted options. For example, they have funds that allow you to invest in:

- Taiwan
- South Korea
- Brazil
- Russia
- Malaysia
- South Africa
- Saudi Arabia
- China

- India

And many more.

What we've found is that international investing is entirely accessible using ETFs and you will find it's the same for mutual funds. You can select targeted or broad investments, and since you're using a U.S. traded fund, you've got a lot more protection than if you tried to do it alone. If you are looking to invest in specific international companies, you are best off seeking out international companies that are foreign based but trading on the New York Stock Exchange.

CHAPTER 10
Bonds And Government Securities

Bonds are a form of debt, with the investor playing the role of a bank. Bonds are issued by a wide variety of entities, from municipal governments to corporations. The most famous bonds are those issued by the United States federal government. In this chapter, we will give an overview of bonds and how they work.

Bonds in detail

When you take out a loan, the bank gives you a sum of cash. You make payments on the loan, which will include paying some of the principal back with interest. A bond is a form of a loan, but instead of banks making the loan, investors loan the money. They don't work exactly like the type of loans you are used to; however, because the entity issuing the bond doesn't pay back the principal until the end of the life of the bond. And of course, if you want a car loan, you don't issue bonds to the bank.

Bonds are used to raise cash. A government may need cash for a wide variety of needs. Local governments can issue bonds to build roads, repair school buildings, or build new county hospitals. Typically the bonds are voted on in local elections, and if voters approve the municipality will issue bonds to investors. Historically, municipal bonds have been a favored investment used by the wealthy, since they provide a tax shelter in addition to providing regular interest payments, hence generating income.

The federal government has used bonds, called U.S. Treasuries, to find budget shortfalls. As everyone knows by now, the U.S. government is in massive debt and yet continues to spend more money than it takes in – so it's continually issuing new bonds. Since their inception, bonds issued by the U.S. government have been considered to be extremely reliable, if not perfectly reliable. They are backed by "the full faith and credit of the United States." Even with the large debts the U.S. government has amassed, people worldwide remain confident in U.S. Treasuries and continue to invest in them.

The federal government also issues bonds to raise money for emergencies, in particular for wars. U.S. Savings bonds and liberty bonds are two well-known examples.

Corporations also issue bonds. They are often issued by top companies like Apple, Ford, and IBM. When you buy one of these bonds, you're lending the company money, so it is not the same as a stock investment. If you invest in a bond issued by Apple, you have no ownership interest in the company. Apple will pay you interest payments on a regular basis, but when the bond is up (the 'maturity date'), Apple will return your principal.

Some bonds carry more risk than others. For example, there might be bonds issued by companies that have a bad history when it comes to paying the money back. These are called "junk bonds," and because of the higher risk associated with investing in junk bonds, higher interest rates have to be paid. In recent times, some government entities are running into trouble meeting their obligations. On the opposite end of the spectrum from junk bonds that pay high yields or interest rates but carry a risk that you'll lose the principal (or that at some point they won't make the interest payment), are investment-grade bonds, issued by those with a solid record of paying their interest rates and returning the principal.

Bonds are considered relatively safe. In the stock market, in theory, you could lose everything. Generally speaking, that isn't true with bonds since they are required to pay back your principal. For this reason, they are considered a safe investment. Although some governments are running into financial trouble, the taxation power of governments ensures that the investor has high confidence in the government paying back the principal on any bonds it issues.

Now let's familiarize ourselves with some jargon used when discussing bonds:

- Maturity: this is the end date of the bond. When the maturity date is reached, the principal must be paid back in full.
- Par Value: Also known as face value, this is the value of the bond when it's issued by the company or government. It is also the amount of principal you must invest in taking hold of the bond. The par value is noted because bonds often trade on markets after they are issued. Prices of bonds will rise and fall based on prevailing interest rates. If the bonds price on the market is less than the par value, then it's a discount. If the bonds price on the market is higher than the par value, it's a premium. If you buy a bond directly from the issuing entity when it's issued, then you will pay the par value.
- Coupon: This is the interest rate or yield on the bond. Yield is given as a percentage of par value. If you have a $1,000 bond with a 7% yield, then it will pay an interest payment of $70. Yields can

be fixed rate, in which case the rate is constant over the lifetime of the bond, or they can be variable. Variable interest rates are pegged as a spread to some measures in the economy, such as the LIBOR rate which is a rate charged for interbank lending.

- Default Risk: the risk that the principal won't be paid back.
- Callable: A bond that can be called by the issuer at a date prior to the maturity date. Of course, if a bond is called, they have to pay back the principal. Since the issuer can call the bond at any time, the investor assumes more risk, and interest rates on callable bonds are higher.
- Putable: If a bond is putable, the buyer/investor can force the issuer to pay back the principal before the maturity date. Yields for putable bonds are lower.
- Convertible: A type of corporate bond, which can be converted into common stock at a later date. These bonds have a conversion rate, which is the number of shares the investor gets in exchange for converting the bond to stock. Convertible bonds pay lower interest rates. If the price of the shares that is equal to the conversion rate is greater than the par value of the bond, then it's to the advantage of the investors to convert the bond. If it's lower, then the investor would be doing a losing deal. When it's equal to the par value, then that is the breakeven price.
- Asset-Backed Securities: Bonds created that bundle together income streams from assets into a bond.

Corporate bonds – how they work
All bonds work in the same way, so corporate bonds work as described in the previous section. However, since many corporate bonds can carry risk, it's important to know what the risk categories are.

- Highest Quality: Rated AAA by S&P/Fitch, and Aaa by Moody's. These are investment grade bonds. Investors can be confident they will get their principal back and that the issuer will not default on interest payments.
- High Quality: Rated AA by S&P/Fitch and Aa by Moody's. Also investment grade.
- Strong: Rated A by all credit agencies. Riskier, but still investment grade. Will have to pay higher interest rates.
- Medium Grade: Rated BBB by S&P/Fitch and Baa by Moody's. Still investment grade, but higher risk than strong, so will pay higher interest rates.

- Speculative: Rated BB, B by S&P/Fitch and Ba, B by Moody's. Junk bonds. These have some risk of default. They have to pay higher interest rates than any of the above.
- Highly Speculative: Rated CCC/CC/C by S&P/Fitch and Caa, Ca, C by Moody's. Invest at your own risk. Very risky Junk bonds but will pay higher interest rates.
- In Default: Rated D by S&P/Fitch and C by Moody's- the lowest of the junk bonds.

Beginning investors probably shouldn't invest in junk bonds, but there are reasons that speculators do so. The first is to receive high-interest rate payments. Also if the issuer of the bond gets its act together – in part by keeping up with interest payments and improving its rating – then the bond can be sold to another investor at a value that is higher than the par value, giving the speculator a profit. These are high-risk activities with little certainty built into them, so that is why we refer to "speculator" rather than an investor.

Bond Pricing

Bonds are bought and sold on secondary markets but not at their par value. Bond prices move inversely with interest rates. So after a bond is issued, if the interest rate goes up, the older bond isn't worth as much. So it will sell for a price below its par value, or at a discount. For example, if you buy a $10,000 bond with a coupon rate of 4%, which means you will receive a $400 interest payment every year. However, suppose interest rates go up and now the company issues bonds that have a 6% coupon rate. Now, someone can buy a new bond that will pay them $600 a year – so your bond is less desirable and so if you sell it on the market it has to be sold at a discount.

On the other hand, if interest rates drop, that makes the previously issued bond more valuable. Suppose that you buy a $10,000 bond that pays 5% interest, or $500 per year. Then, interest rates crater to 3%, so new $10,000 bonds that are being issued only pay $300 a year. That makes your bond a desirable investment, and investors will bid up the price and be willing to pay more than the par value to get a higher interest rate. In that case, you can sell more than the par value at a premium.

Zero coupon securities

Some bonds are known as zero-coupon bonds or zero-coupon securities. This is a bond which makes no interest payments. Zero coupon bonds are sold at large discounts from the par value. However, the value of the bond appreciates and can be redeemed at face value on the maturity date. This enables the investor who buys the bond to make a profit even though no interest is paid.

What are municipal bonds

Municipal bonds, which are usually called "munis," are issued by state and local governments. Typically they are used to fund capital projects like the construction of a prison, bridge, or library. Municipal bonds are exempt from federal taxes, and often from state taxes as well. As such they have long been used to shelter income from taxation. While government bonds are backed by the taxation power of the issuer, that power isn't unlimited and not all municipal bonds have top ratings. However, some are backed by insurance companies.

Treasuries: Investing in the US government

There are several types of bonds available from the Federal government:

- Treasury Bills or T-Bills: These are short term, with maturity dates ranging from a few weeks up to 26 weeks. The face value is $1,000, but they are sold at a discount and redeemed at face value. There are no interest payments, the difference between what you receive when the bond is redeemed and what you paid at a discount is the interest.
- Treasury notes: these are longer term, available in two-, five-, and ten-year issues. They are issued in increments of $1,000.
- Treasury Bonds: These are 30-year notes. Interest is paid every six months until the maturity date.
- TIPS: These are inflation-protected bonds. They pay lower interest rates, but the interest rate and principal are both routinely adjusted for inflation.
- Savings Bonds: Can be redeemed at any point one year after bond issue. Earn small interest payment every six months which is saved until you redeem the bond. Issued in increments from $50 to $10,000. When purchased, they are sold for half of the par value, so you can purchase a $10,000 bond for $5,000. Those purchased online are purchased at face value but start at half the amount ($25). You can hold a savings bond for 30 years. When you redeem the bond, then you get the accrued interest plus your initial investment back.
- I-Bonds: A type of savings bond adjusted for inflation every six months. They pay interest which is adjusted for inflation.

Advantages and Pitfalls of government securities

Government bonds offer some extra security and some tax advantages. Despite growing problems with debt people remain confident in the U.S. government and still confident in less secure state and local bonds. The tax advantages of munis are an attractive feature of these bonds. However as governments become more and more in debt the attractiveness of government-issued bonds will begin decreasing at some point, although nobody knows when that will happen.

How to Invest

You can buy bonds from a brokerage. Some brokerages are municipal security dealers. You can buy treasuries directly from the federal government. Bonds can also be bought and sold on secondary markets, including through your own personal investment account that you self-manage.

And as usual, you can invest in bonds through either a mutual fund or an ETF.

CHAPTER 11
Playing It Safe With Banking

At the root of the financial system are the banks, and although interest rates have been very low for many years now, many people still find banks appealing for the perceived safety of preserving cash.

Banking in an era of low interest rates

Low-interest rates can be an issue when interest rates are so low that they are not outstripped by inflation. In that case, you have to weigh keeping money in the bank against losing its value through inflation. Obviously, you need to keep some money in the bank for emergencies. Other assets like stock are not as liquid (meaning not as easily converted into cash). However, while in the past people might have loaded up savings accounts and CDs, doing so at the present time is of questionable value. You should keep a savings account that has enough cash in it for immediate emergencies, but having a $250,000 savings account that is barely keeping up with inflation – or even losing value – is not the best idea. Check current interest rates to evaluate this situation.

Money Market Accounts and Funds

A money market account will come with a higher interest rate than a standard savings account. However, it will also have a higher balance and deposit requirements. At the time of writing, even with higher interest rates, money market accounts are only paying around 2%. They also allow debit cards and checks but place a limit of 6 debit card charges and six checks per month.

A money market fund is a mutual fund or ETF that invests in cash. It invests directly in cash, in cash equivalent securities, CDs, and debt-based securities with short term maturity dates. Unlike a Money Market Account, which is an FDIC insured bank account, a money market fund is the same as any other fund – so it does not guarantee principal although they are considered low-risk investments. Money market funds also invest in U.S. Treasuries. You can buy and sell shares of money market funds just like any other mutual fund or ETF.

What is a CD

A CD is a certificate of deposit. They are risk-free investments since they are insured by the FDIC. They are sold by banks, thrifts, and credit unions. Typically, they are held for 1, 3, or 5 years. They may require a minimum deposit, and the longer they are held, the higher the interest rate paid. Some are topping 3 % at the time of writing, which is better but still barely above inflation.

Are banks still worth it?

The answer is yes. Banks still provide a means to access money for day-to-day spending activities and a way to save money. Also while interest rates are low now, there is no reason to expect that to be permanent.

CHAPTER 12
The Investing Mindset

Investing involves some risk. Many of us have been raised to avoid risk. Overcoming that fear of risk is important for the investing mindset.

The mindset of the investor

Getting into the proper mindset of the investor means being willing to accept some level of risk – but also taking steps to mitigate risk. Simply jumping into risky situations is reckless. The investor accepts risk but does not act in a reckless fashion. When possible, the investor looks for ways to hedge or reduce their risks.

Getting into the investing mindset

I grew up in an era when people had parents that had lived through the great depression. The experience of the great depression had a negative impact on many people that discouraged the investor mindset. The 2008 financial crisis had the same impact.

To help get in the investing mindset, you can take practical, and mental/spiritual steps. Taking some practical steps can help you feel more secure and better able to handle risks. Ideally, it will set you up so that if you take a big hit in the market, you will remain basically OK in a stable situation, and not facing ruin or bankruptcy. Some steps you can take include:

- Before you invest a large amount of money, build up your savings, or if you have none open a savings account. Save 3-6 months' worth of money and leave it in the account. Pledge never to touch it and don't use it to bail out your investments – it's for living expenses and emergencies only.
- Start investing small. When you invest small amounts in the beginning, you will increase your comfort level slowly.
- Engage in affirmations. Train your mind to be comfortable with risk and investing.
- Study how investors used hedges to "hedge their bets," that is reduce risk.

What level of investing is for you

At first, a deep level of investing might not be in your interest. Your level of investing can increase with time.

CHAPTER 13
Retirement Vehicles

We've discussed some of these items earlier, but let's have a look at the definitions of options available to build retirement funds. Of course any investment functions in part as a retirement fund.

401k and other employer-based plans

A 401k is a type of employer managed investment plan. Generally speaking, they have replaced pensions in an era when people don't stick to one employer for their entire working life and pensions became too expensive to manage. A 401k lets you make any type of investment, including stocks, bonds, mutual funds, or ETFs and cash investments. You can work with a 401k in the same way you would with any investment plan, and probably receive matching from your employer.

Traditional IRA

As noted earlier, an IRA is an individual retirement account. They have some tax advantages. You can invest up to $5,500 per year, but after age 50 the IRS allows you to make larger contributions. With a traditional IRA, you get a tax deduction on the invested money now but will have to pay taxes when the money is withdrawn. An IRA is an account, so can have multiple securities in it of various types.

Roth IRA

A Roth IRA is similar to a traditional IRA; however, the money you put in is taxed now. When you withdraw it after retirement, it is tax-free. Roth IRAs, however, have some income limitations.

Annuities

An annuity is basically an income stream provided by an insurance company. You invest money with them and receive a fixed payment each month in return. The payment is for life; however, you and your heirs will not have access to the principal once you enter into the annuity.

529 College savings plans

There are college savings plans that work similar to other investment accounts, but you can only use the money to pay for college for your children. The accounts take advantage of the power of the market to raise funds.

Using your investments: when to start making withdrawals, and how much

The favored rule of thumb is you can withdraw 4% of your total investments per year. So, if you have $100,000 (hopefully it's a lot more), then you could safely withdraw $4,000 per year. So if you want to have an income of $100,000 a year in retirement, you'll need $2,500,000.

CHAPTER 14
Advanced Techniques

We've already discussed these topics throughout some of the earlier chapters, but we have gathered the advanced topics here together briefly for a centralized reference. A word of caution – using these techniques can be downright dangerous, making you completely broke or in a spiral of debt.

What is Options trading

An option is a contract that governs the buying and selling of a security. It allows an investor to either buy or sell the security at a predetermined price. So the price is set regardless of what happens to the price of the asset before the maturity date for the contract. It is called an option because this is an option for the investor; they are allowed to make the deal but aren't required to. Options contracts are actually bought and sold themselves on markets where investors do options trading.

Calls

A call is a type of options contract. In a call, the buyer has the right to purchase, but not the obligation, securities at an agreed-upon price on a certain date. The buyer pays a fee to the seller called a premium. The seller must sell to the buyer, even if the price that has been agreed to is lower than the price of the security at the time of the sale.

Puts

A put is the inverse of a call, in that the option now rests with the seller. In a put contract, the seller has the right to sell, but not the obligation, securities at a predetermined price on a specific date. A put option is used to protect stock against falling prices.

Strike Price

The price agreed upon for a call or a put.

Margin Trading

When trading on the margin, the brokerage lends the investor money to buy securities. The investor has to pay the brokerage back the money. High requirements are set for margin trading, and it can be dangerous. Trading on the margin got a lot of investors in trouble when the Great Depression hit.

Day Trading

Day trading involves buying and selling stocks on the same day, with the goal of making short term profits. Day traders often sit at their computers all day long trading stocks. Day trading can be lucrative for experienced investors that know what they are doing. If you are a stock market beginner, you should probably gain a lot of experience buying stocks and studying the markets before embarking on day trading.

CHAPTER 15
How To Invest Large Sums Of Money

Investing large sums of money isn't really any different than investing $100. The same principles apply. Namely, you want to use dollar cost averaging and diversification while choosing specific investment types that help you meet your desired goals. Remember that the risk of losing your principal is always there.

Going all in

Going all in is a bad idea. If you do so with a large sum of money, then your risks are magnified. You can review the common mistakes discussed earlier in the book to go over the details again, but going all in puts you at risk of bad market timing, buying high right before a downturn, and so on.

Going slow, building over time

Although it is tempting to put $100,000 or a million dollars right into the markets if you've not been in stocks before, it is better to follow the dollar cost averaging strategy. You should divide up the money you are going to invest into monthly payments to be invested over a fairly large time period, say 3-5 years. This will help you avoid the mistakes that arise from the volatility of the market.

Second, you should implement the diversity principles outlined in the book. In addition to investing in a wide variety of stocks and possibly foreign markets, take advantage of the fact that when investing a large sum you also have the opportunity to hold some in reserve with money market funds, and can also invest a lot in the bond markets. You may invest a large amount in bonds, and the percentage will depend on your growth goals, but note that with large amounts to invest after you learn the markets you can profit from bond trading as well.

Dangers of investing large sums

The same dangers exist that exist for all other investing. Mainly you're risking wasting money buying high and being forced to sell low, or buying at the top of the market right before a bear market hits – causing you to miss out on low-cost buying opportunities. If you are investing slowly and regularly, when the bear market arrives, you'll be in a position to take advantage of it because you will have capital available for the buying opportunities. If you go all in you might not have it readily available if it's available at all – in fact, it won't be. You will have to sell your own securities at discounts. Also, avoid the emotional panic that sets in and causes people to bail from the markets when they should ride it out. Selling a large amount at a loss to stuff it in the bank for a temporary downturn is a bad approach.

Reducing your risks

If you are a large investor, rather than going it alone, you should seek out the advice of an advisor. You don't even need the advisor to make the investments and can run a self-directed account if that is your desire, but you should talk to a professional about hedging your risks. You don't want to get too anxious and make newbie mistakes that might cost you a large sum of money you currently have access too. Having a large amount of money will actually give you access to financial tools to hedge your risks, and you should talk to a professional about how to do this.

CONCLUSION

Congratulations on making it to the end of this book. We hope that you have enjoyed it and learned a great deal about investing and the options that are available to you! If you found this book useful, we hope that you will take the time to rate the book!

Now is the time for action. It is one thing to learn about investing and the stock market, but if you take no action, you will make no progress. Find the right kinds of investments that meet your goals. If you want to protect the money that you already have, then some mix of bonds, savings accounts, and a smaller level of investment in safer stocks will be in your interest.

If you don't have much money saved and need to grow cash for retirement or want to retire early, then a more aggressive portfolio is in your interest. In that case, while you'll want to use some indexed funds for some protection while still getting good levels of growth, you will also want to invest aggressively in smaller companies and emerging markets. Whatever path you choose, we thank you again and wish you the best of luck!

CPSIA information can be obtained
at www.ICGtesting.com
Printed in the USA
BVHW091629260521
608178BV00003B/690